Conversations with Isabel Allende

Conversations with

EDITED BY JOHN RODDEN

TRANSLATIONS FOR THIS VOLUME FROM
THE SPANISH BY VIRGINIA INVERNIZZI
AND FROM THE GERMAN AND DUTCH
BY JOHN RODDEN

FOREWORD BY ISABEL ALLENDE

AUSTIN UNIVERSITY OF TEXAS PRESS

Isabel Allende

Frontispiece photograph: Horst Tappe/Archive Photos; all other photos courtesy Isabel Allende.

See chapter openings for permissions acknowledgments and copyright notices for interviews published previously.

First edition, 1999

Requests for permission to reproduce material from this work should be sent to Permissions, University of Texas Press, Box 7819, Austin, TX 78713-7819.

(∞) The paper used in this publication meets the minimum requirements of American National Standard for Information Sciences—Permanence of Paper for Printed Library Materials, ANSI Z39.48-1984.

LIBRARY OF CONGRESS CATALOGING-IN-PUBLICATION DATA

Allende, Isabel.
    Conversations with Isabel Allende / edited by John Rodden ; foreword by Isabel Allende ; translations for this volume from the Spanish by Virginia Invernizzi and from the German and Dutch by John Rodden. — 1st ed.
    p.   cm. — (Texas Pan American series)
Includes bibliographical references (p.   ) and index.
ISBN 0-292-77092-8 (alk. paper)
ISBN 0-292-77093-6 (pbk. : alk. paper)
1. Allende, Isabel—Interviews.   2. Authors, Chilean—20th century—Interviews.   I. Rodden, John.   II. Title.   III. Series.
PQ8098.1.L54   Z465   1999
863—dc21   99-6138

Para Pablo

Isabel with the cast of The House of the Spirits, *Denmark, 1994.*

Contents

Isabel Allende, 1996.

Young Isabel with her mother and newborn brother, 1944.

Foreword

When the postman brought me the manuscript of this book I panicked. As a former journalist, I expect press interviews to have a very short life and disappear without trace. Finding a selection of them in one volume—some of them translated from German, Spanish, or Dutch!—was scary. Inevitably, there would be many contradictions. Was I responsible for every word published in those interviews? Or for the journalists' interpretations of my opinions? What did I say in 1983? Was it the same answer in 1997? Impossible. I am not terribly consistent in my ideas, although I believe there is consistency in my principles and sentiments.

I don't know why Virginia Invernizzi chose these interviews in particular or what they reveal about me. I have not read this book for the same reason I don't spend hours looking at myself in the mirror: the reflected image might not be pleasant. But I am very grateful that she allowed me to write a foreword, thus giving me the opportunity to explain a couple of things that no one ever bothered to ask.

Most of my writing is an attempt to bring an illusory order to the natural chaos of life, to decode the mysteries of memory, to search for my own identity. I have been doing it for several years, and I have achieved none of the above. My life is as messy as it always has been; my memory still works in mysterious ways—plus I am losing it!—and I still don't have a clear idea of who I really am. Most people would come to the same conclusion. We evolve, change, age. Nobody is carved in stone, except the very pompous or self-righteous. It is frightening, therefore, to become the victim of so much scrutiny. In the last few years I have seen, with increasing terror, how students' papers, doctoral theses, innumerable reviews, and even guides to understanding my books pile up on my desk. It was bad enough when I was the subject of a question on *Jeopardy*. Being the subject of a course is much worse. Nothing that I could write, let alone that I could do or be, would live up to all these expectations. When I wrote my first novel, *The House of the Spirits*, I had no idea that literature was studied in universities and that people who had never written a book determined the value of others' writing. I simply thought that if a story had the power to touch a few readers, if it planted the seed of new ideas in them, if it seemed true and made a difference in somebody's life, it was valuable. Like most normal human beings, I had never read a book review. Word of mouth was how I chose the books I read.

I never expected that the weird craft of writing would be of any interest to the general public, nor that a writer could become a sort of celebrity and be expected to behave like one. Writing is a very private matter that happens in silence and solitude—an introverted temperament is an asset in this job. Writing takes up an incredible amount of energy and time; there is very little left for anything else. But more and more the publishing industry forces the authors to become public figures and go around talking, reading, signing, and even selling their books. How can one be in the limelight and still write? Books deserve compassion. They are delicate creatures born to be accepted or rejected as a whole; they can't endure dissection under the microscope of the pathologist. Most writers are as vulnerable as their work. If you pin them against the wall and force them to explain the unexplainable, you might break them. I am afraid it's happening to me. I am spending a fortune in therapy to deal with this feeling of being exposed, naked, and vulnerable!

Why do I write? This is a question that I often ask myself, although it is like trying to explain why I breathe. Writing is a matter of survival: if I don't write I forget, and if I forget it is as if I had not lived. That is one of the main reasons for my writing: to prevent the erosion of time, so that memories will not be blown by the wind. I write to record events and name each thing. I write for those who want to share the obligation of building a world in which love for our fellowmen and love for this beautiful but vulnerable planet will prevail. I write for those who are not pessimists and believe in their own strength, for those who have the certainty that their struggle for life will defeat all bad omens and preserve hope on earth. But maybe this is too ambitious . . . When I was younger, I thought I wrote only for the sake of those I cared for: the poor, the repressed, the abused, for the growing majority of the afflicted and the distressed of this earth, for those who don't have a voice or those who have been silenced. But now I am more modest. I think of my writing as a humble offering that I put out there with an open heart and a sense of wonder. With some luck, maybe someone will accept the offering and give me a few hours of his or her time so that we can share a story. And that story doesn't have to always be about the most solemn and transcendent human experiences. I find myself often writing for the same reason I read: just for the fun of it!

Storytelling is an organic experience, like motherhood or love with the perfect lover; it is a passion that determines my existence. I am a story junkie. I want to know what happened and to whom, why and where it happened. Writing has been very healing for me because it allows me to exorcise some of my demons and transform most of my pain and losses into strength. Certainly I write because I love it, because if I didn't my soul would dry up and die.

ISABEL ALLENDE

Young Paula with Isabel's grandfather, Agustín Llona (front); Isabel (left; pregnant with her son) and her mother, Panchita (back), 1966.

Panchita Llona (Isabel's mother) with
Salvador Allende a few weeks before
his death in the military coup, 1973.

Isabel with Miguel Frías, her first
husband, in costume, 1971.

Paula Frías, 1991.

Isabel with her son, Nicolás Frías, 1997.

Acknowledgments

No biography of Isabel Allende has yet been written. My hope is that *Conversations with Isabel Allende* will partially satisfy the urge of Allende's vast reading public to know more about the life, background, and literary and personal opinions of this remarkable woman.

Indeed, this book began in conversations I had with Virginia Invernizzi about the fascinating storyteller behind the stories. Our curiosity was sparked by personal contact with Isabel Allende at the University of Virginia, where she briefly taught as a visiting professor beginning in the mid-1980s.

Allende's presence—her magnetic dynamism, her irreverent playfulness, her lusty love of life—created tremendous excitement among students and faculty at Virginia. Moreover, the exhilarating sense of having discovered and of laying proprietary claim to a major literary figure was in the air: *The House of the Spirits* had just recently been published in English and Allende was only beginning to gain a wide North American audience; her second novel, *De amor y de sombra* [*Of Love and Shadows*], had not yet appeared in English translation. The sense of Allende as "our" writer—an honorary Virginian—was heightened by the fact that her daughter, Paula Frías (who would die of a rare genetic disease in 1992) studied psychology at Virginia during this period.

My first debt of gratitude is to Isabel Allende, who took time from her writing schedule to sit for new interviews for this collection, to pen an engaging foreword, and to grace this book with numerous family photographs, almost all of which appear here in print for the first time.

Theresa May and Carolyn Cates Wylie, who handled the book for the University of Texas Press, exerted just the right balance of patience and prodding as they kept watch over the volume's growth. Magdalena García Pinto and Ester Gimbernat González, both outstanding scholars of Latin American literature, evaluated the manuscript for the University of Texas Press, improving it in diverse ways by sharing their wealth of knowledge about Allende's work and its Chilean context.

Colleagues, friends, and family also generously contributed their time and talents to bring this book to fruition. My academic colleagues in Austin—Chuck Rossman, Virginia Higginbotham, and Chilean-born

Sonia Riquelme-Rojas—read an early version of the manuscript and provided astute advice and timely emotional support. William E. Shanahan III and Clayton Maxwell inspected several chapters and furnished invaluable editorial assistance on questions of English and Spanish usage, respectively. Ann Macom scanned the media for items on Allende in the news. Margaret Surratt and Deanna Matthews, who administer the Department of Speech Communication at the University of Texas, buoyed my spirits with their good humor and facilitated my completion of the manuscript with countless random acts of kindness.

Cristen Carson brought her extraordinary patience and gift for detail to a meticulous reading of the book's contents and a professional handling of the literary permissions. Beth Macom, who incarnates editorial care and is simply the best copy editor (un)imaginable, worked her own Scheherazade-like magic on the manuscript at several stages of its maturation.

My deepest appreciation also goes to my old *compañera* from the Virginia days, Virginia Invernizzi, who studied with Isabel Allende, was personally acquainted with Allende's daughter Paula, and wrote her dissertation on Allende's storytelling techniques. Virginia interceded with Allende to obtain both the foreword and the beautiful family photographs featured in this collection, and drew upon her wide-ranging expertise to scrutinize several interviews for factual accuracy, to conduct a new interview, and to translate Allende's original Spanish-language interviews into English for this volume.

I reserve a final, special thank-you for my family. I am grateful to my parents for their quiet trust and abiding love. And last but not least, I am indebted to my *hermano* Pablo, the passionate poet-fireman-mountaineer in the Rodden house of spirits, who not only read these chapters with an artist's eye for nuance but who also has opened my life to Latino culture.

I dedicate this collection to Pablo.

JOHN RODDEN

All author royalties from Conversations with Isabel Allende *will be donated to three funds established by Allende to honor her daughter's memory: the Paula Scholarships, created in 1995; the Isabel Allende Foundation, an educational trust set up in 1996 and under Allende's direct control; and the Porphyria Research Prize, awarded to a scientist for research on porphyria, the rare metabolic disease from which Paula died.*

Chronology

1942   Isabel Allende (IA) is born in Lima, Peru, on August 2, daughter of Tomás Allende (a Chilean diplomat) and Francisca Llona Barros Allende.

1945   IA's parents divorce. Although her father severs contact with his ex-wife and children, IA will remain close to his family, including her second cousin and godfather, Salvador Allende Gossens, whom her family affectionately calls her "uncle." She is reared by her mother in the home of her maternal grandparents in Santiago.

1953–1958   IA's mother remarries. IA's diplomat stepfather, Ramón Huidobro, whom she calls "Tío Ramón," is posted abroad, and IA lives in Bolivia, Europe, and Lebanon. She attends a private English girls' school in Beirut.

1958   In the wake of political unrest in Lebanon in July, an outcome of the Suez Canal crisis, IA is sent home to complete her schooling in Chile, and graduates from a private high school in Santiago. She meets Miguel Frías, her future husband, an engineering student at the University of Chile in Santiago.

1959–1965   IA works as secretary in the Food and Agricultural Organization (FAO) of the United Nations office in Santiago.

1962   IA marries Miguel Frías, now an engineer, on September 8.

1963   Daughter Paula is born on October 22.

1964–1965   IA lives in Belgium and Switzerland with husband and daughter.

1966   IA returns with her family to Chile. Son Nicolás is born.

1967–1974   IA works as journalist and editor on the Santiago magazine, *Paula*. She writes a column titled "Los impertinentes."

1969–1974   IA is regular contributor to *Mampato*, a Santiago children's magazine.

1970   After three failed presidential campaigns, Salvador Allende becomes president of Chile in September. He is the world's first freely elected Marxist head of state, triumphing via a left-wing coalition calling itself the *Unidad Popular* [Popular Unity Party], with 36.2 percent of the vote. Distrusted by opposition politicians, he is required by the Chilean Congress to affirm his allegiance to constitutional guarantees before he can assume office. IA's stepfather, Tío Ramón, is named ambassador to Argentina by Salvador Allende.

1970–1975   IA is regular interviewer for *Canal 13/Canal 7*, a Santiago television station.

1971   IA's play, *El embajador* [The ambassador], is performed in Santiago.

1972   IA lunches with Chilean poet Pablo Neruda, who refuses her interview request and suggests instead that she abandon nonfiction and write novels.

1973   Army troops, acting on September 11 under orders from General Augusto Pinochet Ugarte, storm *Palacio de La Moneda* (the presidential palace), home of President Salvador Allende, who is alleged to commit suicide rather than relinquish power to the military *junta*. Pablo Neruda dies on September 23.

1974   A collection of IA's humor columns from *Paula* is published under the title *Civilice a su troglodita* [Civilize your troglodyte], by Lord Cochran (Santiago). (Neruda had suggested to Allende two years earlier that she collect and publish her best columns.) IA is dismissed from *Paula* on political grounds.

1975   Concerned that her efforts to assist opposition to the Pinochet regime are endangering her own and her family's safety, IA leaves Chile, legally and with passport, for Caracas, Venezuela. Her husband, daughter, and son follow within weeks.

1975–1987   IA resides in Caracas, Venezuela.

1976–1983   IA writes weekly column for *El Nacional*, a Caracas newspaper.

1978   IA separates temporarily from Miguel Frías, and lives in Spain for three months. Near the Chilean village of Lonquén, outside Santiago, fifteen bodies are discovered in two abandoned mine shafts. This event will become the basis for IA's second novel, *De amor y de sombra* [*Of Love and Shadows*].

1979–1982   IA serves as administrator in the Colegio Marroco, a school in Caracas.

1981   IA receives word that her ninety-nine-year-old grandfather, Agustín Llona, is dying. She begins a letter to him on January 8 that eventually grows into *La casa de los espíritus* [*The House of the Spirits*], her first novel.

1982   *La casa de los espíritus* is published in Spain by Plaza y Janés (Barcelona).

1984   *La gorda de porcelana* [The fat porcelain lady], a juvenile book, is published in Spain by Alfaguara (Madrid). *De amor y de sombra* is published in Spain by Plaza y Janés. The French edition of *La casa de los espíritus* is awarded the Grand Roman d'Evasion Prize in 1984 in Paris.

1985   After selling four hundred thousand copies in France and more than a million copies in Germany, and topping the best-seller lists in the Netherlands, Spain, and Latin America during 1982–1985, *The House of the Spirits* appears in English from Knopf, translated by Magda Bogin, and is chosen as a main selection by the Book-of-the-Month Club. IA is guest professor at Montclair State University (New Jersey) for the spring semester.

1986–1987   IA spends brief periods at the University of Virginia (UVa) visiting Paula (who studies community psychology there) and conducting seminars in the Spanish department.

1986   *The House of the Spirits* is nominated for the Quality Paperback Book Club New Voice Award.

1987   IA divorces Miguel Frías. *Eva Luna*, IA's third novel, is published in Spain by Plaza y Janés in September. *Of Love and Shadows* appears in English from Knopf, translated by Margaret Sayers Peden, and is nominated for the *Los Angeles Times* Book Prize. IA meets William Gordon, a twice-divorced San Francisco attorney, in October; she moves to San Rafael (California) in December.

1988 IA is Gildersleeve Lecturer at Barnard College for spring semester. IA marries William Gordon on July 17 and becomes a U.S. resident. IA is guest professor at UVa for fall semester. *Eva Luna* appears in English from Knopf, translated by Peden, and is named one of *Library Journal*'s Best Books of 1988. Pinochet lifts state of emergency in August, permitting five hundred exiled opponents to return to Chile. IA returns to visit Chile for first time since 1975; Pinochet loses October 5 plebiscite held to extend his presidential term until 1997.

1989 *Cuentos de Eva Luna* [*The Stories of Eva Luna*] is published in Spain by Plaza y Janés (Barcelona). Allende's essay "Writing As an Act of Hope," composed in English, appears in *Paths of Resistance*, ed. William Zinsser (New York: Houghton Mifflin). IA is guest professor of creative writing at the University of California at Berkeley for the spring semester.

1990 Democracy is restored in Chile in March election won by Patricio Aylwin of the Christian Democratic Party, who forms a Center-Left governing coalition.

1991 *The Stories of Eva Luna* appears in English from Atheneum. Paula enters Madrid hospital on December 6; on December 8 she slips into a coma, from which she never emerges. *El plan infinito* [*The Infinite Plan*] (Barcelona: Plaza y Janés) is launched at the Santiago Book Fair in December.

1992 Paula dies in the San Rafael home of IA on December 8, exactly one year after she fell into a coma.

1993 *The Infinite Plan* appears in English from HarperCollins. *The House of the Spirits* is adapted for the London stage in August. On October 22, the screen version has its world premiere in Munich. Produced by Munich's Bernd Eichinger and directed by Oscar-winning Danish filmmaker Bille August (*Pelle the Conqueror*), the production costs $25 million and stars Meryl Streep, Glenn Close, Jeremy Irons, Winona Ryder, Antonio Banderas, and Vanessa Redgrave. The film tops German moviegoer lists in November.

1994 *The House of the Spirits* receives the Bavarian Film Prize (the Oscar of Germany) on January 14. IA receives the Gabriela Mistral Prize, Chile's highest cultural honor, from President Patricio Aylwin in Santiago on March 15. *Eva Luna* is adapted for the stage (under the title *Stories*), and holds its premiere in Denver on March 25. An Argentinian-Spanish coproduction brings *Of Love and Shadows* to the screen in October, directed by Betty Kaplan, an American raised in Caracas. *Paula* is published in Spanish in December. By year's end, IA's writings have sold an estimated ten million copies in twenty-seven languages.

1995 *Paula* appears in German and Dutch in January (subtitled in both languages "A Novel") and soars to number 1 on both nations' best-seller lists for fiction. *Paula*, translated by Margaret Sayers Peden, is published in

English by HarperCollins in April, immediately ascending to number 8 on the *New York Times* best-seller list. Channel BBC1 in the United Kingdom produces *Listen Paula*, a widely discussed special on IA, Paula, and the Allende family's history in September. IA establishes the Paula Scholarships, given to students at the University of San Jose and the Canal Community Alliance.

1996   IA is honored as "Author of the Year" in Los Angeles in January; the city proclaims January 16 "Isabel Allende Day." The award is sponsored by the multicultural literacy program called "Read About Me," a national public library initiative to promote literacy and celebrate ethnic diversity. IA establishes the Isabel Allende Foundation. She receives the prestigious Harold Washington Literary Award, presented by the Printers Row Book Fair and the Chicago Public Library Foundation, in Chicago in June. The award honors "an author's creative use of the written word to address issues of contemporary life." IA is the first Latin American author to receive the prize. *Of Love and Shadows* appears on film, starring Antonio Banderas, in July.

1997   *Aphrodite*, a tongue-in-cheek, illustrated nonfiction book about sex and food, appears in Spanish from Plaza y Janés (Barcelona) in November. The recipes are based on humorous anecdotes about aphrodisiacs, such as the penis-shaped pasta that "grows when cooked." Allende's normally reticent mother contributes Chilean recipes reputed to improve sexual performance.

1998   *Aphrodite* is published in English in April by HarperFlamingo. In October, IA establishes the Porphyria Research Prize, for research on porphyria, the rare metabolic disease from which Paula died. Also in October, Allende is presented with the fifth Dorothy and Lillian Gish Prize. The prize, which is given for excellence in the arts, includes a $200,000 cash award.

Isabel and her husband, William Gordon, 1996.

Introduction

In September 1972, just a year before his death, Pablo Neruda invited thirty-year-old Isabel Allende, then a modest celebrity in Chile as a television and magazine reporter, to visit him at his seaside home at Isla Negra. A gracious host, Neruda praised her humorous pieces, telling her that he even photocopied them and showed them to friends. For her part, as Allende recalls in her memoir *Paula*, she "made meticulous preparations for that meeting; I bought a new recorder, wrote out lists of questions, I read two biographies and reread parts of his work—I even had the engine of my old Citroën checked so it would not fail me on such a delicate mission." Alas, unbeknownst to her, the feckless mission was doomed from the start:

> After lunch it began to rain; the room darkened. . . . I realized then that the poet was weary, that the wine had gone to my head, and that I must hurry.
> "If you like, we can do the interview now," I suggested.
> "Interview?"
> "Well, that's why I'm here, isn't it?"
> "Interview *me*? I'd never put myself through that," he laughed. "My dear child, you must be the worst journalist in the country. You are incapable of being objective, you place yourself at the center of everything you do, I suspect you're not beyond fibbing, and when you don't have news, you invent it. Why don't you write novels instead? In literature, those defects are virtues."[1]

Indeed they are. And fortunately, Isabel Allende ultimately followed Neruda's advice: A decade later, she turned from journalism to fiction, and since then has acknowledged her meeting with Neruda as "a turning point" in her life (see interview no. 11 in this volume). Equally fortunate for her readers—and especially pertinent to the contents of *Conversations with Isabel Allende*—she has "put [her]self through" hundreds of interviews in the last dozen years, a period that has witnessed her meteoric rise to the status of leading female literary voice from Latin America and best-selling female writer in the world.

The appearance in late 1994 of Allende's autobiographical memoir *Paula*, written as a farewell letter to Paula Frías, her recently deceased daughter, marked the publication of Allende's sixth book in a dozen years. Allende's books have topped the best-seller lists in Europe, Latin America, and the United States, selling an estimated eleven million copies in thirty languages (including pirated editions in Turkish, Vietnamese, and Chinese); her first two novels, *The House of the Spirits* and *Of Love and Shadows*, have already been filmed.[2] Indeed, as several interviews in this volume make clear, in one sense Isabel Allende has merely switched roles since the distant day of her fateful meeting with Pablo Neruda: she has gone from celebrity interviewer to celebrity interviewee.

Isabel Allende is a disarming and often hilarious interview subject—and her humor, which is seldom remarked on by critics of her writing, is on full display in her interviews. For instance, she confesses her "passion" for writing, declaring that she prefers it over all other activities. Then she pauses: "Well, what I like most is making love! But then second: writing. Writing too!" Later, in a more serious vein, she responds to a question about critical assessments of her *oeuvre*: "I don't know how to answer in an intelligent, academic, scholarly way. I can only tell you how I feel. I write [my work] with feelings. . . ." (no. 16).

Or, as a character in *Eva Luna* remarks about the art of stories and storytelling: "If you start analyzing them, you ruin them."[3]

Although Allende's experience with and sophistication toward the role of interviewee have increased as the occasions have multiplied through the 1990s, her fundamental openness and straightforwardness as an interview subject are apparent in all the conversations in this volume. Such a collection is a kind of "biography on the pulse," both corresponding closely to the dominant events of the moment in her life and serving as a running history of her rapidly changing circumstances between the mid-1980s and mid-1990s. As such, it is an invaluable complement to *Paula*, amounting *in toto* to an informal autocritique that sheds further light on Allende's life and art: another, quite different and more spontaneous, oral form of storytelling by a master storyteller.

Or as Allende herself puts it in a 1994 interview (no. 25), explaining

that her interviewing skills from her journalism days have proven in-
dispensable to her as a fiction writer, and that she still occasionally conducts interviews to enrich her settings and enliven her character portraits:
"Through interviews you can come up with things that you will never
find in a book."[4]

The same is sometimes true about Allende's life, as the interviews in
Conversations with Isabel Allende testify. They variously provide biographical details, extended self-interpretations, or glimpses into states
of mind and feeling not contained in Allende's own books: e.g., her
heady life in the early 1970s as a Chilean celebrity, her struggles with
anger and perfectionism, and her spiritual awakening in the aftermath
of her daughter's death in 1992. Thus, the interviews collected here
supplement and complement *Paula*, sometimes filling in "gaps" not
addressed in the memoir or even (as yet) transmuted into art in Allende's
fiction.

But should we take everything that Allende says in her interviews at
face value? *Paula* was released as "fiction" in Germany and the Netherlands;[5] and perhaps even Allende herself is unsure of its genre. As she
remarked of *Paula* in one pre-publication interview (no. 25): "It's a sort
of memoir. I think it's nonfiction; however, it reads like fiction." And
Allende issues the interviewer a warning:

> If you ask me to tell you my life, I will try, and it will prob-
> ably be a bag of lies because I am inventing myself all the
> time, and at the same time I am inventing fiction, and through
> this fiction I am revealing myself.

Caveat lector!

Let us heed that warning and, rather than approach an Allende interview as prosaic journalistic reportage, conceive it as a literary genre in
its own right, featuring "Isabel Allende" as protagonist (see no. 20).[6]
For Allende is not only drawing on memory and expressing opinion,
but also engaging in imaginative acts of self-transformation: they are
part of the performative repertoire of a prose fabulist and unprosaic
romancer.

Indeed Allende's mythic sensibility—or mythomania (or "bag of lies," as she calls it)—is part of her Romantic *sui generis* project of endless self-reinvention—whereby even her confession about "lying" may itself be a "lie": still another of the tale-teller's telltale tricks. Implicitly confirming Pablo Neruda's judgment of her, Allende readily admitted to one interviewer (see no. 6) her irresistible urge to embellish, recalling her experience in a Santiago publishing house as a translator of Barbara Cartland-style romances:

> I changed the dialogue a little bit at the beginning so that the heroine wouldn't be so stupid. Then I changed the plot a little bit. By the end, I had the man helping Mother Teresa in Calcutta and the heroine selling weapons in Algeria!

Allende sometimes gives different interviewers different versions of major events in her life—versions that also differ from her account in *Paula*. One example are her "different stories" of how she first met her second husband, William Gordon, which range from her jumping from the Golden Gate Bridge to save him from drowning to her walking up to him at a restaurant table and asking him to dine with her.[7] Or as Allende puts it in *Paula*, speaking of her first night of lovemaking with him: "I am tempted to invent wild erotic rites to adorn my memoirs, as I suppose others do, but in these pages I am trying to be honest." Still, she adds: "We can invent memories that fit our fantasies. . . . [Paula's death] has given me this silence in which to examine my path through the world . . . to recover memories others have forgotten, to remember what never happened and what still may happen."[8]

So Allende's claim that she is indeed the Latin American Scheherazade—"In a weird way, Eva Luna is me or I am Eva Luna" (see no. 25)—should thus be taken not just as biographical testimony (Eva Luna—*C'est moi!* Or *Soy yo!*). It is also yet another warning to the unguarded or ingenuous interviewer. As Eva Luna herself puts it: "One word from me and, abracadabra!, reality was transformed."[9]

Should *Conversations with Isabel Allende* itself, therefore, be classified as "fiction"? Acknowledging the relevance of the question, the careful reader may, I think, suspend an answer and move on to enjoy Allende's performance as interviewee. Whatever their genre, the interviews in this volume offer, at minimum, rich insight into the evolving self-images of Isabel Allende as storyteller, fabulist, exile, writer, memoirist, woman, wife, and mother. I hope that they will also assist the scholar-critic's understanding of the relationship between Allende's life and work—and meet the general reader's desire to know more about the lives of authors: the author as heroine in her own life drama. The interviews in this volume address both of these purposes: they enrich our appreciation of the autobiographical aspects of Allende's art and reveal the woman behind the literary characters. As such, these conversations constitute, however informally, part of what the novelist George Garrett has called "the scholarship of experience."[10]

Organized chronologically by date of publication—to highlight both the development of Allende's literary career and the evolution of her political and social thought—the thirty-four interviews in *Conversations with Isabel Allende* divide themselves roughly into three periods.

The first period covers the mid-1980s and constitutes chiefly literary interviews by well-informed scholar-teachers of Latin American literature, most of whom are frank admirers fascinated by Allende's rise to international success. Living in exile in Venezuela during this period, Allende published *La casa de los espíritus* (1982; *The House of the Spirits*, 1985) and *De amor y de sombra* (1984; *Of Love and Shadows*, 1987).

A second group of interviews—which might be termed the "Eva Luna years"—spans the late 1980s to 1991. These years witnessed the publication of *Eva Luna* (1987; *Eva Luna*, 1988) and *Cuentos de Eva Luna* (1989; *The Stories of Eva Luna*, 1991) and coincide with Allende's second marriage in 1988, her relocation to San Rafael in California, and her transition to American life. Interviewers' questions during this period turn increasingly biographical, now that Allende has become not only a literary celebrity, but also an American resident.

Finally, a third phase of interviews opens in 1991, and it spans the sickness of Allende's daughter Paula during 1991 and 1992, the appearance of *El plan infinito* (1991; *The Infinite Plan*, 1993), and the publication of *Paula* (1994; *Paula*, 1995). In this period, interviewers focus above all on Allende's relationship to Paula, who died in December 1992 of a rare metabolic disorder. Quite often, the interviews from these years are not just biographical but frankly personal, even intimate; Allende reveals that she wrote *Paula*, a mother's heart-rending memoir about her existence before and after her only daughter's death, partly to assist other families who have suffered similar overwhelming losses—and that she regards the sharing of herself in her interviews and public engagements as a chance to aid her readers.

1984–1987: A LATIN AMERICAN LITERARY CELEBRITY IS BORN

Isabel Allende's first book, *The House of the Spirits*, created an immediate sensation on the international literary scene in the early 1980s, and by the time of its English translation in mid-1985, Allende's novel had occupied the best-seller lists in several European countries for more than a year. The novel was quickly chosen as a Book-of-the-Month Club selection and given a royal welcome by the *New York Times*: "With this spectacular first novel," began Alexander Coleman in his rave review, "Isabel Allende becomes the first woman to join what has heretofore been an exclusive male club of Latin American novelists."[11] During these years—the early and mid-1980s—though she traveled frequently and even accepted a guest appointment for a semester's teaching at Montclair State College in New Jersey, Allende was still living in Venezuela.

As the *New York Times* review suggests, the American as well as European press took immediate note of Allende: feature stories in *People* accompanied author profiles in Spain's *El Pais* and Germany's *Der Spiegel*; *Vogue* serialized chapters of *The House of the Spirits*. Because most of the interviews from the mid-1980s were conducted by academics and published in literary or scholarly journals, however, the literary interview— rather than the personal or celebrity interview—predominates, with questions focusing on the imaginative worlds of *The House of the Spirits* and *Of Love and Shadows*, or the relationship between the novels and Allende's family history.

Broadly speaking, two related themes pervade interviews from this first period of Allende's reception: Allende's status as both a successful female writer and as a relative of former Chilean President Salvador Allende.

For instance, in the opening interview in this volume, Allende herself emphasizes that one of her major goals is to write to and for women— and as a Latin American woman. Speaking to Marjorie Agosín, a Chilean-born poet-critic and professor of Latin American literature at Wellesley College (see no. 1),[12] Allende emphasizes the femininity of her feminist characters: "I chose extraordinary women who could symbolize my vision of what is meant by *feminine*, characters who could illustrate the destinies of women in Latin America." Noting that *The House of the Spirits* had already been reprinted twelve times by 1984 in its original Spanish edition, Agosín asks probing questions about Allende's family background and literary imagination, so that her interview serves as an excellent introduction of the novelist to her growing international public.

Agosín's in-depth interview (conducted in 1984)—which was translated into English even before the publication of the novel in English— is characteristic of the expertise exemplified by scholar-interviewers in the mid-1980s. Here, in the Agosín interview, as well as in subsequent conversations, Allende discloses the autobiographical dimensions of *The House of the Spirits*, as she reminisces about her childhood in her grandparents' home and reflects on how her maternal grandmother served as the model for Clara de Valle in *The House of the Spirits*. Nor is Allende reticent here about making political pronouncements, predicting that "Pinochet and the evil ones who are with him" represent merely "an accident in the long life of my country. They will go into history as a misfortune that darkened the sky, but they will go."

Such political statements constitute the most controversial elements of Allende's interviews during the mid-1980s, which were conducted before the 1988 plebiscite that removed General Augusto Pinochet Ugarte from power in Chile. In these interviews, Allende's ideological/ feminist critique of Latin American power politics revolves around a cluster of attributes, among them "feminine solidarity," the "military mentality," and *machismo* (no. 2). Commenting on themes that soon would be apparent in her second novel, *Of Love and Shadows*, Allende elaborates on these interconnections in an interview published in 1986 (no. 3): "I have two obsessions, two recurrent phantoms: love and violence, light and darkness. . . . They are always present in my life like two antagonistic forces." Allende asserts here that her "natural tendency" is "toward socialism." As a member of "a privileged social class," she insists, she feels "a double responsibility" to campaign for social justice.

As Allende became a more visible figure in the United States, above all in American university departments of Spanish and Latin American literature, and also a more available one—especially after ending her twenty-five-year marriage to Chilean engineer Miguel Frías and publishing *Of Love and Shadows* in 1987—U.S. interviewers addressed themselves to Allende's political responsibilities deriving from her dual status as an Allende family member and a now-famous woman writer. Increasingly, interviewers cast her not just as a feminist voice but as a spokeswoman for Latin America. Challenged in 1987 by two conservative student journalists to advise U.S. youth on how to approach Latin American culture and politics, she replies: "Try and be open-minded . . . because I'm a very intolerant person. I have only become tolerant after suffering. And probably you will never suffer that much" (no. 4).

As this pronouncement suggests, Allende occasionally rose to the invitation extended by her interviewers to speak as a political authority or Latin American voice. The line of interviewers' questions discloses how utterly Americans were fascinated, from the very outset of her literary career, both by the Allende surname—which functioned as a brand-name tag to endow her with the aura of Revolutionary by Blood Connection—and by her conception of the political legacy she had thereby inherited. The glow from Allende's family heritage radiated outside left-wing academic and political circles into the literary sphere, where, simply because she was an "Allende," critics and reviewers occasionally treated her with awe, lavishly praising her work as comparable to that of Cervantes, James Joyce, and Edith Wharton, not to mention Gabriel García Márquez.[13] Or they approached her as if she were the incarnation of Salvador Allende himself, a phoenix arisen from the ashes to hurl down verbal thunderbolts on the murderous Pinochet tyranny.[14]

Most academic interviewers did not treat her with such awe. Quite accurately, they presented her as the newest addition and only woman in the "exclusive male club" of first-rank Latin American writers of the postwar "Boom," a literary movement whose members combined realism and fantasy to produce what became known as "magical realism" (e.g., Jorge Luis Borges, Alejo Carpentier, Julio Cortázar, Carlos Fuentes, Gabriel García Márquez, and Mario Vargas Llosa). Unfortunately, especially in later years when journalists have subjected her to variants of the "celebrity" interview, many interviewers' questions tend to cast Allende less as a serious writer than as a "personality"—a famous exile, the "niece" of a fallen Marxist hero,[15] the first and only woman writer in Latin America who has ascended to international prominence, or the only Latin American feminist writer who has employed magical realist techniques to depict her continent's history.

To indicate Allende's popularity, I have included a few samples of such "celebrity" interviews in *Conversations with Isabel Allende* (nos. 6, 7, 12, 21, and 30), even though such approaches, of course, beg the issue of the quality of her work, leaving such serious matters to the scholarly journals that Allende's vast public are unlikely to read. Whether deliberately or not, such "celebrity" interviews—given that they have been delivered against the backdrop of the great historical sweep of Allende's real-life drama and the saga of *The House of the Spirits*—have helped confer upon her an outsized, even mythical image that the scholars too have had to confront.

It also bears noting that, in the literary interviews in this volume, Allende frequently addresses the topic of her public image (nos. 12, 16, 17, 19). Already by the mid-1980s, Isabel Allende was known not just as Latin America's leading female voice but in some circles—quite exaggeratedly—as a socialist (or even quasi-Marxist) spokeswoman and feminist revolutionary.

The questions comparing Allende with the Latin American Boom writers also reflect, however, the interesting topic of her literary debts and writing habits. Allende's most extensive, substantive conversations on these topics during the mid-1980s occurred in three interviews with Michael Moody, who met with Allende in Caracas. Speaking with Moody in an interview published in autumn 1986 and included in this volume (no. 3), Allende addresses the influences on her of García Márquez, of the family sagas of writers such as Russian-born Henri Troyat, and of Neruda. Asked whether she is "bothered" by the frequent comparisons between her first novel and García Márquez's *Cien años de soledad* (1967; *One Hundred Years of Solitude*, 1970)—an analogy soon to be so relentlessly voiced that it would indeed annoy her in later years—Allende says, "Not in the least. I admire him. I love him dearly."[16]

Allende discusses, with mixed emotions, the effects of fame on her work life. Feeling both excited and ambivalent, she acknowledges that she is starting to get frequent invitations to travel, and that this involves the challenge of balancing writing against other activities. "Literature is like love, a full-time occupation. It does not accept distractions" (no. 3). Allende also discusses her workmanlike, journalistic sensibility, noting that she has no fear of "the blank page" (no. 2). And she mentions work habits that she applied during the composition of *Of Love and Shadows*—habits that continue to intrigue her interviewers into the mid-1990s. Among them are her "research method"—i.e., clipping bizarre stories from newspapers and popular magazines (no. 3)—and her self-admitted "superstition" that January 8—the date on which she began composition of *The House of the Spirits* and thereafter started to write all her books—is her "lucky day" (no. 8).[17]

And here too, as yet another Allende interview crosses self-reflexively into the subject of interviewing itself (e.g., nos. 15, 19, and 20), Allende stresses the importance of interviewing to gather "research" for constructing her fictional universes. To write *The House of the Spirits* and *Of Love and Shadows*, she made use variously of letters to her mother, old diaries and notebooks of her grandmother, journalistic articles and recordings from her days as a reporter, and conversations with fellow Chilean exiles in Venezuela.

While following Neruda's advice and becoming a novelist, therefore, Allende nevertheless has also remained a journalist—and even an interviewer.

1987–1991: THE EVA LUNA YEARS

"I try to live my life as I would like . . . like a novel," says the title character of *Eva Luna*, a TV soap opera heroine, near the novel's close.

Eva's creator has often said that her own life resembles a novel—or, indeed, a magical realist *telenovela* [soap opera]—and never was this truer than in the *annus mirabilis* of 1988, when the plot twists and character changes in Isabel Allende's life story took a radical new turn—and world events impinged, oddly and yet again, on her personal history. "Out of Venezuela" might serve as a suitable title for a memoir of Allende's life during these years.

How much Allende maintained a "narrative control" over these narrative leaps is hard to say, but fueling the headlong changes was her love life: Ironically, just a few months before the Chilean plebiscite of December 1988 that ended Pinochet's rule—and which would have facilitated Allende's return from her self-imposed exile to Santiago—she fell in love with William Gordon, a San Francisco attorney. Now that she could easily go back home and live in a more hospitable political climate, surrounded by her extended family and old friends, her life seemed elsewhere—in California, *El Norte*. Choosing love over politics, she married Gordon in July 1988 (after sending the lawyer "a contract, listing all my demands, and the few concessions I was willing to make"—and giving him twenty-four hours to think it all over.[18] And then, Allende—despite her publisher's worries that her imaginative juices would desiccate in California suburbia (no. 8)—resolved to build a new life in the United States as a writer, wife, and stepmother of two young boys.

Allende's relocation to the United States and the Spanish publication in 1987 of her third novel, *Eva Luna*—the similarity of Allende's own whirlwind romance to her title character's epic love adventures and storytelling gift prompted critics to dub the author "The Chilean Scheherazade"[19]—ushered in a second, more biographically oriented phase of interviewers' concerns. Allende's life changed radically and the focus of interviewers' questions altered accordingly. This period—which I am terming "the Eva Luna years"—featured numerous explorations of Allende's relationships to her characters, especially Eva Luna herself,[20] and reflected the international acclaim in 1989 through 1991 that greeted the appearance of Allende's first story collection, *The Stories of Eva Luna*. Approaching her work as "woman's writing," interviewers highlighted her treatment of the complex relations between feminism and femininity. American press interviewers—no longer were most of her interviewers Latin American literature specialists—hailed her work as much for what it said directly to Americans, especially to women (who comprise Allende's chief audience, as she herself notes in these interviews) as for its relationship to Latin American politics and history.

Because her transition to American life was so hectic and her professional and family responsibilities so many, Allende said, she did not immediately attempt to write another novel, but rather limited herself to stories, which could be written in short bursts of concentration (no. 12). She began writing the exotic tales that eventually would form *The Stories of Eva Luna*. Permanently settled in the United States, she now also felt that invitations to teach and lecture in the United States did not greatly interfere with her work; during 1988–1989 alone, for instance, she taught at the University of Virginia, Barnard College, and the University of California at Berkeley. One also notes her increasing comfort with English during this period; after 1990, even with native Spanish speakers, she conducts most interviews for English-language publications in English, preferring to speak English rather than have her words translated from Spanish.

A central theme in Allende's interviews is the consequence of her new American life for her international status as a Latin American voice. In a *Mother Jones* interview in late 1988 (no. 8)—conducted when she was halfway to completion of *The Stories of Eva Luna*—Allende identified three major practical changes in her daily life entailed by her move to the United States, all of which posed immediate and significant challenges for reorganizing her work life: her new role as a suburban housewife and mother, without the benefit of the inexpensive live-in household help that she enjoyed in Santiago and Caracas; her sudden accessibility to the American media and academy; and her "split life" linguistically, i.e., as a day-to-day English speaker and Spanish author.

Allende chose to stress the last two issues, seeking to transform them into opportunities: More consciously and deliberately than before, she would embrace the role that Fate had granted her and address Americans on political and social issues. She would step up to the world stage and, standing on the raised platform of literary fame, speak out on the topic of "politics and the writer" in a Latin American vs. North American context (see no. 12).[21]

One representative example is her statement in *The Kenyon Review* (no. 16), in the immediate aftermath of the 1988 Chilean plebiscite. Asked if she has "something special" to say to U.S. readers, Allende replies:

> Yes. You do not live in a bubble. You are not privileged. You are very spoiled. You think you will be saved when this globe explodes. You will not. We all share the same planet; this is a rock lost in space. We are all parts of it. There are no superior races. . . . [Latin Americans are] not [living on] another planet. They are not on Mars. It's our planet. It's our land, and these borders are just illusions. We trace them on a map, but they don't exist. We all share the same planet.

Or as she told *New Perspectives Quarterly* in 1991, responding to the interviewers' comment that Americans possess a Disneyesque outlook whereby "everything will have a happy ending," "The attraction of Disney is undeniable. . . . I have been living in the U.S. for three years and what I really miss about my Latin American culture is the sense I had there of belonging in a common project, of being part of a coherent group, with a common set of values. . . . Due to our history we have a sense of fate, or destiny, that the U.S. lacks" (no. 17).

Such political outspokenness has elicited sharp and sometimes condescending rebukes, especially from a few conservative critics, who deride Allende's politics as black-and-white and simplistic. It is easy to see how her summary of the history of the Pinochet regime in *New Perspectives Quarterly*, a left-liberal magazine, could contribute to such dismissals: "All the violence, repression, and brutality came from the military. And the people responded with nonviolence, pacific protests, solidarity, and organization." But Allende is unfazed by critics' hostility toward her work, whether political or literary. Responding to charges that her work is kitschy, she says: "What do I do with my truth? I write it" (no. 16). Indeed she even goes so far as to run through a dismissive catalogue of her critics' complaints:

> Contradictory things are said all the time. I couldn't please everybody, and I shouldn't even try. . . . One "bad" thing people say is that I discovered a very attractive mixture of melodrama, politics, feminism, and magic realism and I throw it all together. . . . Another "bad" thing is that I'm very sentimental and that I'm not detached, I'm not cold; therefore I can be very kitschy, very campy sometimes. What other bad things can I remember? Oh yes, that it resembles García Márquez. (no. 8)[22]

Despite her cooperativeness with individual critics, Allende makes it clear that she takes a dim view of them as a species:

> Critics are terrible people. They will label you no matter what, and you have to be classified. I don't want to be called a feminist writer, a political writer, a social writer, a magical realism writer, or a Latin American writer. I am just a writer. I am a storyteller. (no. 25)

Allende acknowledges in interviews after 1988 that her transition to American life has put her at a mental as well as geographical distance from political events in Latin America. But she holds that "exile" yields

literary advantages. In general, exile is "good" for a writer, Allende believes, precisely *because* it generates imaginative space and multiplies
perspectives—and because one learns to "understand that your roots
are within yourself."[23] Allende herself possesses a "double perspective"
by living in the United States and writing from her Latin American past;
she says she now has a valuable distance from both places. Another
advantage of "exile" is, however paradoxical it may sound, the upheaval
it creates in one's life. Allende says that her own crises have shaken her
complacency and made her a more questioning, self-aware person and
artist (no. 32).

Not only U.S. but also Latin American interviewers have addressed
the topic of Allende's adaptation to life in California. Indeed it is interesting to see the changing response of selected Latin American interviewers to Allende after her relocation to the United States. In some
cases, they begin to look upon her less as one of their own than as a
cultural mediator and spokeswoman for U.S.–Latin American relations,
i.e., they start to treat her much as did the American press in the early
1980s. One example of Allende's elevation to the status of cultural
spokeswoman in a Latin American interview appears in her 1991 conversation in the journal *Mester*. Asked to assess the "future" of Latin
America, Allende says that the continent has an important role to play
in the evolving "collective consciousness" of the world (no. 15).

Related to the Latin American motif during this second period of
Allende interviews is the topic of her feminism and what might be termed
her "personal mythology." The publication of Allende's two Eva Luna
books gave both U.S. and Latin American interviewers the opportunity
to explore Allende's fantasy life as a real-life Scheherazade, a spinner of
magical Latin American stories. Not only do interviewers express curiosity about Allende's family background, therefore, but also about her
powerful and compelling identification with her autobiographical heroine, Eva Luna.

As we have already seen, Allende freely acknowledges that she identifies with Eva Luna. She has often described how she used to read stealth-
ily what her family ordained to be "forbidden literature"—above all,
the Arabian romance *A Thousand and One Nights*—all of it stashed in
her stepfather's closet in Beirut, which was off-limits to her. (In *Eva
Luna*, the heroine herself carries a copy of the romance with her, deem-
ing it "essential baggage for my travels through life," and *The Stories of*

Eva Luna begins and ends with quotations from *A Thousand and One Nights*.) To several interviewers, it does indeed seem as if Allende's tumultuous life were a seamless story, reality transformed; i.e., from *reading* about Scheherazade as a girl to *becoming* "the Chilean Scheherazade" as an adult woman.

Allende is well aware that her image as a humorous, ironic Scheherazade accounts in part for her tremendous international following, particularly her high standing with educated American women. Diffidently yet forthrightly, she explains to *Mester* in 1991 that her U.S. popularity is "partly due to the great interest that there is here for women's literature," partly attributable to the Anglo-Saxon fascination with magic realism, and partly because her work is not "baroque" and therefore "easy to read in comparison to other Latin American novels"—all of which has led to her books being "read and studied in universities" (no. 15). By 1991, Allende had published five best-sellers in twenty-seven languages. Asked to explain her phenomenal international reception, Allende generously, and with a touch of humor, attributes it to her excellent translators, who invariably "improve my books" (no. 12).

While interviewers of the early 1990s are chiefly concerned with the topics of Allende's feelings in the present and her adjustment to U.S. life, they also plumb her past more deeply than in the previous decade. Much of the curiosity stems from the simple desire to know who Allende was *before* she metamorphosed—Abracadabra!—into the Eva Luna of San Rafael and began weaving her Scheherazade-like fantasies.

Where did this extraordinary woman come from? readers now wanted to know. Some interviewers, therefore, concentrate on Allende's background, inquiring about Allende's Chilean days, i.e., the years before her international celebrity; for example, the writer Alberto Manguel asks about her writing before the 1973 coup, including her activities as a playwright. Manguel also addresses her participation as a contributor and staff member on publications such *Magazine Ellas* and *Paula*, the latter of which was the first Chilean publication to address taboo social topics such as abortion, divorce, and drugs; and also her involvements with the children's magazine *Mampato* and her TV programs and short films. Already at the age of twenty-nine, in 1971, Allende had a much-discussed play *El embajador* [The ambassador] performed in Santiago, along with a play titled *La balada del medio pelo* [The parvenu's ballad] (no. 13). One literary/biographical interview (no. 19) shows Isabel Allende to possess a wide variety of expressive gifts, and here she delves into her literary and theatrical activities in Santiago in greater detail than in *Paula* or her fiction (see also no. 13).

The main outcome of the "Eva Luna years" for Allende herself was that she came to feel more comfortable with herself as a woman and as a writer. As she confides in a 1988 interview, the writing of *Eva Luna* vouchsafed her "a new attitude about being a woman": "I had to finally accept that I was always going to live in this body with this face and be the person I am." And she had taken significant steps to confront and cope with her "anger" toward her grandfather and the oppressive patriarchy of her Chilean years (no. 8). In a 1991 interview, she speaks of an "enraged intimacy" between herself and her maternal grandfather (the model for Esteban Trueba, the family patriarch of *The House of the Spirits*). "We never agreed on anything but we adored each other. I saw him every day while I was in Chile, until 1975" (no. 13). She had also refused to take her husband's family name because of her anger. "My anger towards male authority . . . continued even after my marriage. And it endures even today" (no. 13). This is another topic that Allende takes up at greater length after Paula's death (no. 32).

Allende also affirms that *Eva Luna* led to her self-acceptance as a "narrator of stories," i.e., as a professional creative writer (no. 11). With *Eva Luna* and *The Stories of Eva Luna*—and just as she is starting to write *The Infinite Plan*—Allende finally judges her apprenticeship as an imaginative writer to be over. With increasing confidence, she discusses her admiration for the work of Borges and Cortázar, disavows critics' speculations that she deliberately parodied García Márquez's *One Hundred Years of Solitude*, concedes the admittedly limited capacity of writers to affect world events, and replies to feminist critics who find her female characters stereotyped or weak (no. 11). She also admits in a 1991 interview that life in an English-language environment is affecting her writing: "My sentences are shorter, there's less ornamentation, fewer adjectives. The language is more straightforward, and . . . the text is more restrained" (no. 12). Working on *The Infinite Plan* in 1991, Allende notes that, as she has switched from Latin American and Caribbean settings in her first four works of fiction to a California setting in *The Infinite Plan*, she has moved away from magic realism to a more straightforward literary realism (no. 12).

One final comment of Allende's about her writing merits emphasis here, a comment that leaps out at the reader and makes it seem as if, once again, Allende's life of upheaval is a seamless story that reflects a storyteller's careful design. As though Allende were anticipating her daughter Paula's tragic fate and her own decision to write *Paula* partly just to cope with the loss, she speaks in May 1991—fully five months before Paula falls ill and is hospitalized, and with no awareness of her daughter's impending sickness—about writing (in the characterization of her interviewers) as an "act of remembering to forestall death." Thus does the topic that will dominate interviews of the mid-1990s arise explicitly here for the first time: spirituality. "I believe that there is a spirit, a spirit of life in everything that surrounds me," Allende says. "I try to be in touch with that" (no. 20).

1991–1995: PAULA AND THE BEYOND

But the Spirit of Death was to envelop Isabel Allende and her family first. Attending a Barcelona book party on December 8, 1991, for the publication in Spain of *El plan infinito* [*The Infinite Plan*], she received word of a cataclysmic event that would alter her life abruptly: her twenty-seven-year-old daughter, Paula, who had fallen sick on December 6 and entered a Madrid hospital, had slipped into a coma. Paula would die precisely one year later to the day. Like Alba in *The House of the Spirits*, who followed the advice of the spirit of her grandmother Clara, and wrote to "survive" the ordeal of her rape and her family's anguish, Allende coped with Paula's death by heeding the counsel of her mother, who told her: "If you don't write, you'll die."[24] Allende explains of the note-taking that led to *Paula*: "I was not thinking of publishing . . . my only goal was to survive; that is the only time that I have written something without thinking of a reader" (no. 25).

The interviews from this third period focus on Allende's personal life and on her loss of Paula; even the interviews conducted before the appearance in 1994/1995 of *Paula* devote attention to Allende's loss. Indeed, given that Allende's two books during this period are based on her husband's life (Willie Gordon is the model for Gregory Reeves, the protagonist of *The Infinite Plan*) and on Allende's relationship to her daughter, it is unsurprising that interviewers highlight Allende's roles as wife and mother.[25] What emerges is less the outsized heroic, even "magical realist" portrait of the feminist and socialist in the mid-1980s, or the exotic Chilean Scheherazade of the late 1980s and early 1990s, but rather a more subdued, humanized figure.

Put another way, it is as if we see Allende close up in this most recent round of interviews, rather than against the giant mural of Latin American history or through the gossamer fantasia of Eva Luna. The mid-1990s mark what might be called "the family period" of Allende's interviews. Some of these interviews have a familiar, even confidential tone, making them truly "conversations"; more so than in earlier years, we encounter the private woman behind the public persona. Allende says several times in these interviews that the death of her daughter had "changed" her; one interviewer remarks that Allende's recent experience had "erased all the unnecessary barriers that separate human beings" (no. 26). During my own interviews with her in April and May 1995 (nos. 31, 32, and 33) I found Allende to be a noticeably different woman—more reflective, less goal-directed, more self-revealing, less guarded—than I had in my earlier interview, conducted in 1988. At fifty-two, Isabel Allende seemed suddenly to have taken a mystical turn—and discovered a new House of the Spirits.

And with that discovery have come "lessons" that Allende has drawn from the harrowing year of Paula's sickness: the words "destiny," "trust," "acceptance," and "openness" come up again and again in interviews after Paula's death. Indeed one notes that the whole cast of her conversation has shifted to the spiritual realm:

> Life is like a very short passage in the long journey of the soul. It is just an experience that we have to go through, because the body has to experience certain things that are important for the soul. But we shouldn't cling to life and the world so much: we shouldn't cling to the material aspects of the world, because you can't take them with you. You will lose them no matter what. (no. 24)[26]

Throughout her book tours of 1994/1995 to promote *Paula*, Allende spoke about learning to "let go." As she put it in one interview: "When I said, *dead*, [Paula's death] became real and I could deal with it" (no. 23).

Elsewhere Allende has spoken of another, more mundane "death," or form of "clinging," with which she also still copes: literary ambition. "Ambition is like a bottomless pit," Allende says. After the publication of *The House of the Spirits*, she "had the sensation that I had done something in my life and I could now die in peace," but soon the hydra-headed monster returned to haunt her: "One becomes ambitious and wants more and more" (no. 13).

Asked in another interview to sum up what she has learned as a result of Paula's passing, Allende makes her spiritual discovery even more explicit:

> Your approach to the world is different. . . . You become more detached. . . . You gain a sort of spiritual dimension that opens up completely your world. (no. 28)

Or as Allende put it in another interview: "I finally understood what life is about; it is about losing everything. Losing the baby who becomes a child, the child who becomes an adult, like the trees lose their leaves. So every morning we must celebrate what we have."[27]

Allende is speaking about learning a different kind of exile—a leavetaking of the temporal world—and it seems that she is approaching the sense of peace and acceptance implied in the words told to Eva Luna just moments after the death of her mother: "Everyone dies, it's not so important."[28] For Allende, the death of Paula eventually became—the paradox is only apparent—both all-important and "not so important." "Godspeed, Paula, woman. Welcome, Paula, spirit," Allende closed *Paula*. Paula Frías had merely gone to her spiritual home, joining those intrepid women who govern the Trueba mansion—or, even better, those beneficent ghosts that watch over them.

But perhaps Allende's spiritual turn has not occurred quite so suddenly as it might appear, nor been precipitated by Paula's death alone. For Allende was already working through her fiction on the "lessons" that the harrowing year of 1991/1992 would bring home conclusively. Indeed the lessons from Paula's death that Allende draws in her interviews—Destiny, Trust, Acceptance, Openness—are all thematized (though treated somewhat skeptically) in the quasi–New Age evangelical Christianity propounded by preacher Charles Reeves in *The Infinite*

Plan, whose title Allende borrowed from a book of that title written by her husband's itinerant mystic-father, upon whom the character of Charles Reeves is based. Reeves proselytizes and peddles "The Infinite Plan, or The Course That Will Change Your Life," a package of lectures designed to put the recipient in tune with Cosmic Forces. Listeners flock to Reeves, and are "comforted by the certainty that their misfortunes [are] part of a divine plan, just as their souls [are] particles of universal energy."[29] And indeed, when Allende speaks in the interviews about "karma" and "Fate," it is as if she is sometimes quoting Charles Reeves—but this time sincerely, not ironically or parodically. It is as if she were preparing herself for the news about Paula—and the writing of *Paula*.

"I believe that there is a destiny. I also believe that you can do much to modify it," Allende remarks in one interview (no. 26). And so she ultimately comes to an opposite conclusion from that of her protagonist, Reeves's son Gregory, who says at the novel's close to the Allende-like author-narrator:

> I realized that the important thing was not, as I had imagined, to survive or be successful; the most important thing was the search for my soul. . . .
> [I never imagined] that one day I would meet you and make this long confession. Look how far I've come to reach this point and find there is no infinite plan, just the strife of living. . . .[30]

I have the impression that Isabel Allende might today say instead: "Look how far I've come, only to realize that there's more to life than the strife of living—there may even be some Infinite Plan!" I find her openness to a change of heart in matters of the spirit both courageous and refreshing.

Allende's "courage" resides, I think, precisely in her heightened awareness and commitment to relinquish tight self-control and open herself to the possibilities of a providential Design beyond her own will. And such a change does seem to be one of "heart" rather than "head"—or rather, a form of growth reflecting a greater capacity to connect her heart and head. For Allende already, by the time of composing *The Infinite Plan*, seems to have possessed the cognitive ability to recognize the existence of an Infinite Plan; Gregory Reeves reports that the Allende-like author-narrator had countered his chastened conclusion that "there is no infinite plan, just the strife of living," with words of hope: "Maybe . . . maybe everyone carries a plan inside, but it's a faded map that's hard to read and that's why we wander around so and sometimes get lost."

Allende's courage and openness have also extended to a greater capacity for self-disclosure about her private demons. Fearlessly yet modestly, she now abandons reticence in her interviews and discusses her struggles to renounce perfectionism, to nourish intimacy, and to silence her stern, unrelenting conscience and "inner voices" of Authority (no. 32). In these later interviews, readers gain a deeper understanding of the paradoxical woman behind the work: a woman who, though private, likes to be seen and noticed; who luxuriates in solitude yet possesses a flamboyant, extroverted sensibility and lives life intensely; who is a careful planner yet glories in the moment; who has a steadiness and an iron will dedicated to work, and yet also a spontaneous emotional life and a tendency to act on impulse; who has a shrewd pragmatism and keen sense of responsibility, and yet is ruled by passion and does not wait for Life to happen but rather provokes her Destiny.

And yet: What also about the other Allende—the writer behind the woman? How has she been affected "after Paula"—and after *Paula*?

"All sorrows can be borne," Isak Dinesen once wrote, "if you put them into a story or tell a story about them." In advising Allende to write about the agony of Paula's dying, Allende's mother seemed intuitively to have grasped Dineson's insight—and indeed, writing the story of her confrontation with Paula's death has not only effected her spiritual transformation, but also affected Allende's writing. As yet, she is not quite sure how, except that she is less concerned with the literary "product" (no. 32).

In several interviews of the mid-1990s, Allende is, understandably, in a backward-looking, pensive mood—not only because she is discussing *Paula*, but also because she has built a substantial body of work—six books in a dozen years—that she wants to assess, especially now that she has learned to grant herself the honorific title "writer." Summing up her literary development in the 1980s, Allende told one interviewer that "each one of my books corresponds to a very strong emotion." She associated *The House of the Spirits* with "longing," a desire to recapture a lost world; *Of Love and Shadows* with "anger" in the face of the abuses of dictatorships; and *Eva Luna* with "accepting myself, finally, as a person and a writer" (no. 13).

The early and mid-1990s were also a time for Allende to reflect in her literary interviews on both her vocation as a writer and her literary successes and shortcomings. Implicitly conceding the force of some critics who found the politics of her second novel intrusive, Allende says: "If I were to write *Of Love and Shadows* again, I would do it differently. It is not subtle enough and I feel it is too direct" (no. 13). Although she says that it is easier to be a woman in the United States than in Latin America—since the feminist movement has advanced farther in the United States, Allende tells her feminist critics: "I don't invent characters so that they serve as models for radical feminists or young women who want to be feminists, but I simply tell how life is. Life is full of contradictions" (no. 26). More extensively than before, she also discusses the autobiographical background of *The Infinite Plan*, particularly the similarities between her husband William Gordon and the novel's protagonist, Gregory Reeves. Gordon served as the "model" for Reeves, who "is a survivor. In real life Willie is too. . . . The people who bend but never break are always fascinating to me" (no. 23).[31]

In the aftermath of the American publication of *The Stories of Eva Luna* in 1991, Allende was often asked about her plans to write more short fiction. She tells one interviewer that she's not going to write any more short stories. "I would much rather write a thousand pages of a long novel than a short story" (no. 25). And also: "I'm scared of short stories, very scared" (no. 23). Allende confesses that she has difficulty writing "erotic" scenes. "Every writer of fiction," Allende asserts, "should confront these three challenges: write short stories, an erotic novel, and children's literature" (no. 13). Allende has already written a story collection and a children's book; although she has certainly written several erotic *scenes* in her fiction, and devoted a whole new book (*Aphrodite*) to sex and food, the challenge of the erotic *novel* remains. "I really would like to write erotic novels. Unfortunately, I was raised as a Catholic, and my mother is still alive, so it's difficult. However, I feel that there is a part of me as a person that is extremely sensuous and sexual" (no. 25; see also no 23).[32] As so often, Allende's tone is overtly quite sober—and yet also slightly playful. The reader is not certain how seriously to take her—which is doubtless the way she wants it.

A related topic that engaged interviewers was Allende's response to the film versions of *The House of the Spirits* and *Of Love and Shadows*, both productions of which she admired and enjoyed. Allende's statement to one interviewer on seeing the film version of *The House of the Spirits* attests again to her necromancer sensibility:

> Now the fiction has replaced the real story of the family, and we live this sort of fantasy that these things happened. When I saw the movie, I realized immediately that the fiction of the film is ten times bigger than the fiction of the book. Very soon, we will have the photographs of Jeremy Irons and Meryl Streep on the piano. They will be my grandparents. I will have all these famous people as my relatives.

Like Eva Luna, Allende also said that she would one day like to try her hand at writing screenplays herself. But, for now, prose fiction—novel length—is enough. And through all the vicissitudes of her romantic and family life, novel writing remains the great solace and tonic for Allende. "Writing is never a burden," she says. "It is pure joy. Life tends to be a burden, because it has very grave moments, with a very heavy karma." But she still jokes that she'll never discuss work in progress—as if such a lack of reticence might also boomerang with karmic vengeance: "It's like boasting about a boyfriend—someone may take him away from you."[33]

Life is loss, Allende admits—but she insists that she will not accept losses without putting up a good fight.

Although the leitmotif of this third period of interviews is less literary than spiritual, less humorous than contemplative, the "lessons" that Allende draws from the loss of Paula also have to do with love. Whereas in earlier interviews Allende had invariably used the word "love" in connection with sexual passion, she speaks after Paula's death also of maternal and filial love. For example, Allende says that, before Paula's death, she had practiced only conditional love, but that through Paula's departure she learned true "love" as "giving":

> I even rarely trust a lover. . . . It is very difficult for me to open up, to fully abandon all in an intimate relationship. I begin from the premise that I will be betrayed. . . .
>
> Up [until the last days of Paula's illness], all my relation-

ships, even the relationships with my children, had been a two-way road. . . . But I was left with the everlasting treasure of the love that I gave her and that I know I am capable of giving. (no. 22)

This knowledge has been acquired by Allende at a very painful price, and for this reason she values even the pain itself: "I do not want to lose this pain," she says. "It makes me a better person" (no. 22).

In speaking of herself as a "better person," Allende is not referring to virtue in the ordinary sense, but rather to a perception that she is humbler, more clear-sighted, more forgiving, more empathic. The loss of Paula also taught Allende to let go of the urge to plan life; her new attitude of fearlessness and openness to the future is a marked change:

I have no plans for the future. . . . If you have no plans for the future, you cannot fear it. You are not afraid of being unable to carry out those plans. I try to live today as best I can. That way I have the feeling that I have finished everything. (no. 22)

And Allende observes in an interview published in December 1994:

My daughter died, and she's with me in a way that she never was when she was alive because she had a life of her own and she had a destiny of her own. She still has them, in the spiritual world she's doing things, but the memory of her lives in me. I carry it with me and it's part of my life in a very vivid way. So vivid, in fact, that when I come here every morning I light a candle for her. I have her photograph and her ashes there and I feel her presence very strongly. There's a lot of sadness still going on, but I know that I will get over that and there will be a point when I will understand the spiritual life better and will not be stuck in the loss. I will probably be connected better to who she is now. (no. 28)

Or as Olga says in *The Infinite Plan*:

The dead go hand in hand with the living.

By the time of the appearance of *Aphrodite: A Memoir of the Senses* in April 1998, Allende no longer seemed "stuck in the loss" of Paula's horribly tragic death. Although she had told at least one interviewer in 1995 that she might never write again (no. 33), the act of composing *Aphrodite*, as Allende explained during her U.S. book tour in the spring of 1998, helped her rediscover a capacity to live in the present. She had written her memoir of her daughter's death; now she would write a celebration of life: a "memoir of the senses." *Aphrodite* is, she said in one interview, her "healthy reaction to mourning and writer's block" that followed Paula's death.[34]

In another interview, she discussed her struggle to emerge from her "long tunnel" of grieving,[35] a battle that forms a prominent theme in *Aphrodite*: "After the death of my daughter, I spent three years trying to exorcise my sadness with futile rituals. Those years were three centuries filled with the sensation that the world had lost its color and that a universal greyness had spread inexorably over every surface. I cannot pinpoint the moment when I saw the first brush strokes of color, but when my dreams about food began, I knew that I was reaching the end of a long tunnel of mourning and finally coming out the other end, into the light, with a tremendous desire to eat and cuddle once again."[36]

On Allende's own account, she recovered her artistic powers and her feeling for the sensuality of language by immersing herself joyously in the world of amour and appetite. Revive the senses and the imagination, counsels Allende, and you will revive the spirit too! So Isabel Allende affirmed life by relishing two of its earthiest appetites—sex and food—and in a light, delicate, feminine, playfully poetic way. "When I wrote *Paula*, about her death, I cried every day," Allende told an interviewer for *Ms.* "Now, when I was putting together *Aphrodite*, I finally laughed. A lot . . ."[37] Mixing the carnal and the culinary, *Aphrodite* connects Allende's love of writing to the prime drives that create and perpetuate life and make it pleasurable—and thereby reconnects the author to her deepest creative wellspring as a storyteller.

In literary terms, *Aphrodite* is virtually unclassifiable.[38] Viewed biographically, however, it is clear that this lavishly illustrated cookbook served as a literary aphrodisiac for Allende's dormant literary powers. And here we can witness the Latin American Scheherazade assuming the persona of the Greek goddess of love and beauty. Indeed the new work is the author-grandmother's personal recipe for summoning the love goddess within, a self-help book on how to recover a keen taste for life's sweetness—and, yes, its bittersweetness.

As in the case with her earlier books, Allende credits her family— and her familial House of Spirits—with assisting her completion of her new book (most of the recipes were developed by her mother, Panchita Llona). And, she insists, they have also guided her through the "tunnel of mourning" into "the light": "I don't believe in ghosts. But I do believe in memory. When I say somebody's spirit helps me, I mean that when I need poetic inspiration, I think of my grandmother and the crazy character she was. When I need something to be from the heart, I think of Paula, who had such generosity. When I need courage, my grandfather, this stubborn Basque, carries me through. I have photographs of them, all over.[39]

Memory, of course, is the memoirist's prize resource. And it is significant that Allende's two books in the mid-1990s have been memoirs, i.e., that Allende wrote another work of "non-fiction"—rather than fiction—after *Paula*. While memory had returned, aided by her family spirits, the imaginative powers through which her novels emerged still had not. Indeed, as Allende admitted to one interviewer, throughout the mid-1990s she simply could not write fiction, because "it just wouldn't come": "Fiction, for me, just happens, I let the story unfold itself. I don't think of a plot, an outline, characters. I allow them to appear before me. After Paula died, it just wouldn't come like that. So I did nonfiction: first I wrote about her illness and her death. And now, this" (*Aphrodite*).[40]

Allende has always maintained that while her nonfiction—like her journalism—is an act of will, her fiction "just comes," arriving unbidden and on its own schedule, a gift from beyond. The gift of fiction had been absent from Allende's life for a long time. Eventually, however, it did "just come." In 1998, having emerged into "the light," Allende started her sixth novel—once again, on January 8.

NOTES

1. *Paula* (New York: HarperCollins, 1995), 181, 182.

2. For information about these productions, see the following: Sarah Provan, "The Shooting of 'Spirits,'" *Europe: Magazine of the European Community*, no. 327 (June 1993): 41–42; Brian D. Johnson, Review of *The House of the Spirits*, *Macleans* 107, no. 15 (April 11, 1994): 69; John Powers, Review of *The House of the Spirits*,

New York 27, no. 15 (April 11, 1994): 56; and Bodo Fruendt, "The Chilean Trag-edy," *Süddeutsche Zeitung*, October 5, 1994.

3. *Eva Luna* (New York: Knopf, 1988), 223. That admonition, of course, could have come from Allende herself, and it warrants mention here how much Allende's feelings resemble those of her fictional characters. In numerous author profiles with the mass media she speaks through the voices of her characters, straightforwardly quoting one of her fictional characters' statements, without "attribution," as an ex-planation of her own ideas or states of mind—and which interviewers then cite accordingly, unaware that the line actually comes from one of Allende's literary characters.

Consider, for instance, the following statement that Allende made in a 1988 in-terview with Susan Benesch ("Mixing Fantasy, Reality," *St. Petersburg Times*, De-cember 11, 1988, 7D): "Writing novels is my private orgy. I'm never afraid of the white paper. It is something like a clean sheet recently ironed to make love."

The interviewer concludes her profile with that stunning metaphor, apparently unaware (despite the title of her article) that the line comes from the mouth of Eva Luna herself: "I took a clean white piece of paper—like a sheet freshly ironed for making love—and rolled it into the carriage. Then I felt something odd. . . . I wrote my name, and immediately the words began to flow, one thing linked to another and another" (224).

4. So not only are we readers indebted to Allende's willingness to "put up with" interviews; Allende herself is also indebted to the numerous men and women she has interviewed to sharpen her understanding of events or round out characters' personalities. Allende has noted that Rolf Carlé (in *Eva Luna*) is based on the son of an SS officer whom she interviewed in Hamburg; and especially in her research on portions of *The Infinite Plan* (New York: HarperCollins, 1993), Allende has acknowl-edged her debt to interview subjects—the most important of whom was her own husband, who served as the model for the novel's protagonist Gregory Reeves. She elaborated in her 1994 interview with Farhat Iftekharuddin: "It is much better to research with interviews of real people who have experienced the event, whatever that event may be, than going to a library and looking at books. . . . Journalists are in the streets hand in hand with people talking, participating, and hearing."

Understandably, given Allende's professional past, the topic of interviewing itself surfaces occasionally in her interviews. Her interviewers like to ask how it feels to have the tables turned on her, now that she must answer, rather than ask questions. And one sometimes also has a sense that Allende may be playing with the interview, sometimes embroidering or inventing episodes, or just testing out new *personae*—much as Jorge Luis Borges was wont to do.

Indeed, Allende's "reinvention" of herself in her interviews places her within an already well-established Latin American literary tradition. As Ted Lyon remarks: "Borges turned the interview into a literary genre, a game, a personal art form that he often controlled more directly than the interviewer." And, of course, the tradi-tion is not just Latin American; William Faulkner was famous for telling tall tales and conflicting stories (including even various statements about his birthdate) to interviewers.

On Borges, see Ted Lyon, "Jorge Luis Borges and the Interview as Literary Genre,"

Latin American Literary Review 22, no. 4 (July–December 1994): 74–89. On Faulkner, see James B. Meriwether and Michael Millgate, eds., *Lion in the Garden: Interviews with William Faulkner, 1926–62* (New York: Random House, 1968).

5. For one German reviewer's puzzlement over *Paula*'s classification, see "'Paula' ein Hymnus an das Leben," *Focus Magazin*, 28 March 1995.

6. When the interviewers for *Contemporary Literature* suggested to Allende, however, that her interviews constituted "a kind of storytelling for readers interested in literary interviews," Allende responded: "Let them read fiction."

Perhaps oddly, Allende maintains that interviews themselves—especially literary interviews—hold little interest for her. Told by *Contemporary Literature* (no. 20) that she was becoming "a best-selling interview subject," Allende claimed that she herself "would never read a literary interview." She is only interested in the interview for journalistic purposes—to provide information or to aid her construction of fictional worlds: "I'm not interested in what other writers have to say, only what they write."

Allende does acknowledge, however, that many people are as interested in what she says as in what she writes, and that her frankness with her interviewers sometimes yields unsettling results. For example, Allende relates this funny story: "A man who said he was a doctor came over after a lecture and said he'd listened to several of my interviews, read several interviews, listened to me on the radio, and now he'd heard me in this lecture, and he was convinced that there was something wrong with me. That I didn't have a line between reality and fantasy; that that had a name in psychology; and that I should see a therapist!" For her part, Allende reflects, she would rather remain "sick" than become "cured"—because then she would have no neurosis out of which to write (no. 20).

But Allende is indeed indebted to the interview genre for her new career: She willingly and often recounts for interviewers the aforementioned story of her encounter with Pablo Neruda—which she confirms was a "turning point" in her life— and sometimes does so in an even more spontaneous, ingenuous way than in the already-quoted passage from *Paula*. In a breathless style that is echoed by the starstruck commentary of some of her own interviewers of the 1990s, Allende tells *Confluencia* in 1990: "We had lunch, and when I was driving there, I thought, 'This guy won the Nobel Prize. The most important poet, the most important writer of Latin America, and maybe in the world wants me to interview him!' Of all people, me! I always thought that I was great, I had a big ego at that time. After lunch, I said, 'I'm ready for the interview.' He said, 'What interview?' I said, 'Well, the interview.' He said, 'What interview? Look, my child, I would never be interviewed by you, you are the worst journalist in this country. You never tell the truth. You are always in the middle of everything, you are never objective, why don't you switch to literature.' Neruda was right" (no. 11).

Allende's homage to Neruda has been open and frequent. For instance, she quotes Neruda as the opening epigraph of *The House of the Spirits* and mythologizes him simply as "the Poet" in that book's poignant funeral scene. And the epigraph to the Spanish edition of *Of Love and Shadows* is a famous line about Chile from Neruda: "I carry our nation wherever I go, and the oh-so-far-away essences of my elongated homeland live within me."

7. Allende in a 1991 interview (no. 20): "I'm always inventing my own life, so I find that in different interviews I tell different stories about the same subject. My husband says that I have twenty versions of how we met, and I'm sure the twenty versions are true! His version is not true! So I can't tell you if they are accurate or not. My life is fiction too." By 1994 (no. 23), the story had grown: "I have fifty versions of how I met Willie, my husband. He says they are all true."

8. *Paula*, 231.

9. *Eva Luna*, 15.

10. Quoted in William Butts, ed., *Interviews with Richard Wilbur* (Jackson: University of Mississippi Press, 1990), xiv. Commenting on the emergence of the literary interview as an independent genre, Butts notes: "The form of the literary interview has come into its own, with no less potential for strengths and weaknesses than any other form" (xiii).

11. Alexander Coleman, "Reconciliation among the Ruins," *New York Times Book Review*, May 12, 1985, 1.

12. Agosín is also a human rights activist and fiction writer. Perhaps her best-known works are two short-story collections, *Happiness* (1993) and *Woman in Disguise* (1996). Agosín, a Chilean-born German Jewish writer who was educated in the United States, is sometimes classified with Allende as a Latin American "magical feminist"—along with such writers as the Puerto Rican Rosario Ferre and the Argentine Luisa Valenzuela.

13. Patricia Hart, "The Stories of Eva Luna," *The Nation*, March 11, 1991, 316.

14. And such heroine-worship sometimes provoked a reaction among left-oriented critics, one of whom called *The Stories of Eva Luna* "the populist pipe dreams of a bourgeois Latin American leftist who struggles to recover through literature a lost link with the exotic native culture she somewhat disingenuously claims as her own." Daniel Harris, "The Stories of Eva Luna," *Boston Review* 16, no. 2 (April 1991): 28.

15. Allende's father, Tomás Allende, who abandoned the family when Isabel was a small child, was actually the first cousin of Salvador Allende. Isabel Allende is thus actually a second cousin of Salvador Allende, who was also her godfather and, as the *paterfamilias* of the Allende clan, gave her away at her 1962 wedding. But Allende made it clear to me in a personal communication (May 6, 1998) that she and her relatives have always thought of (and referred to) Salvador Allende as her "uncle."

16. A few years later, however, she would become visibly frustrated by critics' imputations that *The House of the Spirits* was derivative, a mere knockoff of *One Hundred Years of Solitude*, with García Márquez's Macondo transposed into Allende's unnamed, semi-mythical "half-forgotten country at the end of the earth."

On this view, Allende has written a family chronicle that is merely imitation García Márquez, right down to the magical realist techniques and even its parallel characterization, with Rosa the Beautiful based on Remedios the Beautiful, Clara on Ursula, Nicolás and Esteban on Jose Arcadio Buendías, Blanca on Amaranta, and Tío Marcos on Melquíades.

As Allende's defenders have noted, however, such dismissals ignore the feminist perspective—what Patricia Hart has called Allende's "magical feminism"—and the journalistic sensibility informing *The House of the Spirits*. For instance, Allende stresses that she takes historical documents or reportage and uses them as background for her fiction. Máximo Pacheco Gómez's book *Lonquén* (1980), which summarizes an independent investigation of the disappearance of fifteen Chileans in the village of Lonquén, served as the source material for *Of Love and Shadows* (see nos. 3, 5, 11, and 13).

17. Allende discusses the significance of January 8 in *Paula* (p. 280), and in nos. 2, 19, 21, 23, 24, and 31 in this volume.

18. Elizabeth Mehren, "Allende Weaves Novels of Private Pain, Public Passion," *Los Angeles Times*, February 10, 1988.

19. See, for instance, Alan Ryan, "Scheherazade in Chile," *Washington Post Book World*, October 9, 1988, 1–2.

20. In some ways, these explorations constituted a new round of legend-building: an opportunity for Isabel the Storyteller to engage in a different form of self-mythologization. As she confessed in 1988: "What I dream at night is sometimes more important than what happens during the day. When I met my husband, I recognized that I had dreamt of and written about someone like him in Eva Luna. I invented him before I met him" (no. 7).

Or as she closed another 1988 interview: "Writing *Eva Luna* was imagining how the world could be if I accepted myself—and if I had love. I imagined that happening for Eva Luna, and then it happened to me—a year later."

To which the interviewer deadpans: "Please be very careful about what you write next" (no. 8).

21. As she declared in an address, titled "Why I Write" and delivered at the University of Virginia in April 1988: "I write about the things I care about: poverty, inequality, and social problems are part of politics, and that's what I write about. . . . I just can't write in an ivory tower, distant from what's happening in the real world and from the reality of my continent. So the politics just steps in, in spite of myself."

The language, the social commitment, the will to bear witness, and even the artist's reluctance to make a political statement echo George Orwell's famous essay of the same title. (Allende later published the address as "Writing As an Act of Hope," in *Paths of Resistance: The Art and Craft of the Political Novel*, ed. William Zinsser [New York, 1989], 39–63.) She elaborated on this theme in an interview published in 1994: "I feel I have a mission. I belong to the lowest of the low in the social classes in this country. I am Latina and I am a woman. But I have a platform to speak in English about my culture" (no. 22).

22. By contrast, she is contrite about some difficulties in her personal life, e.g., the breakup of her first marriage and her decision to divorce her husband: "There was no reason for not loving him, he deserved love, but you know, love has no rules" (no. 8).

That 1988 comment, which marks Allende's first reference to Miguel Frías in any published interview, also points to the paradoxical fact that, while Allende does openly cultivate a myth of herself, she also insists on her privacy. She keeps a low public profile and does not associate much with other writers, let alone California celebrities; she draws a tight circle around parts of her private life and does not expose them to public inspection.

23. Elizabeth Mehren, "Private Pain, Public Passion," 5.

24. *Paula*, 45. Allende adds: "It was destiny—and it was bad luck. After they told me, I went on writing because I could not stop. I could not let anger destroy me."

25. Noting that Gordon's reading *Of Love and Shadows* had piqued his interest in Allende and led to his wanting to make her acquaintance, Allende deadpans: "I am convinced he married the book, not me" (no. 13).

26. Such remarks may smack of watered-down New Age mysticism to skeptical or sophisticated, academically oriented readers. But Allende's confessional tone possesses both credibility and charismatic power precisely because she has lived through an agony—the loss of a child—that moves people deeply. I witnessed just how deeply people are moved during Allende's dramatic presentation at the University of Texas in April 1995. Many listeners in her audience of twelve hundred were left alternately weeping and laughing by her emotional honesty, as she addressed topics ranging from dying to karma to the non-causal "synchronicity" of events—topics that are rarely touched upon in public by literary figures, particularly in academic settings.

27. Margot Hornblower, "Paula," *Time*, July 10, 1995, 65.

28. *Eva Luna*, 41.

29. *The Infinite Plan* (New York: HarperCollins, 1991), 15.

30. *The Infinite Plan*, 381, 379.

31. Allende interviewed her husband formally and informally, along with others (especially one Vietnam veteran) whose stories might enrich her narrative. She became a journalist again—but now with a substantial difference: not only were her reportorial skills again put in the service of her emerging fictional worlds, but she now relied on interviews to create characters, gain cultural literacy about American history, and fill in large knowledge gaps (e.g., she interviewed several people about topics such as the California counterculture and the antiwar protest movement of the 1960s).

32. On this theme in Allende's work, see Maureen E. Shea, "Love, Eroticism, and Pornography in the works of Isabel Allende," *Women's Studies* 18, no. 2–3 (September 1990): 223–231.

33. William A. Davis, "The Magic Realism of Isabel Allende," *The Boston Globe*, April 14, 1991, A40.

34. Zillah Bahar, review of *Aphrodite*, *The San Francisco Examiner*, May 20, 1998, 13.

35. Diane Carman. "Recipe of Sensuality Focuses on the Physical," *Denver Post*, April 5, 1998, F5.

36. *Aphrodite*, 24–25.

37. Claudia Dreifus, "On Erotic Recipes, Love and Grief, Writing, and Life," *Ms.*, March/April 1998, 39–40.

38. The genre is, however, not unknown in Latin America (though it is usually associated with fiction). The best-known example is Laura Esquivel's *Como agua para chocolate* (*Like Water for Chocolate*), published in 1992.

39. Fred Kaplan, "Angel of Gluttony and Lust," *The Boston Globe*, April 1, 1998, D1.

40. Dreifus, "On Erotic Recipes," 39.

Note on the Selection

Most of the thirty-four interviews contained in *Conversations with Isabel Allende* originally appeared in scholarly books and journals, literary reviews, intellectual journals of opinion, and mass circulation periodicals. Given that some of the interviews were originally published in little-known academic publications, this collection aims to make Allende's conversations about her life and work more accessible to her real public: the general reader.

The volume also includes four previously unpublished interviews, three interviews that I conducted in April and May 1995 and one that Virginia Invernizzi conducted in June 1995, in order to bring the story of Allende's life up to the time of *Paula*'s American publication and the author's spring 1995 book tour.

A special feature of this collection for the American reader is the inclusion of translations of foreign-language interviews with Allende (in Spanish, German, and Dutch), all of which were originally published in non-U.S. periodicals and are made available here to English-language readers for the first time. These interviews offer revealing glimpses of Allende's literary reputation outside the United States, which has been high not only in Spain and throughout Latin America, but also in Europe.

The interviews are ordered chronologically according to date of publication rather than date of occurrence. One reason for this choice is practical: the precise date of a given interview was sometimes difficult to establish. But my main rationale has to do with this collection as a contribution to literary history. And what concerns us in this book is less the woman's life than the role of her interviews in the writer's unfolding literary reputation: the public perceptions of the writer as shaped and reflected in her interviews. Not the raw biographical events in Allende's life history but those events in her "interview history" significant for her "reputation" history command our attention. The schoolgirl's years in Bolivia and Europe and Lebanon, the young woman's first marriage to Miguel Frías, her work as a journalist and editor and TV interviewer in Santiago, her 1971 play *The Ambassador*, her relationship to her uncle Salvador Allende, her self-exile to Caracas and schoolteaching and writing for *El Nacional*: these landmarks, though obviously decisive for Isabel Allende's personal development and early, word-of-mouth reputation, became part of her "interview" history only long after their occurrence.

Not until the mid-1980s, after the publication of *The House of the Spirits* in the major European languages, did Allende's literary reputation begin to emerge, whereupon she quickly attracted the notice of interviewers—and soon shifted her role from celebrity interviewer to celebrity interviewee.

As I have noted in the introduction, this collection offers glimpses into the evolution of this process. The interviews selected for the volume have been culled in order (variously) to identify the milestones in Allende's interview history, to spotlight the diverse faces or personae that Allende the interviewee has presented to her readers, and/or to draw attention (where pertinent) to certain recurrent metaphors and questions that have contributed to Allende's literary reputation.

All republished conversations are printed uncut. While this results in occasional slight repetition, I believe that the comprehensive overview that emerges is valuable, for it suggests the key areas of biographical interest in Allende's work. To read the recurring questions that preoccupy interviewers over the years—and to note how their questions subtly shift with each new publication or event in Allende's life—illuminates our understanding of Allende's self-image and public images—as do, even more so, Allende's varied responses to those questions.

Information about the original publication of each interview is given at the head of each interview; the exact date on which the interview was conducted is also provided when that date is known. In their original appearances, many of the interviews were prefaced by short introductory notes. I have included these notes when they contain significant biographical data or useful information about the circumstances under which the interview occurred.

Pirate, Conjurer, Feminist

INTERVIEW BY MARJORIE AGOSÍN
Translated from the Spanish by Cola Franzen

Reprinted from *Imagine* 1, no. 2 (Winter 1984): 42–56

The House of the Spirits,[1] first novel of Isabel Allende, is already, after barely two years of existence, a critical as well as a popular success. It has gone to twelve editions in the original Spanish and has already been translated into French, German, Italian, and Norwegian. The English translation is scheduled for the spring of 1985.

It seems as though *The House of the Spirits* has been protected by a benevolent and tender sorceress similar to the central character of the book, Clara del Valle. Isabel Allende herself says her novel "was born under a sign of good fortune,"[2] and adds, "Some months ago, when the book was first published in Spain, I saw it for the first time displayed on a table in a bookstore. I huddled in a corner, timid and frightened. I was afraid for my novel. I knew that it no longer belonged to me; I could do nothing to help it. But with the passage of time I have calmed down and now I believe there actually exists a spirit that watches over the book."[3]

To enter the magical, enchanted territory of *The House of the Spirits*, to become accustomed to seeing clairvoyant, clear-eyed Clara in her white tunics floating through the rooms and causing beautiful melodies to play on the closed piano, to see her at a table of light-colored wood writing entries in the notebooks of life, is to become part of this invisible strand where a free-wheeling imagination is joined together with a lucid, true story.

The House of the Spirits is the imaginary world of its picturesque characters, of Esteban Trueba, the feared but finally benevolent patriarch, a man possessed of an out-of-control sexuality; or the Mora sisters with their aroma of lavender and lemons bringing omens of good and bad news. The novel is also the history of a Latin American country, scourged by the tyranny of a monstrous dictatorship. The country is not named but we know it is Chile. We recognize its Cordillera and its implacable seas, its earthquakes that besiege this lost frontier of the planet. In masterful fashion the accomplished writer Isabel Allende leads us page af-

ter page through the intricate labyrinths of Chilean history from the
end of the last century up to the present day.

Between the lines, or rather overlaying the text, the pattern of the
ages-old domination of the land by the oligarchy becomes clear; then
the first signs of agrarian reforms of the 1960s emerge, ending in the
triumph of Salvador Allende, followed by his downfall, plotted and
carried out by the forces of the political opposition both from within
Chile and without. Throughout the nearly four hundred pages of the
book the history of Chile is clearly delineated, from the era of the great
landowners to the revolutionaries who were to end their lives in prison
cells reduced by fear, injustice, and impotence.

Thus *The House of the Spirits* is a double text. On one level we have
the story of the Trueba family and its unforgettable progeny, both legitimate and bastard. On the other level we have the political and social history of Chile from the end of last century to the present-day
tyranny of Pinochet.

Among the most interesting protagonists of the novel the winsome
Clara stands out—Clara who chose to remain silent for nine years. She
deliberately chose silence not out of passivity or fear but rather because that was the only way for her to create her own space composed
of hidden signs and signals, and three-legged tables that could levitate
as she herself could. But in addition to her clairvoyant alchemy, Clara
is the center of a dynasty of women dedicated to aiding the dispos-
sessed, women-bearers of tenderness and nurture for all the indigents
who pass through the immense house on the corner.

The comparison of Clara with Ursula of *One Hundred Years of Solitude* is inevitable. Both women maintain an ancient family line and
keep order in the family not only by means of their domestic skills but
also by means of spirits whose invincible powers they manipulate. From
the line of Clara and Esteban Trueba, Blanca is born, and then comes
Alba, the daughter of Blanca, who inherits the powers of her grandmother to carry on a tradition of the family, the noting down of life in
enormous notebooks, tied with colored ribbons, and "divided according to events and not according to chronological order" (p. 380).

The woman-centered history of these three women encloses the history of the country. In the book various family members constantly
move back and forth from the country to the city. This kaleidoscopic
to-and-from erases the line between the unbridled fantasy of the fic-

tional characters and the true demented history of the country; they become intertwined.

Isabel Allende describes not only the mad geography of Chile with its arid deserts and its earthquakes, but she describes at the same time the hatred and violence that the monied upper class unleashes time and again against the ordinary people of the country. Toward the end of the novel she also makes mention of the victory and defeat of the popularly elected government of Salvador Allende.

The House of the Spirits brings out many real facts about the military dictatorship that are well known by Chileans and Latin Americans. Among these true events that are also events in the novel is the death of Pablo Neruda, known in the book as "the most widely translated poet in the world." In the fictional character of Pedro Tercero, lover of Blanca and father of Alba, we recognize the folksinger Víctor Jara, whose hands were mutilated before he was assassinated a few days after the coup. It is sobering for the reader to see behind these events and to realize that they were not invented. They are part of the true history of Chile. The hatred, the houses of torture are real. Alba as a prisoner invokes the spirit of her grandmother Clara who advises her to start noting down life, using as an aid Clara's own notebooks that recorded fifty years of real and imaginary events. Now Alba, like Clara, will recover the past and will survive the horror of transient nightmare.

The House of the Spirits arrived in Chile by a clandestine route. Months later when the censors permitted dangerous books to enter the country, the novel returned to its place of birth, to the denseness of volcanoes and forests, "to this country accustomed to the dignity of pain" (p. 370), but whose faith in hallucinations, magic, and liberty will allow the dictatorship, death, and exile to be erased. No doubt Alba will write in the notebooks of life that the nightmare of tyranny was a cataclysmic plague-ridden wind, but one that will be overcome forever.

From Venezuela Isabel Allende, in the midst of correcting the galley proofs of her second novel, has answered our questions regarding her novel and its own spirits, which are also our own.

---

66 *When Chileans or Latin Americans read your novel,* The House of the Spirits, *we read about verifiable events at the same time: the deaths of Allende and Neruda, the assassination of Víctor Jara in the National Stadium, all of them characters who appear in your book.*

We would be interested to know how you intermesh the historical with the fictional in The House of the Spirits.

For me it is difficult to draw a line between fiction and reality in literature. A novel is made up partly of truth and partly of fantasy. The author uses something of experience and knowledge and something of his or her own angels and demons to create a personal version of life, a personal vision of the world. If the author succeeds in making the story believable, even within the limits of the improbable, a literary truth has been created. In *The House of the Spirits* the phantoms of the past are so intermeshed with the events that have left such a mark on my country that it is very difficult for me to separate reality from fiction. In my intimate contact with books, first as reader and later as writer, I have come to the conclusion that it isn't worth the trouble to make a boundary between the events that occur within the pages and those that take place outside. Daily life is brimful of fantasy and at the same time books are saturated with reality. I feel that all things float within the realm of the possible. As a reader I let myself be carried away by the enchantment of a story, without worrying too much about its authenticity. As a writer I abandon myself in the same way to the necessity of telling, convinced that if something is not exactly true at this moment, it may be so tomorrow. That's the way I have found it to be in my work.

How and where would you place your novel within the present-day Chilean narrative and especially within the area of exile writing?

Perhaps others, more knowledgeable about literature than I am, could respond to this question. I feel like a pirate who has boarded the ship of letters at an age when other women my age are taking care of their grandchildren. I write out of impulse because it gives me pleasure. I have no idea where my work belongs.

Did you ever imagine that The House of the Spirits *would be so successful, with critics as well as with readers? How do you feel about this novel of yours that has traveled so far?*

When I was writing *The House of the Spirits*, I thought it would be published, but there were many jokes about it in my family. My children said they would go out and peddle the book on buses, and my husband was sure that he would have to pay for the publication. It was a big surprise for all of us that the spirits of the book had such good luck.

> *Did you decide ahead of time to write a saga of a family? That is, how did you choose this way of telling your story, and do you yourself see a connection between* The House of the Spirits *and* One Hundred Years of Solitude? *Were you influenced by* Hundred Years?

When I left Chile, after the military coup, I lost in one instant my family, my past, my home. I felt like a tree without roots, destined to dry up and die. For many years I was paralyzed by a kind of stupor and by nostalgia, but one day in January of 1981, I decided to recover what I had lost. I sat down to write the story of a family similar to mine, the story of a country that could be mine, a continent resembling Latin America. . . . It was almost the act of a conjurer. I have always loved family sagas, especially those written by French and North American writers, who are outstanding in this field. *One Hundred Years of Solitude* influenced me as it has influenced almost all writers of my generation in this part of the world, but I was not thinking of the Buendías while I was writing the story of the Truebas.

> The House of the Spirits *begins and ends with the same sentence. Could you say something about why you chose this strategy for the book?*

I visualized the book as a string of beads. Each anecdote, each character, was a separate bead strung on one string. That is why I wanted to close the book where it began, as if one had fastened the clasp of a necklace. I also wanted to show that life goes in a circle, that events are intertwined, and that history repeats itself. There is no beginning and no end.

> *How did exile, nostalgia, and memory contribute to the conception of your novel?*

I believe I have answered this question earlier in my response to question four. Perhaps the only thing I might add is that if there had been no exile, no pain, no rage built up over those years far from my country, most likely I would not have written this book, but another.

Clara, Blanca, and Alba are luminous, extraordinary women. Do you think that each one of them represents an aspect of the Latin American woman, and if so, which aspects would these be?

In general, fictional characters are special people. Ordinary people do not provide good material for novels. Therefore I chose extraordinary women who could symbolize my vision of what is meant by *feminine*, characters who could illustrate the destinies of women in Latin America. All of them somehow managed to escape from the daily routine, from the limitations placed on them as women. Clara finds fulfillment in the spiritual world and in helping those around her, in charity. Blanca is saved from mediocrity through that great love that she experiences as a tragedy and that marks her every step. Alba belongs to the younger generation and is turned more toward the outside world, toward work, politics, the preoccupations of our present-day society. All these stances are common to the women of our continent and have always been so. I invented nothing. I only chose the most obvious examples.

Why did Clara choose to remain silent for so many years?

The character of Clara del Valle is based on my grandmother. She was a radiant, extravagant woman, and at the same time a spiritual being. But she was bored by the small nuisances of daily life, she could not bear meanness, she fled from violence and vulgarity. When she felt that the atmosphere around her became charged with negative influences, she would submerge herself in her interior world, pull up the bridges that connected her with the outside world and remain silent. She could be silent for days on end. It seems a beautiful idea to me and for that reason I attributed to Clara that ability to escape from the world through silence.

Your work is permeated with the magical atmosphere of childhood. Tell us something about what your own childhood was like.

I grew up in the large and shaded house of my grandparents, surrounded by eccentric uncles and ancient maids. I was a sad and solitary child, but my childhood was full of magical things, strong emotions, changes and upsets, ghosts that roamed through the rooms and escaped through the mirrors. I had a reclusive and formidable uncle who slept in a room crammed full of books. His books multiplied all by themselves, like rabbits, and spilled over into the corridors, the attic, the basement, and all other rooms of the house. I read, at random, everything that fell into my hands, in accordance with my grandfather's theory that no one will read anything that doesn't interest him and if it interests him, he is old enough to read it. This reading fueled my imagination. My mother was an extremely beautiful and solitary woman, to whom I was very attached (as I still am today) by a bond stronger than the umbilical cord. She also stamped my destiny by her unconditional love. The years of my childhood are a treasure that I keep with me and that I recovered intact in order to put them into the pages of *The House of the Spirits*.

> *Do you see Clara as a feminist, settled in her own space, and is that the reason that she resorts to the techniques of clairvoyance and witchcraft, which are typical methods of escaping from a patriarchal society?*

All the women in my book are feminists in their fashion; that is, they ask to be free and complete human beings, to be able to fulfill themselves, not to be dependent on men. Each one battles according to her own character and within the possibilities of the epoch in which she happens to be living. Clara lived at the beginning of the century, when divorce was unthinkable, as was working outside the home. She was subject to a despotic husband whom she did not love, but she freed herself from him by the only path possible for her: the path of her spiritual life and her preoccupation for the poor, the helpless. She was naturally outraged by every form of injustice, but she did not have sufficient information, and possessed neither the power nor the tools necessary to bring about a "women's liberation," as we understand the term now, a half century later.

> *What does the word* Chile *mean for you?*

Pablo Neruda said that Chile is a large flower petal. . . . This word evokes for me the landscape of my country: the Cordillera with its purple peaks, the sea, wild and cold, a silent and suffering race, the aroma of pines in bloom and apples. I love this land and when I say *Chile*, my voice breaks. But after so many years of exile I understand that my country is all of Latin America, that all of us who live in this continent are brothers and sisters. Our stories are similar; our earth is the same.

Do you see a possible return to democratic values in Chile?

Democratic values have never disappeared from Chile. We must not confuse the Chilean nation with the dictatorship that is ruling it now. Chile is its people, its land, its past, its present, and its future. Pinochet and the evil ones who are with him are an accident in the long life of my country. They will go into history as a misfortune that darkened the sky, but they will go.

What is your feeling when you see The House of the Spirits *in other languages?*

About my book in translation, it is surprising to me that Esteban Trueba and his extravagant clan are going around the world speaking different languages. I can't imagine them loving and hating in Norwegian, for example. However, I do realize that human beings are the same everywhere; the differences are not so great. This story of the Trueba family could have happened anywhere.

How much has your experience as a journalist influenced the writing of your novel?

My work as a journalist has been fundamental in my literary creations. Journalism taught me to know and love words, the tools of my trade, the material of my craft. Journalism taught me to search for truth and to try to be objective, how to capture the reader and to hold him firmly and not let him escape. It taught me to synthesize ideas and to be precise about events. And above all, it rid me of any fear of the blank page.

NOTES

1. All the references to the novel are from the edition of the Spanish original, *La casa de los espíritus* (Barcelona: Plaza y Janés, 1982).

2. Testimony of Isabel Allende in *Discurso Literario* 2, no. 1 (1984): 67–71.

3. Isabel Allende, *Discurso Literario*, 68.

"The World Is Full of Stories"

INTERVIEW BY LINDA LEVINE AND JO ANNE ENGELBERT

Review: Latin American Literature and Arts 34 (January–June 1985): 18–20. Copyright 1985 by the Center for Inter-American Relations, Inc. Reprinted by permission of the Americas Society, Inc.

During her stay as writer in residence at Montclair State College, Chilean writer Isabel Allende talked with Linda Levine and Jo Anne Engelbert about her novel, *The House of the Spirits*.

> *The four generations of women in* The House of the Spirits *are really remarkable. Are Nívea, Clara, Blanca, and Alba intended to be representative of their respective generations?*

Not really. All four women in the book are extraordinary. They all break away from tradition. You wouldn't expect to find the mother of fourteen children standing in front of a factory teaching feminist theory in South America. That's inconceivable!

So each of the women finds her own way of breaking free?

Exactly. Nívea escapes through her social involvement, her activism; Clara is another woman who simply doesn't fit into conventional molds. She escapes through her contact with the spirit world, through her charitable work. She's a remarkable woman for another reason: With her personality she manages to control the power her husband has over her, quite a feat! Blanca, who is a less-flamboyant character, has the experience of a great love. She lives this experience as if it were a novel and escapes living a humdrum life. Alba, of course, becomes an activist, and that is her salvation from a mediocre existence.

Did you model these characters to some extent on women you have known?

Yes. The book is dedicated to the extraordinary women who have always surrounded me—my grandmother, my mother. In a way, the novel is a homage to all Latin American women, all Chilean women. Women who, in a crisis, are willing to risk everything.

Latin American women who have been heroic . . .

Incredibly heroic. In Latin America we've seen that in situations of extreme danger the people who take the greatest risks are often women. They are capable of total selflessness, total courage. When the time comes to make a revolution, women are there in the front lines . . . but afterwards, of course, when it is time to divide up the power, they are inevitably left on the sidelines.

That sounds familiar enough. What the women in your novel have in common, then, is more important than what separates them.

Yes. They have so many things in common that sometimes I think they are all the same woman transferred from era to era. The first thing they have in common is a bond of blood that goes beyond mere biology; it's a chain of love that goes from mother to daughter and which conveys some special qualities that are not transmitted to men. I'm talking about feminine solidarity—something I believe in because I've seen it, I've experienced it.

Do you think it's universal?

Absolutely. It links together all women who've had similar experiences and makes them capable of understanding, of making sacrifices. I've found women to be very loyal to one another, for example. Rivalry and competition are not the norm in relationships among women—at least not in my experience. That's why I feel like laughing when I see those incredible women in *Cosmopolitan*, sex objects who are always portrayed as if they were fighting with each other to get the richest or best-looking man, because in real life these women show tremendous solidarity; they help each other. They are sisters whose similarities are much more important than their differences.

Perhaps there's another link as well; all the women in the book are artists of one kind or another; they're all creative people.

Yes, it was important to me that they be creative, not because creativity is the exclusive patrimony of women nor anything of the sort, but because women's creativity has been hidden for so long. There is also a kind of symbolism in the fact that they all do the same thing: In some sense they all invent a world. When they put two parts of an animal together to create a monster, for example, they are inventing worlds—declaring that they do not need to live within a world of masculine values, that they can incorporate their fantasies, their feelings, into a world, a universe they create themselves. I think that men and women are really not so different. If we were left alone, if we were not mutilated, so to speak, by an education that alters our course of development, we would all be persons who did not have such rigid roles and would lead happier, fuller, more integrated lives.

> *So you think a woman's education alters the course of her development?*

I think that what is mutilated is our intellectual potential, along with ambition, energy, strength, power, aggressiveness . . . , but while this part of us is being mutilated we are allowed to have that other part of ourselves, so that we won't be complete vegetables, I suppose, and that other part somehow saves us. A woman who is a fighter can acquire that other part for herself if she makes the effort.

> *That's what your women do, in different ways. And they have an impact on those around them. People are fascinated by the evolution in Esteban's character, for example. By the end of the book he has not only come to terms with his machismo, he has even adopted Clara's vehicle of expression; he begins to write as she does.*

The relationship Esteban has with Clara is the relationship he has with the rest of the world. He wants to possess her completely, from the first lines of the book when he sees her for the first time. He marries her, and on their honeymoon he tells her that he wants to possess her absolutely, to the very essence of her soul, to the point where she will have nothing that does not come from him. In this desire to possess her he loses her. He had lost her from the start, really, and for the rest of their life together he goes on losing her more and more. The loss is complete when she dies. Then, as he grows older, he begins to realize that he has lost her world around him, he has lost his children, he has lost the country, he has lost everything. At this point, he begins to become more human. He realizes that the relations he establishes with the world and with human beings must not be relations of power but of sharing and understanding. He begins to change, and as he changes, Clara appears to him. Her ghost becomes more and more real until the moment comes when he sees her as if she were alive. He says that Clara touches his hair, that Clara sleeps with him—lays her head on his shoulder and sleeps with him; she finally belongs to him when he stops wanting to own her, when he sees that they belong to each other. But this is twenty years after her death.

Machismo, then, is a global attitude that has political consequences.
Of course. Have you ever seen anything more *machista* than the military mentality? It is the synthesis, the exaltation, the ultimate exaggeration of machismo. There is a direct line from machismo to militarism.

How conscious were you of structure as you were writing The House of the Spirits? *There are so many reflections in this mirror that is the novel.*
When I wrote *The House of the Spirits* I knew a little less about literature than I know now, that is, nothing at all. I wasn't thinking about good literature but about telling a story. In my second novel I did do more planning. I do more planning now, but at the same time when it comes time to sit down and write, I just let myself go. I sit down before the blank page and I write and write. Afterwards I cut and rewrite, but at the point of creation it is completely instinctive. It is like making love. It really doesn't help to know all the techniques and to have Masters and Johnson on the night table—when the time comes, you're on your own.

How wonderful it must be not to fear the blank page . . .
When I finished *The House of the Spirits* I thought "I'll never have another idea." I did have a dry period for a while, a kind of post-partum blues; this is a time when everything seems gray and you are gather-

ing strength from your own roots in order to begin to move again. When I finished the second novel, I felt the same way. But deep down I knew that wasn't really the case. It was a matter of setting myself a deadline, so I said, "On January 8 I'll start—and on January 8 I started. The world is full of stories to be told, of people to bring to the pages. If you open your ears and your eyes you'll never run out of things to write about, because you don't have to dredge everything up out of yourself—you can capture things in the air, from other people, from what people tell you. Mama calls me on the phone to tell me that she went somewhere to have tea and heard a story, which she proceeds to tell me, or she says, "Listen, I read in the obituary column that someone named Apulenio Naranjo has died; what a lovely name . . ."

On Shadows and Love

INTERVIEW BY MICHAEL MOODY
Translated for this book by Virginia Invernizzi

First published in Spanish in *Discurso Literario: Revista de Temas Hispánicos* (Paraguay) 4, no. 1 (Autumn 1986): 127–143

3

Isabel Allende's two novels, *The House of the Spirits* (1982) and *Of Love and Shadows* (1984) have achieved a type of success not commonly seen in the publishing world. They have been best-sellers both in Western Europe and in Latin America. The English version of the first novel, *The House of the Spirits*, was published by Alfred A. Knopf in May 1985. In a few weeks it made the best-seller list in *The New York Times Book Review*. Isabel Allende did not leave Chile for more than a year after her uncle, Salvador Allende Gossens, fell from power due to a military coup in 1973. It was a very difficult time for her yet it was a time which was preparing her for the second novel in which she treats the theme of the "desaparecidos." She now lives in Caracas, where I interviewed her many times in her house in June 1985. What follows focuses, in large part, on the origin and the context of *Of Love and Shadows*.

" *I understand that with the great success of* The House of the Spirits, *you receive many invitations and you travel frequently.*

Yes, I receive many invitations, but turn down the majority. I realized that if I accept all the invitations that I receive, I don't have any strength left to work. Literature is like love, a full-time occupation. It does not accept distractions. It is difficult for me to return to my writing every time that I interrupt my rhythm. I have to start from the beginning. I have to do it all over again. It's as though the characters were in the shadow lands and the daily work brought them out of the shadows into the light to gain volume, voice, texture, personality. When I leave they disappear slowly, and sometimes, when I return to my house, I do not find them.

What type of invitations do you receive?

Many are from the publishing houses that have printed my books in different languages. Others are conferences, seminars, talks. I try to leave for few days, and I avoid those where I cannot contribute anything. In general the invitations enrich me greatly, but on the other hand, the need to write is so strong in me that I have to weigh the benefits of the trip and then make a decision.

Are you finding time to continue writing with so many activities of that type?

I am a hard worker and a workaholic. I wake up very early and I lock myself up in the little "hole in the wall" room where I work. I love what I do. It is like a daily party, an orgy. I have never experienced the "torment" or the "anguish" that writers supposedly suffer. On the contrary, it is always a profound pleasure. I steal time from my other activities to write. I do it on weekends, at night. When I travel I take a notebook like Clara del Valle's notebooks in *The House of the Spirits*. Curious things happen to me; for example, people approach me and want me to write down their lives. Here, write it, they say. It is a beautiful present and I receive it and am very thankful thinking that it may be useful in the future for a short story or a novel.

How long does it take you to write a book?

I wrote *The House of the Spirits* in a year. Of course, it was a year of very intensive work. . . . At that time, I worked twelve hours a day in administration in a school. I could only write at night. But when I sat down at my typewriter, the words flowed like a torrent, because they had been inside me for a long time. That book is based on my life, my family, my country. Everything that I narrate there I know very well and therefore it required very little research. On the other hand, I had a lot of backup material. I had letters that I had written my mother over the years, old diaries and notebooks that belonged to my grandmother. I had also kept some of my journalistic articles and recordings. The last chapters in the book, those that talk about prison, torture, the dictatorship, are recordings and interviews of survivors of exile that I made clandestinely before leaving my country.

So you recorded stories of well-known people in Chile.

I left Chile fifteen months after the military coup and during that period I continued working. I was fired from the magazine *Paula*, but I carried on with my journalism. A large part of the material that I gathered could not be published in my country, so I brought it with me to Venezuela thinking that it could serve as testimony later on. At that time I had not remotely thought of writing a novel. I thought that those documents could be useful some day when it was possible to accuse the guilty. They were proof of the brutal violence that took place in Chile. There was a great silence in my country then—and it is still there—but I knew that silence would not remain forever. Sometime public knowledge of those horrendous events would surface, and when that happened, the stories compiled by me would not have been lost; they would serve as historical testimony.

What spurred Of Love and Shadows?

My second book is based on an event that happened in Chile, in the locality of Lonquén, about fifty kilometers from Santiago. Fifteen corpses of *campesinos* (assassinated during the military coup) were found in some abandoned brick ovens. This discovery was kindled by the Catholic Church in 1978, when I was in Venezuela. It took me a long while to gather all the material to write my story. In my book I do not mention Lonquén or the real names of the people. Similar cases of violence and impunity have occurred and continue to occur in Latin America. They have discovered clandestine graves in Argentina, Uruguay, Brazil, in many countries. Assassinations are daily occurrences in Central America. We are living an immense communal tragedy. My book is the story of the violence, the horror, and parallel to that, it is the story of the love and hope that are always present in our lives. I worked very hard on that book. I researched, I read, I searched.

Was there much published in the press about that incident?

There was a lot published in 1978 about those deaths and after that new evidence surfaced. It was not the only case, nor the first. But up until then, it was possible to keep throwing dirt on them and keep the murders in the shadows. That was the first time that open information came out about the crimes of the dictatorship. This was due to the intervention of the church, which did not allow for these crimes to be covered up as had been the case up to then. Mr. Máximo Pacheco Gómez, a lawyer of the Vicaría de la Solidaridad, in Chile, published the documents of the trial. His book came into my hands and it was very useful to me. There are certain parts in *Of Love and Shadows* that are almost literally taken from the declarations of the military and the witnesses; for example the confession that Lieutenant Colonel Ramírez gives. That was not his real name, but his words are in my book. I changed the name of Lonquén to Los Riscos, and other details, but the rest is almost all taken from reality. This does not mean that the book is a report. There is much fiction in it and the book is constructed as a novel. But my trade as a journalist helps me in literature; reality is often richer than the imagination. For example, in *The House of the Spirits*, the burial of the Poet is exactly what I lived through in September of 1973, when I walked behind Pablo Neruda's coffin with a bundle of red carnations in my hand. That night I wrote a letter to my mother telling her how I felt. She kept that letter, and years later I used it in my novel. That type of document is very important to me. My memory remembers the events, but often forgets the depth and quality of emotion. I was able to recreate with precision the details of the burial thanks to that letter which was written the very same instant that things happened. I think that firsthand testimony is of utmost importance.

Do you have a clear idea of what is documentation and what is fiction in Of Love and Shadows?

As a writer it is very difficult for me to know how much reality and how much fiction there is. The thin line that divides both is ephemeral and can disappear with only a breath. I suppose that some of the main characters are based on well-known people. Irene Beltrán is the synthesis of three Chilean women, journalists like herself, who worked investigating the atrocious reality of the dictatorship. I had a psychologist friend who ended up taking pictures for a living because he was out of work. He was Catholic and actively worked in the opposition. He helped a lot of people, the same way that Francisco Leal did. I think that with Francisco I wanted to pay homage to my friend, and others who, like him, put their lives on the line for what I believe is a desire for human solidarity, rather than for political conviction. Those people risk their lives for brotherly love. I think that's admirable. The Flores family is a product of my imagination. In real life, there were five members of the Maureira family who were assassinated in Lonquén. As I read that in the newspapers in Venezuela, I had a terrible feeling. I couldn't stop thinking about the women in that family. I felt they had acquired the characteristics of the Greek tragedies. I saw them as a choir of mothers, sisters, wives, matronly women dressed in black, searching for their men for five years, standing in line, asking about them in the military quarters, hospitals, prisons, reading the lists of the dead, visiting the morgue, bribing the soldiers, knowing deep down in their souls that at the end of that labyrinth all they would find was despair, but without being able to pray, cry, or bury their dead. And finally, one day they went to a patio where they saw, on huge tables, the rest of a horrible puzzle, the pieces of a macabre mystery: this is a piece from my brother's mouth, this is his comb, this is a piece from my father's vest, his blue vest, this is a shoe that belonged to my husband or my son. Thinking of those women and feeling their pain in my heart, I would wake up startled at night; they appeared in my imagination during the day. At times my mind would wander while driving and their memory would assault me along with an adrenaline rush. I understood that I had to exorcise this pain and leave testimony. That is why I wrote the book, even though the story did not seem very attractive. It seemed too sordid, too political. Fortunately, in the process of writing, I discovered that in contrast to extreme violence there is also extreme love . . .

So you had never had a personal relationship with that family?

No. I only know them through what has been published in the press. One of the daughters in the family went to Geneva and spoke at the commission on Human Rights. . . . Her words as a Chilean *campesina* are touching, moving. The entire drama of the *desaparecidos* is saturated with dreadful nuances. In many cases, uncertainty is worse than the reality of death. Ariel Dorfman, another Chilean writer, published a beautiful book, *Viudas* [Widows], where he deals with the problem of the women searching for their loved ones. It takes place in Greece, but it is like what is happening in Latin America.

There are certain scenes in your book, especially the ones in the morgue, that remind me of the movie Missing.

After the military coup, I had to go to the morgue with a person who was looking for a family member. The morgue is an atrocious, a violent spectacle. My book coincides with the film because they both narrate a reality. They are not fiction.

It made me think of the movie not only because of the experience of entering a morgue, but the mental process that Jack Lemmon's character suffered. He seemed . . .

Like Beatriz Alcántara, Irene Beltrán's mother.

Yes, someone who simply could not accept such an arbitrary and brutal reality. He always searched for the logical explanation within his own democratic context. Your novel also recalled Joseph Conrad's famous work, Heart of Darkness, *with that somewhat mythological voyage into evil.*

I have two obsessions, two recurrent phantoms: love and violence, light and darkness. That is where the title for the novel comes from. They are always present in my life like two antagonistic forces. Violence is a possibility, another dimension of our reality. There is an invisible frontier that separates the apparently orderly world where we live and whose laws we believe we understand, from another world which exists simultaneously, that surrounds us and covers a most terrible orbit. It is the world of violence whose laws we must improvise. At times, by chance, without mediation of our own will, we can cross that border and enter into contact with violence. Then, all that matters is survival. The rules of the game change, the values change. . . . Very few people can emerge from that experience undamaged. The panic, the terror . . . are such great forces that they can leave us deeply distressed. Some can possibly return to who they were before the experience, but deep in their hearts they know how much cowardice, betrayal, weakness, and cruelty there can be within them. There are many forms of violence: illness, poverty, old age, delinquency, drugs, and of course, the tremendous violence of a dictatorship. A dictatorship grants power and immunity to certain people, and allows them to air their maliciousness with no consequences for them but terrible consequences for others. That is what I wanted to narrate in my book: a voyage into violence and horror taken by two innocent people who have nothing to do with all that, who do not even suspect any of it. My protagonists are searching for love in the midst of a radiant spring. They meet, they love each other, they desire each other. All of a sudden they see themselves involved in a situation from which they cannot escape.

You mentioned that you have lived experiences of this type before. Would you care to comment on this?

I have lived skirting violence, escaping it with very much luck. People very close and dear to me have suffered prison, torture, death, and exile. I am not an exile in the complete sense of the word. They did not make me leave the country and I did not ask for political asylum in an embassy. I left because I could no longer stand the fear. I felt a visceral terror in Chile. It is difficult to talk about that. It is difficult to understand fear when you have not lived it. It is something that transforms us, that takes over completely. At the beginning, after the military coup of 1973, many people did not realize what was happening because we were not used to repression. Our country was an old democracy, we didn't know what a dictatorship was and even presumptuously scoffed at the "Banana Republics" where puppet tyrants ruled. We never imagined that could happen to Chile. The press was censored. Only rumors circulated; rumors about the tortured, the disappeared, the dead. Soon my job as a journalist allowed me to get closer to the sources of information, and that was how I was able to learn about the new reality better than others. Most of the people in the social strata that I moved in were like Beatriz Alcántara. They had supported the coup and celebrated the death of Salvador Allende and many others. That was the reason that afterwards they did not want to see the consequences, because they could not have borne the guilt. All the proof stood before their eyes, but they refused to look. I began to work with the church. I am not a practicing Catholic, but the only organization that remained on its feet after the blow of the military coup was the Catholic Church. The church became the channel through which help was given to the most needy, the ones in prison, families of the disappeared, the widows and the orphans, especially in marginal areas where unemployment reached the incredible number of eighty percent. That meant hunger for many. Soup kitchens were organized in order to feed at least the children. My job was to obtain food, so I went to the houses in the better districts, to the industries, restaurants, factories. Every day I crossed that line that separates the upper-class neighborhood from the lower-class ones. The contrast was so great that I slowly became ill from the pain and the shame. The underclass received the impact from the "politics of shock" imposed by the new economists from the Chicago School. The rich became richer. That situation was possible thanks to the regime of terror. The helicopters hovered like prehistoric flies above the shanty towns. The police and the army raided the working-class neighborhoods. Stray bullets killed children in their sleep. Every day they took away countless detained, and most never returned home. I saw bodies floating in the Mapocho River. I saw walls stained with blood. I saw the detained being shoved into the military vehicles. All that was there to be seen, but the people in the upper-class neighborhood lived as though all that were someone else's nightmare. They hid away in their houses, their clubs, their restaurants, their beaches, and their luxurious stores. My God, when I think about all that I still tremble. . . . At the beginning, soon after the military coup, it was possible for me to be in solidarity before all that pain, that injustice. There was space to move because the repression took a while to become efficient. I gave asylum to a few people. I had a very primitive vehicle, a Citroën painted with huge flowers in different colors. Sometimes I would pick up someone being persecuted by the authorities, hide him for a few days, and as soon as I could I would show him to an embassy where he would usually have to jump the fence to get in. I didn't realize the danger to which I was exposing myself. Soon afterwards, I understood how the repression worked. If they had arrested any of those people, they would have been tortured and made to confess where they had hidden. In that case my family and I would have been detained. I had two small children and had heard of parents whose children had been tortured before their eyes. Can you imagine something like that? That was an experience that I did not want to go through. It was more than any human being can resist. And so a great feeling of fear took over and something gave in inside me. Fear is a paralyzing feeling. . . .

I couldn't remain in Chile the way others stayed and are still working and fighting to overthrow the dictatorship, helping those persecuted by the government. I didn't have the courage. I stayed fifteen months and finally my husband, my children, and I left. I had lost a lot of weight, my skin was full of hives, and I couldn't sleep at night because I heard the screams, the laments. I saw horrendous scenes, I could feel the sound of the boots, and the screeching sound of the military cars (the only ones permitted on the street after curfew) halting to a stop. That is why I say that I know how cowardly I am. I know terror. It changes people. It is something that can tear apart a family, a society, a country. The most awful things become part of normality, and in order to survive in that climate of terror, it is necessary to accommodate reality: not to see, hear, or know.

> *You say that you are not Catholic, but your work is so full of love in many different dimensions: romantic and physical love, love as a defense, and even love that leads to political reconciliation. I was thinking that perhaps you had a religious orientation. If it is not so, how did you, then, come to own the beliefs that you do hold?*

I come from an anti-clerical family. I was not educated in Catholic schools, but in English Protestant schools. Religion never particularly attracted me. I don't practice a religion and I cannot believe in rites. I have not been touched by the magic wand of faith. I don't believe that earthly problems will be solved through divine intervention, but with our own effort, our love, and our magnificence. The solutions lie within the men and women who live in this world. It was experience that made me understand the power of love, especially those months in Chile under the dictatorship. Love is an extraordinary force, capable of confronting violence. For every one torturer, there are a thousand people ready to risk their lives in order to save another. For every soldier who shoots in a neighborhood, there are a thousand *compañeros* who help and protect each other. Most people feel solidarity towards others; that becomes clear in crisis situations. There are moments in the history of a country, a society, sometimes of an entire continent or of humanity itself, when the forces of evil seem to triumph. Evil carries with it great shamelessness, great impudence. When someone acts in an evil manner, they do it boldly; that is why it is so obvious. Kindness, on the other hand, is discreet and tender, but no less effective. Just like in the movies, I believe that the good guys are going to win. I have no doubt about it. When I travel, especially to Europe or the United States, that is, in the most developed societies, the young people talk to me about their disillusionment. They feel anguish about their world, about their history. They feel they cannot control anything, that they are prey to a nuclear catastrophe, that we will all be blown up into little pieces and that no one can do anything about it. . . . They feel that life must be lived all in one minute because there is no tomorrow. When I listen to them I feel like crying, shaking them, shouting at them that the lack of hope is the worst trap. I believe that I can change the world and I try to do that every moment of my life. I try with all my might . . .

If you are not Catholic, then do you consider yourself a Christian?
No, I feel the same respect for all religions.

How do you define yourself politically?
I do not belong to any political party. I am deeply democratic. I abhor all dictatorships no matter what color or tendency they may be. I believe that we can find original solutions in Latin America, that we can build more just and freer societies. Capitalism does not work for us, and neither do the communist regimes. You cannot take what has worked in other countries and apply it rigidly to Latin America. The Third World lives mired in abuse, misery, corruption, ignorance, social inequality, and extreme exploitation from the developed world (the imperialistic countries). You cannot apply the system that seems to work so well in the United States of free enterprise and absolute capitalism to the Third World. This same system is ruthless in the poor countries and only works to build up pressure and violence until one day all that blows up. The systems like those of the Soviet Union or China have also proved ineffective strategies in Latin America because our reality is different. As I said, we have to look for our own solutions that correspond to our history, our culture, our needs. . . . That should be our task, not only the governing body's task, but the task of every man and woman in this tortured continent. Because of all the misery and injustice that I have seen, my natural tendency

points towards socialism. I belong to a privileged social class; I have never been hungry or lacked basic needs. I have had access to education, travel, culture, and health. That gives me a double responsibility. I am placed right smack in the middle of this reality, of the poverty of our people. These are my people, the ones that come to my house each day begging for a piece of bread because they are hungry. I cannot hide behind a wall to forget the responsibility that befalls me in a time of great changes. On the contrary, by being privileged, my duty is greater than others.

So, as far as politics is concerned, you don't subscribe to one doctrine.
No. We are searching for new solutions because we cannot apply what works in other places. I did support Salvador Allende's project. How could I not? He proposed a revolution in freedom. In Chile there had never been as much freedom in all aspects of national life as when the government of the Unidad Popular was in power. There was even debauchery in the press. The right would publish aberrations, cropped pictures of the president, absolute infamy. But there was freedom. Ah, for sure there was that. . . . It was a great awakening for large masses of people, an ebullience of the social classes that historically had been held back. It was a rebirth of popular culture, of ideas, of projects. There was political voice and economic revival for the lower classes. But unfortunately that magnificent project did not turn out to be. If it had worked out, if they had allowed Allende to go through with his project, if the CIA had not interfered and the opposition had had better historical insight, then possibly that idea of a socialist revolution in freedom would have spread throughout Latin America and the Third World like wildfire. And what is wrong with that? How does that jeopardize national security in the United States? Why do we have to divide the world into East and West, capitalists and socialists? There are alternatives, there are other solutions. Without social justice how can you avoid the increase of violence? It is impossible to repress three-fourths of humanity for an indefinite amount of time. This is a time bomb that will no doubt explode. Allende's project was original and it deserved an opportunity. I am sorry it did not work out . . . the enemies were too powerful. I am not only referring to the United States' international policies, but to the internal enemies that Allende

had: the bourgeois, the oligarchy, the right-wing business and invest-
ment groups.

> *Taking into account what happened in Chile, do you agree with those
> that say that only an armed struggle can make a revolution?*

No. There are other ways. But without a doubt there are times in the
history of a country when it is necessary to oppose revolutionary violence to institutionalized violence. That is happening today in Central
America. What does a country like Nicaragua, which has lived for
years under a dictatorship, do? Only through an armed struggle can it
overthrow tyranny. In Chile, the opposition is searching for a negoti-
ated agreement in order to attain democracy. I hope they succeed because otherwise there will be years of war.

> *The reviews of your work have placed much emphasis on the com-
> parison with García Márquez and the literary context of Magical Re-
> alism. What do you think about this?*

I find it difficult to objectively critique my own work. Nothing that I
say will be valid. I write as I can. I sit down and cast out the story because I like to tell stories. I am trained as a journalist and this helps
me to observe reality. Journalism gave me a way of confronting the
word, of capturing the story, of looking at the world and synthesizing.
In journalism you have little room to narrate. You have to say it all in
a few lines. You must trap the attention of your reader in the first
paragraph and retain it. That helps me in literature. I also worked in
the theater and there I learned about the importance of emotion, of
making the public laugh or cry, of constructing credible characters
that seem fully real. That also helps me when I write novels. I don't
compare myself to other writers. I take many of them as teachers, possibly all those whom I have read, especially Pablo Neruda. He truly
marked my vision of the world. He taught me to see the small things
and to approach reality through the senses: smell, taste, touch, and vision. I suppose that when I was writing *The House of the Spirits* I recalled the Russian family sagas. There is a French writer, Henri
Troyat, who was born in Russia and had to flee with his family after
the revolution to Paris. He tells beautiful stories about his family, his
country, the revolution, the exiled who lived awaiting the return to

their land and could never return. It baffles me that when thinking of a family in literature people can only remember the Buendías. There are others in world literature. . . . On the other hand, I am also marked by the fact that I live in this continent. Here, strange and bewildering things happen, and you, the outsiders, call that "Magical Realism." But for us that is everyday life. Would you like me to give you an example? I have just moved out of my house and I had more than one hundred boxes of books. The movers refused to touch some of the boxes which contained copies of my book in different languages. I had labeled these boxes "good spirits." They thought that inside those boxes lay something magic, something dangerous, possibly some poor spirits trapped in the moving. I had to open the boxes to show them that they only contained books. It is only a small detail, but it shows that in our world spirits can be as real as you or me.

And that happened with the "good spirits." I wonder what would have happened with boxes marked "bad spirits."

[*Laughs.*] I look over the news every day and cut out the bizarre news, the more peculiar things that happen. If I then put them in a book, people think I invent them and ask me, "Where do you get your remarkable imagination?" They don't believe me when I tell them that it was all published in a newspaper. I go to the periodicals and newspapers library to read old newspapers and I discover genuine treasures of the absurd, for example the woman who gave birth to a two-headed monster, one head was white and the other black. If I put it in my book, I will have to come up with many explanations for my readers to believe it. In *The House of the Spirits* the head of the grandmother lies lost and forgotten for twenty years in a cellar. That idea came from two real events. The parents of a good friend died in an automobile crash and the mother was decapitated in the accident. The head rolled under some bushes and the sons had to retrieve it themselves. When I was a child, there was a skull in my grandparents' house. It was probably made of plaster, I don't know, but anyway I used it in my witchcraft games. When I wrote my novel, I simply united the two stories and that was how the head in *The House of the Spirits* was born. I live in a continent where we don't need to invent much because reality is always surpassing our imaginations. It is a land of hurricanes, earthquakes, tidal waves, political catastrophes. It is impossible to imagine something more ridiculous and atrocious than some of our politicians and heads of state. It is not strange that Latin American literature is full of incredible dictators. Our nations were formed from the merging of all the races on the planet. They arrived here from everywhere bringing their legends, their customs, their languages, their dreams. We are marked by fantasy and violence. Our history is wondrous and our reality often seems that way as well.

When you reveal this magical reality, doesn't the constant comparison with García Márquez bother you?

Not in the least. I admire him, I love him dearly. . . . I hope to meet him some day. If they compare me to a Nobel Prize winner, to a man capable of writing those marvelous books, how could that bother me? I feel very proud!

Of Hunger, Hope, and Democracy

INTERVIEW BY SHANNON JONES AND BILL PRILLAMAN

4

Reprinted from *The Virginia Advocate* 3, no. 101 (October 1987): 11–13

" *Jones: Let's start with your books. Your first book,* House of the Spirits . . . *is it autobiographical?*

Well, in a way it is, because my family is in the book—my mother's family. Really, when I started writing, I didn't know it was going to be a novel. I thought, at the beginning, that it was a letter to my grandfather. My grandfather was like the main character in the book, like Esteban Trueba. I loved him very much. He was a very special person and a wonderful character for a book. But he was very old, very, very old, and very lonely in Chile. And he decided that he wanted to die. He was nearly a hundred years old. He sat in his armchair and he refused to eat or drink. He didn't accept any medical attention. Everybody respected his wish. Finally, they phoned Caracas, the family, saying that he was going to die. And I started a letter for my grandfather. I wanted to tell him that he could die in peace because I had forgotten nothing. All the things he had told me, all his memories, would live with me. I wanted to prove that. That's how I began with the story of Rosa. Rosa was the first fiancée of my grandfather. She died in the way it is told in the book. I went on writing, and writing, the whole year; working at night only because I had a very hard job in school at that time. And there I put everything that I remembered about my family, and then afterwards, about other families, and about my country, about things that had been very important in my life. But I am not in the book.

> *Prillaman: One thing I wanted to ask you: when you start writing, do you have in mind a general idea that you want to convey or do you have a pre-planned plot?*

I had a pre-planned plot but I can never stick to it. For example, my

second book is the story of a political crime, something that really
occurred in Chile, and I wanted to tell this terrible story. So I made a
lot of research, and I could have written, with all the investigation I
did, I could have written a document probably. But finally fiction
took over and it changed completely. The facts are there but it is fiction—it's a novel. When you start working in a novel, somehow the
characters start living. They become present in my life, in my house,
and I can no longer order them. They live their own lives—at the end
of course, after a year or so.

> *Jones: So your motive for the first novel was very personal. It started
> with a letter. But the second one was with more intention to write a
> book?*

It's always very personal because in the second book, the main character is Irene. She's a journalist and she works in a women's magazine. That's exactly the life I had in Chile after the coup. I also
belonged to a very conservative family, let's say an upper-middle-class
family, like Irene does in the book. It takes her a long time to realize
what is happening around her, and to really get involved in the world
around her. She would have never done it if she was not a journalist.
I lived those experiences very closely.

> *Jones: I have another question about* House of the Spirits. *I read*
> One Hundred Years of Solitude *and then your first book. The com-
> parisons are great—it seems that there is a good deal of influence of
> Gabriel García Márquez in your work. The use of the magical . . .
> and the supernatural: was that deliberate?*

No, it was not deliberate. On the other hand, this magic tint in Latin
American books is very common. Our life is very strange. We live in
a continent where all races have mixed; with a very overwhelming
geography; with a terrible political, economic, and social situation—
a world of contrast . . . of extreme misery and extreme riches. In the
United States you have a few people who have a lot of money, a very
big middle class, and then a few people who are on the bottom. The
situation in most of the third world is completely different. Literature
in the third world is less narcissistic than European or North American literature. We are so immersed in a world of so much violence

and so many problems that a writer cannot keep himself apart. Literature in Europe or the United States is more a personal matter. A writer writes practically for himself, and about himself, and about how hard it is to write. We don't have time to think of that.

Jones: What changes do you look for in the relationship between the United States and Latin America?

First of all, more understanding. In Latin America, you can't say that the problems can be traced to Communist ideology. You can't divide things between East and West. The main problem is not a problem of ideology, it is a problem of hunger. It is a problem of extreme misery and exploitation. That's why there is so much violence. In those societies there is so much contrast. With that violence, injustice, corruption, very easily you can start a revolution. This is unthinkable in a country like the United States. There is no need for that. You will not understand that unless you see it.

Jones: It seems to me that one of the problems in Latin America is having groups that agree on the fundamental level, parties that agree on having a democratic government, and can disagree on the finer points. Parties that will be able to accept an alternation of power, rather than having polarized positions.

There are countries like Venezuela which have learned that lesson. Venezuela lived under dictatorships for fifty years. When finally it obtained its democracy, they are very much aware that they have to defend it. They agree. There are practically no leftist parties in Venezuela. The Communist Party and Socialist Party are very small. There is a big Christian Democratic Party and a big "ABECO" which is very similar to PRI in Mexico . . . it is a popular, democratic party. They both agree on the basics and they say no, we have to be careful and not provoke the militarists. Anything is better than dictatorship and we will do anything, even alternate power, to avoid dictatorship. Yet there are other countries where you cannot possibly understand what is the matter. For example, in Argentina, in the last sixty years, not one civilian government has ended its period. They have all been overthrown by militarists. The situation in Chile is very, very strange. We were the country that had the longest democracy—160 years of democracy. We had a very long tradition and political consciousness. The people were very much involved in politics in Chile. There were many political parties. The tendency was always towards the center . . . democratic socialist, in the center. Allende presented himself as a candidate four times, and the fourth time, he was elected. He was not elected by the Socialist Party, which was his party. He was elected by the union of parties from the center and the left, which was called the Unidad Popular. After Allende's death, and after the military coup, these parties, which were officially united during the period of Allende's government, could not achieve any form of union in the opposition. In that sense, Pinochet is very clever. He managed to keep them divided. He has divided the opposition so well that it is practically impossible to oppose him legally.

Prillaman: Do you think the situation is more radicalized now?

No, on the contrary I think that most Chileans want a democracy— any democracy would be OK now, at this stage, we'll see after. I really believe that the left in Chile has been practically obliterated. Of course, the Communist Party has grown, proportionally. It is forbidden, it is a clandestine party. The two social forces, the better-organized social forces, in Chile now are the Catholic Church and the Communist Party. The Communist Party is not big compared to the Christian Democrats or the Socialists or any other party in Chile, but it is very well organized. I think they have absolutely no hope of coming to power in Chile.

Prillaman: Salvador Allende said, in 1972, that he was not the President of all Chileans, and several days later he made a statement at a press conference that he stood with those who wanted to pave the road to socialism. That scared American policymakers. Who do you perceive that it scared more, Chileans or Americans?

Both. It would have been impossible for the CIA to overthrow Allende without the help of a strong opposition in Chile. Allende was elected with thirty-six percent of the vote. After three years of a very hard and difficult government, he raised his popularity to forty-three percent in 1973. At that moment, the CIA and the opposition in Chile thought that they would never destroy Allende with an economic crisis. They had to provoke the military. That would have not been possible without opposition in Chile. At that moment, half of the country was against him.

> *Prillaman: In Salvador Allende's interviews with Regis Debray he said that his agreement to uphold democracy was a tactical necessity that he planned to uphold just for the time being. Do you personally think that Salvador Allende planned to transform the democratic system of Chile into a socialist system?*

Allende was a socialist. He always said he was a socialist and everybody knew he was a socialist. He wanted to make very deep reforms within the constitution but he never changed the constitution and he respected all liberties in Chile—we had absolute liberty. I think he was a very strong democrat. I knew him personally. I don't think he would have done anything against people's will. I don't think he was cheating on the people. He said, "I was elected president and I will remain constitutional president for the rest of my period."

> *Prillaman: So do you think he would have upheld the statute of democratic guarantees if he had been able to serve out his term?*

I think that's what he intended. But I don't think that was possible any more in Chile—the situation was too violent. I lived in Chile before, during, and after the military coup and if I were to describe in one word those years, I would say that they were very violent.

> *Jones: Earlier, we were talking about the polarization in Latin America. Do you think the Chilean people are yearning for a pluralistic democracy?*

Of course, yes. All the political parties that existed before, and some new ones, are existing today. It is a pluralistic society. That's how it has always worked in Chile and that is how it will be after Pinochet. . . . I think the people in this country are basically honest. When they know the truth about something, they act honestly. People in this country have been misinformed for a long time about the situation in other countries. But as soon as this news breaks down, when people get to know what's really happening—they see movies, they read something—they react honestly. They exert a lot of pressure on their government. That's why we in Latin America are very hopeful.

> *Jones: What do you think about the Catholic Church's influence on the people of Latin America?*

Well, there are practically three Catholic churches . . . one Catholic Church, but it acts in three ways. One is the Vatican and it is so removed. It's in the other world. Then there is the Catholic Church that believes in the spiritual life and has been with the people in power always. That is the type of church you can find in places like Argentina. And then there is another church. The church of the priests that work in the slums, that work with the peasants and the Indians. They are those people who are in contact with the terrible reality and they think, well, we can no longer expect heaven. To solve these problems we should be involved with social changes. In Chile that church is very strong. After the military coup . . . the Catholic Church was the only door that was open through which Chileans could do something to help. From the very first day, the church started to help the prisoners, the widows, the orphans. That church has become very strong in Chile.

> *Jones: So it's not just the laity; you're saying that it is the clergy?*

Yes, the cardinal even.

> *Prillaman: Argentine writer José Donoso spoke here last year and said that, looking back at his work, he realizes now that he didn't mean much of what he said, that he just wanted to provoke certain responses or to make the reader think. Do you do that?*

Not consciously. I started writing five years ago and I don't know what will be my opinion in twenty years if I'm still alive. I don't do it on purpose. I am really very honest and very naive when I face a piece of paper. I have a very naive attitude. I am not detached or ironical. I might be wrong, of course.

> *Prillaman: Did you notice a difference in attitudes having lived in a country like Venezuela that is perceived to be one of the most demo-*

cratic, egalitarian Latin American societies compared to your last two years in Chile, which were incredibly violent and very tense? Did you see a difference in the attitudes of people?

Yes. There are differences. But you can blame those differences on many things. The racial mixture in Venezuela is different, the climate is different, the history is different. Latin America is very complex and fragmented society. I think that Chile is living a crisis . . . a historical accident. Chile has walked a long path and it has been interrupted. But then it will continue, and develop into the society it used to be. I liked that society very much. In a way, I think that we had more freedom, and more equality than most Latin American countries.

Jones: What would you tell a student here about Latin America?

I would tell you: try and be open-minded . . . because I'm a very intolerant person. I have only become tolerant after much suffering. And probably you will never suffer that much. It will be very hard for you to become tolerant. But if we can be open-minded it is easy to understand.

NOTE

The *Virginia Advocate* would like to thank Professor David T. Gies, Chairman of the Department of Spanish, Italian, and Portuguese, for his help in arranging this interview.

Chile's Troubadour

INTERVIEW BY MAGDALENA GARCÍA PINTO
Translated from the Spanish by Trudy Balch and Magdalena García Pinto

Reprinted from Magdalena García Pinto, *Women Writers of Latin America: Intimate Histories* (Austin: University of Texas Press, 1991), 21–42

5

> *" Where does your personal chronology begin, Isabel Allende?*

I was born in Lima (because my parents were diplomats), but by nationality I'm Chilean. I was so young when my parents separated that I have no memory of my father, and when it came time for me to identify his body in the morgue, twenty-five years later, I couldn't do it because I'd never seen him. I grew up in my grandparents' house—a somber place—huge, drafty, marvelous. I grew up surrounded by eccentric adults. I wasn't what we could call a happy child, but I did have my mother's unconditional love, and vast intellectual freedom. I learned to read when I was very young, and books were my companions throughout my childhood. There were so many in that house that you couldn't count them, organize them, or keep them clean. And I had access to them all, so I can't say which ones influenced me the most. My head is full of written words, authors, stories, characters, everything all mixed up together.

> *What kind of relationship do you have with your family now, particularly with your mother?*

My mother was the most important person in my childhood, and she has been the most important person in my life. She's my friend, my sister, my companion. We laugh at the same things; we cry together; we tell each other secrets and share the fun of writing novels. She made a very strong impression on me. Her love has always nourished me, and I'm sure I wouldn't be who I am now without having had such an extraordinary relationship with her.

Was your grandmother very special to you?

Yes. My grandmother also occupies a special place. She was the guardian angel of my childhood and still watches over me, even though she died thirty-five years ago. She was adorable, a refined spirit, a complete stranger to anything vulgar; she was delightful, with a wonderful sense of humor and a love of truth and justice that turned her into a hurricane when it came time to defend those principles. She died when I was very young, but she stayed with me. She never abandoned me. She is Clara del Valle in *La casa de los espíritus* [*The House of the Spirits*].

Are there certain childhood memories that have stayed with you and have colored your life in some special way?

One of my most vivid memories is of my grandparents' cellar, where I used to read by candlelight, dream of magic castles, dress up like a ghost, invent black masses, build forts out of an entire series of books that one of my uncles wrote about India, and then fall asleep among the spiders and mice. That dark, damp cellar was full of discarded objects, broken furniture, worn-out things, and ghosts. Time was suspended down there, trapped in a bubble. A cavernous silence reigned, and even my most tentative sigh sounded as strong as a gale. It was a beautiful world where the imagination knew no limits.

What part do your husband and children play in your life?

My husband's name is Miguel Frías. We met when he was nineteen and I was fifteen; we were complete children, absolutely truthful, with no secrets. We swore eternal love to each other with the certainty of those who know nothing of life. We've always been together, and it hasn't always been easy. We've fought and made up, we've destroyed and rebuilt, we've killed illusions and given life to children. We're growing old together. He gives me support, loyalty, love, confidence, tenderness, and freedom. I make him laugh.

By 1985, you had published two titles. The first, La casa de los espíritus, *has been through seventeen printings in Spanish and has been translated into almost every language in Western Europe. The second,* De amor y de sombra [Of Love and Shadows]*, has already had five printings in Spanish. So the name of Isabel Allende has become synonymous with tremendous success in Latin American literature. Also, you probably are the first Latin American woman writer who has become a best-selling author overnight. These two facts lead me to inquire about the beginning of your literary vocation. At what point did you start thinking about becoming a writer?*

The truth is that I'm a journalist and I've always worked as a journalist. I never had a literary vocation until I left Chile, my country. I think that the desire to write flares up inside me when I feel very strongly about something. There are people who say they need an image or an event before they can start writing. I need to feel a very deep emotion. In the case of *La casa de los espíritus,* it was knowing that my grandfather was going to die. For many long years after I left my country, I felt a tremendous paralysis. I felt I'd lost roots, that I'd lost my native land, that I'd lost my whole world. My friends were scattered: many had disappeared, many others were dead. One day I got a phone call from Chile saying that my grandfather was dying, and that he had told the family he had decided to die. He had stopped eating and drinking, and he sat in his chair to wait for death. At that moment I wanted so badly to write and tell him that he was never going to die, that somehow he would always be present in my life, because he had a theory that death didn't exist, only forgetfulness did. He believed that if you can keep people in your memory, they will live forever. That's what he did with my grandmother. So I began to write him a long letter, elaborated from the awful thought that he was going to die.

Do you see a close relationship between your journalism and your literary creativity? Do you think that being a journalist helped prepare you to write these two novels?

People say that all journalists want to be writers and all writers have been journalists. I think journalism is important, because, first of all, it teaches you to control language, which is your basic tool, and second, because it is a form of communication. I think communicating is terribly important for a writer, because a book begins to exist only when another person picks it up. Before that it's only an object, some pieces of paper glued together that become a book only after someone else picks it up. That's why journalism is so important—because it forces you, in very little time and usually in very little space, to grab your reader and not let her go, so that she becomes involved with whatever news you have to offer. It's good training for writing literature. I think theater helped me a lot, too. I'd worked on four shows in Chile. I don't like to claim I'm a playwright, because it seems an exercise in vanity. Theater is really something you create as a team. At least that's how I did it, and it was a fantastic learning experience that later helped me with character development.

When were you involved in theater?
From 1970 to 1975.

In other words, you were doing journalism and theater at the same time. What kind of journalism were you involved with?
Every kind, except politics and sports. From horoscopes to advice to the lovelorn, features, interviews, even recipes.

Working in both journalism and literature is very common, especially among Latin American writers, not only in order to communicate, but also as a way of earning a living. In what way, specifically regarding the use of language, do you consider that your journalistic career has contributed to your literary formation?
Well, as far as language goes, it didn't teach me much of anything, except that it refined my capacity for observation, my powers of synthesis. I think that's more important.

And when did you start out as a journalist?
The truth is that I almost don't remember, because I graduated from high school when I was sixteen and started working as a journalist right away. I've always worked in journalism, so it was almost like a continuation of school work. That's why I don't feel as if my work in journalism began one moment and ended the next, but rather that it's like marriage, a natural state—at least for me—because I married very young.

In spite of the fact that you're not interested in politics, politics has played a fundamental role in your life. I'm referring to the 1973 military coup that interrupted Chile's constitutional history, and, as with many others, interrupted your life in Chile as well. And you had to leave, didn't you? How and when did you leave Chile?

Well, I feel that the military coup split my life in half with the blow of a hatchet, just as it split the lives of so many thousands and thousands of Chileans. In my case, I was deeply affected because my family was particularly involved. Nevertheless, I didn't leave Chile immediately after the coup, partly because I didn't understand what was going on and partly because I didn't have enough information. Even though I was a reporter and I did have access to information, at least more than other people had, we Chileans weren't used to governmental repression. We hadn't been trained for terror. We didn't know what a military coup was. We had had many years, many generations, of democracy in Chile, and it always seemed to us that these things happened in other countries, not in ours. We were very proud of that. There was a very strong civic sensibility in Chile. I, for example, had never heard the word *torture* in connection with any familiar or contemporary situation. For me, torture was part of the Inquisition, the Middle Ages—a part of history. I couldn't imagine that it could exist within our reality or could touch us; nevertheless, hours after the military coup, all the repressive apparatus was in place. They were already torturing people, already killing people. Everything was organized, and we didn't even realize it. We were waiting to hear that it had been a historical accident and that at any moment the soldiers were going to go back to their barracks and that the democratic process was going to be reinstated. Then we kept on waiting, like a lot of people, for this to happen, and meanwhile there was tremendous, tremendous poverty. Many people were persecuted, and there was a tremendous need for solidarity and mutual support. A few months went by, and then I realized that there wasn't much any single person could do. I'm not very brave, and after a few months I came to believe that any direct action would mean an enormous risk for me and I became so terrified about it that I began to break out in rashes. I couldn't sleep. I had asthma and a whole series of physical symptoms. One day, my husband and I finally made the decision to leave. We spread out a map of the world on the dining room table and looked at where we could go. We looked for a country that would be a democracy, where Spanish was spoken—because I'm a journalist and I needed to work in my language—and where there was work. At that time, half of Latin America was living under fascist dictatorships, so we discarded those countries. In other places it was hard to get a visa, or else it was impossible to work because of the country's economic situation. That's how we ended up in Venezuela, without knowing anything about the country, with tourist visas and twenty kilos of luggage. We left everything behind—the past, our entire lives, grandparents, friends, my country's landscape, everything. Nevertheless, we've been very lucky in Venezuela, much luckier than other exiles in other parts of the world. We were welcomed with generosity and hospitality in that warm, green country, where you can put down roots and make another home.

> *How do you think being in exile has affected your writing? Also, how do you see your relationship with Venezuela?*

Exile has had an effect on hundreds of thousands of human beings. We live in an era where masses of people come and go across a hostile planet, desolate and violent. Refugees, emigrants, exiles, deportees. We are a tragic contingent. This situation, which we became involved in through a fluke of fate, has changed our lives, but I don't have any complaints. We've been very fortunate, because we've stayed together and we were able to choose what country to go to. We live in a democracy, in a warm, green land where we feel free, where we belong, which we love like a homeland.

> *Did the name Allende help you when you left, or rather was it a burden?*

Well, my name is always a problem, in Chile as well as in airports. When I have to cross a border and show my passport, there are always some officials who call others over and look through some thick books to see if I'm in any of them. On the other hand, I'm very proud of the name I bear, and I think it's helped open the hearts of many people to me. I think of the name of Salvador Allende as a banner and not a stigma.

Then, as you said earlier, your literary vocation, triggered by politics, has come alive in exile. You mentioned earlier that your literary vocation was triggered by a family situation. You said that it started in the form of a letter addressed to your grandfather. How does a letter grow into a five-hundred-page novel? Is there anything else you can tell me about this phase in the evolution of your writing career?

I've always needed to write because I've always been writing—journalism or theater or something. I've always been connected to the written word. When I began to write *La casa de los espíritus*, I wasn't thinking about composing a novel, just a letter, and when the letter got to be five hundred pages long, my husband suggested it would be better to think of it as a novel. That's how the idea gradually came to be a book, but I had had no experience with literature. I didn't have any publishing contacts. I didn't know anything about it, and the only thing I could think of was to take those five hundred pages, tie them together with a string, and take them to publishers whose addresses I found in the yellow pages. But no one wanted to read it. No one was interested. They told me it was too long, and they suggested a lot of cuts—in some cases, about two hundred pages' worth. It seemed a pity to me to cut it, because I thought if it hadn't all been important I wouldn't have written all those pages in the first place. Coincidentally, I was reading José Donoso's *Al jardín de al lado* [The garden next door], in which one of the evil characters in the novel is a literary agent. Someone told me that such a character really existed: her name was Carmen Balcells, she worked in Barcelona, and she was responsible for getting the Latin American literary Boom off the ground. I, who have always been daring, thought, why shouldn't I get lucky? I went to the post office to mail my manuscript to Carmen Balcells. Curiously enough, the postal officials told me that same thing the publishing houses had: "This is very thick. Cut it in half, and we'll put it in two envelopes because you can't send more than one kilo by air mail." So I put it in two separate envelopes and sent it to Spain. Of course, my cover letter was in the first envelope, and the first envelope got lost. The second envelope got there. And in spite of that mix-up, or maybe because of it, Carmen Balcells agreed to be my agent. Six months later, the book was published in Spain. And from then on, it has been like the Star of Bethlehem was shining on the book. I've been extremely lucky.

> *Truly. You say it was a letter to your grandfather, but it's a five-hundred-page novel, so you must have spent some time planning that letter. How did that letter become the magnificent narrative of* La casa de los espíritus?

It began like a letter, but along the way I began to forget it was a letter. My passions, my obsessions, my dreams, and all those other characters I stole from other families, other lives, started getting into it. I think that somehow I wanted to tell the story of my country. I wanted to describe what had happened. It was a kind of therapy for me, a way of drawing out all the sadness that had built up inside, of trying to share the painful experience that I didn't go through but so many other Chileans did: the experience of a military coup, of all those years of repression. When I began to feel it as a book, I also visualized it as a mural, an enormous tapestry, a canvas on which I was going to embroider a very complicated story with many characters, a story that shifts through time and begins to change color as it gets closer to the present. It's a tapestry that, in a far-off time, say at the turn of the century, has that smoky sepia color of antiques, of old things, of things told. And as we get close to the present, the colors grow brighter and brighter, until they acquire the almost brutal colors of the reality of Alba, the present-day narrator of the story. That's the way I saw it, like a very complex mural where I knew the order but had a hard time explaining it.

—— Around the age of eighteen, Alba left childhood behind for good. At the exact moment when she felt like a woman, she locked herself in her old room, which still held the mural she had started so many years before. Next she rummaged through her paint jars until she found a little red and a little white that were still fresh. Then she carefully mixed them together and painted a large pink heart in the last empty space on the wall. She was in love. Afterward she threw her paints and brushes into the trash and sat down to contem-

plate her drawings, which is to say, the history of her joys
and sorrows. She decided that the balance had been happy
and with a sigh said goodbye to the first stage of her life.
(from *La casa de los espíritus*) —————————————

Sometimes some student will tell me that the novel has a spiral
structure, because it moves forward in a series of circles, one always a
little ahead of the other. I think that's a nice way to read the novel, but
I don't see it that way. I see it as a gigantic tapestry in which everything is all mixed together and some things are topsy-turvy. On the
other hand, the second book, *De amor y de sombra*, reminds me of a
bicycle wheel, and that's how I saw it from the beginning. There is a
central event, which is the hub, and all the spokes converging on it
are the characters, the situations, all the parts of the narrative.

In La casa de los espíritus *you use the letter-chronicle whose writers
are all female. As each one of the women writes in those continuing
diaries, each starts to redeem herself, each begins to give a perspective of history and of life at the same time, of fiction and of reality.
Besides, the novel begins and ends in the same way, with the same
words, right? That's why some people say it has a spiral structure.*

Or that it's a circle.

*What led you to choose the color white as a link in a chain of the
name of all the women in the Trueba family: Nívea, Clara, Blanca,
and Alba?*

I wanted to symbolize a state of purity. Not the purity that means virginity, normally assigned to women, but the purity of facing the world
with new eyes, free from contamination, without prejudice, open and
tolerant, having a soul capable of being moved by the world's colors.
That's why the women's names are colorless, because the color white
includes all the other colors. And that's what I wanted to symbolize.
On the other hand, every one of those names, even though they're
synonyms, still has its own meaning, the significance it's built up and
shared, all that it has lived, and it stands out in a new world, in a new
dawn.

Keeping diaries has been a very traditional way for women to express themselves. Did you choose that writing technique because this was a novel about women?

No. And if I'd known it was a feminine technique, I wouldn't have used it.

Why not?

Because I don't think literature has any gender, and I don't think it's necessary to come up with a plan to write like a woman, because that seems like a kind of awkward self-segregation to me. I think you have to write as well as possible, and you have to write like an authentic person as much as possible, like an open human being, tolerant and educated. And those qualities are independent of gender. If people pick up any one of my books and don't see my name on the cover, they have no reason to assume that a woman or a man wrote that book. They could say whether or not they liked it, but they don't necessarily have to guess my sex.

Would you agree that La casa de los espíritus *is about women and that it is, in many aspects, a feminine novel?*

It's a novel where the main character, the spinal column of the novel, is a man, a patriarch, and throughout the narrative frame of the story he's surrounded by a succession of women. In some way, the women narrators are the voice of emotion, the voice of the subjective, the voice of the most human, the voice of the soul, that is telling the underlying story, not the story everyone can see. Esteban Trueba speaks of life and the world, and he tells the story from an intellectual, rational point of view; he represents the voice from the outside, always trying to construct the world. The women, on the contrary, are trying to understand the world. They're trying to seize it and participate in it, and they have another vision of the world. And, yes, they're the narrators, all right, but I don't feel that means I write like a woman. Rather it may mean that I express a feminine point of view about life. To be sure, I'm a woman and I have to have a feminine point of view.

There is an important debate over whether it is possible to claim that there's a feminine way of writing that is different from a masculine

*way of writing. Do you think it's possible to distinguish these two
types of creative writing?*

I think there's a feminine way of feeling and a masculine way of feeling, but these differences fade more and more as time goes by. Perhaps
at the turn of the century, when Esteban Trueba came to life, along
with Clara del Valle, the roles were very clearly defined. It's not like
that today, fortunately, and my children and my nieces and future
grandchildren will be less and less aware of that barrier. And each one
of us will feel more like a human being and less in agreement with a
role previously established by gender.

> *It's precisely the distinction you've just made, in discussing the char-
> acter of Esteban Trueba, where you've outlined the man of action, the
> man-builder of the world, a world of his particular design. He's the
> doer. He turns nothing into something. He puts the world together and
> starts to populate it. He builds a farm, he builds a town, and he builds
> a world emanating from that huge house in the city. But, as you said,
> it's the women who besides recording the intimate history of the fam-
> ily (precisely the mark of a feminine world) also begin to provide a
> vision of inner space, to furnish that world with particular forms that
> stem from the masculine ambition to shape the universe. Women try
> to fill in the gaps in the world. They furnish it with details, with inti-
> macy, with family love. That is, as they leave their own particular
> mark, they humanize it. In that sense, we could say that* La casa de
> los espíritus *is a feminine novel insofar as it gives a voice to that part
> of the world that doesn't have a voice.*

But many people do that, not only women. Men do it too. Just recently, a critic said I would never truly become a writer of worth until
I was capable of creating a masculine character with as much strength
as the feminine characters I created; until then I wouldn't have dem-
onstrated that much craftsmanship. I wonder how many male writers
have good female characters. Very few. And that doesn't mean that
they write badly or that they aren't recognized as writers. Perhaps
their masculine characters are much stronger because they're men
themselves and that's how they feel. But that doesn't count for or
against their quality as writers, their literary quality. That's what I'm
trying to say. I don't want my worth as a writer to be decided from a

female point of view or a male point of view. It's possible that my female characters are stronger or that I have a feminine point of view. But literature, language, structure, and the final product that a book is, should be accepted for its intrinsic value, for its literary quality. I'm not asking for any concessions because I'm a woman, nor do I permit superfluous demands to be made of me because I'm a woman.

> *Precisely. I don't think it's about making or not making concessions; rather, it's about differentiating a way of being and existing in a woman's world that until recently had not been taken into account or, better yet, acknowledged. Now, with women writers of your caliber who are imagining and creating worlds from the female perspective, who elaborate fictional worlds from another point of view, readers will discover worlds that speak to the feminine experience. That's an important distinction that engenders different ways of working with language. The comment that critic—a man—made to you comes from a phallocentric way of looking at the world that is rejected within a feminist perspective. In any case, feminine literature seems to be engaged in restructuring, revising, rethinking all these ideas. How did you develop the dominating theme of your second novel?*

The origin of *De amor y de sombra* goes back to a newspaper story that moved me very deeply. I extracted from it a case, exemplary of so many that have happened and keep happening in Latin America: people who disappear and die, graves that, when opened, are found to contain dozens of corpses. This story wasn't very different from the others, but it made a big impact on me. In an abandoned mine, they found five corpses from the same family: a father and his four children. When I read that, I immediately put myself in the mother's place and felt an emotion so intense, so strong, that it haunted me for a long time. For two years I tried to exorcise that image, that sorrow, through writing. Although Chile is never mentioned, the story comes from a highly publicized incident that occurred in 1978 in the Lonquén mine, an abandoned mine shaft fifty kilometers outside of Santiago. And it happened just as my book describes it. Although segments of the story have been fictionalized, it really happened in just that way. There are even parts in the book that are almost exact copies of the court records or taken from testimony presented at the trial.

That's how the novel grew, out of a newspaper story and some strong emotions I felt. Afterward came the literary elaboration, shall we say, when I combined characters and actions together in time. *De amor y de sombra* is an example of the way I always work: I take something from real life, something from the papers, things I know, interviews I do, and I add fiction to it. I put things together that aren't usually related. In this case, Evangelina Ranquileo is a real person I wrote about when I was a journalist a long time ago in Chile, but she doesn't have anything to do with what happened in Lonquén. I simply put these elements together, though they don't go together in real life.

—— Isolated from the Leals' grief, Irene Beltrán borrowed her mother's automobile and set out alone for Los Riscos, determined to find Evangelina on her own. She had promised Digna that she would help her in her search, and she did not want to give the impression that she had spoken lightly. Her first stop was the Ranquileo home.

"Don't keep looking, señorita. The earth has swallowed them up," the mother said, with the resignation of one who has endured many afflictions. But Irene was prepared, if necessary, to move heaven and earth to find the girl. Later, looking back on those days, she asked herself what had propelled her into the world of shadows. She had suspected from the beginning that she held the end of a long thread in her hands that when tugged would unravel an unending snarl of horrors. Intuitively, she knew that Evangelina, the Saint of the Dubious Miracles, was the borderline between her orderly world and the dark region never explored until now. Irene concluded that it was not only her natural and professional curiosity that had driven her forward, but something akin to vertigo. She had peered into a bottomless well and had not been able to resist the temptation of the abyss. (From *De amor y de sombra*) ——————————————

We could think of De amor y de sombra *as a political novel, but to call a novel "political" is to run the risk of turning it into a pamphlet, an accusation. It seems to me that one of the successes of* De amor y de sombra *is that you work through—and maintain—that tone we referred to a moment ago. You succeed very well in creating a structured fiction; it may even be better structured and more elaborate than* La casa de los espíritus. *It's a world, the current world, of Chile in which all the characters—with their individual stories—eventually become united in the narrative's core. I particularly wanted to ask you about the group of characters who are members of the military: there's a sergeant, there's a lieutenant, there's a foot soldier, and there's a captain. They are sympathetically and humanely represented. The captain is developed according to the canon of the romantic hero. He's right out of a Hollywood movie, very strong and tough, very idealistic, and physically perfect. He's treated with great gentleness. How did you decide to give the military element, which is precisely what is creating the problem of oppression in Chile, such benevolent literary treatment?*

Well, it's very hard for me to see the world in black and white. I think there is always some shading. There are many colors in between. And every person has good points and points we could call bad, if we wanted to put an adjective to them. I'm sure Pinochet is a charming grandfather and his grandchildren adore him and maybe his friends do too. The fact that he is what he is in the eyes of most Chileans and of the world—that he represents tyranny, torture and death, and exile and prison for so many people—doesn't mean he's not a human being. And if I had to describe him in writing, I'd have to capture all the aspects of his personality. I think that people come in many different shades, and I try to see all of them. For me, it's very hard to make a character black or white, totally good or totally evil, perhaps because in real life I've never found anyone who's completely one thing. I can have more or less sympathy for one or the other, but in the end, I love them all. And after living with these characters for two years, after you begin by pulling them out of the air, when they're like ghosts haunting your brain, all out of proportion, they start taking shape as you work with them, so much so that by the end you know the sound of their voices, you know how they smell, how they look. You know everything about them. They may be closer to me than my own children. Then I have to love them. Whoever they are, I end up loving them. In *La casa de los espíritus*, I worked a lot on the character of the torturer, and, of course, I felt all the horror that any person facing someone with those characteristics would feel. But I ended up loving him because he was one of my characters. It's like a mother with a re-tarded child who has to love that child more than the others at times.

Irene is a character that evolves through the narrative. She seems to share some features with you, with Isabel Allende. She's a journalist, she's very decisive and clear in her activities and intentions, and she finally commits herself to her political reality and suffers the conse-quences of that critical position, which forces her to leave her country. Are there some autobiographical elements in Irene?

No. I would like to be like Irene. You always want to be like your fa-vorite character. I'd wanted to be like Clara and to be like Irene, but I'm not. Irene is like many, many Chilean women journalists I knew and still know, who have lived a similar destiny, and, deep down, that character is an homage to all of them. At no time am I there. The only thing that could be autobiographical in Irene is her life at the maga-zine where she works, which was a lot like my life at *Paula*, the maga-zine I worked on in Chile, but besides that, Irene is not me. Rather she's a kind of homage to my friends.

You seem to be making the same point you already made about La casa de los espíritus, *that the autobiographical material isn't there.*

The only autobiographical element in *La casa de los espíritus* is the whole household: that family, those people, are like mine, but I'm not there. I'm not Alba, though many people think I am. So many people think I'm Alba that when I was invited to the Frankfurt book fair in Germany, people looked at my hair to see if it was green, and they looked at my hands to see if there was a finger missing because they wanted me to be the character, but, unfortunately, I'm not.

What relationship is there between your work and García Márquez's narratives, especially Cien años de soledad [One Hundred Years of Solitude]? *It's frequently been pointed out that* La casa de los espíritus *is strongly resonant of* Cien años.

If you're talking about the family saga, I really wasn't thinking of

García Márquez when I wrote *La casa de los espíritus*. Or when I turned that letter into a novel. García Márquez is very important to Latin American literature, and I think he's a very powerful influence on me. Nevertheless, I wasn't thinking about him, but rather about Henri Troyat, the French writer who left Russia after the revolution and wrote the story of the many Russian families who lived that exile in Europe, especially in France. I was thinking of Stendhal. I was thinking of our very own Latin American families. I live in a continent where the family is very important, so it seemed natural to tell the story of a country and a continent through the eyes of a family. My theory is that in my continent the state is generally my enemy. It's every single citizen's enemy. You can't hope for anything from the state. You can only hope for repression, taxes, corruption, inefficiency. Where is your protection, your security? In your family, and to the extent that you have your tribe around you, you're safe. That's why the family is so important, and that's why it's constantly present in Latin American literature, not only in *Cien años de soledad*. It's always there.

Is your intention to tell the truth through fiction?

Yes. I'm not trying to get across a specific message or accuse anyone or give testimony or capture the world with what I write, but I do want to tell the truth. It seems to me that truth is important because—that's what I learned in journalism, I think, with the first story I wrote—only the truth touches people's hearts. People instinctively know the truth, and it's impossible to fool them forever. They immediately recognize truth, and so for me it's very important to touch readers, move them, bring them over to my side. And for that I can only use the truth, because tricks don't work.

Then your connection with García Márquez would be related to the narrative techniques used, together with the attempt to develop a saga that could be interpreted as a representation of the Latin American world. But I think you're different in that you adopt the position, perspective, and tone of an involved chronicler. The vision you articulate seems to start out with a very personal view of Chile, of a Chile you never name in either of the two novels but that we can see on the skin of the female narrator, the one I call the chronicler, which is very much like the tone of Neruda in Canto general *[Canto general] or* Memorial *or* Las piedras de Chile *[The stones of Chile]. Would you say you consciously intended to create this tone in order to get closer to or, rather, not to get farther away from Chile?*

There I do accept direct influence. The only book on my nightstand is always a book by Neruda, and Neruda has been present in my life since I was very young. He was a friend of my grandfather's, and he visited our house many times. I saw him a few days before he died, a few days before the military coup. His funeral is in *La casa de los espíritus,* and it's a very powerful influence. Neruda taught me, I think, to value small things, to find poetry in an onion, a carrot, in conger stew [a typical Chilean soup]. It's very important in my life, that feeling of "I am." It's the relationship with the world of small things that inspires a vision of big things. It's a sensory and sensuous link with reality. That's what's most important in my writing. Whenever I get ready to write about a situation, a love scene, a scene of violence, or simply a description of a landscape, Neruda comes into my heart, and I think of the aroma, I think of the murmur, I think of the flavor—not just of what we can see, because we have a tendency to relate to the world through our eyes and forget the rest. Neruda, I think, constantly reminds me of that.

——The Poet was dying in his house by the sea. He had been ailing, and the recent events had exhausted his desire to go on living. Soldiers broke into his house, ransacked his snail collection, his shells, his butterflies, his bottles, the ship figureheads he had rescued from so many seas, his books, his paintings, and his unfinished poems, looking for subversive weapons and hidden Communists, until his old poet's heart began to falter. They took him to the capital, where he died four days later. The last words of this man who had sung to life were: "They're going to shoot them! They're going to shoot them!" Not one of his friends could be with him at the hour of his death; they were all outlaws, fugitives, exiles, or dead. His blue house on the hill lay half in ruins, its floor burnt and its windows broken. No one knew if it was the work of the military, as the neighbors said, or of the neighbors, as the military said. A wake was held by those few who were brave enough to attend, along with journalists from all over the world who came to cover his funeral. Senator Trueba was his ideological enemy, but he had often had him in his house and knew his poetry by heart. He appeared at the wake dressed in rigorous black, with his granddaughter Alba. Both stood watch beside the simple wooden coffin and accompanied it to the cemetery on that unfortunate morning. Alba was holding a bouquet of the first carnations of the season, as red as blood. The small cortege walked on foot, slowly, all the way to the cemetery, between two rows of soldiers who had cordoned off the streets.

People went in silence. Suddenly, someone hoarsely called out the Poet's name and in a single voice everyone replied, "Here! Now and forever!" It was as if they had opened a valve and all the pain, fear, and anger of those days had issued from their chests and rolled onto the street, rising in a terrible shout to the thick black clouds above. Another shouted, "*Compañero* President!" and everyone answered in a single wail, the way men grieve: "Here! Now and forever!" The Poet's funeral had turned into the symbolic burial of freedom. (From *La casa de los espíritus*) ——————————

How did you react to the tremendous success of La casa de los espíritus?

No one thought that *La casa de los espíritus* would be as successful as it was: not my family, not my editors, not even me. The manuscript was appalling: a book by an unknown journalist, too long and with a complex theme. It's not at all strange that it got rejected several times. When I finished writing it, my children joked that we'd have to publish it ourselves and sell every copy in bus stations and coffee shops. What made readers receive it with such generosity? It's really a mystery. Maybe a guardian angel is watching over me, or else certain books have a life of their own.

How did you learn to handle the tremendous popularity this book has brought you?

I don't handle my "tremendous popularity." Instead, I'm isolated in a house high on a hill. I write in a tiny room full of books, photos, toys, and plants. I'm very selective about my friendships. I spend a lot of time with my family, and I only assume the role of writer when I travel.

> *How do you react when critics put you beside our best writers? What do you have to say to novelists of your generation and to the ones who'll come after you?*

When critics put me among good writers, I feel a great responsibility, which I assume with pleasure and pride. I can be the voice of the many who are silent. I can convey the truth of this magnificent, tortured Latin American continent. I have nothing to say to the women novelists of my generation. That would be unforgivably pretentious. I want to hear them and learn from them.

> *Do you realize you're the first woman who has succeeded in entering the publishing market on such a grand scale?*

Maybe I'm one of the first Latin American women to do it, but in Europe and the United States women occupy almost the same place as men do in literature. For Third World women, it's difficult, but we're getting there. We need to overcome a lot of prejudice: critics ignore us; editors aren't interested in our work; college professors don't study us. Add to that cultural backwardness, social pressures, hard labor, poverty, bearing children, housework, and submission to men, and you can see it requires superhuman talent and assertiveness to stand out in any field, especially in the arts.

> *When and how did your first novel appear in Chile?*

My first novel appeared in Chile as soon as it was published, underground at first and then openly. At first, people photocopied it, and there were long lists of people interested in reading each photocopied edition. The books that crossed the border without covers or hidden in diaper bags went from hand to hand, from house to house. They served as a topic of discussion and told a generation of children the story that the dictatorship had tried to erase from memory. I received hundreds of letters from Chile, all of them very moving. I realized I'm not far away, that I live in my homeland still and no one can take it away from me. I have it with me. In the middle of 1983, book censorship was suspended in Chile because the dictatorship wanted to improve its image. Now you can buy—although they're very expensive—the books that were forbidden before, and they are, of course, very sought after. It's just like what happened with pornography—prohibiting it was enough to arouse everyone's curiosity.

How was your second novel, De amor y de sombra, *received in Chile? Can you buy it there?*

My second novel got a terrific reception from the Chilean public, bad reviews from *El Mercurio*, silence from the official media, and excellent reviews from professors, intellectuals, and literary journals. They say it's more well-written than the first one, better structured, a more mature book. The theme is painful in Chile, and no one is indifferent to it. Some people feel solidarity, and others deny it happened.

And the reception in general?

They've told me that people remember me in Chile and hold me in high esteem. My name isn't completely unknown, but I haven't been able to find out for myself because I haven't gone back.

What has the reaction been in non-Spanish-speaking countries?

I've been lucky with all my translations. The reaction has always been very good. In Norway, they sold 40,000 copies in a few weeks, and that's a country with four million people. In Germany I was at the top of the best-seller list for almost a year. In France the Club du Livre alone published 350,000 copies. It seems vain to talk about all this, but that's how it's been. And I don't look at it as a personal success but as more recognition for Latin American literature. Our continent has considerably more to say; we've hardly begun to talk, to write.

To what do you attribute the universal success of your two novels?

I've thought a lot about why my novels have been so successful, without discovering the formula. Someone told me I write about feelings, values, and emotions that are common to all human beings at any point in history. Love, hate, justice, violence, the search for truth, for passions and obsessions, concern everyone.

Taking up the theme of feminism again, what do you think of the feminist movement? Do you support it or oppose it?

I'm a feminist, of course; no woman who stops for an instant to think about her future cannot be one. But I don't look at the women's liberation movement as a fight against men, a battle to replace machismo with feminism. Not at all. I believe it's a war both men and women are waging to build a more just and free society. That's how the world is conceived. We are all victims; we are all prisoners. Very few have the opportunity to grow, to love, and to develop creativity. We have mutilated each other, all of us. Machismo hasn't made men happy either, and though we women are the main victims, the man's role is also very hard—to be the provider, to be superior, to always be strong, not to cry. Poor creatures, living dissociated from their own nature, from their emotions, estranged from tenderness, relating to the world and to women through power, possessiveness, domination. What a bore! What a waste!

I'm not opposed to women organizing themselves in liberation movements. On the contrary, I believe it's the only way to get what we ask for. I don't belong to any such groups because I'm incapable of accepting group discipline. That's why I don't belong to any churches, political parties, or clubs.

Is feminism important in Venezuela? Are there feminist groups there?

Laws in Venezuela favor women more than laws in other parts of the continent. Half of the students at the Universidad Central are women. Women hold important posts in the country's administration, in business, in science, and in the shaping of national culture. Of course, I'm talking about women who've had access to education. Working-class women, peasants, and poor women live in the same backward conditions as in any other Latin American country. Venezuelan women are strapping specimens, tremendous females. They stride like goddesses—their breasts and hips swaying like flags—proud of their bodies, ready to win any beauty contest. This is a very macho country, but I've seen the freest, most shrewd, most stable women here. It's as if deep down they make fun of those rules that men try to impose on them; they shake them off with a swish of the hips and a flick of the eyelashes. There are a few small feminist groups, and they publish a small feminist journal. Although I don't see a growing, important liberation movement, I perceive that women are gaining ground every day. At any rate, we're very far from equality.

What kind of journalism do you do in Caracas? Are you still working as a reporter or are you devoting yourself exclusively to creative writing?

Until recently I was working at the Caracas daily *El Nacional,* but I had to leave because I travel too much and my new commitments won't let me keep it up. I only work in literature—if you can call that work.

How do you view your future as a writer?

My future as a writer? I don't think about it. I keep putting one word after another, and so I do a little every day.

Do you know any Latin American writers personally? How have they reacted to your work? Have you met García Márquez?

I know Ernesto Sábato, Mario Vargas Llosa, Pepe Donoso, and others. Antonio Skármeta is a friend of mine, a tremendous man, full of talent and generosity, who praises my work and stimulates me, which is rare in the world of literature where people are fairly egocentric. I don't know García Márquez. I think I'd be overcome if I could shake his hand someday.

Do you think it's important to integrate yourself into this group of writers?

It's important for Latin American writers to be in contact with each other, to be involved with each other, to help each other, and also to help young writers who are struggling to write and get published. All

of us have a very important task: we have to tell the story of our continent, be a common voice, put into words the tragedy and the
dreams of our people who have been tortured and forced to submit. If
we are united, if we work along the same lines, we can contribute to
building a different world.

For whom do you write?

I write for a reader. I always try to tell the story to *one* person. I don't
imagine who the person is, but I always try to make the tone I'm going to use as intimate as possible. I feel like one of those African
storytellers who go from village to village and sit in the middle of the
village and the townspeople sit around him and he tells the stories
and the news he brings from other places. And then the people give
him a chicken or a tomato so he'll add the news of that village to his
repertoire, and then he'll go to another village and will tell the same
story plus the news he has of that last village. And that's how you find
out that so-and-so died, that so-and-so got married. You find out that
there was a war, you find out the news.

Like a troubadour?

Like a troubadour. . . . That's how I think of myself. That's how I feel.
I want to go from village to village, from person to person, from town
to town telling about my country, telling about my continent, getting
across our truth—that accumulated suffering and that marvelous expression of life that is Latin America. And that's what I want to tell. To
Latin Americans and everyone.

*And do you have a particular purpose in your literary activity? Why
do you write?*

Because it's like celebrating something! I love it. It's a lot of fun. I like
it as much as making love—that's why I write. And if it weren't for
that, I wouldn't do it because it's very hard work.

What kind of project are you working on now?

Right now, my project is to go on writing. I'm immersed in another
novel, but I have to put up with a lot of interruptions. And every day

I find it more difficult to find the peace and quiet to do it. Sometimes I miss the cellar in my grandparents' house.

NOTE

Since the date of this interview, Isabel Allende has divorced and remarried. She is now living in the United States and has published a new novel, *Eva Luna*, and a collection of short stories, *The Stories of Eva Luna*.

Speaking Up

CA interviewed Isabel Allende by telephone on November 7, 1988, at her home in San Rafael, California.

> 66 *The dedication to your 1988 novel,* Eva Luna, *reads, "To my mother, who gave me a love of stories." Was it the storytelling that gave you the impetus to write?*

I don't know. I think that I had been approaching literature since I was a child; I had always been on the periphery of literature without daring to say to myself, I want to be a writer. The storytelling of my mother, the books I read, the love of words, this desire that I've always had to communicate—all of that was a part of it. So I started as a journalist. I wrote some theater plays, I wrote short stories for children, I did many things that were somehow near literature, but not exactly literature. Finally, after the military coup in Chile, when I had to leave my country, I couldn't work as a journalist, and for many years I remained in silence. I had no possibility of writing, or trying to communicate anything. So I did all sorts of odd jobs until 1981, when I sat down to write a letter to my grandfather. And that's the letter that became *The House of the Spirits*.

> *Was journalism something you had prepared yourself for, or did you just luck into it?*

It just happened. I was very young, seventeen, and I started working in FAO, the Food and Agricultural Organization of the United Nations. I started immediately with the information department, working with journalists.

Somewhere I read that you once translated Barbara Cartland novels, which is hard to imagine. Is that true?

I don't know if they were her novels or those of somebody very similar. They were love stories. But I was fired very quickly, because I changed the dialogue a little bit at the beginning so that the heroine wouldn't be so stupid. Then I changed the plot a little bit. By the end, I had the man helping Mother Teresa in Calcutta and the heroine selling weapons in Algeria!

When did you realize that the letter you kept writing to your grandfather was turning into a novel?

I think I knew from the beginning that it was not a letter. What I didn't know was if I was just writing my memories, writing to salvage fragments of the past that I thought were becoming very blurred by time and distance. I wanted to get back all I had lost. But I didn't tell anybody, not even myself, that it was a book. I would just sit down and write. When my children asked what I was doing, I would just say, "Writing," and they wouldn't ask any further.

Were you afraid that admitting it was a novel might have spooked it away somehow?

It was embarrassing. It was pretentious. It has taken me a long, long time to admit that I am a writer. I usually say that I am a storyteller or I am a journalist. When I have to fill out a form, I can't put "Writer."

The diaries of Clara, a character you've said is based on your grandmother, provide the stories that make up The House of the Spirits. *Were there any family journals for you to take inspiration from in writing the book?*

No.

At the end of The House of the Spirits *Alba, the granddaughter of Clara, has just been released from prison, where she has been tortured and raped, and she says that she is writing instead of hating, instead of perpetuating the chain of revenge. Writing, for her, is an affirmation of life. Do her feelings about writing represent your own?*

Yes, absolutely. The end of the book was very important to me because, in writing that final word, that epilogue, I could put everything together and justify to myself what I was doing, why I was doing it. It became clear to me that writing was, in a way, very subversive. And it meant a big change for me; something very deep inside me changed. In my first novel I overcame hatred, probably, and a sense of nostalgia; with my second novel, anger.

In that second novel, Of Love and Shadows, *the photographer Francisco is a major character and his work plays a crucial part in the plot. There are photographers elsewhere in your work too. Are you a photographer, by any chance?*

No. But I'm always fascinated by the movies and by photography. In an image you can tell in one second more than you can in six hundred pages of a book. The power of images is so great that it's always amazing to me.

You have acknowledged Gabriel García Márquez and Pablo Neruda as inspirations. Are there other writers who made you want to write or whose work you especially admire?

I think I was greatly influenced by the books I read when I was a kid. Those first books gave me the sense of adventure, the love for strong characters and deep emotions. I like plots, rich plots, something happening all the time. As you might have noticed, I'm not in the modern tradition; I'm old-fashioned, completely nineteenth-century! I like storytelling. Now I'm writing short stories, and I've been reading a lot of modern short stories. I find myself so far away from these new tendencies. What is important now is the tension, the tone, the emotion. So you have a man walking on the beach at night. He walks on the beach and he walks and walks and he goes back home. Nothing happens. I'm always expecting a shark to come out and swallow him up! But nothing happens, so that's not a story to me. I need people to be raped and beheaded. I've tried very hard to be modern, but I can't.

It's impossible to talk about your first and third novels without bring-
ing up magic realism. How useful and valid does the term seem to
you?

It's useful, but it's not a literary device. I think that not only in Latin
America but everywhere in the world there are things that are invisible that we systematically deny: emotions, passions, dreams, superstitions, myths, legends. They are everywhere all the time, and they
affect our lives. It's the same in Germany or in the United States as it
is in Latin America and Africa and India. But it seems that in what
you call the Third World we are willing to accept those realities too.
We cannot control everything in our reality. We know that there is a
dimension of uncertainty in which we move constantly, and that is
what in literature has been translated as magic realism.

I wonder if that ability to accept the unseen realities is educated out
of us in this country.

But this country is full of channeling and psychics and palm reading
and tarot and satanic sects. Why? I'm not sure about that.

Magic realism has rarely been tried in movies. Do you think it's pos-
sible to translate it from writing to that visual medium? And would
you like to see it done with your novels?

It has been tried, but it's very tricky to do magic realism in movies.
For example, with *Cándida Eréndira*, the story by Gabriel García
Márquez, they have made three movies, one commercial movie that
everybody has seen and two others that are experimental movies,
which I have seen. You can't translate it into images; it doesn't work.
That wonderful story is just destroyed. My first novel will be a movie
very soon. The Swedish are going to produce it, with the Danish director Bille August, who won the Cannes Film Festival [in 1988]
with a movie called *Pelle the Conqueror*. I think a certain magic realism was very well done in the movie *Fanny and Alexander* by Ingmar
Bergman. There are certain little things in that movie that are very
magic-realist, and they do work wonderfully. So I think it can be
done, but only very cool people can do it—Scandinavians mainly!

Eva Luna seems to me, of your three novels so far, the most spell-

*weaving. Was writing that third novel different for you in any way
from writing the first two?*

Yes, very different. First, it was probably the first time I acknowl-
edged to myself that I was writing a novel, so I planned it and I knew
what I was going to say exactly. I wanted to write a novel on several
levels, that could be read as a story, as *A Thousand and One Nights*, as
a picaresque novel, but also as a story about writing, about
storytelling, about being a woman. It had a different tone from the
other two novels because it's placed in the Caribbean, and I wanted
to give the impression of that warm, chaotic, green atmosphere, that
confused reality.

*There's a wonderful device you use in your books, which is alluding
to an event that will happen in the future, but not telling too much
about it. It has the effect, at least for me, of speeding the reading on,
creating great anticipation. Is it a deliberate device? How does it work
in your writing?*

I don't know how it works. Maybe because I know what will happen,
I just say it. Sometimes I consciously avoid it, because it's a tendency
that I have even when I talk. I use it a lot. But I know it can become a
formula so I try to avoid it.

*Do you feel the political concern of your books sometimes keeps re-
viewers from reading them as fully and dispassionately as they should
be read?*

I don't know. Politics are in all Latin American books, and maybe it's
the same with books from other underdeveloped countries. We are
immersed in a world where there's so much violence, inequality, poverty, illiteracy. Those things appear constantly in our lives and in our
books; we cannot avoid that. Even if I tried—which I don't—I would
not be able to. And the fact that I am a woman is so important to me,
and I care so much for everything that has to do with women, that it
always appears in my literature.

Do you consider yourself a feminist, whatever that word means now?

I do, but I think we should define the word, because it has a different meaning in South America. In a way, the feminist movements in the United States and Europe have gone very far. In Latin America we're still struggling with the basics. We're struggling with changing the law, with having the same moral standards for men and women, with having the same job possibilities and the same salaries for the same jobs. But most of the time, these struggles for women's rights have not been a war against men. We know that we have to change the society, and men and women are part of the society, so we all have to change. And we will all benefit from the change.

You mentioned earlier your long period of silence after you moved from Chile to Venezuela. Did that have something to do with Clara's long silences in The House of the Spirits?

In all my books there's a character who is silent, for different reasons and for shorter or longer periods of time. I don't know what it means, but it has been pointed out several times, and I have papers here from students and professors and critics who have talked about that. In a way, maybe it is because I feel that, in my continent, women have been condemned to silence, and speaking up, having a voice, is a very subversive thing for a woman.

Are you active in Amnesty International or other such organizations that struggle for human rights?

I collaborate whenever I can. I don't belong to any group, political or religious or social.

Is it a matter of keeping your own voice?

It's not that. It's just that I am a very chaotic person. I think I'm an anarchist! I can never accept the rules and I'm always defying all forms of authority. Everything that's organized, I'm always against. So I'm a terrible member of anything.

Are your books being read widely now in South America?

Yes. They're available in several countries in Spanish editions, and sold everywhere. They've become very popular—after they were popular in Europe, of course. You have to prove yourself abroad first.

Yes. It is amazing that your first book was not more quickly published in this country. But now you're established, and I believe there's a fourth book, isn't there?

Yes. I'm writing these short stories, and I'm starting another novel. Eva Luna, in my last novel, is a storyteller, but the stories she tells are not in the book. Except for one time, it always just says that she told a story, or she told about such-and-such a thing. So now I'm telling her stories. That book will be called *Stories by Eva Luna*.

Do you still write in Spanish?

I always write in Spanish, except lectures or letters. Fiction, always. I can spend a whole morning looking for a word, looking for a noun that will substitute for three adjectives. I can't do that in any other language but Spanish.

Have you been happy with the translations of your books?

Yes. I have had very good luck, I think. The German translations are excellent, all of them. The French, I know because I have read them, are excellent too. And my two translators who do the English versions are very good.

So the next book published will be the short stories rather than the novel.

I think so, though I can never plan anything. My life is very strange.

Do you prefer not to plan?

It's not that, but rather that things don't work out the way I've planned them. I have an idea of what the future should be, and it usually works out to be quite different—not bad, but different.

Are you living full-time now in the United States?

Yes, and that's part of the adventure of the future. I was on a lecture tour, I met a man in a restaurant, and we got married. So now I am living with my husband in the United States. I never thought I would live in this country. I never thought I would be speaking English. And cooking for a gringo—that's strange. But he cooks for me too.

Do you still want to go back to Chile?

Yes. I will go back in December, and we hope to spend some time there. Now that the situation in Chile is changing quickly, I think we may be going there a lot. That's so important for me. All my roots are there. I have felt a foreigner everywhere in the world since I left my country. It's a very subtle thing, but it's there.

Modern Politics, Modern Fables

INTERVIEW BY ALVIN P. SANOFF

" Some people can sing; others can run; I can tell stories. Story-telling is a way of preserving the memory of the past and keeping alive legends, myths, superstitions, and history that are not in the textbooks—the real stories of people and countries. I have tried desperately to do that in all my novels. *The House of the Spirits* is an attempt to rewrite seventy years of the history of Chile, my native land. That was a very pretentious goal, but I was naïve at the time. In my second book, *Of Love and Shadows*, I tried to keep alive the memory of just one event; I wanted to save from oblivion the story of fifteen people who were murdered in Chile. In my new book, *Eva Luna*, I have tried to include tales that are in the memory and the hearts of people. Some appeared in the newspapers and were then forgotten; others were passed on to me by the people themselves. I invent tales, but they do not come from my soul or womb. They are the voices of others whom I talk for.

My fascination with storytelling goes back to my childhood. When I was about twelve, I lived in Lebanon, where a young girl couldn't leave the house alone. But through the window I saw the life in the streets, the music, the sounds, the smells. I was awakening to sensuality and fantasy while locked inside, as if imprisoned.

My stepfather owned the book *Thousand and One Nights*, which he hid in a closet because it was considered erotic literature. Young girls were not supposed to read it. Of course, as soon as he went out, I ran to the closet, took out the book and read fragments very quickly. My awakening to eroticism and imagination was marked by that book. It left me with a love for storytelling and a love for the sensuous world it portrayed.

When I started writing *Eva Luna*, I knew that I was going to write about a storyteller and what storytelling means to me. "Tell us a story to pass the night" is the line that starts every story in *Thousand and One Nights*—and it is at the beginning of my book; it sets the tone. As I wrote, I felt just like *Eva Luna*, who says that when she puts the first sheet of paper in the typewriter, she thinks of the page as being like a clean sheet ironed for making love.

It took me a long time to realize that I can use stories to embellish not only the lives of others but also my own. I can make my life romantic and adventurous, even though it may be just as dull as everybody else's. I can create my own legend. So, don't ever read my memoirs, should I ever write them.

Like many storytellers, I live in the world of the invisible as well as the pragmatic. I listen to the voices inside, to the dreams, to the feelings. What I dream at night is sometimes more important than what happens during the day. When I met my husband, I recognized that I had dreamt of and written about someone like him in *Eva Luna*. I invented him before I met him.

This isn't the first time that what I have written has come to pass. In *Of Love and Shadows*, I tried to symbolize the anger of people who faced a terrible injustice. They took a big pig into the street, dressed him in the attire of a general and scorned him until the pig was killed. The cape, the hat, the sword, and all the emblems of the general ended up in the mud and in blood stamped by the people.

Not long afterward, I was invited to Spain for publication of the book. Nobody had read the story except my mother, myself, and my agent. But I saw in the newspapers that in Chile a mob had taken a pig into the street, dressed him in the attire of a general and, finally, killed him. It couldn't have been copied from my book, and I couldn't have copied it from life because it had not happened yet. This was a terrifying experience because I didn't know if it was somehow prophetic. Perhaps I simply feel things that are in the air, internalize them unconsciously and then translate them into words.

Isabel Allende Unveiled

INTERVIEW BY DOUGLAS FOSTER

Reprinted with permission from *Mother Jones* magazine, © 1988, Foundation for National Progress

Isabel Allende is trying to get through to Chile over a fuzzy telephone line, and it's not easy: she dials again, taps her foot in frustration, and then peers out the window as if to conjure up her home country. Dozens of her relatives (including her cousin, Isabel, with whom the *New York Times* occasionally confuses her) have recently left exile in Mexico to campaign against Augusto Pinochet, the dictator who overthrew her uncle, President Salvador Allende Gossens, fifteen years ago. She's concerned about their safety, and wondering how to respond to the family pressure on her to join them.

Just as life is tricky for the characters in her novels, so is it complicated for the forty-six-year-old Isabel Allende. She is a writer, after all, not a politician, and her third novel, *Eva Luna*, has just been published in English. Her publisher, Alfred Knopf, wants her for a publicity tour. She recently married and moved from Venezuela into her husband's suburban home in Marin County, California, becoming a stepmother to his eleven-year-old son. And stacks of letters begging for interviews, inviting her to speak, and asking her to write fill her purse.

Still, a return visit to Chile in the middle of this commotion would close the circle of a dramatic journey for Allende: until the military coup d'état in 1973, she was happily working as a columnist in Santiago. Only because she was unable to find work as a journalist in Venezuela—where Allende, her two children, and her first husband moved after the right-wing takeover—did she decide to try her hand at fiction writing. An historic tragedy led to international acclaim and best-seller status for novels that celebrate the values of her martyred uncle—*The House of the Spirits, Of Love and Shadows, Eva Luna*—and ended up with the heroine becoming a suburban housewife: that's the kind of irony Isabel Allende credits, and often celebrates, in her fiction.

     ❝ *The plebiscite is over, and the opposition won, limiting Pinochet's continuation in office.*

I just received a letter from my mother that made me cry. She was right in the middle of it, living with Hortensia Allende, the widow of Salvador Allende, during the campaign. She documents, hour by hour, the day of the plebiscite. At first, the government falsely claimed it had won. Then the true numbers came out and there was an outburst of celebration.

Now comes time at the bargaining table, to see if there will be real democracy. The opposition has moral force, but the government still has, of course, the effective power and the kind of arrogance to ignore moral force. So it's a wonderful time, a scary time too, filled with anxiety.

    What has been the cost of your exile?

A cost in pain. I didn't move at first. I thought that, due to our long democratic tradition, a military coup was just a terrible historic accident and the soldiers would go back to their barracks and we would have elections again. Most Chileans thought that that was going to happen. We never expected fifteen years of dictatorship. So I thought, as many others did, that I had to just stand the situation for some months and then everything would be better. I was involved with the opposition and I had been taking some risks, and after nearly two years I was so frightened and so horrified with the situation in Chile that I could stand it no longer. After we were threatened, my ex-husband and I decided to leave; and so in 1975 we left.

After we left, we had no money, no friends, no visa, nothing on the table or under it either, and we started again from the very bottom, in a warm, hospitable country fortunately. But it was very hard. I was extremely unhappy and I had the feeling of failure, constant failure, because I couldn't find a job as a journalist.

But I cannot complain, because what came after has been a wonderful experience. First of all, when you go into exile (I have to make clear that I'm not really in exile—that is, I could go back if I wanted to because I have a Chilean passport) I had to search for strength inside me, a certain energy or strength that I didn't know I had. It grew within me and it made me stronger. I'm a very strong person and very determined and I was not that way before. I had prolonged adolescence, and all of a sudden I became a grown-up woman. I have a wider vision of the world now. I can look at my country and my continent with a new vision. Chile's like an island. I lived immersed in that little reality and I couldn't see through those immense mountains.

But when you lose everything, everything that is dear to you—your family, your friends, your house, the objects that had surrounded you, your landscape, your language, your accent—memory becomes more important. You never think about the past in normal times, but when you have to leave everything behind, the past becomes central because you have to put your roots in the past and not in the landscape or in a place. That's what I achieved with *The House of the Spirits*—the recovery of those memories that were being blown by the wind, by the wind of exile. Therefore, exile has been a wonderful experience for me because I have things that I would never have had without it.

> *You said recently that writing* Eva Luna *marked, in yourself, the emergence of a new attitude about being a woman. What did you mean?*

I never had accepted the fact that I was born a woman, because it was like being handicapped in many ways. In that macho culture where I was brought up it was hard. I had to struggle and make double the effort to get half the recognition. I would have liked to be a man. If I could not be a man, then, I tried to be this stereotype—that is, the tall blonde—and it didn't work with me because I don't have the raw material. So when I was forty I had to finally accept that I was always going to live in this body with this face and be the person I am.

> *What accounted for the change?*

The books. The books. Writing is like a catharsis; it's a way of getting inside the past, inside your own memories. And when you write about other people you write about yourself. Why do you choose those characters? Those anecdotes? It's because they're meaningful to you. While writing the books I learned a lot about myself and the world became more tolerable. Living with myself was more tolerable too.

> *How was your upbringing different from that of the key female characters in your novels?*

There are more similarities than differences. I was brought up without a father, and you will never find a loving father in my books. I can't really imagine a loving father, although I have a wonderful stepfather—but he came later in my life, not in my early childhood. My characters have very crazy families and that is how I was brought up—in a family that was very liberal intellectually but extremely conservative, Stone Age I would say, in other aspects. The main difference is that those characters have courage, they are brave women, very determined. They know exactly what they want from the very beginning and they do it. It took me a long time to start knowing what I want. But they know what to do, and that's the way I would like to be. Eva Luna says in one part of the book that she writes the way she would like life to be—and I think that I do that too.

> *Eva is tolerant, even admiring, of outcasts and rebels. . . .*

Yes, she identifies with the marginals.

> *But it's more than that. The guerrillas in your books, for example, are nearly perfect—selfless, brave, determined, sensitive, and even terrific lovers.*

Yes?

> *What is your own view, these days, about armed struggle, about people who are in the mountains all over the hemisphere?*

I have a very ambivalent feeling. I have this romantic sympathy for them, although very few guerrilla movements have succeeded in Latin America. I don't think that a guerrilla movement can be justified or explained in a democracy, but it is fair that they exist in a dictatorship. How can you oppose the violence of the state if it is not with violence too? In Chile now something very strange and wonderful has happened. All the violence is done by the government, and it is the opposition which presents an opportunity for reconciliation. The opposition is like Gandhi, talking about unity, harmony, reconciliation of the Chilean family. I hope that our society will be rebuilt on those bases and not on the basis of revenge.

But it's only fair that young people, after fifteen years of struggling against this incredible violence and terror of the state, would form guerrilla movements—which are very weak in Chile, by the way. I respect them. I have to respect them.

> *You also treat other social outcasts with respect—gay people, transsexuals, prostitutes.*

Of course. Absolutely. But I don't write about those characters in a very self-conscious way. I don't say to myself, "This is the way I should feel towards this." It just *is* the way I feel.

> *Among the critics, there seem to be two schools: one that criticizes you for being too heavy-handed. A* New York Times *reviewer said you "cast everything in terms of white and black, good and evil, love and shadows." Then there is another school that says you're too soft: John Updike wrote that "fantasy and truth intrude as a softening veil that allows us to take the protest more lightly."*

Contradictory things are said all the time. I couldn't please everybody, and I shouldn't even try. Many things have been said about my writing. One "bad" thing people say is that I discovered a very attractive mixture of melodrama, politics, feminism, and magic realism and I throw it all together. I produce these books that look so different— the three of them are different—but if you search, you might find the formula in the three of them; that's one of the supposedly bad things. Another "bad" thing is that I'm very sentimental and that I'm not detached, I'm not cold; therefore I can be very kitschy, very campy sometimes. What other bad things can I remember? Oh yes, that it resembles García Márquez.

> *Some have called your writing "imitation García Márquez."*

Look, if you're trying to be a dancer and someone says it's bad because you dance like Nureyev, wouldn't you feel wonderful? That's the way I feel when people say I write like García Márquez. I think he's the great writer of the century, so it's wonderful if I'm compared to him—although I doubt he would like that.

Do you know García Márquez?

No, never met him, never talked to him.

Someday.

No, I would be so overwhelmed by admiration that I don't think I could talk to him. That happened to me with Germaine Greer. I met her in a hotel, in a little hotel in Paris, and I was so embarrassed to approach her that I could just stare at her from a certain distance. I could never get over my own embarrassment to say, "Hello, I admire you, your books have changed my life." All the things that you should say I couldn't. And this was three years ago; I was a grown-up person by then.

You've just remarried.

Yes. It's very unexpected. I divorced my husband and I thought that my future would be alone because I have a hectic life and I travel a lot and then I need long periods of silence. . . . Long periods of silence, because the books build up inside me little by little. It's like expecting a baby for some time and during that time I can go on working, lecturing, doing many things. But then there is a moment and I don't know when that moment happens, all of a sudden I feel like words are choking me, that I will die if I don't write. And then I have to lock myself in a place and really forget about everything else and be in silence. It's not being alone that's important. It's the big silence, it's the silence of emotions, because I have to live through the characters. I have to give them life—feel for them, talk for them, act for them, and that can take a long time.

Let's get back to your life for a minute, though. How did you get transformed into a suburban Californian?

Well, I had divorced my husband, the father of my children. He's a wonderful man, a good man. There was no reason for not loving him, he deserved love, but you know, love has no rules. Separating was very painful and I felt very insecure because I'm very bad at being alone.

I started traveling on one of these crazy lecturing tours, and I ended up in San Jose. Imagine, of all places, San Jose. [*Laughs.*] And then somebody introduced us—William had read my second book, *Of Love and Shadows*, and he had liked it very much and he wanted to meet me. And so we just looked at each other and fell in love immediately. In the first meeting.

That doesn't happen anywhere except in the movies.

Well, I think Frank Sinatra was singing "Strangers in the Night" in the restaurant and maybe that helped. And then we had a wonderful pasta. Maybe those months of chastity helped too, you know.

But then, he had been a bachelor for a long time. He was used to having many different women and I was leaving for Venezuela—and Venezuela is very far away. So, I left thinking that I had met this wonderful man and I was in love but it was too far away. California . . . oh my god! So when I reached home my son said, "Mother, you look strange, what's the matter with you?" "I'm in love. It's very embarrassing but I'm in love." And he said, "You're too old to suffer the pains of love, so get on the next plane and I'll take care of everything." He thought I would be gone for a week and I left him with the house and my books and the mail and the bills and everything. I came here and I never went back. He's still there and he's complaining now. [*Laughs.*]

How has the move changed your life?

First of all, being in the United States means among many other things that I am suddenly available. I receive seven invitations per week to lecture in different parts of the country. Of course, I cannot accept them, because that would mean I would be on a plane all the time. This is a very big country and I would not be able to write anymore. Then I have many offers for teaching which I cannot accept for the same reason. I have a lot of information now that I didn't have before. And I am a suburban housewife, which is *awful*. In Caracas I had two housekeepers living in the house, so I didn't have to worry. Here I have to wash clothes, vacuum the house, and do many things I absolutely, totally hate. I'm a suburban housewife and I am a stepmother, which is also a hard job because I had finished with my children and being a stepmother is not like being a mother. It's different, very difficult, and I'm a natural, nasty stepmother and intend to be one for the rest of my life.

What does your stepson say?
Oh, he loves me. He's a masochist. [*Laughs.*]

And how will this move affect your creative imagination? The House of the Spirits *and* Of Love and Shadows *are so clearly rooted in Chile's geography. But* Eva Luna *feels more generically Latin American. Should we expect a novel set in Marin County from you next?*
I don't know. First of all there's a problem with the language. Talking and listening all the time to a foreign language is very hard, and I work with words; the subtle nuance of each word is so important to me, and I can't have that in English, so it's difficult. I don't know what to expect from my next novel, but now I'm writing short stories because *Eva Luna* is a storyteller and the short stories that she tells are not in the book. So now I'm writing the short stories. It's called *Short Stories by Eva Luna*. And they're all set in Latin America.

And when will you shut yourself away for another "long silence"?
I have had very little time since I married. This year I divorced, I moved, I got married. I have a stepson, I'm lecturing. I've been trying to adapt myself to the United States; many things have been going on. But I'm finishing with everything on October 15 and I will lock myself in my house now for a couple of months at least.
   I have fourteen stories written already, but I want to have at least six more. I already know, more or less, what they will be about. They are all love stories—but sometimes so twisted that you can't find love. I mean, you have to look for it very carefully. That's the com-

mon thread that all the stories have, and I hope to have that book ready for next year because I have another novel growing inside me and I want to start that next year. I always have to start a book on January 8. I know it's very superstitious, but I started *The House of the Spirits* on January 8 and all my books have begun on that date. It's a lucky day.

> *Are you less angry than you were when you wrote* The House of the Spirits? *In the first novel, women pay a high price for the folly of their fathers, from the poisoning of Rosa in the beginning of the book to the rape of Alba in the end. There is less violence in* Eva Luna, *more softness, more love. . . .*

There is less violence because it's a different book, but I don't think I've overcome, completely, my anger. I feel terribly angry at the world. I think that the world is a crazy place, very unjust and unfair and violent, and I'm angry at that. I want to change the rules, change the world. I know it's terribly pretentious. I have also become softer, but—look, I want you to understand: when I wrote *Eva Luna* I wasn't in love like I am now, so you can't blame the softness on that. Please!

> *I know you finished the book first—and then lived it, instead of the other way around.*

Yes, yes! In a way, that has happened with all my books. Writing *Eva Luna* was imagining how the world could be if I accepted myself—and if I had love. I imagined that happening for Eva Luna, and then it happened to me—a year later.

> *Please be very careful about what you write next.*

Very. Very careful.

Women's Stories, My Stories

INTERVIEW BY VIRGINIA INVERNIZZI AND MELISSA POPE,
UNIVERSITY OF VIRGINIA

Reprinted from *Letras-femeninas* 15, nos. 1–2 (Spring/Fall 1989): 119–125

**" *Pope: Where do you think you got your sense of storytelling?*

In the kitchen. Listening to the maids tell stories. Listening to the radio. In Latin America there is a long tradition of soap operas that started with "The Right to Be Born." Imagine what that was! I remember being very small and coming back from school running to hear the next chapter of the soap opera. Always very tragic stories and very sad stories too. I have that in *Eva Luna*. When Eva Luna is a child she lives in the kitchen. She is a maid, and she listens to the radio. That's the only contact she has with the world. And all the stories that she hears she believes are true stories—I believed when I was a child that they were all true stories. So I thought that the world was full of very interesting people and it was just me that was always bored. Everybody else was having these wonderful love affairs except me.

Invernizzi: When did you start telling stories?

When I was very small. My mother says that I terrorized my brothers with horrible long truculent stories that haunted their days and filled their nights with nightmares. After I had my own children I also told them stories. They would give me the first sentence and immediately I would start the story. I was trained then. I've lost that training now. I've always liked it. I remember always having told stories—and making them up and inventing and exaggerating and lying all the time.

Invernizzi: Lying?

Yes, they were not lies for me because I thought those things really happened, but my mother says I was a terrible liar. I was always punished for lying.

> *Pope: How would you describe the difference between lies and truth?*

For me, I can no longer say. At the beginning there is some truth always. For example, I just went to Switzerland and I received an award. It was a bronze statue. I no longer know what size the bronze statue is. When I received it I think it was more or less like this [*holds hands a foot or so apart*] but then I started telling the story and now it is this big [*opens arms wide*]. Very soon it will be a monument. I no longer know what is the real size of the statue. But at the very base there is some truth. With *Of Love and Shadows* I was very respectful of truth. It is a real story, a terrible, real story and I did not have to make up much of it because the story itself is so truculent and macabre that the final product was incredible. So you have fiction just by writing the truth. With the rest, with *The House of the Spirits* and *Eva Luna*, I no longer know how much is true and how much is invention. There is some basis of truth for both of them I hope.

> *Invernizzi: In* The House of the Spirits *you pay homage (very explicitly) to Neruda, Allende, Víctor Jara, for example. It seems to me that in* Eva Luna *that does not happen. Does it?*

No, no.

> *Invernizzi: Is this a conscious effort to make your literature less explicit in some way?*

In *Eva Luna* I base the characters on some real historical characters—people that someone who has studied history of that part of the world might identify. But I think that ambiguity and distance might be good sometimes for literature and that's what I intended with *Eva Luna*. It was not so at the beginning. In the first draft I was very strict with historical data. As I was going through the book afterwards with Paula, my daughter, she said, "Mother, I don't know why, but this doesn't work." Then, when reading it, I realized that you either write fiction or you write an historical book—choose, and once you've made the decision stick to it. That's what I tried to do in *Eva Luna* finally.

You've mentioned repeatedly that you rewrite all the time. What is that process like? How much of the original do you end up with?

It's a very hard and long job. First I write a first draft to get the story written from the first page to the last—then I start writing it properly and when I finish I go through it again and I start putting it nicely, as nicely as possible. That is, taking care of the form—making sure that it sounds right. I usually read it aloud to hear the sound because I think that in a text there should be melody, music, and you have to try to hear that music. Sometimes you don't have to read it aloud but often you do. Reading it aloud, I can hear if two words clash together or if I have to change an adjective or if a sentence is too short or too long. That's important also for me. And after I have done that, I go to another part of correcting—that is, having a very efficient language. I have spent a long time now trying to put it nicely; most of the time I destroy it because I realize that more important than having a nice sentence is that the sentence have an effect upon the reader—that the sentence produce in the reader fear or love or tenderness or some emotion that I want to provoke. Sometimes the way I put it is very nice but it is not efficient so I change it again. I worked on the last novel with a word processor. That allows you to go on correcting forever. I think sometimes that I should go back to the typewriter.

Pope: How do you feel about having your books translated? Do you worry that something might be lost in the process?

No, no. I think it is such a fantastic opportunity to be translated that I don't mind if it is not well done. Just the opportunity to be read in another language is something that I'd never thought of before. I'm always very grateful. I think that to translate is terrible because I worked as a translator once.

Invernizzi: Tell us about that.

I was expecting my second child and I was feeling very badly and had to stay at home, so I left my job as a journalist—but I needed money so I started translating love stories, romances. Do you know Barbara Cartland? That's the Corin Tellado of England. Women that meet these incredible men in airports and go to Polynesian islands, and oh, incredible stories. I had to translate them. But they were so boring.

After the third novel they were all exactly the same. So I started changing things. Some of them ended up quite tragically with the hero caring for lepers in India and she selling guns in Sicily. So finally I was dismissed from my job.

> *Invernizzi: Today in the United States many creative writers like yourself are often and increasingly connected with universities as visiting professors, occasional lecturers, whatever. This of course makes them have more frequent and closer contact with the critics. Do you feel that this is a good thing?*

No. It is good to be in contact with the university, but I don't think it is good to be in contact with critics. Very honestly, I didn't know that critics existed before I wrote *The House of the Spirits*. I had never read any literary criticism whatsoever and I think most people never read it. Critics write for critics and for students. But not for common people because common people are not interested in criticism—they are interested in books. They buy books because they've heard that someone told someone else that they'd read the book and they liked it. And that's how books circulate. Not because critics say that they are good or bad. Critics are so ferocious sometimes that they can paralyze a writer; that has been the case with me very often. So now I don't read critics anymore. After *The House of the Spirits*, half of the critics were very enthusiastic but many said horrible things about the book. The same thing happened with the second book and I'm sure the same thing will happen with the third. If I paid attention to every bad review I wouldn't be able to write another word. I would feel terribly shy and timid. Fortunately I don't read too many of them.

> *Invernizzi: So the criticism has affected your writing. How much?*

At the beginning I think quite a lot. And then I think that I realized that, although I made jokes about them, part of what they do is very important. Sometimes I read critics that analyze what I have written, and I find out about things that I didn't know I had put there. But then I don't know if it's good to find out. It's much better to ignore it so you can go on writing. If a critic finds out, for example, that I use certain symbols, and I think about it, I might not be able to use them again. I become aware that those symbols exist, and that's not good for me as an author.

> *Pope: So there's a difference for you between doing what you have called "putting chaos in order" and actually analyzing it.*

I don't want to analyze. If I start analyzing it's not writing with joy and feeling free any more. I'm doing something for someone to evaluate it. I don't want that. If you write very spontaneously it is much better. You have, of course, to correct, but you must let it go.

> *Invernizzi: You spoke earlier about editing your work.*

Yes, because in Spain or any Latin American country editors don't exist. That is a North American invention.

> *Invernizzi: That is where I was leading. What role do editors play in your works?*

They don't exist. An editor is someone that takes the manuscript and puts it in print, but I've never had anyone say change this or that, never. That goes for my editors or my agents. And when the other editors buy the book that has already been printed in Spanish, they can't change a word. So there is no editing from any other person except me.

> *Pope: How did you get your first book published?*

I sent it to Spain by mail. I sent it to my agent. She was a woman, and because she was a woman she was interested. She read it and she liked it. Then she started struggling to have it published because nobody wanted it. Imagine, a first novel by a Latin American woman, who wants it? And it was five hundred pages! But then, something very interesting took place. She was selling a manuscript of a very well-known Spanish author to a very important publishing house. She said, "Okay, I'll sell you the manuscript but you have to also take this woman." And they said, "No, why should we?" But then she just forced them to. They finally published it, and I've published all of my novels with the same publishing house.

> *Invernizzi: So the second time the publishing house took you.*

Immediately, immediately, because *The House of the Spirits* had sold so well.

> *Invernizzi: You've mentioned that some of the critics didn't like your work, and some of the editors wouldn't touch your work because you are a woman.*

Well, not because I am a woman but because nobody knew me.

> *Invernizzi: What do you think it is that makes people love your work, because, obviously, the readers are loving it.*

I think it is because I speak of things that are common to everyone. Emotions. I found out afterwards that there are things that are common to humanity. Even if you live in Finland, or in the United States, or in Germany, or even in Chile, or in a small village in Chile. People feel the same, they feel fear, love, hatred—the same emotions. We all react very similarly. And I write about those things. Not about goals, but about the process.

> *Invernizzi: So do you think this makes your literature more universal?*

I wish it would be so. I hope so.

> *Invernizzi: What direction do you think Latin American literature is taking now?*

I think that new authors—I don't want to say young authors because most of us are not young anymore—I think that we are marked by exile. Not only political exile. Remember that we have a decade of dictatorships. But also this feeling of being marginal, the feeling that you are not accepted. And that form of internal exile, that people just can't find air to breathe in their own countries and they have to leave. Sometimes it is that they are so repressed by the dictatorship that they have to leave. That is very important. But I would say we are more optimistic. We are not apocalyptic anymore. As our predecessors were. There is a new tone, less baroque and more humble, more humorous, more detached. We don't have so many explanations for everything. I think we ask more questions and we have fewer answers. I would say that the fact that so many women are writing now is important too. That's a new perspective in literature. We have better and stronger female characters in books than we did fifteen or twenty years ago.

> *Pope: Speaking of predecessors: you did meet Neruda. Can you tell us about that?*

Oh, he was a friend of the family's, and that's how I met him. Then years later I met him in Isla Negra because that's where he was living, near the coast. He invited me to his house. I went and we had lunch together. He thought that I was a terrible journalist, absolutely terrible.

> *Pope: Did he say why?*

Yes, because I would always put myself in the middle of everything. I was never objective. I was always thinking about myself. He said that I should abandon journalism and become a writer because all of those faults were virtues in literature.

> *Pope: Did you listen to him at the time?*

Of course not. I thought his mind was just drifting away. He was too old.

> *Invernizzi: If you had to do it over again, would you do it the same way, journalism first and then become a novelist?*

Yes, yes. I think it's very good training. For me it was. Very good. If I look back at my life, there are very few things I would not do. I have suffered a lot and I think that's good too. I have had a wonderful life, really. Someday, when I get very old, if I do get old, I hope to write an autobiography. Of course, it will be full of lies. Full of lies and insinuations and I will change everything and it will never be objective. But that will be the best part of it.

> *Invernizzi: Are you working on a project now?*

Short stories. But they are very difficult. I do not know if I will ever finish them, I'd much rather write a novel.

Pope: What's the difference between writing short stories and writing novels?

Oh, much. With a novel, you can get an idea and you just work on that idea. For a long time, work, work, work. But with a short story, you have to get a new idea for every one. And then you have a few pages and you have to be very clever so that you will trap your reader and not let him go. Just to keep his attention you have to have some surprise, something special. It's difficult.

Pope: Where did the idea for Of Love and Shadows *start?*

I was at home in Venezuela reading the newspapers in 1978—that is years before I became a writer—and I was working at a school in Venezuela. I read the news that fifteen bodies had been found in an abandoned mine in Chile. They were peasants killed by the military during the military coup in Chile in 1973. So, these bodies had been in that mine for five years. I started thinking about the relatives, the women, that looked for the men. Especially the Maureira family, because four sons and the father were found in that mine. And I thought about the women, the mothers, the daughters, the wives, the sisters of those men that for five years went around asking for them in the morgue, in hospitals, in concentration camps, in prisons, and they never got an answer. Somehow they represented the tragedy of the disappeared in Latin America, not only in Chile, everywhere. I couldn't stop thinking of these women, and I thought that it was such an interesting case that I began keeping clippings—everything that was published on that case. I just cut it out, without knowing what I would do with it. When I finished *The House of the Spirits*, and I wanted to write another book, I didn't have to think about it. I knew exactly what that book would be; it would be the case of these people, I had done a lot of research before, but then I started doing serious research because I wanted to get all that was published and not published about this case in the trials and to find out what really happened—interviews and all that. At the very end of the book, the main characters, Irene and Francisco, leave the country. They cross the Cordillera. When I finished the book, I thought there were parts that needed to be very accurate, to have the feeling of nature, the feeling of how people talk, of how people feel. Because I could not go

back to Chile, my mother went. I have a very close, intimate relationship with her, and I know that if she goes it is just exactly as if I were
there. Because she can look through my eyes and I can look through
her eyes. She went with a notebook, and she crossed the Cordillera in
the South. It's described in the book. She took notes on the names of
the trees, and how the earth smelled and how the sky looked. I have
this incredible notebook, my mother's notebook. I wrote the last part
of the book through her eyes. That's why the book is so dear to me,
because it's a story that lived with me for such a long time. And finally when I started writing, I think that the emotion that really got
me to do it was this feeling of impotence, of fury about these crimes
and what was happening in Chile. Then I started talking with people,
interviewing, and I realized that it was not only a story of violence,
but that it was mostly a story of love and solidarity. That's how something changed inside me. I no longer feel this terrible hatred that I
felt before. Somehow I feel whole.

"If I Didn't Write, I Would Die"

INTERVIEW BY MARIE-LISE GAZARIAN GAUTIER

Reprinted from Marie-Lise Gazarian Gautier, *Interviews with Latin American Writers* (Elmwood Park, Ill.: Dalkey Archive Press, 1989), 5–24

**" *What books did you read as a child?*

I read Emilio Salgari, Jules Verne, Charles Dickens, and all the detective novels I could lay my hands on. I also used to read pocketbook "historical novels" on the Roman Empire—I loved anything that had violence in it. When I was about nine years old, the man who would become my stepfather, and was then courting my mother, gave me the complete works of Shakespeare in a single volume made of thin Bible paper. I used to make cardboard figures out of each of Shakespeare's characters. I read his works as adventure novels; I wasn't aware that they were literature.

What works have influenced you the most?

If I have to acknowledge real influences that affected me deeply, they would be those works that I read as a child, such as adventure novels, because I longed for things to happen, for blood to be shed and for the characters to get married and have children. The influence of Pablo Neruda began to be felt after I left Chile. I took along a suitcase, photographs of my family, a small bag filled with soil and one volume of the complete works of Pablo Neruda. Every time I felt the need to recover my country, I read Neruda because he is Chile, he is the voice of Chile. It is a beautiful metaphor that he died following the military coup. With his death, the voice of the people and the voice of freedom grew silent.

You speak a lot about Pablo Neruda, but has Gabriela Mistral had no impact on you?

Gabriela Mistral's poetry is masterful and I first understood it when I recorded one of her albums and I had to read her work with great care. I identify with some of her poems, but I cannot relate to her tendency to indulge in suffering. This can be explained by the upbringing of women of her time and the literary mores of that period. Since I am always fighting against pain and suffering, I cannot identify with her on that count. By contrast, Pablo Neruda is a poet of emotion and sensuality. Although he is lacking Gabriela Mistral's mystical bent, I feel very close to his way of approaching, smelling, touching, tasting, and walking the world. I like this very much.

What about French writers?

I feel close to the work of Henri Troyat, a White Russian who emigrated to France. His literature, like mine, is stamped by the loss of a world and the dream to recover it. He wrote long sagas and I have read all his work.

What did your uncle, President Salvador Allende, stand for?

Allende was proposing very deep reforms. He had a dream. He was a socialist, a Marxist, the first socialist Marxist president ever to be elected by a democratic free election. He wanted to institute these reforms within the bounds of Chile's constitution. We continued to enjoy all the civil rights we had before: freedom of the press, speech, education, and religion. Within the constitutional framework, he tried to redistribute the land and that meant taking it from rich landowners who owned half the country. He also attempted to regain control of Chile's copper mines from the North Americans, and do many other things that were very important to our economy and for our dignity as a country. It was a fascinating process and a beautiful dream. Before that, Chile had been a democracy, but without social justice. How can you have a social democracy if there is such great inequality that a few people have all the opportunities and all the wealth while the great majority does not?

Why is Latin American literature always concerned with politics?

I would say that Latin American literature was born with the first Spaniards who arrived in America, discovered the New World, and started writing the chronicles of the Indies. In the letters they sent to the King and Queen of Spain and to their own families, they recounted what they saw. They came to conquer, they invented a utopia and spoke with effusive praise of this new continent. Since then, Latin American literature has been marked by political and social restlessness. A major political upheaval resulted from the almost complete destruction of a world on which a foreign culture, religion, and race were imposed. This produced a wave of feelings and emotions that have always been present in our culture and which have affected its political aspects. For five hundred years, we have been exploited and colonized, first by Spain and Portugal, then by other European countries, and nowadays by the United States. The latter is a more subtle form of colonization, but colonization nonetheless. It is impossible for writers to separate themselves from this reality. How could I write without being aware that I come from a society rooted in inequality? I don't think this is solely a Latin American trait, however. It is characteristic of certain times and certain places throughout the world. All the literature that was written after the Second World War was marked by war: all Jewish literature is marked by the Holocaust, and much of the literature that is being written today has been marked by the Vietnam War. These have been crucial moments in the history of nations.

What relationship do you see between exile and literature?

Exile is something that has marked our literature significantly. My generation was kicked out of Chile for political reasons. If we had stayed, they would have killed us. The literature prior to ours reflected another form of exile: people who could not stand mediocrity—intellectual and otherwise—in their countries, left them. In my case, I would not have written novels had I not left; I would have continued as a journalist. I communicated through journalism and I had no need to write literature. But when I left Chile, I couldn't keep working as a reporter, so I turned to literature.

In Of Love and Shadows, *you speak of Irene as follows: "She was saying goodbye to her country. Next to her heart, beneath her clothing, she carried a small bag with soil from her garden that Rosa had sent so she could plant forget-me-nots on the other side of the sea." What is it like for you and your characters to live in exile?*

For me, exile has been a brutal and painful experience, but it has also been very beneficial. I have become strong, and I didn't know I had that strength within me. One learns more from pain and failure than from happiness and success. But it is also true that in fifteen years of exile I have not been able to shake off all my feelings of nostalgia for Chile . . .

Has the transition from journalism to writing novels been a difficult one?

I didn't choose to make that transition. If I had remained in Chile, I would not have written novels. What happened was that when I left Chile I could not find work as a journalist because journalism is a profession that is very difficult to carry from country to country, except as a correspondent. A journalist is a person who interprets society, its laws, its way of behaving, and its language, and then writes about these things with the subtlety of everyday expressions appropriate to that culture. When I went to Venezuela, I tried to work as a journalist and the only job I could find was to write satirical articles for a newspaper. I couldn't make a living with that. So I worked at many other things for a few years during which I remained silent. Perhaps the fact that I could not work as a journalist left me no resort but to write books. I started writing purely by accident, after I had returned from working a twelve-hour shift at a school, on the first day of classes following vacation break. It was the eighth of January. When I got home, I received a phone call from Santiago saying that my grandfather was very sick and he was going to die. It's not really that he was sick so much as that he was old; he was almost one hundred years old. One day he sat on his rocking chair and decided not to eat or drink anymore. He wouldn't allow a doctor to see him either because he wanted to die, and my family respected his decision. So when they called me, I sat down and began writing him a letter. I knew that the letter would never reach him and that I would never send it. Deep down, I knew I was writing that letter for myself but I didn't yet realize it was going to be a book. I sat down at my typewriter and wrote the first sentence of the book without any idea of what it meant; it was as if someone dictated it to me. It went like this: "Barrabás came to the family by sea." Barrabás was our very large dog. When people ask me about the meaning of the dog in *The House of the Spirits*, I reply that he symbolizes nothing. Some critics, however, say the dog symbolizes Pinochet, while others maintain that he represents Clara's innocence because he appears in her life when she is a child, and he remains with her throughout her childhood. When Clara falls in love and gets married with her white dress on, Barrabás is murdered in a pool of blood, which critics view as symbolic of the sexual act. I think there are things that writers are not aware of having put in their books, and it is the task of you people to discover them.

Has journalism helped you in the writing of your novels?

Yes, I use the techniques of journalism, such as interviews, research, the concise use of space, synthesis, suspense, etc.

You have said of your mother: "She gave me a notebook to jot down life at an age when other girls played with dolls. She also allowed me to paint whatever I wanted on one of the walls of my room." What did you write in that notebook and what did you paint on that wall?

I painted landscapes, friends and animals, and wrote about fear, sex, injustice, inequality, violence, and loneliness. That's pretty much what I am still doing in my books.

What do you write about?

What does anyone write about? The things that happen and matter to you. The three novels I have written, as well as my short stories, are marked by two obsessions that are present in Latin American literature: violence and love.

Why do you juxtapose rape and love in your work?

That's a very strange question. In the literature of the so-called Boom, there is one constant: there is always a house of prostitution involved. Curiously, rape has become a dominant theme in the works of Latin American authors of the 1980s. I think there is a symbolic element in this. When I left my country in 1975, half of Latin America was ruled by dictators. We endured years of human rights violations when people were murdered, mutilated, tortured, exiled, or made to "disappear." I think rape represents the worst humiliation and the worst transgression against a person, and this theme has become prevalent in the stories, novels, and movies that are being done nowadays. It is as if in the collective unconscious the rape of a woman has come to symbolize the rape of all of us as a species, continent, and race. At the end of *The House of the Spirits*, Alba has been raped and is awaiting the birth of a child, and she doesn't know whether it is the baby of her love Miguel, or the offspring of all rapes, and she doesn't care. What she is interested in is that it is her child, it is a being that is going to be born and which is the product of accumulated and shared suffering. But it is a being that is also born out of love. The point of all this is that without forgetting the horrors of the past and by forgiving them, we can build a new society based on love.

Why do you write?

I come from a family of storytellers, an oral tradition, and that helps a lot. As women, we were kept silent in public, but we had a private voice. And now, because others have made it easier for me, I write about the lives of my people. It is the voice, not of the winners, but of the little people, us, my mother, my grandmother, not my grandfather who wrote history with big capital letters. I never write with a message in mind. I want to tell a story that in some way resembles life and reality. I write to communicate, to survive, to make the world more understandable and bearable, so that people may be moved by the things that matter to me, to firmly establish the need for a collective endeavor to build a world where there is room for love, solidarity, laughter, the pleasure of the senses, the growth of the spirit, and imagination. I write because if I didn't I would die.

Your prose has a poetical musicality. Do you write poetry?

No, I don't. How I envy poets! In seven words they say more than I do in six hundred pages.

How did you develop your capacity to wonder and astound?

The world has no explanation. I think what we know is less than what we don't know, and that even those things that we do know, we don't know fully, so we can't control them. The capacity to wonder is always there because it is enough to look at the world to realize that it is unexplainable and ruled by invisible forces. Why do men fight wars? Why does a person fall in love with one particular individual and not another? Why do people hate all of a sudden? These passions have no explanation. Why do we move? Many times we don't even know why we have to stand up or sit down. Everything that happens in the world and in life makes me wonder.

How is a novel born?

From deeply felt emotions I have carried around with me for a long time. *The House of the Spirits*, for instance, was born from nostalgia; *Of Love and Shadows* from impotence and anger; and *Eva Luna* from the pleasure of being a woman and telling stories. In my first novel, I didn't have to construct anything artificially; everything was within me, I didn't need to invent the landscape, the smell of peach trees or anything. My latest novel, *Eva Luna*, takes place in the Caribbean; it is a story that could have happened in Venezuela. Despite having lived there for thirteen years, I had to do extensive research, read practically every paper published in this century, travel all over the country, and speak to people to make *Eva Luna* real. When I say in that book, "it smelled like a mango," I had to buy a mango and smell it first, because even though I eat mangoes every day, they are not a part of me. *Eva Luna* was written after a lot of hard work and thirteen years of living in Venezuela.

Do you think The House of the Spirits *would exist were it not for* One Hundred Years of Solitude?

Yes, I acknowledge that *One Hundred Years*, like the works of Borges, Cortázar, Donoso, Neruda, Amado, among others, opened the road for me.

Do you see some resemblance between your work and that of José Donoso?

No, except for the fact that we are both Chileans and our country has influenced us. But our ghosts and obsessions are different, we belong to different generations, and our sexes have affected both our works.

In Of Love and Shadows *you describe the atrocities that occurred at the mine as if your words had the same visual power as Francisco's camera. How did you manage to capture that horrible world of the dictatorship with your words, and what does the written word mean to you?*

I researched for two years before writing that book. Each fact I detail in it is based on reality. I have lived under a dictatorship; that's why I can speak and write about it. The written word is an act of human solidarity. I write so that people will love each other more . . .

Do you see the novel as a testimony or a documentary?

The novel is a magic trunk where everything fits: poetry, essays, testimonies, fantasies, documentaries, everything! Through it we can give a fictional order to chaos and find the key to the labyrinth of history. A novel is like a window open to an infinite landscape where the written word records memories which cannot be blown by the wind.

Your work is a criticism of the bourgeoisie and a reevaluation of history. Do you see writing as a process of weaving and unweaving? Do you want to rewrite the world?

I want to tell a secret story, that of the silent voices who cannot speak. I want to change the world, not just rewrite it.

How do you manage to transform the reader into a witness?

I don't know if I achieve that, but isn't that the aim of writing? A book is the work of two people: the writer and the reader. So every book is really several books, and each reader is a witness to the reality the author suggests.

*Could we call your narrators witnesses, commentators, or partici-
pants in Chilean reality?*

Participants, I think.

*Who are your narrators and why are they gifted at telling stories and
living them?*

They say that every character is the author. Perhaps that's true and I
am within each of my protagonists. Storytelling and writing are like a
private orgy: they allow me to create and recreate the world according to my own rules and to fulfill all my dreams on the page. I like to
do it from my perspective as a woman who challenges the patriarchal
order, mocks authority, the law, repressive morals, and the thousand
ways they have devised to trap our bodies and our souls.

*Who is your favorite female character: Clara, Irene, Consuelo, or
Eva Luna? Who among your male characters?*

I love all of them: Alba, Irene, Eva Luna, Jaime, Francisco Leal, Professor Leal, Riad Halabí, but especially Clara. Clara is my grandmother. Clara del Valle is exactly the same as my grandmother,
although I exaggerated her a little. For instance, my grandmother
couldn't play the piano with the cover down. But it is true that she
was a spiritualist and a clairvoyant. I come from a family of very
crazy people; I haven't had to invent anything. My grandmother was
the craziest of the whole family, she was wonderful, she lived apart
from all material things in a spiritual world, experimenting with a
table with three legs to speak with the souls of the dead. My grandfather was a pragmatic Basque who totally disagreed with the experiences of my grandmother because he said they had no scientific
grounding. Later on, when I was five or six years old, my grandmother discovered that it wasn't the souls of the dead who were moving the legs of the table but rather extraterrestrials, Martians. My
grandfather felt that this had a scientific basis. The fact that all the
names in *The House of the Spirits* mean the same thing—Clara,
Blanca, Alba—is like saying that Clara is the great spiritual mother of
us all. She is not concerned with braiding the hair of her daughters,
or with whether they are going to get married or not. On the other

hand, Blanca is the great earthly mother, she fulfills all the household tasks. Alba is the great intellectual mother.

> *In two of your novels, you give leading roles to effeminate men. Is it easier for you to write about women and about those men who most resemble them?*

No. I don't like to categorize people by their sexual roles. Women can have "masculine" characteristics (action, courage, rage, ambition), while men can be tender and compassionate. This complexity makes them more interesting in both real life and literature. I also don't have any prejudices against "effeminate" men.

> *Why do many of your characters speak in the first person?*

Because it can't be done in any other way. I know absolutely nothing about literature, and I am not interested. When one knows too much, one can no longer write. But one knows intuitively when something isn't working. When I finished *The House of the Spirits*, I read the text and it felt magical, but the fuel was missing. I read the novel many times without knowing what was wrong. And then I realized that the character of Esteban Trueba was based on my grandfather, he was exactly like him. But my grandfather would never have told anyone, least of all his granddaughter, about his sufferings. My grandfather, unlike my character, would have never spoken about his intimate love for his wife, the violent moment in which he chopped Pedro Tercero's hand off, the time he humiliated himself in front of the prostitute to beg her to save his granddaughter. So how can Alba, who is writing the book, know all these things? It was too easy and artificial that she should know them. So at the end of the novel, Alba says: "I have written this book based on the diaries of my grandmother." With my grandmother something very different happened: she is the only one who speaks in the first person. Initially, the whole book was written in the third person; I told the story.

> *Eva Luna says: "The books, silent by day, open up at night to let the characters out so that they may wander the rooms and live their own adventures." Do you share your experiences with your characters? Who dominates whom?*

Yes, I share them. At the beginning, I think I dominate my characters, but then they fulfill their own destinies and I cannot impose my will on them.

> *You have said more than once that "it is difficult for me to write my biographical information without repeating many things that appear in* The House of the Spirits.*" Where does autobiography leave off and the characters begin?*

Almost all my characters are based on real-life people. A few are the product of my imagination, like Riad Halabí in *Eva Luna*. There is a part of my biography (and that of my family and friends) in *The House of the Spirits* and *Of Love and Shadows*. There are no autobiographical elements in *Eva Luna*, but I think I identify completely with two emotions in that novel: being a woman and being able to tell stories.

> *Is the family of the Truebas related to that of the Buendías?*

The Trueba family is a lot like my own family.

> *Where is the magical world and where is reality?*

I don't know. The dividing line between them is constantly being erased for me. I no longer know whether my life is a novel or whether my novels are like life.

> *Is fantasy a way for you to escape reality, or is it a tool to discover reality?*

It is a means of embellishing it. I don't try to escape from reality but rather to understand its complexity, not just explain it. How pretentious of me! I want to enrich reality and paint it with bright colors, as Eva Luna says so clearly.

> *When do you know you have reached the last stage in writing a novel and that it is time to turn it over to the publisher?*

You have to set a deadline for yourself. In this respect, I got my training in journalism, because there you always have to race against the clock; it is an unalterable deadline. I have learned to work with a certain discipline and to turn over articles at a given time on a given day. And I write like a possessed person until that time. When I think a work is finished, I hand it to my mother—she is my only reader. She then returns it to me with scribbles all over and we begin discussing what doesn't work, and I rewrite the novel. Later I separate myself from the book and let it rest.

How do you feel upon ending a novel?
Twenty minutes of sadness because I am breaking up with the characters. Then I feel euphoria at the prospect of starting a new project.

If you had to give a geometrical shape to your novels, what would it be?
A whirlpool, a hurricane!

What do you plan to write when democracy returns to Chile?
I don't know what I will write when democracy returns to Chile, but I know that I would not have written any novels had it not been for the 1973 military coup because I was forced to leave the country as a result. The loss of that world and my roots and a feeling of nostalgia led me to write *The House of the Spirits*. My second book is based on a crime committed during the military coup, while the third was written in the Caribbean. I would not have gone to Venezuela were it not for that coup; I would still be in Santiago. The political future of Chile is a democracy, without a doubt. Pinochet is not eternal; immortality is going to fail him at any moment.

Why are women in your family so strong?
It is true that I have a greater knowledge of women because I am one, because I have worked with women all my life, and because I come from a family where women are very strong. My great-grandmother, my grandmother, my mother, my daughter, and I all communicate with each other telepathically, even after death. My grandmother died thirty-seven years ago but she still speaks to me. My mother who lives in Chile also speaks to me telepathically because calling by phone is very expensive. So there is very much of a female focus in my work

because of my understanding of women. But I am also interested in the perspective of men because I think it is impossible to imagine a world where we are divided. I believe that machismo and sexism harm both women and men. Of course, we women were victims first, but men are also victims. I think that sex, eroticism, and love are extraordinary forces in human beings. A man who does not consider a woman as an equal cannot live life fully. His life will always be incomplete.

Do you think you have had to struggle harder as a writer because you are a woman?

I would have liked to have been a man because they lead much more comfortable lives. But due to the absence of one ridiculous little chromosome, life has been made much harder for us. At least, I come from a continent where women have had to make twice the effort to obtain half the recognition in any field. And there are some areas where women have not been accepted at all, the world of ideas. A woman is allowed to be an artist, dancer, singer, actress, musician, or painter, but she is not permitted to handle ideas. Fundamentally, literature is a concept, it is ideas. You can adduce all the arguments you want, but behind them there are still ideas. Gaining acceptance into the world of ideas has been the hardest task for women.

Do you consider yourself a feminist writer and do you believe women have their own language?

I am a different person since I read Germaine Greer's *The Female Eunuch* because she expressed what I felt with a great deal of humor. All my life I had experienced feelings of anger, impotence, and injustice without knowing why. Suddenly I felt someone understood me and I could finally cope with my emotions. This marked not only my writing but my life. I read Simone de Beauvoir when I was twenty-six. My generation began to read her before I did. I became acquainted with her works when I was a journalist for an avant-garde feminist newspaper. Yes, I consider myself a feminist and I think that any intelligent woman has to be one. What does it mean to be a feminist? For me, feminism is a fight that men and women must wage for a more educated world, one in which the basic inequality between the sexes will be eliminated. We have to change the patriarchal, hierarchical, authoritarian, repressive societies that have been marked by the religions and the laws that we have had to live with for thousands of years. This goes a lot deeper than not wearing a bra, or the sexual and cultural revolutions. It is a revolution that must go to the heart of the world, and that all of us must fight, women and men alike. Both sexes are on a ship without a course, and we must give it a new direction. On the other hand, I don't believe in equality on the more mundane level; I don't want to be equal to a man, I want to be much better than he and I want him to be far better himself. So I am concerned with the struggle to better ourselves as a species. We have to separate this from other struggles. At the beginning of this century, a lot of people said that women's inequality stemmed from a political system which, as it changed and revolutions were won, would improve the lot of women. This is a lie! Revolutions don't change the basic sexual inequality that was established in prehistoric times and which is still present today. Venezuela has some of the more advanced laws as far as women are concerned. They have just changed Venezuela's constitution to give women all the rights that men have. Half of the university students in that country are women, and Venezuelan women occupy important positions such as bank managers and executives, although not yet the presidency of the nation. This contrasts with the macho appearance of Venezuelan society. Chilean society, on the other hand, appears more matriarchal and liberated, but not according to the letter of the law. Women have now learned to develop a voice using male tricks. But I don't think that one can talk of female or male literature as if literature had a sex.

It has been said that Luisa Valenzuela is heir to the Boom. Could we say the same of you, or do you prefer to be seen in some other way?
I can't classify myself. That's the job of the critics. I don't know anything about literature, the Boom or the post-Boom. I don't think that those labels are important for an author, at least not for me.

Do you consider your voice that of the Latin American continent?
I don't pretend to be anyone's voice. I have been very lucky to be published in Europe, and I say lucky because there are women who

have been writing in Latin America since the seventeenth century, like Sor Juana Inés de la Cruz. The problem is that few people ever talk about them. Their work is rarely taught at the universities, there is no literary criticism on them, and they are not published, translated, or distributed. In Latin America, no one wanted to read my novels, so I sent them by mail to Spain, and that's where they were published. As a result, they were promoted and became known. I think European publishers are opening their doors to many Latin American women authors, even those who have been writing long before me but have not yet been published. I am just one of them. I am bold enough to believe that I have a gift for telling stories, as other people do for singing. This gift came from the heavens! So I must use it to benefit those who don't have a voice. That's why when I speak I always refer to the political and social aspects. How can one not talk about war, violence, poverty, and inequality when people who suffer from these afflictions don't have a voice to speak? I have also been lucky to have been translated into other languages.

What do you think of the future of Latin America?

It is very difficult to speak of the continent as if it were a bag into which we have all been thrown. Every country, but even more so every social class, has its own reality. If I talk about the middle class in Chile or Colombia, I am certain that there are reforms to resolve basic problems. If one speaks about the poorer classes in El Salvador, Guatemala, Nicaragua, Chile, and Peru, however, there are many years of abuse and anger that must be turned inside out and changed. It is neither just nor natural that some people have everything while the great majority has nothing. The privilege of the few when many are starving is an obscene thing.

> *Eva Luna said: "I pretended that a ray of moonlight struck my back and I developed the wings of a bird, two large feathery wings that allowed me to take flight." Listening to you speak is like seeing your wings, and reading your work is another form of witnessing that flight.*

When I write, I fly to another dimension. Like Eva Luna, I try to live life as I would like it to be, as in a novel. I am always half flying, like Marc Chagall's violinists.

The area of Monte Grande in the Valley of Elqui was Gabriela Mistral's favorite. What is your favorite spot?

All of Latin America. I seek epic dimensions, I am fascinated by our history and our magnificent geography, and I identify with the mix of breeds, the *mestizo* people that we all are. But on a deeper level, which in truth determines my existence and my writing, my favorite spot is to be in the arms of those I care for deeply.

Who is Isabel Allende?

A happy person, because I always had a lot of love and I have not yet lost the hope that the world can be changed.

Of Love and Truth

INTERVIEW BY INÉS DÖLZ-BLACKBURN, GEORGE MCMURRAY, PAUL REA, AND ALFONSO RODRÍGUEZ

11

Reprinted from *Confluencia: Revista Hispánica de Cultura y Literatura* 6, no. 1 (Fall 1990): 93–103

This interview was conducted at the University of Northern Colorado on February 14, 1990.

> " *In treating historical themes, do you intend to shed some light on historical events, to clarify historical notions, to transform reality or do you have other intentions?*

I don't have any intention. I write because I cannot avoid it. It's an overwhelming passion. I just sit there and pour everything. Of course, I write about things I care for. Things that are important to me, that's why there are six issues that always appear in my writing: love, historic events, social issues, women's issues, ecology, peace. All those things that are part of my life naturally appear in my writing. I have been marked by historical events in my country; my whole life has been determined by those events.

So, in a sort of catharsis, my first novel deals with that, and my second novel too because my second novel is based on a political massacre in Chile. All of the facts are true, I researched them. Although it is fiction it's not a testimony or a document, and when I say I don't have an intention, it's because I don't want to clarify anything. The only thing that a writer can do sometimes, because we are very lucky, is to preserve the hidden memory that is not in the textbooks. If you read the history of Chile in the last fifteen years, you won't find any of that, but it's in the memory of the people, it's in the suffering of the people. That's what I want to talk about.

One time I talked to a professor of history, and we were talking about a miniseries that appeared on TV, The Winds of War, *and he had read the novel, and I asked about the accuracy of that, and he said that it was pretty accurate. When I asked about the difference between literature that deals with history and a historical essay, he said that in a novel the reader feels more profoundly than in a historical essay.*

I don't think that I write a real history or an essay because it's very accurate, it deals with facts, and I'm not good at that, my mind just drifts away. On the other hand, I've been a journalist for many years, I used to walk in the streets, and talk with the people, and when I write about a historic event, it's always from the point of view of the little people. I'm a little person in every sense, I'm even short. So, I'm there in the streets and finally that is the real history. I mean, what is history finally? It's not an edition of dates, of battles that are won, of defeats, of statistics; it's suffering, and that's what fiction deals with.

Do you find your residence in this country has affected your creativity?

I think that my creativity, or anybody's creativity, is determined by the necessity to adapt yourself. What is creativity finally? It is the capacity to survive in different situations, with original solutions. Why are you creative? Why do you invent a machine? Because you need to solve a problem in an original way. I would have never written my books if I would have not been forced to leave my country, and adapt myself in a new situation. Every time that I have had to do that, I feel that there is a new strength that comes out from inside, that I didn't have before. Or maybe it was there, but it was asleep, it was not active, and the need to survive develops that, activates, or triggers that initiative, and it's an enormous challenge to me. Just the fact that I have to speak in English, just that makes a big difference. Because it's not only trying to translate your thoughts into another language, it's trying to grab a set of references that belong to another culture, another generation, in another part of the planet, that is a tremendous challenge. Very strange.

When do you find time to write?

My writing time is sacred. I get up very early in the morning, and I commute to Sausalito where I have a study, and I work there for ten to twelve hours a day away from everybody, and from everything. If I don't do that, I couldn't write. Because writing is a very solitary pursuit, you do it in silence, in privacy. And it requires many hours in a row.

> *On the issue of Spanish and English, you certainly are a very fluent speaker of English, but I get the impression that at this point, you are very committed to writing in Spanish. Is this the case? Do you always think of yourself as writing in Spanish first?*

Fiction, yes. Now, sometimes I have to write lectures in English, but I have a Gringo husband who corrects the language. And I couldn't write fiction in another language. My training as a journalist taught me that you have to use this tool in a very effective way. In the choice of words you can convey an emotion, you can create an atmosphere, you can do things, that to me, are impossible to do in another language. And then there is something very important, you cannot have any sense of humor in another language. I'm very funny in Spanish! But it does not show in English at all. That's important to me.

Then when I write, for example, I spend many hours in the first draft, which is just pouring out the story, and then it takes two or three years to shape it up, and to put in the language that I think is the best, the best that I can do. They say that you never finish a novel, and that is true. There is a point where you are saturated with the corrections and you have to leave. It could always be better, but language is very important to me. Sometimes I spend three hours looking for a noun that will replace three adjectives, or changing the sentence to see if it weighs better this way, if it sounds more musical the other way. I always read it aloud, and I measure the sentences in a paragraph to see if it flows, to hear the music of the language. How can you do that in another language? Impossible.

> *Well, you must often be quite disturbed when you see a paragraph or a sentence that you polished so carefully, or weighed for the music in*

Spanish, and then in translation in English, all of your creativity seems lost because it's untranslatable.

No, because it's another book.

Is it really another book?

It's not my book anymore. I mean my book is what I produce, and I sent to my agent, and that's it. When it's published then it belongs to every reader, and every reader reads it in a different way. It's not anymore my book, it's our book. And so, I don't know, for many readers the language is not important, only the plot. To other people, it's just the political meaning, for example, of a historical event, or whatever. So I cannot follow up my book in the world. I mean the book, the world has its own destiny, and now, for example, my books are being made into movies. I don't want to read the screenplays because it doesn't belong to me.

You don't want to know?

I don't want to know. It's like my children; I have grown-up children, they can do with their lives whatever they want.

You don't even select translators that help?

No, I have an English translator in the U.S., who is a good friend, and she's kind enough to send me the translation and I read it, and sometimes when there's something that strikes me as awkward, I comment on it. For example, if I use the word "aguardiente" in Spanish, and she translates "whisky." In Latin America, whisky has a very special meaning. It is seen as a Gringo liquor that only people who can afford it can have. So, you cannot have people in the streets drinking whisky in Chile. That would be impossible. Translating is not only changing this to that, one language for another language, it's adapting to another culture. I will give you just one example, in my second book, *Of Love and Shadows*, there is a sentence that was eliminated in the English version because it was impossible to translate it so that it would make sense in English. We belong to a culture where we are very oral in our love expressions, the boleros, the tangos, the poetry, the whole culture talks about love. Actually the "Latin Lover" is just a myth, they don't work. But we have the culture of talking about love. We talk about it and make very little of it, and that doesn't work in English, where they make love and they don't talk about it. So, it's true, the sentence was "Supo entonces que amarla era su inexorable destino," which is very easy to translate, you say "He knew then that loving her was his inexorable destiny." First of all, the concept of inexorability of destiny in Anglo-Saxon culture is too heavy, and it's suspicious. If any man would tell me, in English, that I'm his inexorable destiny, I would run away! But in Spanish, it's acceptable.

I'd like to follow up on something you said about journalism. Your journalism career. Now, García Márquez was also a journalist . . .
All Latin American writers have been.

And I think García Márquez has had special success as a journalist, because he became successful as a novelist, and he has said many times in interviews, that if it hadn't been for his journalism days he would not have become a writer, quote "that they were tremendous training for me," they prepared him to become a novelist. Do you feel the same way? Do you feel that strongly about your work as a journalist?
Naturally. To me, there has been practically no transition. It was very small, because when I write, I have the feeling I am doing what I was doing before, writing for the same audience. The only difference is that I have more time and space to develop things. But first of all, you use languages, and it has to be as effective as in journalism. You have to grab your reader, and you have little time and space to do that. In journalism, you have six lines, in a novel you have six pages. If you don't get your reader in the first six pages, forget it. The guy has paid for your book, you have absolutely no right to bore him.

Then, when I write, I always deal with things that do happen, and you read them in the newspapers. Sometimes they sound very extravagant, or extraordinary, because of the way they are told. It's a trick of the language, but not of the facts. If I talk about *Eva Luna*, for example, many people have said that it is a totally fantastic book.

And you did the same thing in Of Love and Shadows.

Well that's different because that was a real case, and I had all of the documents, and that was of very special concern.

But you used the newspapers to get some of the documents.

Well, and the documents from the trial, because the military that were involved in those killings were brought to trial justice in Chile. And that was because the Catholic Church opened the mine and found the bodies before the police could stop them. There was a long military trial and I got many of the documents.

How did you get them?

Well because people knew that I was writing the book and lawyers that were involved in human rights endeavors helped me, and there was a book that helped me a lot that was written by Máximo Pacheco about that case.

Speaking of the journalism connection, your somewhat difficult journalistic encounter, when you attempted to interview Pablo Neruda, was that anything of a turning point for you?

Yes. He was the one who said I was a terrible journalist. Pablo Neruda, at that time, during the three years of Allende's government, Pablo Neruda was an ambassador in Paris. He was already old and sick, and in 1972 he won the Nobel Prize for literature, and he went back to Chile because he was feeling already very sick and tired. And he went to live on the coast in a little house he had in Isla Negra. He liked some humorous articles I wrote in a magazine, not because they were good, because I had absolutely no competition. Very few people did humor in Chile, I don't know why, we are very tragic! And so, he liked them and he called the magazine, and said he wanted to meet me. He didn't remember that our families had been very close before, he didn't know who I was really and that I had known him when I was a child.

I went to his house. It was winter, and he was alone in his house. We had lunch, and when I was driving there, I thought, "This guy won the Nobel Prize. The most important poet, the most important writer of Latin America, and maybe in the world, wants me to interview him!" Of all people me! I always thought that I was great, I had a big ego at that time. After lunch, I said, "I'm ready for the inter-view." He said, "What interview?" I said, "Well the interview." He said, "What interview? Look my child, I would never be interviewed by you, you are the worst journalist in this country. You never tell the truth. You are always in the middle of everything, you are never ob-jective, why don't you switch to literature? Because those faults are virtues in literature." Neruda was right.

> *Right now, we are facing in Latin America, repression, torture, the disappeared, death, poverty, hunger, violence, illiteracy, guerrillas. What do you think you can do as a writer, as one of our best writers, to reach people?*

Nothing, nothing. Books are important, art is important, and I'm go-ing to talk about this tonight. I want to be an agent of change but I'm very conscious of how limited my possibilities are. I come from a country where fifty percent of the population is illiterate. Of those fifty percent that can read and write in Latin America, only very few can afford a book. And of those who can afford a book, very few have the habit of reading. So, how many people can you reach with a book in Latin America? Very few. You can do more with a song, with a painting or a poem, that the people can see or memorize or sing.

> *But if you consider your North American readership, your audience in this country, perhaps your impact can be considerable when North Americans become more aware of the conditions that their tax dol-lars may be contributing to in South America.*

If I'm very lucky I might touch the hearts of two or three people, but what is really making a difference in this country is the press. Now, it's like the Vietnam War, for eight years, people ignored what was going on in Vietnam, until the press reported, and you could see, while you were having your coffee in the morning, you could see the people being killed in Vietnam. Although it was reported from a very repressed point of view, and very directed, people got to know about it. And finally there was a widespread movement in this country that changed the attitudes towards war.

The same thing is happening now in El Salvador, it's happening in

Guatemala, because journalists are going there, students are going there, just common people are going there. And these people come back and report. What they have to say is extremely important, and is making a big difference.

> *But you know, writers may have contributed to that consciousness. I'm thinking particularly of Carolyn Forché and her wonderful, thin, but very powerful book of poems from El Salvador. And Carolyn alone has done a lot to call attention to poetry of writers.*

But the movies have done a lot too. Movies like *Salvador* have done for the cause more than any writing.

> *Your books have also made people aware of the conditions in Latin America, problems that were completely unknown before they read your novels, and they want to know about what is going on there. At least, that has been my experience when I have taught your books. They want to know more about it, and they want to do something about it.*
>
> *Your books are so readable, and the characters are so wonderfully believable that this keeps a general reader going to the end of the book and exposes such a person to very different perspectives on foreign situations than they might get from most newscasts. Because American news is really, as you're well aware, at least limited if not narrow and biased. So I think that your books may be more important than you think.*

Well, I hope so, I don't want to think about that because then you get ideas. It is better to just write the best you can.

> *When Pinochet was in power many people looked at the creative artists, writers like you, and Jorge Edwards, Donoso, Skármeta . . . to see what they were going to write, what kind of allusion they were going to make about the regime. And now that democracy has been restored in Chile, I suppose the literature will take on different modalities. Do you know what those might be, since the Enemy is not there anymore?*

Well, first of all, we will have a formal democracy back in Chile that will start in March. But the military and economic structures still remain intact, and it will take years to dismantle them. Pinochet is there and the whole military structure is there, so repression is still there, and the new government will have to be cautious.

Right after the military coup in 1973 there was a wave of testimonial literature by the people who had suffered the repression directly. People who had lived in concentration camps, people whose relatives had disappeared, people who had been tortured, raped, etc. . . . It took several years to internalize that suffering, and transform it into art.

At the beginning it was just testimonial literature. I believe that I had the information to write *The House of the Spirits* in 1973 but it took me nine years to get over the pain, and to take enough distance to be able to write fiction. At the beginning I would have written a testimonial of what I had lived. I think that will happen to writers of this generation that will live in a democracy in Chile. They will have to exorcise the demons we have, to look for the truth. There is a whole period that has lived in ignorance of what has really been going on. We have to recover all of that. Dig in the dust, the mud, in the blood, to recover ourselves and find our own identity. I think that the writers and the artists of the next decade will have that mission, so it will be a different kind of writing.

> *Well now, Jorge Edwards has been here a few times and one of the things he said when he was here the last time was that during the Pinochet era, what writers started to do was looking at certain historical documents, and viewing history from a different point of view, and trying to evaluate it. Now if we are beginning a new era in Chile, do you suppose that there might be other modalities, other characteristics that were not there during Pinochet, in the literature?*

I don't know what's going to happen when for a long time people in Chile have had the feeling that they have lived in a period of darkness during these fifteen years. That culture was dead, I don't think that happened, I think that it had to find a way of getting around censorship and every form of art had to find a way of defying the system and getting away with it. That created a language, a set of symbols. It's very strange because there always was opposition press in

Chile during those years. Yet you have to live in Chile to read between the lines, to learn the key words that give you the message. The same thing happened in all the forms of art. Now that's not necessary anymore, so a new form is going to appear. But I think that during these sixteen years, much has been done in the shadows that was never published, that never saw the light, and that will come out now. I think that there will be a renaissance of art, of literature especially, because Chile is a country of writers, of great poets.

> *But the other side of this could be a situation parallel to Argentina, where in books and movies, like* The Official Story, *we've seen such soul searching and examination of how in many ways people were accomplices to the crimes.*

That will happen, that is happening now in my country.

> *How would you define your exile from Chile? Do you think that if you had remained in Chile you would have written novels?*

I don't know, maybe I would have written other novels. If I have to define my exile, first of all I have to say that it was a very privileged one, because I chose the place of exile. I went to Venezuela out of choice, I could take my family with me, I had a passport, none of my children were ever tortured, or disappeared. I was a very privileged person. I have seen, I have traveled extensively in the last years, and I have seen the exile of Chilean people. Everywhere, in wonderful countries like the Scandinavian countries, or Germany, where they are treated as political refugees. They live permanent suffering, because they are always looking back to their own, to what they left behind. They are rootless, they will never find themselves at ease in these countries, and they will try desperately to go back. I have seen people who lived in the slums in Chile, and now live in perfectly decent neighborhoods in Norway, and yet they want to go back to the slums! Because that is where they have their extended families, their language, their roots, their food, everything that belongs to them.

When I say that I'm privileged, it is because my parents were diplomats, I traveled all my life, I could adapt myself more easily. And then, I am one of the privileged people that out of suffering developed a new form of strength. Many people are destroyed by the experience of exile, it's death for them, very few develop this strength that I think I would have never developed in Chile because I didn't need it. I was a happy adolescent all my life, until the military coup, and I was already thirty. All of the sudden, in twenty-four hours, I realized that there was evil in the world and I had to deal with it. My whole life changed. Later, when I was threatened I had to leave, for many years I thought that I was going to die. I wanted to die every day, until little by little you grow, and you become stronger.

So I think that it was a very good thing for me and for my kids too. My kids were very unhappy, and I would talk with them, they were little and I would say: "Look this is very good, out of all this pain and out of all this loneliness, you will be better." And they are better people.

Do you have any plans to join your family who are emigrating back to Chile to take part in the changes there?

I'm living in a very happy moment of my life, I'm in love. It sounds terrible, I shouldn't be saying that, but it's Valentine's Day today. It's true, that changes also my whole experience of life, my vision of life. I've learned something very important, that maybe is the best lesson of exile, to live one day at a time. I don't make plans for the future, only for today. I want today to be a perfect day. I don't know if tomorrow will ever happen, maybe not. The Indians in Chile, the Mapuches, and Araucanos . . . say that the past is in front of you, you can look at it, and you can draw experience and knowledge from the past, and you can use it in your present. The future is at your back, you cannot see it and maybe it's not there because you will get hit by a truck today, so the future does not exist.

Will you tell us a bit about your next publication?

In the last couple of years I've lived a very hectic life, because I moved to this country. I had to adapt myself, and clean up the mess in my husband's life. I have two stepsons, and so it's a difficult time. And I couldn't find enough time and space for a novel that requires so many hours and so many months and years. And I decided that I would write a collection of short stories. It was my first experience with short stories, and I hope, well I think, it will be the last. It's much more difficult to write short stories than novels. A novel is an accumulation of details that creates a world. You don't need any inspiration, just patience. In a short story you need inspiration, a short story is something that is round, whole, it has a tension and if you don't get it in the first line, and if you don't know exactly when it will end, it's lost. It's very easily destroyed, one sentence can destroy it, you can see all the faults there. In a novel you can make many mistakes, and nobody notices. In a short story you can't! Everything is visible, it's like a poem, it's very difficult. And so, I wrote this collection of short stories with great effort, and it's going to be published next week in Spanish, and by the end of the year in English.

What's the name?

Tales by Eva Luna; in Spanish we don't have the difference between tales and stories. Tales have that magic fairy tale idea, folktales, and that's what I wanted, that meaning. But we don't have it in Spanish, it's *cuentos.* It could be *relatos,* but it doesn't convey the meaning at all.

Are there other writers of short stories that you particularly admire, that maybe interested you in the genre?

Yes, Borges. And Julio Cortázar wrote wonderful short stories.

As you know, Latin America has a certain perception about North America, and vice versa. Those perceptions are sometimes true, and sometimes false. Has your perception of North American society changed since you've been here, and about Latin American society?

Not about Latin American society, because I know it from inside. But now I'm beginning to learn a little bit about this country. This is a very complex society, just as complex as Latin America. And just as North Americans have a vision of Latin Americans as a whole, and they think we're all sitting under a cactus, under a sombrero, the same way we have an idea about the "Bad Yankee," and that's not at all like that. This is a multiracial, multicultural society, where you can find anything. The best and the worst, very dynamic, everything happens here, and what doesn't happen here, doesn't happen in the rest of the world. It is just like a melting pot, everything is boiling.

I'm fascinated by it because I'm learning a lot. When I came for the first time to San Francisco five years ago, I went back home saying, "I've been in a place for ten days, and I haven't met one normal human being." I was fascinated, and I'm back there. I've been there for two years, and I still have the same opinion. I haven't met one normal person. They're all in channeling, organic chicken, in Buddhism, Zen, in bus stops, it's incredible! And so, I have modified my vision of this country. I had the strong prejudice against the U.S., because we are the first victims of North American policy. Living here I realize, although you choose your representatives, therefore, you are responsible for everything that happens, and there is a free press, and you have all the possibilities of being informed, yet there is a huge number of people who do not agree with the foreign policy. People don't want their taxes to go for weapons in El Salvador, they don't! And that has been a revelation, a big revelation.

Can I ask you a question about Of Love and Shadows? *This book is usually read as a combination of love story and political intrigue, and political violence. But feminist critics have treated this book as an indictment against female repression in Chile and Irene's character as a portrait of female liberation. Did you have this in mind when you wrote the book?*

The first time that my mother said "Sit with your legs crossed," I realized that I didn't want to be a woman. I wanted to be a man. It's much easier to be a man, you have to make half the effort to get double the recognition that any woman does. And then, I was brought up in a very patriarchal society, in a very macho family. With very strong males and very victimized subdued females, although they were very strong characters.

This feminism appears in all my characters, all my books. But I wasn't planning it that way, what I wanted to show in Irene's change is what happened to me. That is the political awareness that I didn't have before. I became aware when all of the evidences were there too late. Three years before the military coup, I should have realized what was going on in my country, because I was old enough to do that, and I was a journalist.

Where was I? I was on the moon! Then the military coup happened, and you realized. In twenty-four hours, in a country where I had never heard the word torture . . . ? Very often, when I was teaching at Berkeley, I told my students "Beware! This dimension of violence is here. It can be triggered by a little excuse, by something very small, and the fascists will take over." The people who are self-righteous, who have the weapons, and who think that they have the truth, they need a very little excuse to take hold. And this has happened in the most civilized countries in the world.

Then for you Irene's character is more a question of awareness, becoming aware, rather than of liberation?

Yes, I belong to the first generation of women in Chile who belong to women's lib. There were many women before that who struggled for women's issues, but in a very isolated way. We were the first to really get together, to work for a magazine, and say "OK, this is what we want." We had to endure a lot of pressure, aggression, loneliness, isolation, all our marriages were broken up, we had to break with the family, because we were outlaws.

How has it happened that the main characters in your novels are women?

I think that one writes about what one knows, and being a woman in a society where in many ways men and women are segregated, I know better the world of women. And therefore, it's easier for me to write from that point of view. It has been said, for example, that most Latin American writers who are males, at least the ones from the Boom, don't have good female characters, they are stereotypes, the mythical woman. That is because especially that generation was brought up in a segregated world where men and women went to different schools, we only danced together, we didn't even sleep together very often. And so, we knew about each other very little, and you seldom find conflicts or well-developed female characters in Latin American literature. Most of it has been written by men, except a few of them like Jorge Amado, for example, who had great female characters. And I think that literature written by women in Latin America has better knowledge of our feminine reality.

Is this also going to happen in your short stories, that we're going to find a lot of women as main characters?

No, it didn't happen that way with the short stories.

One critic that knows your work very well, much better than I do, says that even though you declare publicly that you are a feminist, that your writing is actually masculine writing.

What is masculine writing? I mean does language or literature have sex? Writing is writing. Language is language, and you write from a human point of view. There's no such thing as masculine or feminine literature. Why would we segregate ourselves, segregate men?

I've been attacked by feminists because I'm not aggressive enough, or because I don't dress like a man. I don't know, they want things to be extreme. They want to change a patriarchal society for a matriarchal one. Pants for skirts, that doesn't work. We need a society of partnerships, where we can all be better human beings, where we can get the best of both parts and share. I can do anything that a man does, everything. And a man can do everything that I can do.

Now they say for example, the feminists, the extreme feminists say, that my characters become aware, politically aware, because they fall in love with a guerrilla, for example. That at the end of *The House of Spirits*, that she goes back to the house and she waits for the world to change, for better times to come, and she's expecting a baby from the rape. And that's not a feminist attitude, she should go out on the streets and fight.

Well, the characters in my books defy the first rule in a patriarchal society. The first thing that women have to do, is to stay in their house and be quiet in your home. They defy the rule of silence, and they write.

What does Alba do in *The House of the Spirits*? She goes back to register the memory, the collective memory to write. And this book is the product of her writing, of her defying the rule. She waits for better times, as she expects the baby. Not because it's the baby of a rapist, and she's a victim, but because the baby symbolizes the book, the new generation that is marked by violence, it's marked by the rape of the society. And that kid will have to live with that pain but also with the hope, and the love and the experience, possibly of a better society; and that is what the baby symbolizes in the book. In *Eva Luna*, she's also a victim because she lives in a patriarchal society, she's orphaned, she's poor, and she's a woman. But she defies that, and she writes, and she becomes independent and free.

It seems that all your women reach illuminations, through human concerns; do you do this consciously or is this imposed on you?

I look at the problem in the world, and people are that way. That happens with suffering. Everybody, I don't invent that, it is that way.

One of the most delightful and diverting aspects of Eva Luna *is the ingenious integration of stylistic devices, evocative of García Márquez; here I'm talking about the use of hyperbole, paradox, the juxtaposition of concrete and abstract words to describe the characters' state of mind, and the flights of imagination from objective reality. My question is when you wrote* Eva Luna, *did you have any idea of a parody of* One Hundred Years of Solitude?

No, no.

Who are your favorite writers these days?

I'm a very disorganized reader, I read different things. When I'm writing I only read things related to the book I'm writing. Because, if not, I get cluttered with other things. Now I'm discovering North American writers. I hadn't read many women writers before. The best literature in this country now is being written by minorities, black women first, Chinese Americans, Chicanos, Japanese-Americans. These people are writing wonderful literature that totally defies the standards of WASP literature that is always in the *New York Times*, and I love it.

"Magical Realism," what do you think about that, what is that?

The first person to name that movement "Magical Realism," to give a label to that, was Alejo Carpentier. He was living with the surrealists in France and the surrealists were inventing this wonderful new thing of printing together on a dissecting table, a sewing machine and an umbrella, and that was surrealism. And Alejo Carpentier realized that this was an intellectual process that had its roots, and he could see the umbrella and the sewing machine on this dissecting table in Latin America because it was part of our culture. Kafka would have been a realist if he would have lived in Mexico. So Alejo Carpentier realized that, and he abandoned the surrealists and searched in our roots, in our history, in our legends, in our folklore. He was the first one to label it. And it was wonderful because it was like giving permission to other writers to finally use their own voices. Because before that our writers were always trying to imitate Europeans, or North Americans, and were denying all our Indian background, our African influence, our own languages, and legends, and myths. This was just an open door for all that. I think that was the beginning of the Boom. That really gave a lot of people permission to do anything. But it's not a literary device, it's part of our life.

The magic is still there. Because magic, in my case, stands for emotions. The spirits in the house are not really ghosts, the spirits are the passions, the obsessions, the dreams of the family, and of the country. Maybe we deal with them in different forms, but we all feel them in the same way, and that's what the spirits stand for in *The House of Spirits*.

The tone of the first third of the book is very much like a dream, because the narrator was not yet born, Alba. The narrator of the first book is not born until the first third part of the book. At that point she tells what she has been told, so it has that dreamy tone. Then she's born, and there is one part of the book that has her vision as a child, so that has another tone. With a tone of a child telling about a war that she doesn't quite understand. And she cannot make the difference between what is real and what is fantasy.

And then the last part of the book is when she is an adult, and there is repression, and she has been tortured, mutilated, raped, her whole world is destroyed. Reality is so overwhelming that she can't go back to the spirits. There is a scene in the book when she is in this sort of cage, the dog house, and she has been terribly tortured, and she's dying and she calls her grandmother, and she calls her for help, and she tries to call the spirits to bring back the happy memories of childhood. They don't come because reality is so terrible, that there is no space for dreams. The spirit of the grandmother comes not to console her, or to pamper her in any way, nor even to help her die. She comes with a very strong voice to say: "Everybody will die, there's nothing new in dying, nothing strange or extraordinary. The real miracle is surviving, and you have to find a way to survive. And that's the only thing that you have to do now." Her voice is very powerful when she says that. I think that in a way I was talking for myself, and for many people who lived my experience. You can always die, you can always be depressed, the miracle is to survive, and find the voice to talk about it.

> *In your work, memory is very important. Is memory kind of a way to survive?*

For many years after I left Chile, I felt totally rootless, and as long as I felt that way, I couldn't do anything for myself, or for anybody else. I was dry, I couldn't nurture myself, I had no reason. And then I slowly realized that my roots were not in a country, not even in my family, they were in my memories. And I think that I made up my memories, most of them. I no longer know what is true, what is not. Sometimes when I confront a relative, who doesn't speak to me anymore, I realize that maybe there was some truth there, but I'm not sure. I created this memory in a way to plant my roots there.

There is a wonderful sentence, a statement, by one of Bertolt Brecht's characters, he says: "I am that man that goes around with a brick in his hand, to show the world how his house was." And that's the way I feel about my books in a way, that they are my bricks. I can show people what I believe my world was, so I've not lost it.

> *Then there is a beautiful line from a poem by Antonio Machado, the great Spanish poet; he says: "También la verdad se inventa" [the truth is also invented] and that's what you have done.*

Can you say how much we invent, and how much was real? Maybe I have had a very dull life, that I had to invent it. So, I will have wonderful memories when I die.

Transforming Stories, Writing Reality

INTERVIEW BY JOHN BROSNAHAN

Reprinted from *Booklist* 87, no. 20 (June 15, 1991): 1930–1931

Isabel Allende's novel *The House of the Spirits*—a family chronicle that revealed generational and political forces in conflict—introduced a new and vibrant voice from Latin America. Allende knew her subject firsthand from growing up in Chile and from witnessing the 1973 military coup that resulted in the assassination of her uncle, Salvador Allende, the country's president. The end of democratic rule ultimately forced Allende and her family into exile in Venezuela, where she began her career as a writer in 1981. Two other novels, *Of Love and Shadows* and *Eva Luna*, followed in 1987 and 1988. Allende's latest book, *The Stories of Eva Luna,* is a collection of short stories that takes its name and inspiration from the title character of the novel that immediately preceded it. Eva Luna, not unlike Allende herself, is a marvelous storyteller who has made her life a source of imagination and invention. Now Eva Luna has resurfaced once more to charm readers with a further series of adventures and tales that are set in the landscape of contemporary South America but that deal with universal themes: social warfare, political corruption, sexual battles, passionate and tender love.

Allende now lives in California, from where she spoke to *Booklist* just after the publication of her latest book.

❝ *What is the relationship between your two Eva Luna books?* ❞
Well, the reader can read both books separately. They are not so closely related that you have to read the first one to get an idea of the

second—not at all; they are two separate books. When I finished *Eva Luna*, I thought it was over, that was it, and that I would never go back to those characters. But many people asked, "Well, where are the stories? This is a story of a storyteller and the stories that she tells are not in the book." So I thought that maybe it was time to face that challenge that I think every writer has once in their lifetime, and that is the short story, which is such a difficult genre.

My life at that time was very hectic. I had recently moved to the U.S.; I didn't have a room of my own; I didn't have long periods of time that I could dedicate to a novel because I was teaching and working and traveling—really, my life was a mess then. But I had fragments of time, let's say two weeks, a month. So I thought, well, short stories are perfect for this kind of schedule because I can really lock myself away for a couple of weeks and finish one story—you cannot do that with a novel. So that's how the idea of these short stories came to me. Later, when I started working on them, I wrote many more stories, but again I made a sort of selection. Without really having anything in mind, I realized that all the stories that I had chosen were somehow related: they were all love stories, first of all. Then, they all belonged to a common sort of geography, to the same space; they all took place in the same universe, which was very similar to *Eva Luna*'s universe. And I also wanted the voice of Eva Luna to narrate the stories, but it didn't happen exactly that way. That is, all the stories aren't in the same voice or person; for example, one may be told in second person, and there are others in first or third person, so it's not always distinctively Eva Luna's voice, but it's her tone. And that is the only relationship that both books have. Now there are characters from *Eva Luna* that appear in some of the stories, but they come in such a way that the reader who has not read *Eva Luna* would understand the story. . . .

When *The Stories of Eva Luna* was published in Spanish, people said that they were like stories written many years ago. There's a whole tradition in Spanish called the *picaresca*, and they said these stories remind them of the *picaresca*. But I had never read any *picaresca* before because I didn't read that kind of story when I was young. So it happens sometimes that you just tune into something that's already there.

What are some of the sources of these stories? Are they from things that you witnessed yourself, or did other people tell them to you, or are they entirely imaginary?

I don't have any imagination. I just watch and listen and read. In this book I would say that half of the stories happened in the U.S.; I just transplanted them to another environment.

In the final story ["And of Clay Are We Created"], a young girl was buried in a collapsed building, either from an avalanche or an earthquake. Did you live through the San Francisco earthquake, and did that inspire the story?

I was in California at the time of the earthquake, but that story happened in 1985 in Colombia. There was an eruption of the Ruiz volcano, and an avalanche of mud, snow, and stones completely covered a village. Many people died, and it was a real tragedy. And this little girl, Omaira Sánchez, was buried in the mud for four days, and the television cameras and the media from all over the world went there. But the rescuers couldn't find a machine to pump the water and save her life; we could see her agonized face on the screen for four days until she died. So, I saw that story on television; I saw that little girl buried alive, and I have a photograph of her on my desk. Her black eyes have haunted me for five years. I thought that by writing the story I could get rid of her, but I haven't. She's still there.

Another story in the book describes a woman who is locked in a basement by a jealous lover for nearly fifty years ["If You Touched My Heart"]. That happened in Venezuela; I read about it in the newspaper. I had to imagine what her life was like, but the story was already there. There's another story of a little Indian boy in Central America, who's given in adoption by a mother who thinks that he will be much better off with a rich family in the U.S. ["The Road North"]. But in reality, the boy is sent to a clinic where his body will be sacrificed for organ transplants. That story also happened and is still happening now in several countries in Latin America where children are sold to organ banks.

You said it was difficult for you to write these short stories. Is it more difficult for you to write stories than novels?

Oh, yes. Once you have an idea, a novel is just work. You sit there everyday, you add detail, and one day it's over. It's like embroidering a tapestry—you need patience, but it's just work. But writing a short story is much more difficult, like aiming a single arrow. You have one shot only. You shoot the arrow, and it needs precision, direction, speed, and good luck. And that's the way it should be written—in one impulse. I don't really know how to write short stories so I invent and write like a novel, but then I cut and cut until it's down to fifteen or twenty pages. But I always have a thousand more things to say.

> *Frequently, the reader has the impression that your story came to an end; it wasn't actually the end of their story.*

Yes, I would like to tell their whole lives and what happened afterwards. That's why I feel so much more comfortable in a novel. I feel that the short story is closer to poetry. You really don't have any space or time, and you have to be very precise with language. In a short story, everything shows. One adjective that is too much, the reader notices. In a novel, you can make all the mistakes you want, and very few people notice.

> *I've read that you began your career as a journalist and that you've also written plays and children's books. Was the transformation from journalist to novelist difficult for you?*

It happened smoothly yet rather dramatically; smoothly because I didn't have a choice and dramatically because I was practically forced to abandon what had been a career for me. I had been a journalist all my life; I loved it. I had the feeling that I participated in the world, that everything that happened to anybody happened to me. It was like the whole world was my home: I was always in the streets, always there in the middle of the action. And then after the military coup in Chile, I had to leave my job and my country. I went to live in Venezuela where I couldn't find a job as a journalist, and for many years I would say that I lived in silence. I couldn't write, and I was used to expressing everything in writing, so when I don't write something, it's as if it didn't happen.

In 1981, many years after the military coup in 1973, I began to write a letter to my grandfather. My grandfather was dying, and this was a spiritual letter because he was not going to receive it before he died. But in that letter, I poured out everything that had been accumulating inside me for eight years. And it happened more or less in the same tone, and in the same way that I wrote when I was a journalist—without thinking too much. It just happened and that's how I became a writer, using practically the same techniques I did before as a journalist. By the way, I was a lousy journalist.

Well, I haven't seen any of your journalism published.

It was terrible. I was always putting myself in the middle, I could never be objective, I lied all the time. And if there was no news, I would invent some. No one ever caught me, fortunately.

I read that early in your career you translated Barbara Cartland–style romances, and you got into trouble because you would change the dialogue, the plot, and the characters.

Well, you see, at that time I was a feminist—I still am. So the idea of translating those romantic stories in which the women were so stupid bothered me so much that I changed the endings. I was fired.

But I hope you have better luck with your own translators.

Yes, I hope so. In fact, I think that the translations really improve my books. They sell so well in translation that I'm sure that the translators do a splendid job.

They've been translated into English, French, German, and what other languages?

Twenty-seven languages, including Chinese, Vietnamese, Japanese— all sorts of languages. I have several editions of my books written in alphabets I can't even read.

Booklist recently did an interview with the South African author Nadine Gordimer in which she contends that in her writing she is not interested in politics. She is concerned about politics in her private life, but not in her novels, which she believes must focus on the personal. Do you feel the same way about your writing?

I have never belonged to any political party, and I'm not active in politics now. I was during the military coup, though, because as long as it lasted, the people of Chile had no freedom. Now I am not involved directly in politics anymore. I'm not a political creature at all. But I'm interested in everything that happens to people, and that's what I write about. I write about the things I care about: poverty, inequality, and social problems are part of politics, and that's what I write about. My books have been accused of being too political. I'm not aware of that. I just can't write in an ivory tower, distant from what's happening in the real world and from the reality of my continent. So the politics just steps in, in spite of myself.

That corresponds with what I experienced about two years ago when I led a women's group in a discussion of The House of the Spirits. *This group was from a fairly wealthy suburb of Chicago, and they loved your novel. But the problems they had with it were in the second half when you were describing the political turmoil in Chile; they had a hard time accepting that.*

In the U.S., writers are not supposed to mingle in politics. To be considered a political writer here is an insult; North Americans believe that literature should be art for its own sake and should not be involved with political reality. In my continent, in Latin America, that's impossible. I'm not just talking about recent events in Chile, because even before the military coup, it was the same. The situation in our continent is so terrible—with the violence, the poverty, the inequality, the misery—that writers have necessarily assumed the voice of the people. What else can they write about? If they want to represent somebody, what else can they write about?

Then do you think that much of the great writing that has come out of Latin America within the past several decades—and equally out of South Africa—has been prompted by the political turmoil and revolution there?

I think that there has been an element of politics that has made these books important. Many people, especially in Latin America, read novels because they are the real history. You don't find anything in official textbooks that tells you what life is about; you find it in literature. Our great writers have become like prophets, like shamans for our continent. That's a status that you never achieve as a writer in Europe or in the U.S., but you do in Eastern Europe. So where the situation is dramatic, writers become very important because they say what the press can't say. And if you can't live in your own country, you live in exile.

> *That's my next question. You're a resident in the U.S. now, but you have been back to Chile within the past several years. Do you think that living in the U.S. is going to have any effect on what you write about and how you present it?*

In my last book, the short stories were all written in the U.S., and half of them happened here. I just transplanted them. So what I have discovered after three years of living in California is that people are very much the same everywhere. Passions, obsessions, demons, angels, legends—it's just the same. I mean, there are so many more similarities than differences. The air is loaded with fantastic stories; I don't have to invent anything. I don't think I will ever write in English, at least not fiction. Because to write fiction for me is something very organic; it just happens to me, and it happens in Spanish, like dreaming. But I have noticed that in these short stories there's a change in the language. My sentences are shorter, there's less ornamentation, fewer adjectives. The language is more straightforward, and I think that is the influence of not only speaking English all the time, but of reading American authors. And I like it. The text is more restrained; I like that very much. I hope I can go on with that in my next novel.

The "Uncontrollable" Rebel

INTERVIEW BY JUAN ANDRÉS PIÑA

Translated for this book by Virginia Invernizzi

First published in Spanish in *Conversaciones con la narrativa chilena* (Santiago, Chile: Editorial Los Andes, 1991)

13

> **" ** *Even though you are Chilean, you were born in Lima. Why were your parents in Peru at that time?*

My father, Tomás Allende, was a diplomat. I was born in Lima during one of his official missions. After I was born, my parents separated and my mother returned to Chile; once there, she realized that she was pregnant. Due to family pressures, she returned to her husband. My brother was born in Peru as well, and we remained there enough time for my mother to become pregnant again. My father left for good and the Chilean consul saw to it that my mother returned home. My father disappeared completely. I never saw him again. The only time that I knew anything about him after that was when they called me from the morgue to identify his body: he had died on the street of a heart attack. Even though he lived in Santiago, we never saw each other.

Why?

I never knew. It is one of the mysteries of my life and I haven't tried to find out, because I prefer that it remain in a sort of misty poetics. Besides, he had very little to do with my life. The only thing of his that I had was a trunk—with his name engraved on it—full of books, that remained in the basement of my grandfather's house where I lived for many years. I grew up reading those books which were mostly young adult fiction. That was my only inheritance. Later on my mother married another diplomat, Ramón Huidobro, the same consul who had helped her return to Chile.

> *You have said that he wasn't your biological father, but he was your spiritual father.*

He was my true father. We traveled widely with him and he was the one who formed me. I owe him my intellectual inquisitiveness, my curiosity, and my discipline. My stepfather—I feel strange calling him that—has asked me at times why he is not in my books. I answer back that it is because he has common sense. People who have common sense are not good protagonists for novels, but they are fantastic to live with. He had a Jesuit upbringing, and somehow he transmitted that: the dialectic, the rigor, the ability to set a goal and walk straight towards it. He has been the only person in my life with whom I can talk about absolutely everything and without a mask: sex, money, sin, work. I can talk about those topics without worrying about hurting or bothering him.

> *How long did you live in your grandparents' house?*

For my first ten years, more or less. About then my mother married Ramón Huidobro. It took them a while to marry because they had to settle their previous marital status. After the marriage, we left for Bolivia, then Europe, and finally ended up in Beirut. When the revolution began in Lebanon, and the American Marines were sent over in 1958, the local government asked all diplomats to send their families home because they could not take responsibility for them. They sent us, the children, back to Chile. So I returned again to my grandfather's house. My mother remained in Lebanon with my stepfather as long as she could, and when things became quite difficult, they both left for Turkey. He went as a businessman. So I stayed for a very long time at my grandfather's. I finished my studies in Santiago and when I was seventeen I began to work.

> *How did you deal with the distance between you and your mother?*

My mother and I began something that we still keep up today: a permanent epistolary contact. We wrote every day. Since then my relationship with her has been very special, intimate, very rare between mother and daughter: we are a combination of comrades and accomplices. Lately it has become somewhat of a literary relationship because she is the only person who knows my books before they are published. After she reads the original, she corrects me, proposes changes, suggests that I enrich certain characters, and gives frank opinions. Now that I live in the United States and my Spanish has deteriorated, she also corrects aspects of the language.

> *It seems by your books that your grandparents' house and those years of youth were very important to you. What were those years like?*

My grandparents' house was on Suecia Street, number 081. When I was a little girl I saw it as a great mansion, but when I visited many years later I saw that it was just a common old house. Life there was very important to me. Most important was my relationship with my grandmother, Isabel Barros Moreira, who died when I was very young, and who left an indelible impression in my memory. These recollections are partly true, partly inventions made up of everything that I heard about her after she died. I made up the memories from stories that I heard my grandfather, my mother, and other people who knew her tell. They kept her alive in some way. Maybe all those stories were full of fantasy, but everyone who knew her told extraordinary tales about her.

> *A person with extraordinary powers like the protagonist in* The House of the Spirits?

Obviously the character of Clara is based on her, though quite exaggerated. My grandmother had extrasensory powers: she was half prophet, half clairvoyant, telepathic, and she could even move objects without touching them. She had a group of friends, the sisters Mora, who were quite famous at the time. They would get together with my grandmother and have spiritual séances. My grandmother did all this with a great sense of humor, openly, without allowing it to become macabre, solemn, or dark. It was a game that shone as though it belonged to the fantastic. It was something very open, pleasing, ironic. She was a very frail woman, physically as well as spiritually. She didn't walk on earth: she would float among things. She left a permanent mark in the house and also in me.

In what aspects especially?

Stories, fantasies. It was something spiritual above and beyond material things. I also inherited from my grandmother her social restlessness. Politics came into my life much later. I did not have much contact with the Allende family except for Salvador Allende, who was closer to my mother and a good friend of my stepfather's. I looked upon Salvador as another uncle whom I saw on vacations or outings. I didn't have political inclinations because my mother's family is very conservative and Catholic. At my grandfather's house you just did not talk about politics, or religion, for that matter. My grandmother practiced what at that time was called Christian charity, and today is called social restlessness. She was saddened and anguished by economic injustice, poverty: she went to the slums and spent her time sewing and collecting money for the poor.

The second time that you lived with your grandparents was upon your return from Beirut.

When they sent me from Beirut I was about fourteen. My grandmother had already died, and my grandfather, Agustín Llona, had remarried. I did not have much of a relationship with that second wife, but I had a wonderful relationship with my grandfather. I call it our "enraged intimacy."

What do you mean by that?

That we never agreed on anything but we adored each other. I saw him every day while I was in Chile, until 1975. I went by for tea and if I ever missed our date he was truly hurt. I remember that the day I had my first child I went to visit him at the last moment because I couldn't miss my date. He would tell me things in those conversations. I had a special type of fascination with everything that his life had been. Imagine that he was born before electricity came to

Santiago. Talking with him was like taking a seductive voyage into the past. I attempted to recreate that world in *The House of the Spirits*.

Was he a good narrator?

Yes, of course. He would seize your attention and was full of stories. He had a powerful personality: he was a strong man who represented traditional values, that in some way were like the platform or the skeleton that sustained me, but before which I rebelled continuously. After the military coup in 1973, I would tell my grandfather of the gruesome events that I knew about and I had seen, and he would shake me and ask me why I had to get involved in that. He would tell me that I had nothing to do with all that. He would tell me not to get involved and that all that was not my life or my reality. It was the same thing that he would tell my grandmother when she went to the slums. It was really his fear that the world would take the people that he loved and destroy them. We had a relationship based on love, pain, and constant confrontation. He died in 1981, just when I began to write *The House of the Spirits*.

What was your experience with literature when you were a child?

I lived in a house where the walls were covered with book shelves: they would multiply, reproduce, because my uncle Pablo brought books all the time. There was no television and we listened to the radio very little. I read a lot and without censorship. I could read what I wanted. The books were only an arm's length away. I read a lot, and actually, at home everyone read a lot. The books that first interested me were the ones in the cellar, the trunk that belonged to my father. All that had to do with my father had not been explicitly prohibited, but he had disappeared from my life completely: there were no photographs and no one talked about him, and if I ever asked, the answer was always the same: "Your father was a very intelligent gentleman." Nothing else. And so everything that had to do with my father had a very attractive mysterious quality to it. To top it all off, the cellar was always closed because there were spiders and mice, and it was humid and disorderly. I would always sneak downstairs to play in the cellar, alone, and that was when I found my father's trunk.

Inside the trunk were books that I could have found in other places, but the mixture of a forbidden place and something that belonged to my father was like embarking on a forbidden adventure. I read almost in the dark with only the light from a candle. The books were for young adults and we didn't have them in the house because no one bought that type of literature: Jules Verne, Salgari, Dickens, and others. I read all of them.

> *You also read the Marquis de Sade, quite an unusual author for a young girl.*

Yes, but that was later when I was in a Quaker school in Lebanon. At home I found de Sade's *Philosophy in the Bedroom.* When I began reading it I realized immediately that it was not the type of book that I could just carry around because most probably my uncle Ramón (that's how I refer to my stepfather) would take it away from me. I made a cover for it and took it to school. I also read Shakespeare when I was about nine or ten, not for its literary quality, but for the story itself. I would draw the characters on cardboard, cut them out, paste a stick behind them and act out the plays.

> *What was your experience like in that Quaker school? Somewhat sinister?*

No, it was a good experience even though it was a tremendously strict school. They thought that even wearing buttons in your clothing was frivolous. We studied the Bible exhaustively—we memorized it. Everything was regimented. The difference between good and evil was perfectly clear. There were a million things that were sinful. But even with all this rigor, I was very happy. Maybe I needed such definite and rigid structure. I had come from a past with many changes and uncertainties. I was always going from one place to another, changing friends, schools, family, and home. Those years in the English school gave me a structure.

> *How did that rigid structure affect a young girl entering adolescence?*

Things have changed much since then. When I was twelve or thirteen and my hormones started to explode, I was locked away in that school. In Lebanon, girls don't go out alone in the streets. You didn't go out in a group, you could not dance to rock music or have male friends. Life was austere. The only man in the entire school was the bus driver. Everything was oriented to keeping you as ignorant, virginal, and chaste as possible.

What happened when you returned to Chile?

Since I hadn't done my schooling in Chile, upon my return I had to take an exam, and that was how I received my high school diploma. I had good marks and could have easily entered the university.

Why didn't you?

I don't want to blame any one, but I was educated to be a housewife and not a professional. I had no inclinations towards a career or towards university studies because no one ever expected it. I finished high school very early, at sixteen, but I never imagined that I could study beyond that. I had no idea what I could study for. I was totally confused. Uncle Ramón told me that if I wasn't going to study, I should work at least for a year, to find out what I wanted. That is what I did, and since I already had a boyfriend, the idea was that I would get married, have children, and take care of the house. I have been working since I was seventeen. The only interruption was for six months when I had to stay in bed because I had problems with my second pregnancy.

Where did you first work?

As soon as I finished school, I started working as a secretary for the Forestry Department, for the FAO [the Food and Agricultural Organization of the United Nations]. It was terribly boring. All I did was to copy forestry statistics. After that there was a job at the Department of Information, and they took me. Two journalists who worked there taught me to write in Spanish because I hardly knew it. I had had a very uneven education in French, English, and a bit in Spanish. A short time later television came to Chile. Channel thirteen offered the United Nations fifteen minutes to explain the World Campaign against Hunger, which was very popular at the time. My boss couldn't do the first program which was, of course, live. I called the channel to let them know, and the producer told me that he was very sorry but that someone had to be there at three o'clock to fill the space. I had an Italian movie on the United Nations campaign and I quickly edited it (trying to guess the time), I added text according to what the images said to me, and I went to the station. It was aired, and I have no idea how I did it all. In those days I was quite daring. But, anyway, after that I was offered a weekly spot on TV, and that was how I got started as a journalist. When I exhausted the topic of the campaign, I began to talk about the United Nations, the FAO, forestry, all topics that related to my work.

You were still a secretary in spite of all that.

Of course. I was hired as a secretary, but my dream was to one day enter into the category of the experts who work on information. But that was impossible because I didn't have enough training or schooling. Meanwhile, my husband, who was a civil engineer, and was dying to see Europe, received a scholarship to study in Belgium. I also arranged to take a course in Belgium related to radio and television and hoped that would allow me to go back to work at the FAO but to a better job. I can say all this with certain clarity today, but at that time everything was very confusing. I lived constantly pulled by the desire to stay home, to be a mother to my children and an exemplary wife with the starched place setting for lunch, and a terrible desire to accomplish something. I also felt guilty for wanting to do so much. I feel that I have been a feminist all my life, even though back then I could not articulate it. I didn't have the words to express it. What I felt was a rebellious anger towards everything, against machismo, against the fact that my husband had advantages and rights that I simply did not have. I refused to use his last name, due more to anger than to an idea.

You say that you felt you were a feminist. In what sense did you feel a feminist? I ask you because that term has been charged with so many different meanings.

First of all, when I was a little girl, I felt anger towards my grandfather, my stepfather, and all the men in the family, who had all the ad-

vantages while my mother was the victim. She had never been prepared for the world out there, and she still had to go out and work to
take care of her three children. She had to please everyone and everyone told her what to do. If my Uncle Pablo came home at three in the
morning, nothing happened, but if my mother got home at eleven my
grandfather would have a fit. All my life I felt I was at a disadvantage
with respect to my brothers. I don't remember any instance when I
didn't perfectly understand that having been born a woman was a
curse. The first clear recollection is from when I was about five years
old. I was sitting in the living room while my mother was teaching
me how to knit. I am not very good at those things, and I had trouble
working the yarn around the needles, twisting it, etc. I was sitting in
front of the window which looked out to our back patio where there
was a poplar tree that my brothers used to climb. And in the midst of
all that torture my mother said to me, "Darling, sit with your legs together." That is, not only did I have to twist that cursed yarn around
those needles, but I had to sit with my legs together!

While your brothers played outside.
Of course! While my brothers played outside—and all this because I
was a woman. I was a tomboy until my breasts grew and my female
condition was no longer concealable. When that happened I was so
angry that I wore a gray suit and I refused to accept femininity. Of
course, there was another side to me. . . .

The one that liked boys and wanted to be liked by them. . . .
I wanted them to like me, but I was so sure that that would never
happen, that I did everything I could to be as ugly as possible. I even
wanted to become a nun so no one would know that I couldn't catch
a husband. But, isn't it ironic, at fifteen I met a boy who fell in love
with me and opened doors to another dimension. When he took my
hand for the first time I felt a whole world was opening its doors to
me. His name was—his name is—Miguel Frías and that is the man I
married. My anger towards male authority and all types of authority
continued even after my marriage. And it endures even today.

Did your "feminist" vision continue after your marriage?

When I married I felt it was unfair that my professional life was tied to my husband's professional future: go wherever he went, accept whatever he did. And I could maybe do something but always under his shadow. I also thought it was unfair that they had only prepared me to be a housewife. I adored my children, but I lived with the sense of guilt that being a mom was not enough. I wanted to do a million other things. In my youth all forms of rules and hierarchy infuriated me: the police, the government, my parents, my husband. If there was a red light in the street, I wanted to go right through. That has subsided with the years, but it has been with me all my life.

What were you looking for when you studied in Belgium?

I would be lying if I told you that I thought my studies in Belgium would lead to a career. What I wanted was to get out of the house. I studied for one year there thanks to some scholarships that the government gave to citizens of the Congo. All my classmates were black men. The first months were very difficult because I not only encountered reverse racism, but rampant machismo. That experience affirmed my feminism. Since I was sure I wasn't the only one who felt that way, I began to do some research on the topic. Just then I met the journalist Delia Vergara in Geneva, who was traveling with her husband. She was the first person who spoke to me about feminism. It was the end of 1965. Delia quoted from books by American feminists, and that was when I listened to this intelligent Chilean woman from my generation, articulating the thoughts that for me had only been an organic, visceral anger. I began to research the topic.

How did your professional relationship with Delia Vergara, from the magazine Paula, *begin?*

Delia read a letter that I had sent to my mother in Geneva, and when she returned to Chile, and began the magazine, she called me. She said that she had found the letter very funny and she thought that I could collaborate with the magazine in a section dedicated to humor. This was towards the end of 1966. It took us six months to begin and the magazine came out in August of 1967. Delia's team was essentially Malú Sierra and Amanda Paz, and at the beginning I was a collaborator. The first piece I wrote was a type of classification of the different types of husbands. It was actually quite offensive to men, but people liked it. I kept that column for many years. I also answered letters giving readers advice on love problems. I signed with the pseudonym Francisca Román: Francisca for my mother and Román after my uncle Ramón.

The magazine Paula *marked an epoch in Chilean journalism for its confidence and brazenness. It broke the mold of the typical magazine for women. Do you feel that way about it too?*

Absolutely. And I refer to the *Paula* of those years, not the current one. It was the first Chilean publication that dared to speak about divorce, abortion, virginity, sex, drugs, corruption within the government. It delved into politics, reported on radical movements around the world, and, in general, it touched on all that which had been untouchable up to then in Chile. When I wrote, I could say many things because I used humor; otherwise they might not have accepted it. We were together until 1974. Soon after the military coup, they fired the team and the magazine became another of the many publications for "young ladies."

You also wrote for the children's magazine Mampato *which belonged to the same journalistic staff.*

Yes, I collaborated on both simultaneously. I loved *Mampato*. When the director, Eduardo Armstrong, died, I replaced him, because there was no one else close by who could hold that post. While I was there I wrote some children's books which I think should pass on to oblivion. The language was not well crafted and it was overall not good writing.

And during those years you still worked on television.

Also simultaneously I had a television program which had different names during the years such as "Fíjate qué" [Listen up!] and "La media naranja" [My better half].

What was the structure, the idea, behind that program?

The idea was to present every week a focused theme, but with a bit of humor. Half of the programs had to do with machismo. We used different approaches such as candid camera and theater. After a while the program improved radically thanks to Margara Ureta's participation. I didn't know her and one day she gave me a call. She told me that I had to give her a chance to be part of the team. She said that she had great ideas. She was right. She was able to change the tone and make it much more daring. She was an actress who could do the craziest things on the street and not care.

What, for example?

Well, for example, one day she drove the wrong way on Pío Nono street at midday. There was a huge traffic jam and all the while I was hidden in a truck with a camera filming what was happening. Of course a policeman came. We were waiting for him. We wanted to prove that they won't give you a ticket if you are a woman and you work on the policeman. When the policeman came, Margara started to plead, "Oh please my sweet police officer. You can't give me a ticket, you just can't." People had already gathered all around, and as always, they were against the police officer and on Margara's side. The program ended with the police officer trying to make his way out of the crowd looking for another officer to help him. Meanwhile, on the ground, Margara was holding on to his foot, and the man had to walk with her dragging behind amidst all the insults from the people.

Did you always try to show something, prove some thesis?

Our goals always had a critical perspective, and I think that was the reason for part of the success of the program. On another occasion, for example, we tried to prove that men are so foolish, that they don't notice the significant feminine attributes. Instead they notice the artificial ones. Margara put on a pair of old blue jeans and a simple blouse and took walks down the street. Of course, no one looked at her. Then I showed the "exterior details" that she would later put on: stockings with a line down the back, false eyelashes, wigs, a mini skirt, etc., and then we repeated the same stroll down the street with the same attitude. Of course a big commotion arose and we filmed the men who said things and followed her.

You also did some short films. What were they like?

It was called *Magazine Ellas*. A man had the idea that you could film short news clips to be shown with previews at the movies, and that we could run the clips at least ten months in the theaters. The idea was to exhibit them first in Santiago and then in the provinces. Since they could run for so long, they brought in good profits. I came up with the ideas and directed them. I'll give you an example so that you can see the stupid things that one can do when ignorance gets in the way. A birth control device which had to be injected into the woman's arm, and which was called Pelet, came to Chile. I, of course, was in favor of it, and asked the camera man to film, very close up, the actual injection of the device into the arm. The camera man said it would be counter-productive, but I insisted until he filmed it. When it came out in Technicolor, on a huge screen, Pelet had all the likenesses to a horrible missile. Well, no one dared to use it and the sale of the birth control device failed for years. So in the end, the news clip served precisely the opposite function of what we had planned.

> *This job on television and your columns in the magazine* Paula *made you into a public figure for a few years. Was that spontaneous or was there some form of marketing that gave you your status?*

I had what I was talking to you about before, an uncontrollable rebelliousness. All those years seem so strange to me now, because my life was so bourgeois: loyal wife and housewife, mother of two children, the one who complied to all the rules. But simultaneously I dressed like a hippie. I had a car painted with flowers and angels, and I went everywhere with my dog. I had all the appearances of rebellion, but in truth I haven't met anyone who was more bourgeois. At *Paula* I seemed like the craziest of them all, but I was the only one who did not divorce and who led a life which was much more standard than that of my colleagues. I was married to the most formal man in the world, angelic and absolutely understated. But in spite of all this conservative family, on television I did a series of wild things. It wasn't marketing, because I didn't know that existed. I suppose it was a desire to scandalize. It was a form of channeling that rage, that rebelliousness that I felt.

In 1971 your play The Ambassador *opened. What was the origin of that experience?*

Not long before my uncle Ramón was named Ambassador in Argentina, they had kidnapped a diplomat in Uruguay. I began to think about my uncle being kidnapped, and at dinner one night we began to imagine what would happen in a situation like that. I was very shaken and that night I dreamed that they had kidnapped him. I woke up very distressed, I got up and wrote a draft of a situation where the kidnappers and the hostage live together for a year in a basement and eventually learn to understand and love each other. I liked the idea and I locked myself up for two days at home, without going to the office, in order to write the play. It was very strange. In that period of time I lost three kilos, as though I had been slowly dehydrating. It was a type of organic process that happened again later with literature. Things are felt in the gut, not in the head, a bit like giving birth. Your entire body passes through a creative process that, in my case, resembles pregnancy and birth.

How did you stage the play?

When I finished it, I showed it to the actress Malú Gatica, who is also my aunt. She then showed it to the Compañía de los Cuatro, who then staged it. The merit is not mine at all. I gave them a first draft. When I listened to them going through the first reading, I was very ashamed. They taught me to be consistent with each character, to respect a certain harmony. What I learned about constructing characters has served me well throughout my career. I always ask myself who the protagonists are; what their past was like; what they eat; how they smell. . . . I became obsessed with the theater; it was my passion and all I wanted was to be there every night. Sometimes I had to take my children, but I never missed one rehearsal.

Your passion lasted a long time because after that your play La balada del medio pelo *[The parvenu's ballad] opened.*

A group of actors sought me out to write something based on what I did in journalism for them. We produced a play with music by Vittorio Cintolesi. It was a spoof on the Chilean middle class, on all

the biases that the petit bourgeois in Chile hold. It was very successful, but not on account of my text—which was really a pre-text—but
on account of Tomás Vidiella's direction, the work of the actors, the
music which was marvelous, and the fullness of color that they gave
the production. Since things went well, we then staged "The House
of the Seven Mirrors," also with Tomás Vidiella. For the title we took
the name of a brothel in Valparaíso, we came up with different
sketches that focused on different moments of life in that place, even
though they had nothing to do with the original Seven Mirrors. It
was a parody of *costumbrista* aspects of Chilean society. One thing
that was very popular was the "ballet de gordas," a dance performed
by overweight ladies, directed by Malucha Solari. I wrote and we re-
hearsed that play before the military coup, but it was staged after.
And what I find interesting is that many people interpreted some of
the scenes as a critique of the new political situation. But it would
have been impossible to inject this meaning, since when we re-
hearsed we never imagined that there could be a military coup.

*You have said that something similar happened in September 1973
with the magazine* Mampato. *Can you tell us about that?*

The color pages in the magazine had to be prepared four months earlier. The issue that came out the week of the coup had been practically ready since July. In it there was an article on gorillas, and on the
cover there were three adult gorillas and one baby. Of course everyone said that represented the three branches of the armed forces and
General Mendoza (of the carabineros). It was a nightmare for the directors, but we couldn't do anything because the issues were already
circulating.

*What is your vision of your personal and professional life at that
point?*

During all the time that we've just been discussing, I lived in absolute
bliss. I was a perpetual adolescent. You can tell by the fact that I was
always in costume and in a car painted with different colors, without
measuring consequences and without knowing what I would do
next. My feminist attitudes did not offer any alternative. They did not

propose anything in exchange. It was a confusing and happy time because I felt strong and that nothing could happen to me. The fact that people recognized me on the street—for having been on TV—gave me the sensation that I could knock on any door and enter, like one who walks very firmly on his own ground. After the coup I helped to house people. And I didn't do it for political reasons, but because someone asked me and I thought it was the right thing to do. I didn't think about what could happen to me. I was a very arrogant person.

Arrogant? In what sense?

Well, in the sense that I thought nothing could happen to me. It wasn't that I thought I was the center of the universe, I was. I felt that I was acting out of good faith, and that protected me from any criticism, mistake, or any malicious deed against me. I felt untouchable and invulnerable. After going through very painful experiences I realized that reality doesn't function that way.

And then you went to Venezuela.

We left Chile in 1975 because things were very difficult by then. I couldn't stand the dictatorship. I lived in constant fear and horror. We went to Venezuela, one of the few countries that kept open borders and where it was not difficult to obtain a visa. There were already a few Chileans in Venezuela who had fled the law in Chile for fraud. They went to Venezuela because there was no extradition treaty between the two countries. Many of them had become very rich and were doing very well. Then those that fled Allende in 1970 arrived, and after that the political exiles following the coup. Finally those in exile due to the economic situation in Chile appeared in 1980. Since there were so many Chileans in Caracas, it was easy to run into them daily, and the typical question was "How long have you been here?" From the answer you decided whether you would talk to them or not—if they belonged to "your" group of exiles.

What was your experience in Venezuela like?

Venezuela was very welcoming to all of us, but I had not closed the previous stage. I couldn't adapt. The past was lost as we left Chile. I have never again had the feeling of belonging to a place, of understanding the codes in the language and the culture. I lost it and I will never recover it because my life took an unpredictable direction. The event that marked the definitive passing from one epoch to another was the publication of *The House of the Spirits*. It was the ultimate closing: in that novel my life, my past, are bottled and sealed.

Did you want to return to Chile or were you planning to stay in Venezuela for good?

When I left for Venezuela, I was planning to return to Chile soon. I never unpacked my emotional bags. I only looked south, reading Chilean newspapers, hanging on every word I read. I had only Chilean friends. It was very difficult to adapt. At the beginning things did not go very well because my husband had to work far from the city. In 1978, when total anguish had overwhelmed me, I decided to unpack my bags, understand that I wasn't returning to Chile, and try to fit outside my country. It was my step from adolescence to adulthood.

Why do you specifically refer to 1978?

Because that's when my marriage fell apart and everything went to hell. I went to Spain in order to find work and I couldn't even get permission to stay. I returned to Caracas humiliated. There I got together with my husband again to try to rebuild this family. Our separation was final in 1988.

But during many years you worked at the newspaper El Nacional.

In Caracas I couldn't work as a journalist. I only collaborated on the Sunday magazine to *El Nacional* while the journalist Julio Lanzarotti was there. Julio Jung, the actor, took me there. I met him on the street and he was as lost as I was. After we asked each other when we had arrived in Venezuela, he took me to speak with Lanzarotti. What I earned wasn't even enough to pay for postage. When I returned from Spain, a friend offered me a job as administrator in a school which ran all day. They offered primary school in the morning and secondary in the afternoon. I worked the two shifts from seven in the morning to seven in the evening. It was the only way to earn more for the family. During my separation I learned the most important lesson in my life: feminism and freedom cannot exist if one cannot support oneself. Any freedom begins with economic freedom. If there is economic dependence, there is no freedom. I had worked and earned some money, but due to a lack of foresight and ingenuity, I didn't have that money or that freedom. I couldn't even support my children.

What was your job like in that school in Caracas?

I can't add, or much less, subtract, but I did the accounting. Don't ask me how the school survived. . . . I was an administrator there for four and a half years. If it hadn't been for that job I think I would have broken emotionally, and I didn't have money for an analyst. After a while I became a member of the school. I began to have a little capital and earn my money. The next ten years that I spent with my husband were not bad ones. He did all he could so we would once again have a home and our family would thrive. He is a very good man, loyal, a good husband and a good father. He never gave me a reason not to love him. I should have loved him and given more than I gave. I don't know what happened. Life is full of mysteries.

You began writing The House of the Spirits *when you were at that school.*

When I was at that school I had to dress like a lady and act like one. But I've always needed a valve to allow the crazy part of me to escape. At that time there was no escape. In 1981, with the excuse of my grandfather's illness and a letter that I would send him, I began writing at night, after work. It was the escape that I was searching for. Everything that I had inside and that had accumulated for years began to spring forth. And that was how *The House of the Spirits* was born. I didn't know that I was writing. What got me through it all was the desire to rescue the memory of my family, my lost world.

Compulsive writing, as though someone were dictating.

That has happened twice, with this novel and with the one I have just finished. It is as though the author does not need to invent anything because all that has been lived; someone lived it. Those characters lived some time and your job as a writer is to take all the loose pieces and glue them together, like those quilts, to give them a shape or form a design. If you can see the design in the confusion of all the pieces, you've got it. The rest is work. That's what happened to me with *The House of the Spirits*. When I sat down and wrote the first sentence, "Barrabás came to us by sea," I didn't know who Barrabás was or why he had arrived on a ship.

Why did you write that sentence?

I don't know. It seemed poetic, it sounded right, and I wrote it down. After that, a ball of yarn, which was entirely already there, began to unroll. All I had to do was to pull the yarn. That's how *The House of the Spirits* was finished in one year. If you had asked me what the book was about when I finished it, I couldn't have told you. It was a type of confused fresco with no connections.

That was in the first version, because after readings and corrections you did know what it was about.

No, no. I only knew what it was about once I read the first reviews. When they said it was a family saga with a patriarchal core, narrated through women . . . oh well, all the explanations that I can give you today are copies of the reviews and the literary studies that have been done on the book. At that time I had no idea of what I was doing.

But you were consciously writing a novel.

I don't know. . . . I was working on something that I didn't dare call a book, much less a novel. I didn't know if it was chronicles, letters, memoirs, or some other thing. At home I never said I was writing a book because I was embarrassed. I worked on the dining-room table, which we did not use for a year. I had all my notes there, separated in groups and held down by stones. Little by little the table became tremendously chaotic. I wrote on a portable typewriter and erased with white-out. Some pages stood all by themselves because they had so much white-out. Nobody knew what I was doing and I never talked about it. It didn't have a title or theme; I did not discuss it with anybody. After a year when I had five hundred pages on the table tied with a ribbon, I read them. I thought they had the form of a book, but I didn't know if it was a good novel. I gave them to my mother and we began to talk. I asked her to help me correct it and she said, "This is the first draft of a book."

Was she very excited?

No, she didn't like it at all. The first thing that she thought was horrible was that the Count de Satigny—whom I based on my father—in the original version was called Conde Bilbaire. It seems that was a family name on my father's side. I didn't remember or I didn't know it. It was necessary to change it for another that took more or less the same number of letters to fit in the space. Otherwise I would have to retype everything. Also, when I finished the novel and reread it, I realized that there were characters that had not aged; characters who at the beginning and end were the same age. Another difficulty, even though there are no dates in the book, was to be true to historical data. For example if I mentioned an earthquake, and right after that I mentioned an event that happened ten years after, I wasn't being historically precise. If I mentioned a car, I had to make sure it was a model made at the time. I had no idea how to do that type of work, and the only way I knew how to work was much the same way I did when I was a secretary. I filed information in file folders. I had a folder for all major characters so as to be consistent with their characters. I didn't want them appearing in one chapter saying things that would contradict what they would say three chapters later. My experience as a journalist was very useful to me.

What aspects of journalism?

I am a person who is full of prejudice. I appear tolerant, but I am very intolerant of everything that has to do with the military, for example, of everything that carries a uniform. Even the Salvation Army irritates me. I also have strong religious prejudice because I was educated in a Catholic, conservative system that is very hard for me to accept. I become very ironic at times because of this background.

And every time I touch the topic of feminism, all my prejudices towards men come out. Journalism taught me to attempt a certain objectivity when conducting interviews: how to look for information, listen, be alert as to prejudice. I used all this in the novel.

Whom did you interview?

All the part set in the country that appears in *The House of the Spirits* comes from interviews with campesinos, people who lived there. For the military parts, I did the same thing, I interviewed military men who had left Chile. I also had recordings of people who had been to jail and had been tortured. I used these in the second part of the book. I spoke with family members who remembered life in my grandfather's time. All in all, an extensive journalistic job.

What happened after you revised the first version? Did it change a lot?

I changed the last name that bothered my mother, I fixed the dates, I edited a lot because the original was quite a bit longer. I cut out unnecessary things because I always tend to digress, and I worked on the language. I wrote the epilogue many, many times because I felt it was kitschy. At last, when the last version was ready, there was still something that felt wrong. As you may know, the model for the principal character, Esteban Trueba, is my grandfather. My grandfather was very much like the protagonist in the book, even though obviously, he was not as bad or as exaggerated. But they both had that patriarchal, proud, honorable, Basque-Castilian personality. My grandfather would never have mentioned certain things; for example, if he ever had a relationship of any type with a prostitute, he never would have told anyone. There were aspects of his life that were substantial secrets. It becomes clear at the end of the book that Trueba's granddaughter Alba narrates the story. I thought it was strange that she knew certain things about her grandfather that were impossible to know. So how could I justify her knowledge? So I thought that in a confession to himself he would mention things he would never mention to anyone else. That's why certain parts of the book are narrated in the first person: his relationship with the prostitute, the scene when he cuts off the boy's fingers. So all those critical moments that he would not have confided to anyone were technically resolved with a monologue.

Do you rewrite much?

Very much, to the point of exhaustion. I read out loud because it is the only way of knowing if I am repeating words, if the sentences are too long, and where the stress in the sentence falls, in order to invert the clauses if necessary. . . . I do this reading at the end of every chapter when I feel it is ready.

Could we say that in your first novel you wrote more from literary intuition than from a knowledge of technical aspects?

Absolutely. Just to give you an example of how ignorant I was about those things, when they took me to the presentation of *The House of the Spirits* in Spain, a critic from an important newspaper from Madrid asked me the following question: "Could you explain the cyclical structure in your novel?" or something of the sort. I stared at him wide-eyed: I didn't know what "structure" was, and I had only heard the word "cyclical" having to do with menstruation. I think the poor man realized that he was before a literary virgin—if that exists—because I could not answer any of his questions. Imagine the surprise when I received literary analysis from all the graduate students, mentioning things that I never even knew I put in the book: metaphors, symbols, use of colors, meanings of the names. It was both a revelation and a dreadful experience. Luckily I had already started my second novel when this happened because it could have paralyzed my writing forever.

When you had the final version of The House of the Spirits, *did you try many publishers before it was accepted?*

I tried many publishing houses in Venezuela, where they all rejected me. There they told me that I had to find a literary agent, that without an agent it was impossible to publish a novel, particularly such a lengthy one as mine. It just happened that Tomás Eloy Martínez was in Caracas, and he mentioned Carmen Balcells, whom I did not know. I Xeroxed the manuscript and sent it by mail in two separate envelopes. At the post office they would not allow me to send it all in one package. Of course, the second part arrived first. . . . Carmen gave it to some of her readers who wrote notes on the literary quality, commercial value, and certain orientation as to who would be interested in publishing it. It seems that *The House of the Spirits* received very good reviews because Carmen Balcells read it, called me, and told me that she would accept being my agent. I signed the contract and in six months the book was published and soon it was beginning to be translated in Europe.

> *The start of a career.*

I am not so sure. In a way it was the culmination of one project. The entire process was a curious one. When the book was rejected so many times in so many places, I became deeply saddened. It was one more failure to add to a string of failures during the past few years. Every time I left it in a publishing house I prayed that they would just read it, but there was no response. When it was published in Spain, I had the sensation that I had done something in my life and I could now die in peace. Of course, after it was published, after it was so successful, and after beginning with the translations, one becomes ambitious and wants more and more. If you have only good reviews but are not on the best-seller list, you become angry. It is curious to observe how a person changes: ambition is like a bottomless pit. But, of course, the emotions that accompany the publication of a first book are simply impossible to relive. It never happens that way again.

> *Your novels, especially the first, have been compared to certain important texts of the '60s and '70s; especially with the work of García Márquez. How strongly do you agree with that connection?*

I knew almost all the authors of the Latin American Boom, but my discovery of them was late, not until the mid-seventies. When I wrote *The House of the Spirits* I was reading García Márquez, Vargas Llosa, Jorge Amado, Carlos Fuentes. . . . I think that their influence is clear only in my first novel, but not in the rest. At first I felt very proud when people noted García Márquez's influence on my work, but now it is beginning to make me mad. I now have five books and harping on that same issue is to deny me any originality, capacity as a writer, and my own voice. I say all this while I hold great admiration for García Márquez, who is a fantastic narrator and a superb storyteller.

> *But there is an obvious connection between your novel and* One Hundred Years of Solitude. . . .

It's clear that there are elements in common between *The House of the Spirits* and *One Hundred Years of Solitude*: they are both autobiographical. The authors felt the need to tell that which we both heard in our youth, sitting in the kitchen. We were both raised in our grandparents' houses and we reconstructed that through family sagas. Anyway, I had read *One Hundred Years of Solitude* when it was published, many years before my novel was published, and I did not remember certain precise details like the fact that one of the characters is named Remedios the Beautiful. At my house we had Aunt Rosa, who was also "the Beautiful," who had died by poisoning and whose picture was on top of the piano. When I wrote *The House of the Spirits* I had completely forgotten García Márquez's character; all that remained was the memory of my aunt. The same thing happened with an uncle of mine who flew in a helium balloon that he himself invented, forgetting that in *One Hundred Years of Solitude* there are characters who also fly. Anyway, the other day something funny happened to me. I read a paper that a graduate student from an American university sent me, where she says that I discovered "magical feminism."

> *After that comes your second novel, a more polemical book:* Of Love and Shadows.

Yes, after that I wrote *Of Love and Shadows*, a book which has nothing to do with García Márquez. It is much more of a journalistic report, much more realistic and testimonial. *The House of the Spirits* was published in 1982, and I had started to write it January 8, 1981. Even while I visited different editorial houses, I was already writing the second book, which I also started on January 8, 1982. I had been gathering a lot of material for *Of Love and Shadows* since 1978.

How was the idea for that novel born?

When the news about the discovery of the Lonquén ovens (where many of the disappeared were found) was published I gathered up all the material that I could. I was extremely affected by the story of the Maureira family, five men (of the same family) who disappeared. I thought it was an extraordinary case and I began to gather everything that was published in Venezuela. Afterwards, some Chilean friends sent me articles that were published in Chile on the case, as well as Máximo Pacheco's book, which was very enlightening. When I decided to write a second book, I was automatically drawn to that story. It was as though the dead were calling me, as though they were impatient ghosts who wanted their story told. I didn't even have to think about what the story line would be. It was right there. There was a need to exorcise those demons through writing. At the beginning it was essentially a horror story; the title was "Of Love and Death." But things slowly balanced themselves out, thanks to the interviews I did.

How did these interviews modify your perception of the case?

I spoke with a lot of people, even with some who had relatives who had disappeared, and others who had been in concentration camps. As I talked with them, the rancor and hate that I had felt before I started writing began to disappear. I saw that the people who had been affected the most and lost the most were the ones who felt the least need for vengeance. They wanted to know the truth and wanted justice to be established, but they did not want to torture the torturer or murder the assassin. I learned a tremendous lesson on love, if one can use that word without it sounding kitschy. . . . Anyway, after those interviews, the title and the book changed.

At that time were you already thinking of quitting your job at the school to write full time?

When the echoes of the first book reached me (the checks, the contracts for translations) I saw that I could live off my writing and I thought of leaving my job. But I didn't dare because if the next one didn't go well, I would be left hanging. Carmen Balcells had told me that anyone could write a first novel, but that didn't mean the person was a writer. When I sent her *Of Love and Shadows*, she then told me I was a good writer. That was when I seriously considered the possibility of living from my writing. But I desperately needed my salary because my husband's office had gone bankrupt; he didn't have a job and was deeply depressed. I decided to wait. That is why it took me a while to immerse myself completely into the world of literature where you can receive one check every month, one every year, or simply no checks at all.

> *How would you characterize the differences between the first and the second novel?*

There are many differences. Foremost is the fact that *Of Love and Shadows* takes place within a few weeks, in a single place and has few characters. If I visualize it, I imagine a bicycle wheel that has a center, the deaths at Lonquén, and everything else is the spokes that converge in that center. The story is narrated like those spokes which jettison out yet converge in that one and only moment of contrast: the love of the protagonists and the discovery of the corpses. Therefore, the narrative technique is totally different from that of the first novel. The tone is not oneiric, like the first part of *The House of the Spirits*, but much more realistic. It is more realistic in the sense that everything in *Of Love and Shadows* is verifiable, as time has shown since then.

> *It wasn't as successful as the first novel.*

No, not the same commercial success. The reviews were also not unanimous, like those for my first novel. Some critics said it was better put together than *The House of the Spirits*, and others said it lacked the charm the other novel had. Some said it was too political, and others that it was not political enough—that the story had lost its tragic sense once it had been turned into a novel. What also happened was that with such an ambitious first novel, the people and the critics were benevolent and generous. With the second one, though, all the eyes are upon you to see if they can screw you, because of your former success. It is very difficult to be successful with a second book. For me, *Of Love and Shadows* was very important, a good school. If I had to do it all over again, I probably would not do it the same way. It is, though, what some of my readers have liked best of what I have written, including my present husband, who wanted to meet me after reading it and we ended up marrying. I am convinced that he married the book, not me. . . .

Contrary to your first novel, where the characters are more complex, Of Love and Shadows *is a story where there is a categorical division between good guys and bad guys. Why is that so? Did reality impose it?*

I don't know. At times reality imposes it; at others it is the burden one carries within. One cannot be absolutely objective and, besides, I am not trying to be. I am a very passionate person and, for me, objectivity is a relative virtue. At times, the story imposes the tone. In *The House of the Spirits*, the first part is like a mist, like an old sepia photograph where things are disfigured by time, by the haze of oblivion. As the end approaches, the focus becomes slowly adjusted, becoming more and more realistic, until we reach the scene in the prison. There, Alba is raped, mutilated, and tortured, and in that story the magical realism of before does not have a place. Even if I had wanted to write it in another tone, I couldn't have done it: the need to tell it is so strong that the style goes to hell. I must admit that after the success that *The House of the Spirits* experienced, the temptation of taking that road again, of changing what I had already written in *Of Love and Shadows*, was strong, but the story did not allow it.

One of the points that caused controversy was the political nature of the novel. . . .

Well, the problem is that it is absolutely and unconditionally a political novel. And this is a mortal sin in the United States. The worst thing that you can tell an author is that one of his books is political. People here aren't even interested in voting.

Then Eva Luna *came out. This is a novel which does not correspond to your Chilean background, but rather to your Central American experience.*

I never would have been able to write that book without having lived thirteen years in Venezuela. The character of Eva Luna can only be Caribbean. The tone is different: confident, green, exuberant, exaggerated. It is the focus on life that Venezuela gave me and that I waited long in accepting and incorporating into my life. Each one of my books corresponds to a very strong emotion that has been with me for a long time. The first is longing, the desire to one day record a lost world; the second is anger about the abuse in these years of dictatorships that we are living in Latin America.

And Eva Luna?

Eva Luna, though it belongs to a very difficult time in my life, because my marriage had definitely broken up and I knew that I had to leave Venezuela, was triggered by a very positive emotion: accepting myself, finally, as a person and a writer. It was the first book I wrote thinking of myself as a professional writer. I knew I was writing "a novel" as I wrote this book, which was something I hadn't done before, possibly just out of modesty. I also felt proud of being a woman, because up to then I ranted and raved against injustices done to women without accepting that I could not change my condition as a woman. But I realized that I would remain a woman, and that as a woman I had been able to achieve many things, possibly more than what many men achieve. In *Eva Luna* I embraced my own femininity and the feminist struggle. I began that book in 1985 and then I left the school and dedicated myself only to writing.

In this book we see a different aspect of your writing: narrative technique.

From that point of view it is a book with different levels, like a chest full of surprises for the reader. The idea was to make one of those Chinese boxes that have another box inside, and then another. You believe that you are reading something that you take as the story of Eva Luna, but then you find out that she is inventing her own biography, and at the end you don't know if what you are reading is that biography or the soap opera that she is writing. What's more, the ambiguous denouement attempts to leave the reader with the feeling that he does not know what he read. It is the magic of the story, the fiction, that takes you on a magic carpet ride to a place where you don't control anything. You play along in the game and simply say "Here I am, take me." I first became aware of that surrender when I read *The Thousand and One Nights* in Lebanon, at thirteen, while I hid in my stepfather's closet. It was four volumes of very thin paper (the type many Bibles are printed on), bound in red with golden letters on the covers. I remember that I couldn't mark where I was because he would have known that I was reading them, and since I never remembered where I was, I just opened the book searching for the parts with sexual descriptions, which was the only thing that interested me, and which are really not numerous in the book. While I searched for those parts, I was caught by the story and then immediately trapped by the genies and fairies. When I heard uncle Ramón approach, I had to close the book. The story would then live within me until I had the opportunity of visiting the closet again. When I returned I would turn to any page, and then that story would come together with the previous one. The entire story was being made as I read. That was what I envisioned in *Eva Luna*, that each story would, in a sense, bite the tail of the previous one. And I think it worked out well, because it is a book that is studied for its narrative technique.

So you used your experience as a reader to write.

Well, I had read a lot, but in a very disorderly fashion and without any type of critical approach. I read for the story. Very little writing will capture me for the form if the story doesn't say something to me. There are writers who write marvelously well. They are great masters at the pen, but their stories are a bore and I'd rather have nothing to do with them. When I read I want passion, plot, strong characters who have things happen to them. Minimalist literature bores me. As a reader I let myself be maneuvered. I wait for the writer to trick me, to convince me, to fill me with passion, to make me cry and laugh. And when I close the book I want to be sad that it is over. As a reader I am not searching for the form or the style. But I also dislike it when the message is too obvious. That's why I said that if I were to write *Of Love and Shadows* again, I would do it differently. It is not subtle enough and I feel it is too direct.

So for your own reading, you have opted for a certain type of literature.

Of course, there are so many good writers who can do whatever they want with the written word, but they tell you stories that are boring. It's like drinking water without any taste, and it's because they were exploring form. Literature per se does not interest me in the least bit. What I want is to take bits of life; the life of the characters. I admire writers who explore language and narrative form, as I admire dancers who do tap. I can't believe what they do, but I can't do it myself. It isn't my trade and I don't pretend that it is. I don't want to go down in history for having worked with form.

What is your goal as a writer? Do you have a specific objective?

My objective is to know my reader. I want my reader to read the first six lines and not be able to put down the book. I think that is the objective in literature, that they read you with passion, believing every word. Now, to be able to tell a story and move your reader and provoke the emotions that you want to incite, you have to know how to do it; you need to know the tools of the trade. You need to use your instrument, language, the best you can. I don't spurn form; on the contrary, I give it much thought, but I will only work with it to enhance the story I am telling. If I need to invent a new language to tell a certain story, well, I will do it. If one of my books ever comes out with a six-page monologue without periods or commas, it won't mean that I am exploring a new literary form, but that there is no other way of telling that story. That's the case with Esteban Trueba's monologue in *The House of the Spirits* when he kneels before the prostitute and asks her to save his granddaughter. In these pages the punctuation is mostly lacking because Esteban speaks with confusion, he is fearful for his granddaughter's life, his pride has been hurt, and he cannot stop talking. All he says gushes out without restraint. That is the reason that the monologue takes that form.

Are you recovering or continuing with the old tradition of telling stories, hearing stories?

The desire to hear stories is insatiable. One day I was talking to a Vietnam veteran who lived in a village with civilians, and he told me that the most important person in the village was the storyteller. The gift of telling stories was held in higher esteem than beauty, courage, power, or money. The villagers would gather around this person who told stories they all knew, because the stories were all legends from the village. But in spite of the fact that they knew the stories, the people were endlessly mesmerized by the magic and the charm of the words. You can tell a child the story of Cinderella a thousand times, and he will always be mesmerized. It's possible that at that level it enters the mythical level, the collective unconscious, of those things that come to us from so long ago.

>*Did you always like to tell stories, even before you started doing it professionally?*

When my children were small, I invented stories for them every night. But they were so naughty that they would conspire to make it as difficult for me as they could. After putting them to bed, when I asked them what type of story they wanted, one would say a story about ants, and the other a story about Martians. It wouldn't take me over thirty seconds to begin unraveling a story in my head. They would make it more and more difficult every time, but I was so well trained that I could ford the difficulty. Some day I hope to do the same with my grandchildren.

>*You have said that* Eva Luna *marks a sort of merging, or consolidating point in your career. Was this consolidation or merging the reason that it took you longer to write than your other books?*

That book took me over two years, which is a lot in comparison with the other books. What happened was that my life had already begun to change. I began to receive invitations to speak, participate in universities in the United States, and do promotional tours. I was no longer a little mouse in the cellar of my house. I began a type of public life which I had never known before. That robs you of much time and energy.

>*What is the reason for writing a book of short stories next?* The Stories of Eva Luna *is your first book of short stories, correct?*

198   JUAN ANDRÉS PIÑA

Short stories were the only thing I could write at the moment. It was the end of 1987: I was living in the U.S. and doing promotional tours for my other books. I didn't have time for anything else and I knew that I had to continue writing. I think that every writer of fiction should confront these three challenges: write short stories, an erotic novel, and children's literature. They are very difficult, and if one succeeds in crossing those three bridges, he or she is a professional writer. Since I am not prepared for an erotic novel—my Catholic background and my mother who is still alive are important problems—and I was far from the children, I decided to write short stories. Another reason was that my time was fragmented. I had two weeks here, a few days there, and those moments determined that my next book would be of short stories.

> *How would you define the short story in comparison with the novel as narrative genre?*

The short story is a genre that needs inspiration. The novel does not, because when you have a theme, what you need to do is work on it. The short story, on the other hand, comes already whole, like an apple, and if in the first sentence you don't already have the tone or you don't know how it will end, you've lost it. The short story requires precision, the right amount of tension. It is very difficult for me to write short stories because I have a tendency to take delight in description, to give details, to create ambiance, and that you can only do in the novel. The novel is a labor of patience that sometimes takes years. The short story is an arrow which has only one chance at the bull's eye.

> *In many of the stories in* Stories of Eva Luna *you recover much of the oral tradition of Venezuela.*

That is true. Eva Luna tells them in the same tone that the novel has. I recapture places, climates, smells of the Caribbean. It is the same environment. Many of the stories are based on cases that I cut out of the newspaper, for example the one about the little girl buried in mud ["And of Clay Are We Created"]. I based it on the case of Omaira Sánchez, who died, with all the TV cameras fixed on her, when Nevado Ruiz erupted in Colombia. There is also the true story which happened in Venezuela of the woman who was buried in a cellar for fifty years ["If You Touched My Heart"]. "Phantom Palace" is based on the dictator Juan Vicente Gómez. They are not stories full of what we call the marvelous, except for the first one, "Two Words," which is a sort of code to enter the book, where the power of the word is so important. It is tacitly telling the reader that if he gives himself to the reading, the weight of the word will lead him to another dimension and another reality. The writer contributes half the book; the other half is created by each reader with his own biography.

> *How has your life in the United States changed your relationship with the language?*

My situation is a bit different from what other writers, like Fernando Alegría, have done. I am not working with the language and teaching it at the university level and I do feel the loss. I suppose that for those writers who do work with the language in classes it must be easier to maintain. I am quite isolated. My American husband and I communicate in a type of Spanglish or Chicano, peppered with Venezuelan expressions that I have added to my vocabulary. My Spanish is less fluent. I used to be quicker with the word. And since my English is not very fluent either, I find myself in a very dangerous limbo. I must spend more time in Chile and Spain, where my daughter lives, and speak Spanish more often. I also have to read more in my own language. These past few years I have wanted to catch up on North American literature, and I read in English all the time.

> *What happened with the language in your last novel—as yet unpublished?*

Now that I have finished the novel, and it is time to work on the last bits, I need to feel the language well spoken, with its nuances, its texture, its beautiful words, its rhythms and its accent. So what I do is to lock myself up for about three or four days to read Pablo Neruda out loud. That helps me a lot for his wonderful use of the language. I dive completely into Spanish.

Beside the sales in Spanish-speaking countries, your books also sell well in Germany, Holland, Sweden, and the United States. Why do you think this is so?

I don't know. The only possible explanation is that the translations make the books better.

Maybe it is due to a return to a more traditional way of writing where the story matters and the experimental aspects are left behind. . . .

That could be, especially in the United States. Here there was over a decade of minimalist literature and now there is a return to the short story. People always come back to the story.

Could you briefly tell us what has been said about your novels abroad? How have they characterized them?

A lot has been said, and I remember very little of it. I prefer to tell you how I see them. I see them as stories which are sentimental and horrible, charged with love and violence, just the way I perceive life. They are a mix of feminism, politics, and melodrama. Without any pretense I can say that they are entertaining and are well written. I like them quite a lot, to tell you the truth. . . .

"We Are a Generation Marked by Exile"

INTERVIEW BY FERNANDO ALEGRÍA
Translated for this book by Virginia Invernizzi

14

First published in Spanish in *Nuevo Texto Crítico* 4, no. 8 (1991): 73–90

In my recent trip to Chile I had the sensation that Isabel Allende was present everywhere: her books are in all the book stores, people read them and talk about them . . . And the Conference on Women Writers that took place in Santiago, her name was mentioned many times, her books were discussed, and I realized that one thing that the dictatorship had unwittingly achieved was that it had united the writers (all the writers, not only those in exile) and the reading public. Today people read and discuss books, their meanings, their themes. And I also realized that a new narrative voice exists in the short story and the novel, and that is the voice of women. These are young women writers whose names I did not know. I brought back some of their novels and I am presently reading them. And so, the first question I have for Isabel is whether she sees her work as part of this new Chilean writing tradition. There is no doubt that there has been a drastic change in the type of literature that is coming out in Chile, and in whether that literature is published or not, and in whether knowledge of its existence reaches the public or not. . . . And all of a sudden a new writer like Isabel appears and that new voice does reach an international market. I would like to ask Isabel to comment on this phenomenon, this new tradition (which may not be a new tradition as yet).

" I find it very difficult to see myself as a Chilean writer. I left Chile twelve, almost thirteen years ago, and the reason I do not live here is no longer political. I feel more and more Latin American. I talk a lot about being Latin American. This, I feel, is a new phenomenon in the continent. During the seventies the military dictatorships closed the borders with culture, thought, and ideas. These governments became progressively repressive, forcing masses of people to emigrate, to leave their own country and live in other countries in the continent. And what came of all that is a phenomenon that we have all lived through, and that is interexchange of cultures in Latin America. As an unplanned reaction to the political strategy of the nationalist dictatorships a true communion of peoples took place for the first time in our history. More and more you hear people saying "I am Latin American," because they have had the opportunity to live in other countries in Latin America. Some have even walked the continent from Mexico to the far south. They have gone and returned many times. This has marked our generation. That is why it is difficult for me to think of myself as a Chilean writer. I feel I am only one of the many voices in Latin America today. I don't think I am only speaking for Chile. When I write about the disappeared in *Of Love and Shadows* I am not only speaking about those that served as the models for my story. I am writing about those that disappear in El Salvador today, those that disappeared in Argentina yesterday, those that continue to disappear in Chile or Guatemala. It is a problem that transcends borders. When I talk about repression, dictatorship, women, love, about those emotions that are so much ours, I don't feel that they are Chilean, nor of a new Chilean voice. I feel the voice belongs to everyone.

A Sniper between Cultures

INTERVIEW BY JACQUELINE CRUZ, JACQUELINE MITCHELL,
SILVIA PELLAROLO, AND JAVIER RANGEL
Translated for this book by Virginia Invernizzi

First published in Spanish in *Mester* 20, no. 2 (1991): 127–143

15

*What do you believe is the key to your success in Latin America and
the United States?*

I would love to know what the key is in order to be able to repeat it,
and I would even venture to say that my editors would also love to
know. I have produced different books in ten years and no one knows
why they are so well liked. I think that I have an explanation for my
first book *The House of the Spirits*. I believe that it worked because
great writers had opened up the market for Latin American literature.
These writers had been publishing for twenty years. They invaded
the world with what is called the Boom of Latin American literature,
and their translated novels had already been accepted and liked. The
market had already been won over. Yet, there were very few female
representatives in that Boom, almost none. And, at that specific moment, ten years ago, there was a new interest in Latin America and
Europe in women writers. And then, my name must have helped.
Chile had been constantly in the news since 1973 and it continued to
be of journalistic importance for many years. There were many
movements in several European countries to help Chilean refugees,
and so the name Chile and the name Allende made history at the
time. When a novel published by someone with that name appeared,

someone who lived in exile, someone who had actual family ties to [Salvador] Allende, many of those factors combined together to make a sort of irresistible mix. I was also a woman and the time was right. The success of *The House of the Spirits* was so absolute and instantaneous that it paved the way for the other novels.

Now in the United States, I believe that my success is partly due to the great interest that there is here for women's literature. Another ingredient to my success is probably the fact that my books are easy to read in comparison to other Latin American novels in general which are quite baroque. Americans are not used to reading books in which the language plays tricks on the reader, books in which the reader has to work hard in order to decipher what in heaven's name the writer is talking about. People get tired of that. And we are very baroque in our writing, in our speech, in just about everything. My books are not as baroque as others, and that is why I have many young readers, for example, high school students. Also the fact that my books are read and studied in universities has helped. That is a captive audience.

> *Could the appeal also be due to the magical realism that so much attracts the Anglo-Saxon reader?*

That could be a factor even though magical realism is part of so many books. Magical realism is found not only in Latin American literature, but also in Scandinavian sagas, in Indian literature, in African literature. And many of those books don't have the same following. There are many books that incorporate magical realism in Latin America which are excellent and they just don't work in the United States, and no one knows the authors. They are only known in universities because they are part of the required reading.

> *You have commented that you believe that to even speak of women's literature is a type of "segregation." Could you comment on this? What do you mean by "segregation"?*

I believe that women have always been segregated and continue to be. Just the fact that when we speak of women's literature you have to add the qualifier "women's" denotes a type of segregation. Why is it that when we speak of literature written by men we don't say "male literature"? In turn, when we speak of women's literature you need the adjective because otherwise you don't know what you are referring to, as though it were a lesser genre. It was assumed for a long time that women's literature touched only certain themes, and women could not write about history, politics, philosophy, or economy. That is why I believe it is better if women attempt to form part of all literature, and not form a small world within the world of literature.

> *Do you not believe, though, that for the simple reason that women write from the margins, this in itself forms a type of literary "mode"?*

I believe that there is a different point of view: women have a different biography from men. They are different biologically, culturally. We have had a different reality; therefore we have a different approach to life, to feelings, to events, and to literature. That makes it all much more exciting. I truly feel that women are writing extraordinary books, especially in the United States, where women's literature carries a force superior to anything written by men. But I feel that part of fighting marginality is not contributing to it. It means taking on the system.

> *Wouldn't then the final epigraph in* The Stories of Eva Luna *be a contradiction to that? It says "And at this moment in her story, Scheherazade saw the first light of dawn, and discreetly fell silent." It is as though women, no matter how much they believe, produce, and elaborate an entire literary discourse, will always be relegated to the most silent and nocturnal zone.*

I did not think of the epigraph in that way at all. The book begins and ends with two quotes from *The Thousand and One Nights*. The main idea within *Eva Luna* and *The Stories of Eva Luna* is based on the woman narrator like Scheherazade who exchanges her stories for what she needs. Eva Luna exchanges them first for food and shelter, later for friendship, and finally for love, because she seduces a man with one of her stories. Scheherazade saves her life with her storytelling. She reinvents reality, she paints it in different colors and while she is at it, she saves her own life. That is what those two actions mean to me. But I never thought of my characters writing in darkness. I also think it is a beautiful image. I will no doubt use it in the future as well.

How do you conceive the role of the writer in Latin American societies?

I think that they have a very different role than the one that writers have in European countries or the United States. And I am not sure which is the role of writers in other parts of the world, in underdeveloped countries like those in Latin America. In our case, though, the writer who lives in an ivory tower, isolated from reality, does not belong anywhere and does not interpret anything. That writer has no readers. No one is interested. Writers have a place in our society and our literature inasmuch as they have made a certain commitment; a commitment to their surrounding reality. All our writers of any importance deal with social realities: myth, legend, history, geography, race problems, the terrible misery of our continent, the inequality in our land. The writers who take that direction represent the people and become great writers. That commitment takes with it certain suffering and effort that the writer must take on. Many times it means incarceration, torture, murder, or exile. Great Latin American books have been written, for centuries, in exile due to the repression in our countries. Repression can take other forms; it is not only political. Many times it is economic as well.

I believe that the role of the Latin American writer is somewhat like that of the *shaman*, the prophet, the one who interprets the dreams, the hopes, the collective fears. That is why the writer holds such an extraordinary position. It would be unthinkable in the United States that a writer, because he or she is a writer, would be a candidate for the presidency like Mario Vargas Llosa. The mere fact of being a writer would annul his or her chances in this country. And in this country, to be labeled a political writer is belittling, an insult. In our countries, a writer must be political, otherwise what can he or she write about? Who will he interpret if he eludes the problems of men and women in Latin America? How can a woman writer avoid writing about the situation of women in Latin America? It is her subject and it will always be her subject.

Even when the message may seem reduced a bit given the number of people who cannot read or write? Don't you feel that is an important obstacle that keeps people from becoming liberated?

It is a tremendous limitation. I am amazed that in spite of those economic limitations, in spite of the fact that people often cannot buy books and that reading is not the way in which many people chose to spend their time, writers still hold that extraordinary position in Latin America.

There is a very beautiful anecdote about Pablo Neruda. Neruda was a candidate for the presidency in Chile in 1969. They were looking for a candidate other than Salvador Allende to represent the left because Allende had already run three times and had lost all three and there were too many jokes about it. He would even joke that he wanted written on his tombstone, "Here lies the future president of Chile." So, they searched for another candidate, and as often happens in Latin America, they chose Pablo Neruda because he was the poet, the Poet. And so Neruda began to travel throughout Chile as the new candidate. They say he traveled all through the south, the north, the mines, the fields, and when the train stopped, he would stand in the last wagon and speak to the people about whatever came to mind at the moment, and then he would recite from his poetry. There were often two or three hundred peasants standing at the train stations listening to him, and to his surprise they began to recite his poetry along with him. These peasants, miners, these very poor people, knew Neruda's poetry by heart! Many of them probably did not even know how to read, but they knew Neruda's poems!

And I am sure that there is no one in Peru who does not know Vargas Llosa, or in Colombia who does not know García Márquez, even if they have not read their works. They are like milestones, they represent something. They represent the people. This is something that will never happen in this country. Being an intellectual in this country is not such a good thing.

You were just mentioning that the majority of Latin American writers have been in exile. What did exile mean to you?

First of all I have to clarify that my exile was a golden exile in the sense that I left my country with a passport and I chose where I was going. Many people leave prison directly to a small village of a Scandinavian country where they will never adapt, where they will never learn the language, and where they will always be marginal. I went to an open and generous Latin American country. I spoke the language, and even though I was alone because I left in a hurry, my family arrived soon after. And I say it was a "golden exile" because I was never really hungry; many vicissitudes, yes, I did experience, but hunger, never. And if I had never left Chile I never would have taken the road that led me to literature. I also would not have matured as a woman; I never would have found the strength that was within me. I needed the challenge of having to live through difficult circumstances in order to know that I had the strength within me. So I cannot complain. Life has been very good to me. I also have the feeling that I am about ninety years old. I feel that it is though I had lived many lives, as though I have had to start over again many times. Something very positive has come out of each one of these stages in my life. When one stage began, my children were born; then when I started yet again, each book was born.

Was there a great impact on your writing when you moved from Venezuela to the United States? If so, in what ways?

There was an impact, but it was not evident at first. Writing is a very slow process. It is like cooking at a very low temperature. I arrived in this country without knowing that I was going to stay. I came because of love, because I fell in love with an American. I was on a conference tour, and I met a man and fell in love with him. Then I came to spend some time with him, but I really thought I would get over him. I never thought it would be for the rest of my life. I arrived with one bag and the clothes I had for my conference tour, and I stayed at his house as a guest. I can't live without writing because something starts to hurt inside, so I found lots of yellow pads, the legal ones (he is a lawyer, so there were lots of them about) and in his room, on a small table and chair, I began to write. I did not have a typewriter, a computer, nor my own space, so I wrote short stories. A novel requires much more time and a different commitment. The advantage to the short story (it is easier for me to write short stories) is that one works in fragments: if you have a few hours, a few days free, you can work. I began to write the short stories while my soul was still in Latin America. I hadn't yet truly made the move to the United States. Slowly the relationship became stronger, deeper, and I ended up married to the American. . . .

The stories take place in Latin America. They have the tone and the language found in *Eva Luna*, because they are also narrated by Eva Luna. But in the last few years I have been working on another novel. I finished it three days ago. And I wrote that novel feeling that I was established in the United States. I had been speaking English for the past four years as well as reading exclusively American authors. And it is a totally different novel from everything that I have written before. It has a different tone, another language, much shorter sentences, much less adornment, less adjectives. It is a much more precise and delineated style of language. The story takes place in the United States. There is much of that Latin world and Mexican immigration. It is a contemporary novel which takes place in California and so has nothing to do with my previous books, and the change is very noticeable.

Exile is also an interesting topic. Now, living in California where there are so many Hispanics who write here, do you place yourself among the Latinos writing in the United States, or among Latin American writers?

I cannot answer that question. When I am asked to analyze what I have written, I cannot do it. That is not my role. I also do not want to classify myself as one type of writer writing in one place, because tomorrow I may fall in love with a Swede (that could happen, you know) and end up writing short stories in Sweden.

What writers have you read from the United States?

I am reading women writers, especially black women writers. I am a good friend of Amy Tan's, so I have read all her work. Also Louise Erdrich, Barbara Kingsolver. They write, as you say, from the margins: a subversive novel, with an anti-WASP tone that I love. Right now I am reading Gloria Naylor's latest book.

Are you in contact with Chicana writers . . . ?

No, nor am I in contact with Latin American writers. I hardly know writers at all. I was very isolated in Venezuela. I hardly know any of the Boom writers. I have met a few of them on occasion, but I couldn't say that I have made friends with any of them because the opportunity has not been there. Besides, don't forget that it is a masculine club.

I was asking about Chicanas because I find very interesting what they are doing, especially their treatment of exile. They appropriate American culture and their literature is a totally syncretic product of the two cultures. I am thinking, for example, of Lucía Guerra's short stories. She is Chilean, yet in those stories she appropriates much of Californian culture, and therefore it is difficult to say that she is strictly a Latin American writer. Have you read her latest novel?

I see it as a novel written by a sniper, a person who does not belong to either culture and is standing in limbo looking outward. And that is precisely how I feel. I feel totally foreign. That is not to say that I am unhappy; I feel very happy, but completely foreign. I live from one discovery to another; and I feel that is a good thing for a writer.

What do you think about the present situation in Chile, with the elections and Pinochet's stepping down to a lesser role?

Well, I think that the "good guys" won, to put it simply. Chile lived seventeen years of a brutal dictatorship during which political and social organizations were dismantled. Even political parties were prohibited, and so people organized themselves from the roots, in a very effective and brave fashion. They finally defeated the dictatorship, and they did it without violence. Chile never had a significant guerrilla movement nor excess of any type. They did not kidnap people. The Chilean people did nothing aggressive or violent that they could be accused of in order to rid themselves of the dictatorship. All the violence and the horror came from the dictatorship itself. Therefore, I think it is quite clear who was right. That is why I say that the "good guys" won.

And, of course, the present government is one of transition. This government now has the difficult mission of slowly dismantling the military hold on everything. This stronghold extends widely, to universities, education, health, and especially the economy. The military is everywhere in the economy, in all the banks, in all the businesses, in all the high places. And the new government has to take away their power, slowly, without angering them so they will not provoke another coup because the military structure is intact and at any moment they can strike again.

I think the government is acting very wisely and they have the people behind them. And this, in itself, is a surprise, because Chile is a country broken up into many different political parties. It seems like a miracle that Chileans have come together and agreed on one candidate, one program, and supported the Christian Democratic Party, which has a lot of enemies on the left (because much of the blame for Allende's death falls on the Christian Democrats). They thought that people were going to come together only until the elections, and once the dictatorship was overthrown, the coalition would break apart again. That did not happen. People are taking it slowly, waiting, taking one step at a time. I view Chile's situation with a lot of optimism. Chile is a country with fewer political, social, and economic problems than any other country in Latin America, and that is not because we had a dictatorship, but in spite of it.

What is happening with the Left now in Chile?

It is very quiet right now because what is important at the moment is for democracy to survive. They have to support the government in order to make the changes slowly, step by step. Some factions on the left are very anxious, they have suffered much repression. Those people feel very anguished and want fast results, but most of the country is progressing slowly, and they are very aware of the dangers. Nobody wants to live under another dictatorship.

What are your thoughts about the present situation of women in Latin America, and how do you see the future? In Eva Luna *you seem to suggest that a social revolution, a revolution of the Left, is not going to solve women's problems because men are also involved in making revolutions and among them is the macho-type of man like Huberto Naranjo. What do you think, then, is the road to find the right level of equality and liberation?*

I have seen some changes in my lifetime. When I was about thirty, nearing the end of the sixties, the feminist movement began in Chile. (I was a journalist at that time.) There had always been suffragists and feminists in Chile, but they were quite isolated. A consistent movement, with a definite voice, publications, and a true presence did not originate until the late sixties. I was part of that movement because I was lucky enough to be working with a group of women who were very articulate and very much part of the avant-garde of the time. And in my lifetime I have seen the changes, from that tiny revolution that we led when we spoke publicly, through the press, the television and the radio, about abortion, divorce, sexual problems, social problems, machismo, inequality in the work place and at home. We spoke about all the things that women fought for and continue to fight for. My daughter Paula will now benefit from the struggle that my generation led, yet, I believe there are many things that she takes for granted. But if my daughter were in the work force, instead of protected in a university setting, she would see the great gap that exists between situations for men and women in the world, and she would realize that the struggle is not over. And when my granddaughter is old enough to work, the fight will still continue.

Women will achieve great changes, but I will not see that in my lifetime, and it does not matter. Because what is important is not so much to see the great changes, but to see the work in progress. This is a process, a long, slow, and painful process that women will have to go through. Nothing will be given to us. Everything that we obtain will be through our own personal struggle day by day in every single field. I have seen the struggle, yet witnessed results in only certain groups of women. These groups of women are those that have access to education and information, those that live in urban areas and who have resolved basic problems of existence. Poor women, peasant women, those in isolated areas, in slums, don't have a prayer. They are still in the same condition they were five hundred years ago. Take a look at Muslim women today, it's as though they had taken steps backwards. There is much to do. Eva Luna says at one point, or, is it

Mimi (I can't quite recall), "This struggle never ends, therefore we have to continue with joy."

Do you see a great difference between the condition of women here in the United States and in Latin America—even when we restrict it to the urban setting?

Yes. Women who belong to the upper middle class have a very different situation in Latin America. One great difference is that they can pay someone to take care of the house and the children. Things are very different here. We are at the very tail end of women's emancipation. And precisely because we are at the tail end we could avoid some of the mistakes that feminist movements in the United States and Europe have made. At times these movements have proposed such a radical and angry struggle, that they have repelled women away from the movement. I believe that is a mistake. You cannot present things that way. You have to solve social problems much the same way that slavery was resolved, or the way many other social issues were dealt with. Humankind reaches a moment in which it agrees on something and achieves a goal only after a long struggle.

In 1983 you were quoted as saying "the history of humanity is an upward spiral" and that "there is a collective consciousness, a genetic memory that leads us down the right path." I wanted to know what you refer to when you mention the terms "collective consciousness" and "genetic memory."

I am referring to all religions and cultures when they function in a healthy and normal manner; I am not speaking of the Nazi movement nor a host of crazies in a sect. The great movements of humanity, the political movements, religious, social ones, always have the same idea of what is correct and what is wrong. Well, let's not call it good and bad in the Christian sense, but what is worthwhile or not, what is advisable or not, what hurts and what benefits at the time. It is as though humanity knew, through a collective consciousness, how we need to act. We all want peace and justice, we all want a nonviolent world, we all want to preserve the planet, we all want the children to be happy, we all want love, we all have a need for affection, and we all have a need for food. In the basic things, the differences are not so great from one culture to the other. That is what I call the great collective consciousness, and it returns eternally from generation to generation, from culture to culture, and creates a type of memory in which we all fit in, to which we all belong, and which we see in myths and legends. The myths of Eden, the great flood, and the father of creation are found most every place in this world.

Every one of us joins with that collective consciousness at some time or other. What does an artist, any artist do? On a subconscious level they merge in with that collective memory and he or she repeats or represents something that is significant to everyone else. That is why their work holds a sort of echo for us. There is no echo when the work hasn't achieved that subconscious level. One cannot force the connection, but if one is very lucky, it happens, and if indeed it happens, it touches a great number of people. It is also what politicians and preachers do. I feel that is a great resource that humanity holds, and that we cannot, or do not, know how to use consciously. It is a great spiritual resource and thank God we cannot manipulate it, or at least very few people can manipulate it. It is ever present, it keeps us alive, it keeps us going forward: we are not in the Stone Age. And I also do not believe that we will destroy ourselves in a nuclear disaster. We have that part of us that says, "This is as far as we'll go." It is happening right now. The world will have to dismantle nuclear arms because the collective consciousness has reached us all: the first one that pushes the button blows us all to pieces.

> *In that same quotation you also say that history is like a "spiral that rides up," that at times it seems as though we are going through the same place, but actually we are a step higher. How can you relate this to the present situation in Latin America and Eastern Europe? At times it seems as though we advance, at others that we take steps backwards. . . .*

We cannot measure things in one year or in two. We want to measure results from one day to the next because we are accustomed to the immediate gratification that television offers, and it cannot be so. But results can be seen and measured in the length of one, possibly two or three, lives. And you must look at history as a whole, not from the perspective of one's life span, the very little that one person is able to live, the very little that one person is able to see. We are so limited, while the vastness of the world, the complexity of the things that are happening, is immeasurable.

And would Latin America have a role in all that?

I think we all have a role. Latin America is a tortured continent, one that has had an embarrassing history of colonization and exploitation, and all that mixed with indigenous theocratic cultures. We are carrying a tremendous weight. But we are not where we were a century ago, nor ten years ago. When I left Chile, half of the population in Latin America lived under a military dictatorship. All were violent dictatorships. Fifteen years have passed and the political situation has changed, I believe almost in an irreversible manner. What has to change now is the economic situation along with the basic structures in the countries. And before we begin to make changes, we will hit bottom in the economic sphere just as we hit bottom in the political realm.

What stands out in your talk, besides the daily personal struggle that you mention, is the collective struggle of which we are all part.

I cannot speak for Latin America in general, but if we look at what occurred in Chile, we can see that during those seventeen years of dictatorship numerous private organizations were formed. These were people who studied what was happening; in other words, we became the great scholars of the dreadful times we were living. We researched the economic situation, the possible democracy, future governments, and grass roots organizations. Everything was re-searched, over-researched, and reinvented. And I think that all that was very good, in part because it produced a collective consciousness that said democracy could only be obtained and preserved if we all took part in the process. Before the dictatorship there was a special feeling in Chile, a feeling that if you elected the right president, ev-erything was going to be taken care of from the top. It was as if all were going to come to us from the top of a pyramid that ended in a king or a plumed emperor who was going to bestow upon us all the benefits that a perfect government would grant. The seventeen years of dictatorship showed us that things are not that way, that we have only whatever each one of us is able to obtain through a personal struggle and a collective organization. I think that has been the great lesson that we learned all these years: the importance of working together.

> *We have already spoken about your work and the project you have at the moment. But, can you comment on how you perceive the evolution of your work up to this point?*

I think that in general what I have written is related to different moments in my life. I never write anything autobiographical: I am not a character from any of my novels or short stories. But each one of those books corresponds to a time in my life and to a very strong emotion that was with me for a very long time and that I could only resolve through writing. I suppose that if I had had the money to go to a psychiatrist, I would not have had the need to devote myself to literature. But since I could not afford a psychiatrist, I sat at the dining-room table and I wrote about what hurt most.

That old and painful emotion that *The House of the Spirits* brought on was the sense of loss. It is a typical book of memory. I recreated a world that was destroyed. I found the friends, the family, the country, the accent that I had lost. When I left Chile I also left everything behind. I found myself naked and rootless in a country where I could not adapt. After the first moments of plain subsistence, of attempting to support a family, of feeding the children, when I had already found a stable job, that was when the anguish began. I felt I did not belong, that I wanted to go backwards, that everything was falling apart. What made me write *The House of the Spirits* was longing. In that book I invented a family that was very much like my own, but was not exactly my family, I invented a country that appeared to be my Chile, but was not—that's why I don't name it—, and a past that resembles mine, but is not.

What made me write *Of Love and Shadows* was the anger I felt towards the abuses of the dictatorship. The theme of the book is the disappeared, but the emotion behind all that is the rage and feeling of impotence before the mistreatment, and the violence that continues and repeats itself and seems interminable. And all that is not measured in my own lifetime, but it must be measured within five hundred years. It is our own historical burden filled with feelings of impotence, with exploitation, colonization, militarism, the abuse of women, the powerful against the poor, the white against the one of color. It took me two years to write. I had a lot of research to do because it is based on a real situation that happened in Chile (what I wrote is almost word-for-word what happened—it is fiction, but the facts correspond to what actually happened). In the process of interviewing people I discovered that my rage was slowly transforming into action, into strength to work against those things that bothered me. I also discovered that for every one of those torturers, there are one hundred, one thousand, anonymous people who are willing to give their lives in order to save another. I learned that for every informer, there are one hundred who open their houses to hide others. That lesson keeps me alive to this day because if I had held the anger I felt in 1984, I would already have died of a heart attack.

In *Eva Luna* we sense two explicit emotions, and they are both happy ones. That is why I love that book so much. The first is that I accepted myself as a woman. I always wanted to be a man. It is so much easier to be male. Being a woman means having to do twice as much work in order to obtain half the recognition that a man gets. I saw that all around me men who did less work, who were less disciplined, less talented, less of everything, had much better possibilities only because they were men. It was very hard for me to accept (and that happened only after I was forty) that I had done the same things that any man could have done, plus all the things that a woman can do, with a lot of effort—it is true—, with a lot of pain—at times—, and for the first time I said, "It isn't so bad after all to be a woman." Besides, I always wanted to be tall and blonde and one day I looked at myself in the mirror and said, "Well, I'll always be short and dark; there's nothing I can do about it." Eva Luna accepts her feminine essence from the time that she is born; she never questions her own femininity, she searches for, and therefore has questions about, women's rights, but she never questions her femininity. And that took me many years. For me to create that character was tantamount to saying to the world and to myself that everything was fine.

I talked about two feelings; the second one was that I accepted myself as a narrator of stories. Eva Luna is a narrator of stories and in the book she says what I always wanted to say. She tells us what it means to tell a story. So many times I don't remember people's names, or the places I have been. I don't know if I have seen Michelangelo in Florence, or if I have been in Venice. I don't remember how many lovers I have had or the names of the men I have married. At times I even forget the names of my own children, but if someone tells me a story I never forget it, not one single detail. My mind is made that way, totally focused on stories, and I see the world through a glass painted in stories and legends. I always thought that was a terrible handicap in my life. I am totally incapable of adding two plus two or of thinking logically. My thought process is one circle after another, and I cannot explain how I reached a specific point. But it works, by instinct or something like it, yet it actually works. Then one day I thought that I was just different, that my thinking went in different directions, and I said to myself, "Well, let's try to accept that, let's make use of it, let's even try to make a living with it." They had always told me that I was a liar, yet it only took writing books and I was not a liar any longer; I became a writer instead.

Each one of the stories in *The Stories of Eva Luna* corresponds to something that has happened to me and that has left a mark. For example, the last story in the book ["And of Clay Are We Created"] is the story of Omaira Sánchez, the little Colombian girl who was trapped in the mud when the Nevado Ruiz erupted. I have Omaira's picture on my desk. The eruption happened in 1985 so I have had her picture there for six years because those black eyes of a little girl buried in the mud taught me a great lesson. I have never again complained about anything. That poor little girl was dying in the most atrocious manner. It took her four days to die with all the television cameras recording every breath she took. And I wondered, couldn't those same planes that brought the television cameras have brought a pump to siphon the water and rescue the little girl? She never became impatient, she never despaired, she never blamed anyone. I followed the story closely on television, and every day as I look at that picture I tell myself that life is like that, like the death of that child.

The character that the little girl moves so deeply is Rolf Carlé. Is it that men need to go through such a process more than women do? Do women feel things more deeply and so understand such great pain without the need of that type of an experience? I was struck by the fact that the protagonist in that story is a man and not a woman.

I think that part of the problem of *machismo* is that it mutilates men and cuts off their emotional part. I don't think it is a biological question, and I don't believe that women are better equipped to feel emotions. It is something that culture propagates or inhibits. In our culture it is often thought of as inappropriate for men to cry. Women are allowed to feel more emotions, and to be more superstitious. I think that is why there are such great women writers in Latin America, because they are much more into the story.

And so, when you create characters that are strong women, who have the responsibility to preserve tradition and memory, but are nevertheless very intuitive, very "mystical" (like Clara del Valle), are you then creating a type of woman that actually exists, and not attempting to portray the "essence" of femininity?

All the characters in my books are modeled on real people. At times I exaggerate the characteristics, or at times I take two people and create one character from them. Except for one character, they are all based on someone that I know or have heard about, so I really don't feel I invent anything; I write it down, but there is a model for everything I write. Whatever impression you have of my female characters, it is because that is what those women I have known are like. Clara, my grandmother was like that, and I don't think that I invented much. My grandmother could move objects on the table without touching them, but, of course, I embellished it a bit: she couldn't play the piano with the top down. Therefore, I don't think that I am looking for the essence of femininity because I doubt that it exists. I feel that every one of us is different, that we all form a collection of particles, but it is very difficult to find a common essence. I don't know what women are like, I have no idea. I don't even know what I am like.

The spiral that you mention that goes upward, does one have to drive it up?

Of course one must drive it. I believe that we have to drive it on a collective and a personal level. Things don't happen by chance; we make them happen. That is one of the aspects that saddens me most about the crisis of values and of education that we are experiencing today in the U.S., in Europe, in Latin America, and truly all over the world. We live in a world in which there are no consequences. People are so isolated, everyone is such an individualist, and there is no sense of community. Like the child who does not understand that everything he does has an effect on those around him, and that every action echoes interminably throughout history. I was raised thinking that everything that you do matters, that all has a cause and effect, that you are responsible for everything. Today in society things seem to happen magically. You steal and you end up in San Quentin, not because you robbed, but because you were caught. Today you buy this shampoo, and tomorrow you will have a line of men outside your door. If you wear this deodorant, people will fall at your feet. If you serve this type of coffee, a man holding a bouquet of flowers will appear at your doorstep.

> *And maybe the crisis we are living is good, because all those stereo-types could possibly be dismantled.*

I don't know, because young people don't have guidelines to judge. People have a very passive attitude and accept all that as very natural. How many people question all that? And how many people truly question it and become enraged and teach their children to question? Very few. People continue on with their daily lives and don't ever see the pernicious effects of all that. As you may know, in Venezuela the most important aspect of the culture is the soap operas. If you don't watch the soaps, you are nobody because you have nothing to talk about, you can't find a boyfriend, you are nothing. At home they banned me from the TV room when the soaps were going on because I would start to comment: "Well, look at that silly woman with false eyelashes in the morning. Look at how ridiculous that man looks painted black. Why don't they use a real black actor?"

> *Is that why Eva Luna writes soaps with a different twist?*

Yes! At that time they asked me to write a soap, but it would be impossible to actually film one based on my script.

You wouldn't be interested in writing one?

I would love to, but you have to believe in the medium. I believe that the soap opera is a fantastic means of communication. But, much like the romance novel, or the detective novel, or thrillers, or the espionage novel, it has a formula. And if you don't give people the formula that they expect, then the soap opera is not a soap opera any more. I suppose that what one would have to do is to introduce changes slowly, but I don't have the necessary patience do that.

It seems to me that you did a bit of that with the romance novel in Of Love and Shadows.

It wasn't my intention; if it came out like that I did not do it consciously. I think that what was behind *Of Love and Shadows* was a great desire to tell the story of the dead in Chile. That was the basic motivation.

When you mentioned that Eva Luna *had been inspired by your coming to terms with your own womanhood, it made me wonder whether the process of "feminization" that Mimi goes through has any relation to that, or is Mimi a character that you created for other reasons?*

I wanted to have a character that would be a parody, a character who would question many aspects of machismo. Mimi does it very well. She parodies what I find is excessive and quite ridiculous about feminine artifice. She also questions virility. The idea for the character came from Bibi Andersen. We appeared on the same television program in Spain and I thought that she was the most beautiful woman I had ever seen. She was about seven feet tall, and had beautiful legs, hair, fingernails, eyelashes, . . . lips, white teeth, firm breasts. . . . I later found out she was a man. I arrived back in Venezuela with my model and I began to read and research all I could about her. That is why I named my character Mimi.

My daughter Paula knew someone in Los Angeles who had had a

sex-change operation, and she introduced us. Since Paula had been taking a course on sexology, I was able to interview many people who had gone through the operation. I then had a model for the emotional side of the character. I also learned a lot about the hormonal aspect and many other aspects of people who have gone through this experience. What I mean is that Mimi's character was not just invented out of nothing. The only character in my books for which I have no model is Riad Halabí. I don't know anyone like that, and I could not tell you where he came from because I don't know.

"The Responsibility to Tell You"

INTERVIEW BY JOHN RODDEN

16

First published in *The Kenyon Review*—New Series, Winter 1991, Vol. XIII, No. 1

Until she was thirty-one, the heroine was living a happy, successful life as a Chilean journalist and mother of two. Suddenly, with the assassination of her uncle, president of the nation, her world was shattered and she left her homeland with her husband and family. Unable to find regular work in her adopted country, she began writing a novel, savagely critical of the dictator's regime. It became an instant best-seller, vaulted her into international prominence, and may even have played a role in bringing down his government.

That could well serve as the plot for one of Isabel Allende's romantic novels of political protest, but it happens to be her life. She's found, however, that the two intertwine in odd ways. In 1987, not long after she was divorced, she met a California lawyer who had admired one of her novels. They fell in love "at first sight," quickly married, and are now living, with his teenage stepson, in Marin County. Only in a novel . . .

Allende is a charismatic blend of romantic, feminist, utopian, satirist, and gifted storyteller. Her novels—*The House of the Spirits* (1982), *Of Love and Shadows* (1984), and *Eva Luna* (1987)—are melodramatic fantasias featuring victimized heroines who come to political consciousness as anti-fascist critics and feminists. Allende's first two novels are set in an unnamed country (recognizably Chile) and express her critical views of patriarchal tyranny and the right-wing Pinochet dictatorship; her third is set in Venezuela and condemns sexist stereotypes and the hypocritical chauvinism of Latin male revolutionaries.

Born in 1942 in Lima of Chilean parents, and raised in Santiago, Allende is the niece of democratically elected Chilean president Salvador Allende, who was overthrown and killed in a coup d'état by General Augusto Pinochet (with the help of the Chilean Right and the CIA) in September 1973. Fifteen months later, fearing for her security and outraged by the repressive new regime and its violence and press censorship, she relocated to Caracas.

There Isabel Allende began to consider a new career. She had previously worked as a journalist for a progressive Chilean women's magazine. Along with her news and feature articles, she had run a horoscope and lonely hearts column. One day in Santiago, she recalls, the Chilean poet Pablo Neruda phoned her, saying that he had been reading her articles and would like to meet her. Allende agreed eagerly. After a pleasant lunch, Neruda told her he would like to share his opinion of her columns. "You are a horrible journalist," he said. She was crestfallen. "But—you are a wonderful storyteller! You have the imagination of a great writer."

That encounter helped give her the confidence she later needed. When Allende, in exile in 1981, received a phone call that her ninety-nine-year-old grandfather was near death, she sat down to write him a letter and thereby "keep him alive, at least in spirit." The letter grew to five hundred pages. It became the basis for *The House of the Spirits*, her Galsworthian family saga of love and rebellion among three generations of Chilean women. After being rejected by numerous Latin American publishers, the novel was first published in Spain, soon ran into more than two dozen editions in Spanish, and was translated into a score of languages. (Although it cost the equivalent of a month's salary for a Chilean earning the minimum wage, the novel reportedly circulated widely on library loan in the mid-1980s, was discussed in reading groups, and aroused resistance to Pinochet's military dictatorship.) Similar success followed with *Of Love and Shadows*, the story of a courageous woman journalist's battles with the Pinochet regime, based on a true story of the discovery of a mass grave found in an abandoned mine near Santiago; and *Eva Luna*, the adventure of a *pícara* who eventually becomes a celebrated soap-opera writer. The autobiographical resonances are clear.

In the Chilean elections of December, 1989, a broad Left-Center coalition (which Allende supported), backing Patricio Aylwin for the presidency, won a decisive victory against a divided Right. A number of legal obstructions, however, may bar the way for the new government to exercise power effectively. Among them is the fact that Pinochet, although stepping down as president, will remain commander of the army.

The following interview took place in October, 1988, at the University of Virginia in Charlottesville, one week after the Chilean plebiscite which ended General Pinochet's chances of remaining in power.

" *Do you believe that there are any special responsibilities of the writer in politics? I mean the writer as an artist, and not simply as a citizen.*

I think that it depends where you are placed, where you live. If you live in the United States or in Europe, probably you can be an artist dedicated to art alone. But if you live in a world like the world where I come from, it's very difficult to ignore the reality that surrounds you and affects everyday life. There's so much misery and violence, inequality, injustice, five hundred years of exploitation and colonization. It's very difficult for anybody to ignore that. And writers are not exceptions in this sense. Maybe they have more responsibility than other people because they have a certain platform from which they can speak for others who are kept in silence. So I feel the responsibility myself. I don't want to talk about other writers. I speak only for myself, not for other people.

Should the writer go so far as to write editorials for a specific political position? In other words, is there anything different about doing your videotape and sending it to Chile [Allende sent a videotape to Santiago in September, 1988, urging Chileans to vote against General Pinochet in the plebiscite] versus writing a novel or a political pamphlet? Is your writing a thing apart that you must not allow to be compromised by politics?

I do not belong to any political party. I have never participated in politics until now. And I do that now because the opposition in Chile is a multiparty opposition—people from the Center, the Left, and some parties of the Right, too. All of us have united to form a coalition and the goal is "Vote No in the Plebiscite." That's the only thing that we agreed on. We will see what happens in the future.

But now, eighty percent of the population in Chile has said "No" to the dictatorship, and I am with them. And I feel that I must adopt a stance of political commitment—that is, against the dictatorship, which doesn't mean that I am working for any particular political party. For the last fifteen years, I have been working against the dictatorship, not in a political party. And my writing is affected by politics. But I have never thought that I could write a novel to promote an ideological cause. I don't think I would be able to do it. I could write a document, or a testimony, but somehow a novel is different.

Is it something you wouldn't want to do then?

It's not that I wouldn't want to do it, I think that I wouldn't be able to do it. Somebody said once that good sentiments don't make good literature, and that's really so. I mean, you can believe in something so strongly, but when the time comes to transform it into art—well, it doesn't work that way. If you plan to deliver a message, it usually doesn't work that way. At least in Latin American literature it doesn't. Latin American literature has been politically committed. Especially in the last twenty-five years. All the Latin American Boom literature was marked by politics. Yet those books possess independent artistic value. You can't say the Boom is political literature alone. Politics are part of the Boom literature, but it's not chiefly political literature.

What are the implications for your politics of your decision to live in exile, outside Latin America?

I have not decided to do that. I have lived in exile in Venezuela. That is in Latin America. And I chose a Latin American country because I feel more comfortable in my own culture.

Are you not now living in the United States?

I have lived in Venezuela. And only recently—some months ago [1988]—I married a North American. But that was, let's say, an accident in my life. I met him in a restaurant, I fell in love. I'm not applying for American citizenship. I have my own citizenship. And I will not be American. I will be Chilean.

How much time are you planning to spend in the United States?

I got married. As long as I am in love, and want to live with him, I will stay. That doesn't break my rules at all. I still speak my language, I write about my country, and I travel all the time.

Do you think your plans [to reside in the United States] might undermine your attempt to be a Latin American voice? Might you be identified with the United States? And might residence here distance you from Latin American problems?

Well, many Latin American writers don't reside in Latin America, or at least they spend long periods of their lives abroad. Carlos Fuentes, for example, has lived for the last twenty years in the United States. Mario Vargas Llosa lives in London. Cortázar lived in France all his life. So I don't think that exile affects so much the writing. Exile affects you as a person.

But in my case—I must be honest—exile has been very good. First of all, I'm not really an exile. When I left Chile I was frightened and afraid, but I left the country with a passport. I did not find asylum in an embassy. And I have not gone back all this time [since 1975] because I do not want to live under a dictatorship. I *do not want* to live under a dictatorship. That's my choice. I *could* go back if I wanted to. I am not—and was not—on the list of people who could not return.

So my situation is somewhat special. It has been hard, it has been painful very often, but it has been a very good experience. It has brought out a strength that I did not know was inside me. It has given me a broad vision of the world, of my reality. The fact that I have had to put distance between my country and myself has made my country clearer to me. Now I feel like I know more about Latin America and our reality than I did fifteen years ago. I've been studying and working on that.

I gather from your earlier comment that you think it is quite possible for American writers not to be political. Can you envision a Latin America that would not involve the duty to write about politics?

There are some countries in Latin America where maybe this is not so—I mean where it's not a necessity. Costa Rica, for example. It's a wonderful country with good leaders. A peaceful country. Maybe a writer there can really produce literature just for the sake of literature. And I can think of a situation in the Latin American future, of course, when this will not be necessary. But I don't think that it will happen very soon.

We Latin Americans still are living in a terrible political crisis. Not as difficult as it was some years ago. We had a terrible decade [in the 1970s] of dictatorships in Latin America. When I left my country in 1975, half the population of Latin America was living under a fascist dictatorship. But the situation has changed. And now in Latin America we have dictatorships only in Paraguay and Chile. The rest of the continent has gone back to democracy. These are fragile democracies, and the shadow of the military is there always. But we are getting better, not worse. We are living in an economic and social crisis, we have enormous problems. But we are better than we were five or ten years ago.

How would you respond to critics who allege that Isabel Allende is writing popular romance, or even kitsch, which is escapist and ultimately conservative because it doesn't fundamentally challenge readers? Some readers have charged that you write literary soap operas. How do you respond to criticism that your work is implicitly conservative because it merely confirms readers' extant world views?

That's not my intention. I write as well as I can. And I try to reach people and tell them what is true for me, what is important for me. I don't experiment very much with literature. Why? First, because I'm not interested in [formal] experimentation. And second, because I want to communicate in a very direct way. I want to tell readers about my country. I want to tell them about torture chambers, about politics, about people who starve to death, and about people who sell themselves as slaves because they have no food. And I don't think that's soap opera.

Soap opera is a melodrama in which you have no political or social concerns. You live in a bubble, away from everything that has to do with the world. Away from poverty, away from all the struggles of humankind. And those are not my books. Maybe they are sentimental very often, and maybe they are kitsch very often. And I'm not afraid of that. I can cope with that. I like it actually.

> *How about the reader who says, "Frequently her evil characters are punished in the end. That's not real life. That's a fantasy world. We're deluding the public into thinking that good will triumph and evil will be punished."*

That is not so. In *The House of the Spirits*, the torturer is not punished. He stays in power. Who are punished? The good ones. The heroine is raped, beaten, mutilated, kidnapped, imprisoned. She escapes alive, but she is terribly punished for no crime. In *Of Love and Shadows*, the murderers of the peasants that were found in the mine were never punished. They are promoted in the army and they are free. The general is still in power, and the protagonists have to flee for their lives. So that's not the case at all. That accusation doesn't respond to my work at all.

> *You remark in one interview: "It comes naturally, I don't look for them, I'm always fascinated by them, I feel very close to them, these marginal characters of mine who are punished."*

I haven't read this interview but that's not so. I'm not fascinated by the people who are punished. I'm fascinated by marginals. Marginals are people who stand unsheltered by the system, who somehow defy authority, defy the stereotypes. These people can be prostitutes, poor people, crazy people, guerrillas, homosexuals—I can give you a whole list—people who must live their lives without being sheltered. And I'm always fascinated by those characters because in a way I think I've always defied authority too.

> *You have said in an interview that your ideal reader would be a girl called Alejandra. She's a Chilean girl, twenty years old, who's read your books so many times that she knows long paragraphs by heart. And she's the perfect reader because she makes you feel responsible.*

Can you elaborate on that? How do you seek to influence this ideal reader politically?

In the case of Alejandra Jorquera, I don't have to convince her of anything. She has chosen to read my books so many times because she feels the way I feel. So that's why I think that she's my ideal reader. I don't have to convince her of anything.

But if I say that I write with responsibility, it's because sometimes I can reach a reader the way I reach a student in my classes here. And by telling him what has been my experience, and by telling him what truth is for me, I can put doubts in his mind and, if possible, in his heart. And I can make that person realize that we all share the same planet. We all have a common destiny.

You cannot live in a bubble away from the problems you think are not yours. That child who is dying of hunger in Africa, the person who is being tortured in Chile, is your brother or your sister. And you are responsible the same way I am, and we cannot ignore reality. We cannot say, "I didn't know." We bear the *responsibility* to know! And I know, as a writer, I bear the responsibility to tell you and convince you that all this is happening. Now what are you going to do with that truth? That is your problem.

What do I do with my truth? I write it. And I go around the world lecturing, and I make these videos. I do whatever I can, I do not take a weapon in my arms and go out and shoot. I cannot do that. I can do other things. And the other things I try to do. I feel that I am responsible not only for my own life, but for yours too. And for everybody's. And for the planet's. And that responsibility is enormous. And I feel it every day. Every minute.

You have said that your female characters are usually feminists. Is there a line beyond which you think you as writer cannot or should not go in promoting "isms"? We are back to politics again. In other words, to what extent can your work affirm feminism, socialism, or anti-capitalism? Is there a point beyond which ideology intrudes, so that it threatens your artistic aims?

I don't know. That's a difficult question for me because I never think of my books as art. Maybe because I was a journalist for so long. I write because it gives me a lot of pleasure. It's the only thing I can do.

And when I sit at my typewriter and I start a book I don't think of the consequences. And I don't ponder if I'm creating something that will be good or bad. I write the best I can. But always with pleasure, with a sense of joy, as if I were playing. I think that you're right. If you are very narrow-minded, and if you stick with "isms," probably that will affect your work as literature.

I consider myself a very tolerant human being. And though many of my woman characters are feminists, there are others who are not. In my books I have the same compassion for these others. I treat them as kindly as I treat the feminist women whom I like more. I even treat the torturer compassionately. Because he's also a product of my writing; he's one of my children. Although he's a twisted child he's also mine. But these questions are very difficult for me to answer because I have never studied literature. I never read my reviews. So I don't know how to answer in an intelligent, academic, scholarly way. I can only tell you how I feel. And the books that I write—I write them with feelings, not with much thinking.

Do you think there's any danger for you that your enormous world-wide popularity in recent years may jeopardize your other "work"—what one might call your social mission?

Well, my celebrity is something that feels very far away. I lived many years in Venezuela, where any sense of mass popularity never reached me. I realized *House of the Spirits* was popular in Europe only when I received my first check and an envelope with clippings. Now I'm aware of the popularity. I'm in the United States.

But popularity is of the moment. Celebrity is fragile. It's something that happens today and can vanish tomorrow. And I am conscious of that. If, in twenty years, you and I meet again, and there are people that are still reading my books, then I can say, "All right, I'm a writer, and some of this has been important to someone." But I started writing only seven years ago. My fame is very sudden. Only time can tell if a book is good or not. The fact that it sold at this moment doesn't mean that it's good. It means at this moment there are a lot of people who need to read this kind of book. Nothing else. How many books can you remember? Very few. So in twenty or forty years we might speak again about my celebrity.

Yet when someone becomes a public figure or a celebrity, obviously there's a special opportunity to speak to the public which may not exist twenty years later. Do you have the conviction that you should seize the moment and address the public about the things that concern you?

Yes, I feel that. And that is one of my greatest responsibilities. And I do it when I speak, when I lecture. And I lecture a lot. I tell American audiences about my continent, I tell them about my country, and about the things which I care about in the world. And about people. I speak about all that. But when I write it's different. Because when I lecture, it's like a conversation with someone, and it's not literary. It's life, it's feelings. But when I write it's different. Then I'm telling stories. Part of what I believe comes through. But I'm addressing a piece of paper, not an audience.

I lecture in spite of the fact that I hate it. I like to be alone in my room writing. That's the thing I like best. Well, what I like most is making love! But then second: writing. Writing too! And I don't like to lecture people, because then I'm up there on a platform. It's a very upsetting situation. I am asked questions that sometimes I cannot answer. And the only good part about it is that I am forced to be very clear about what I feel and what I want. And preparing a lecture can take me months because I try to put in a lecture everything that is not clear to me.

Now, for example, I will have a lecture in December about the meaning of life. Why did I accept that lecture? It will take me six months to prepare it. Why? Because it's the best opportunity I will have clarifying what I think. What's the meaning of life to me, now that I am forty-three years old and I've done all this?

When I lecture about women, I try to be clear about where I stand being a woman in this part of the world at this moment. When I lecture about why I write, I spend months preparing to answer. And then it becomes clear to me that I have grown.

And do you undertake these political responsibilities reluctantly? Or do you finally see them as useful and energizing to your work and life?

The political issues for me at this moment are all related to Chile. The plebiscite, the long struggle against the dictatorship, fifteen years struggling against the dictatorship. I know that I cannot avoid these issues. The rest of what people call politics are social issues. Human rights. Things that concern everybody everywhere, not only in Chile. And that's not the domain of any political party. It's the concern of anybody who thinks, anybody who has an audience. So with those issues I can deal because I think that they are part of life, and I'm very passionate about that. But those issues concerning the dictatorship, the plebiscite? No, they are strictly political, and the specific moment is very stressful for me. I wish we could get through it all as soon as possible. Not for my sake, of course, but for Chile and for everybody.

> *You've emphasized that a Latin American or Chilean writer may have a special political responsibility. Would you extend it further to say any member of a group which is oppressed or underprivileged bears a similar responsibility? For instance, in the United States, might a woman or a black intellectual, or a Hispanic perhaps in some regions, have similar responsibilities? Or do you see this more as a national or continental responsibility?*

I think it depends on the person and on the tradition. I come from a continent where writers have been concerned with politics, have sought from the beginning of the century to "educate the people" about social issues. Then the social issues become political issues. So if you belong to that tradition it's very difficult to ignore it. On the other hand, if you take a look at the literature written in the United States, you would find probably that the best contemporary literature is written by black women. And those black women are writing about being women and being black. And they cannot ignore *that* fact. How can they ignore it when it has affected them all their lives? A writer in South Africa cannot ignore apartheid. Jewish writers cannot ignore their history. Polish writers at this moment cannot ignore the political situation. So it depends on many things. And, once again, I think that the accusation that I am writing soap operas is not fair. I stand for certain things that are important to me. I'm concerned and committed. In a soap opera you have no commitment.

Do you have any particular political message for North Americans in relation to Latin Americans? Is there anything special you would like to say to North Americans?

Yes. You do not live in a bubble. You are not privileged. You are very spoiled. You think you will be saved when this globe explodes. You will not. We all share the same planet; this is a rock lost in space. We are all parts of it. There are no superior races. When I come to this country and see the good things here, when I see how democracy works, how people have most of the basics, I say: So it *is* possible! Why is it not possible for the rest of the world? For us Latin Americans? Why can't we live like this? But you are not Utopia. You are a possibility.

But then we must also consider the reverse. You must look at us in Latin America and say: These people are hungry, these people are oppressed; they live in violence, inequality, misery. That is also a possibility for us! We are not excluded from *that* as our possibility, too. They are not another planet. They are not on Mars. It's our planet. It's our land, and these borders are just illusions. We trace them on a map, but they don't exist. We all share the same planet.

Do you plan to integrate this message more explicitly into your work? Or is it something that you hope to communicate primarily via your lectures?

I don't know. When I have something that is clear to me, it comes out little by little, in drops. And someone might discover it. In my last book, for example, in *Eva Luna*, when I finished the book I realized I had put there things I had been thinking about as a woman for the last twenty-five years. Twenty-five years preparing to accept myself as a woman made that book possible. I put in Eva Luna and the other characters all those things that took so long to grow inside me. Finally I could put them in words. I'm not a very articulate person, I'm emotional. And these characters were born out of a deep emotion that has been within me for a long time. And sometimes they speak for me and they speak about the things that I care for. So maybe if I can't be very clear about this message that we've talked about, maybe some character of mine will say it or do something about it.

I don't know. I don't know what I will write tomorrow. I don't know if I will be alive tomorrow. I'm often asked, What are your plans for next year? I don't have a next year. Every time that I plan a next year destiny comes and just changes everything. I thought that I would be a suburban housewife in Chile all my life, and that I would be buried in a Chilean cemetery in Santiago. Well, that has not been my life. So I'd better not make any plans. I had not planned on marrying a North American, and it happened.

> *When you come to the United States and you say capitalist democracy here seems to work somewhat, does it make you think that this may be in some way a suitable model for Latin American countries?*

No, it has proven that it is not. Latin America is quite a different reality from North America. Latin America is the product of the conquest by the Spaniards and the Portuguese. By the Catholic Church. We have a history of hierarchical, authoritarian government. We have no tradition of democracy. You come from a tradition of Europeans who were already thinking about democracy. You've had that in your genes. It's always been part of your tradition. It's not part of our tradition. So after the wars of independence we tried to copy a model of the utopian republic. And we copied this in our constitutions. Our constitutions are perfect. The people who fought our wars of independence were idealists. They thought they could do something perfect, but when the time came to practice what they had written—it didn't work that way. Why? Because we have a tradition of dictators. We had inherited this terrible social structure that the Spaniards had left. Social classes divide our societies in layers. You cannot move from one class to another.

We have also had five hundred years of different forms of colonization. First politically by the Spanish and the Portuguese. Economically by the British, then by other European countries, and now by North Americans. We have never really been economically free. So we have had a terrible burden, a burden of misery and poverty. We have this terrible burden, and we cannot copy. The models of the Soviet Union and China have not worked in Latin America, and the capitalist model has not worked either. It has only created more injustice, more violence, and more inequality. The rich become richer, and the poor become poorer. And what happens then? You have to repress the poor more and more to keep them quiet. And this creates a horrible situation of violence that's ready to explode all the time. So we cannot copy other models. We'll have to invent something that is suitable for us—considering our past, our tradition, and our problems.

Do you think that Latin America can or should remain non-aligned?

No, the ideal would be that Latin America and North America could be allies. We could plan together something that would be like Europe. We have ourselves many things in common in Latin America: we have a common language, a common religion, and a common history, which is more than Europe had. Of course it took Europe three thousand years of existence and we have only had five hundred years of existence. But we can achieve unity. And once we are strong enough we can be a good ally to the United States. Not only a supermarket, a place where you can take products, or you can sell products, but rather a good ally. But not an ally with those social classes which possess power and use the military forces as their mercenaries. Not that sort of alliance. A real democratic alliance. That has not been possible due to many factors. One of the reasons is that United States foreign policy is awful. You have never understood what the situation in Latin America is.

For example, Nicaragua. During the last century, thirteen times the United States Marines invaded Nicaragua. The United States supported all the dictatorships in Nicaragua until the situation could no longer be held under control. Now it's too late. And the same thing will happen in Peru and in many other places. We must undertake structural reforms to avoid revolutions. One cannot keep the people oppressed forever and profit from that. It's impossible, and it's not moral. It's unjust—as obscene and perverse as slavery ever was. And people have to get up and say "No." Because many people are suffering this enslavement.

The Shaman and the Infidel

INTERVIEW BY MARILYN BERLIN SNELL

17

Reprinted from *New Perspectives Quarterly* 8 (Winter 1991): 54–58

Author of three books of fiction—*The House of the Spirits*, *Of Love and Shadows*, and *Eva Luna*—and *The Stories of Eva Luna*, to be published in January by Atheneum, Isabel Allende is one of Latin American literature's most imaginative and popular writers.

In the following conversation with *NPQ*'s Marilyn Berlin Snell, Allende discusses "magic realism" and the political, historical, and cultural influences on her work.

> ❝ *If one could talk about the zone between past and future where, you have written, children can see into the future and move objects on the dinner table with their eyes, and where "outlaws die of hunger in the Amazon with bags full of emeralds on their backs," it would be a zone of a nonlinear present, a land of opposites, contrasts: Latin America.*
>
> *Is the writer who occupies this physical, spiritual, and temporal space—who can describe a life that shimmers, that borders in the North American mind, at least, on myth—different from other writers on other continents? Is there such a thing as Latin American literature? Octavio Paz has argued that there are Latin American writers but not Latin American literature.*

Of course there is Latin American literature. There is a Latin American culture and its written expression is literature. In a way, this literature has become the clearest expression of our identity, personality, and experience.

For many years our identity was expressed mainly in music and painting. And, of course, always in the crafts. Only in the last thirty years have we developed a real literature. Prior to this, we had great writers, Nobel Prize winners, even writers who became presidents *because* they were writers. However, except for a very few, these writers were imitating the voices of Europe. We had our eyes on Europe and didn't dare speak with our own voice.

The Boom of Latin American literature, which began thirty years ago with the works of Alejo Carpentier, Gabriel García Márquez, Mario Vargas Llosa, and Carlos Fuentes, encompassed a generation of writers that forged a new way of speaking. With few exceptions, the writers before them had tried to express their thoughts with the aesthetic standards of Europe, using the language of the Europeans, and were therefore unable to fully express themselves.

The Boom literature, on the other hand, was like a choir of very different but harmonious voices. For three decades now, these writers have been telling Latin America to the world and to Latin Americans.

I belong to the first generation of writers brought up reading other Latin American writers. The Boom writers paved the way for me. Without fear or modesty, they invented new voices. Further, these writers were not afraid they would be called liars or that their work would be accused of being overdone, baroque, or sentimental. They were not afraid of politics or of addressing social problems.

What I don't believe is that the literary form often attributed to the works of these and other Latin American writers, that of magic realism, is a uniquely Latin American phenomenon.

Magic realism is a literary device or a way of seeing in which there is space for the invisible forces that move the world: dreams, legends, myths, emotion, passion, history.

All these forces find a place in the absurd, unexplainable aspects of magic realism. And this view of life is to be found in practically all the literature of Africa, Asia, and underdeveloped countries everywhere. Magic realism is all over the world. It is the capacity to see and to write about all the dimensions of reality.

Do you think this way of seeing the world through the prism of magic realism—a literary style whose practitioners come mostly from developing countries—can survive in a world that is rapidly becoming more and more tightly integrated both culturally and economically?

Because we are living in a world defined and described by communication, integration is unavoidable. Today, not only is it practically impossible to be isolated, it isn't particularly desirable.

However, until now it has been mostly a one-way transfer—moving from north to south—of information, culture, and moral and economic habits.

Real integration will not exist until north and south *exchange* with one another, rather than the north merely taking things away from us or imposing things upon us—from entire governments to *Dallas* and *Dynasty*.

But, to get back to the question, I don't see any threat to magic realism. Indeed, I see this literary device being utilized beautifully in many industrialized nations, particularly in the U.S.

Today, great writers from minority groups in the U.S. are finding their voice in the wonderful, rich imagery of magic realism. Writers such as Louise Erdrich, Toni Morrison, Alice Walker, and Amy Tan all have a unique, rich way of writing that can be described as magic realism.

These women are among those who have broken away from the style of writing that defines most of the fiction coming from industrialized countries: that pragmatic, minimalist style and way of facing reality in which the only things one dares talk about are those things one can control. What cannot be controlled is denied.

I have been coming to the U.S. frequently for the past decade, but I am seeing a real change now. There is an openness to different kinds of voices. More people no longer automatically accept what the media tell them. This might be the beginning of a new way of communicating, an authentic exchange, and a new relationship between peoples and cultures.

Let's take the acceptance of Latin American literature in the U.S. In that sense, the cultural exchange has been from south to north. What effect does this type of cultural exchange have on the North American mind?

I try to be realistic. I don't think my books, for instance, have had any impact whatsoever. What books do, really?

What interests me is not so much why my work does not have an impact on the North American mind but why literature in general is so important to Latin Americans. The prestige and power a writer in Latin America commands has always amazed me. One cannot compare anything in North America to the respect and celebrity achieved in Latin America by its writers.

In Latin America, a writer can be a candidate to the presidency. Mario Vargas Llosa, for instance, was a candidate because he was a great writer, not because his politics were particularly sound. This, on a continent of illiterates; a continent in which fifty percent of the population cannot read or write in Spanish; a continent on which practically *nothing* is published in most of the indigenous population's original dialects or languages.

Latin Americans embody a desperate need for identification. This is a continent on which the culture, religion, and languages were virtually destroyed through conquest and colonization. There is a great need to took at ourselves in a mirror and find a face that resembles our own. Perhaps the reason we have such great respect for our artists and their works is because we can find our image only through them—through the twisted mirror of art.

Another example of the power and prestige of Latin American artists is that they are always among the first to be silenced when their countries fall to dictators. The first people to be persecuted, killed, tortured, and sent into exile are inevitably the writers, journalists, and artists. Because the musicians, artists, and writers are the prophets and shamans, the interpreters of the dream of the people, they are the enemies of authority. When the government needs to silence the people, they begin by silencing their representatives.

Let me give you an example. In Chile, we had a folksinger named Víctor Jara. He composed very simple songs honoring the revolution, the people, and the social changes occurring in his country. With one

song he could say more than the press would say in a year or a politician could say in a lifetime. And his songs, which were easy to remember and repeat, became weapons against the political enemy.

The dictatorship, headed by Augusto Pinochet, could not allow
Jara to go into exile where he would continue singing. So, in September 1973, in the shadow of the military coup which overthrew President Salvador Allende Gossens, Jara was tortured and murdered by
Chilean soldiers in the National Stadium—used during this period as
a concentration camp.

Our writers present the same kind of threat. Indeed, during the
Conquest, novels were forbidden in Latin America because the Spanish Inquisition thought they would plant subversive ideas in the
minds of the people. The only books allowed during the Conquest
and colonization by Spain and Portugal were religious and scientific
books.

> . . . And in the contemporary era, the writers and poets proved those
> fears to be quite valid. I remember a story Pablo Neruda once told of
> traveling by train to the desert in Chile to read his poem to the copper
> miners. He arrived and hundreds of miners were there to greet his
> train; he stepped out on the back platform of the train and was show-
> ered with roses; he began to read his poetry and found the miners
> knew his work by heart and recited it with him.

One must remember that Pablo Neruda was not only the greatest
poet Chile has ever had, but he was also a communist. He was politically committed and acted as a voice for Chile's workers and peasants. One could be with him or against him but no one could accuse
him of remaining in an ivory tower. Even his love poems reflected
the social and political reality of the country.

Latin American writers are constantly accused of being too political. But if we did not write about politics we would not be addressing
the reality of Latin American life; we would not be interpreting anybody and we would have no echo. When Latin American writers
cease to address reality, we cease to belong to the people, to speak for
the people, and so become isolated and, ultimately, ignored.

Latin America is a continent of great contrasts, of inequality, injustice, corruption, violence, and misery. Eighty percent of the popula-

tion lives very poorly and a handful of people are very wealthy. That fact alone creates a permanent state of violence.

How can I write without talking about the suffering? How can I write about secretaries with big tits and green eyes who run off with the wealthy executive when I am living in a society of contrasts, violence, dictatorship; of repression, exile, torture, and disappearances; of children who are sold to organ banks for their body parts? Our reality is so terrible and so rich in imagery that it is impossible to write about anything else. I only express what exists. I don't invent anything.

> *Ivan Klima, the Czech author who was silenced in his country for twenty years, wrote that "for the writer, there is no useless experience—quite the contrary. The more hideous his experience, the more extreme the situation he enters, the more beneficial it is to his future work."*
>
> *And you yourself have said that exile was very good for you, since* The House of the Spirits *was the result of an effort to "recover memories being blown by the winds of exile."*
>
> *What are we to make of these claims—one from a woman who was forced into exile by Pinochet after he overthrew a democratically elected socialist government, and one from Klima, who was silenced in his homeland for twenty years by the communist government? Both of you say, essentially, that repression has its merits.*

I wish it were not that way, but it is impossible to imagine living in a world without pain. The only place in the world I have been where people think they can live without pain is the U.S.

The rest of humanity, for centuries and millennia, has known that there is no growing, no learning, without pain and failure. One doesn't learn from success and joy. Those are merely slight instances of good luck. In Latin America, the world where I have lived all my life, this is assumed to be a fact of nature. One rebels against it and suffers all the anxiety, pressure, and fear that goes along with this knowledge, but in the end we understand that this is what it means to be alive.

All my short stories and novels have been born of profound emotions I have internalized and suffered in some way. When I am ready to be cured, I write. Though the writing is healing, the pain is necessary to the process of creation.

For instance, the nostalgia for my country and everything I had lost produced *The House of the Spirits*. Anger at the abuse of the dictatorship produced *Of Love and Shadows*. And all the injustice I had to suffer being a woman in a macho, authoritarian, patriarchal society produced *Eva Luna*.

Some of the stories contained in my recent collection of short stories have been inside me for ten years or more but I had not been able to write them. I needed all this time to internalize them, to dream them, to suffer them in some way.

Let me give you just one example: The last story in the collection of short stories ["And of Clay Are We Created"] is about a little girl who dies after being trapped for three days in a mud slide caused by a volcanic eruption. This story really occurred. In 1985, we saw her on every television screen in the world, the face of Omaira Sánchez, one of the thousands of victims of Colombia's Nevado Ruiz volcanic eruption. The black eyes of that girl have haunted me for five years. Sometimes, as I am driving in my car, amidst the beautiful landscape of San Francisco, I see those eyes. I see the girl again. She is telling me something. She is talking to me about patience, about endurance, about courage. She gave me all those lessons looking at me from a television screen.

Since the day I first saw her face I wanted to write an homage to her, but I couldn't. I had not suffered enough. When I was finally able to write the story, I couldn't write about her. The story is not about her; it is about a person who is with her and about a person who is watching the person who is with her. It is a story removed in two and three levels from the pain experienced directly by Omaira Sánchez. She is just the excuse, because I am really expressing what happened to me through her suffering, what she taught me. I endured a little pain, and she suffered a great deal of pain, but one cannot give birth without pain. It's terrible but that is the way life works.

Is that what life is then, and is that what creativity finally comes to be: the art of enduring and expressing our suffering beautifully?

It is more than that. Art exists not only to express suffering but to transform it into something else. Art is an act of alchemy. It is an effort to take the evil of the world and, by internalizing it, transform it into its opposite: hope, love, friendship, solidarity, generosity, all those things that wouldn't exist without the pain and the evil.

Art is an effort to transform the experience of failure, for example, into wisdom. Failure won't make a person rich, won't give them prestige, but it might give them wisdom.

> *Yet, worldwide, the attraction is not toward the view that pain, suffering, and even death are essential parts of life but toward the ideals best illustrated by Disney: the American view that death can be cheated; that everything will have a happy ending. Don't the fairy tales of Disney have a great deal more power today than the philosophy behind Día de los Muertos [the Day of the Dead; the Latin American tradition of honoring and celebrating the lives of dead loved ones on the first day of November]?*

The attraction of Disney is undeniable but sooner or later we have to accept that we will die. We cannot deny death; it is a natural part of the life cycle.

I have been living in the U.S. for three years and what I really miss about my Latin American culture is the sense I had there of belonging in a common project, of being part of a coherent group, with a common set of values.

In Latin America, even though the project of the elite is totally different from the project of the great majority of the poor there is nonetheless the sense that one belongs to a place and everything that happens to that place will happen to you; and everything that happens to your neighbor will happen to you. You are tied to your place.

Due to our history we have a sense of fate, or destiny, that the U.S. lacks. It is a sometimes overwhelming sense that we can only do so much and the rest is fate—a fate we share with the group.

> *Your novels all convey the theme that love is stronger than hatred, that solidarity and hope will prevail over death and torture.*
>
> *How can you still believe this when, as you write, "it is impos-*

sible to speak of Latin America without mentioning violence"? How can you continue to have so much faith in humanity?

Because I have seen it. Let me give you just one example, the example of my country. The Pinochet dictatorship lasted seventeen years, yet it was defeated nonviolently by the solidarity and the love of the people—the love of freedom, the love of the truth.

All the violence, repression, and brutality came from the military. And the people responded with nonviolence, pacific protests, solidarity, and organization.

The dictatorship proposed a plebiscite because it arrogantly believed it would win, since it controlled everything. It also believed that the civilians in Chile's multiparty system—the joke about this system being that if you have two Chileans in a room you will have three political parties—would never be able to agree on one candidate, one program, to face the dictatorship. But they did. And they defeated the dictatorship.

Then the military immediately thought that though the Chilean people did it for the election they would never be able to hold together afterward. But they have. The various political parties put away all their differences to work together, to sustain Chile's fragile democracy. Of course, it will be impossible for the new government to punish all those who should be punished: The torturers won't be tortured; the rapists won't be raped; the murderers won't be killed. And people will have to understand that it is not out of revenge that we will rebuild our country but out of love and forgiveness. Though the memory must be kept alive, we will fail if we attempt to build anything on revenge and more violence.

Sometimes it seems that evil overcomes, that evil prevails. But it is not that way. Instances of evil are moments.

The instances of torture, of dictatorships and abuse, in Latin America are merely moments, aberrations?

No, unfortunately they are not aberrations. They are part of the Latin American reality.

Latin America is a very strange and complex place. It is the product of conquest and colonization, authoritarian European monarchies and indigenous theocracies. The mixture of monarchies and theocracies produced a certain mentality, culture, and way of thinking politically that is very authoritarian, hierarchical, and based on *caudillos*, or "chieftains."

During the independence wars, when our patriots tried to form what are now the republics, they attempted to imitate the republics of Europe by imitating their constitutions and laws. Unfortunately, when the time came to apply those constitutions to a people who had no democratic tradition whatsoever, the efforts failed. Very quickly, we had the *caudillos* once again. And later revolutions merely succeeded in replacing one *caudillo* with another.

Since the beginning of history there has been violence, war, slavery, and torture the world over. But there have also been people who see evil and want something better, who struggle toward this end, and who very often prevail. With them, humanity takes one step forward, a little step.

Indeed, though our revolutions have historically failed to create democratic nations, this pattern is now changing. It may have taken us five hundred years but we now have democracies all over the continent. They are fragile and conditional, but they are democracies all the same.

It is a terribly hard and slow process but this is what life is. We don't have anything better. This is our reality, our world. This is the journey.

As you have said, "to despair only benefits our enemies."
Absolutely. They win. They defeat you. What is the whole goal, the whole purpose of torture and terror? To paralyze the people. If we are paralyzed we are no longer a threat. And so we cannot yield, we cannot bend to the will of the enemy.

There are always people who are willing to give more than they receive. The problem is that goodness is silent and discreet. Evil is so noisy.

When I write, I express the darkness; it comes out all the time because that is part of reality. But I don't think my books are pessimistic. There is a lot of brutality but there is also solidarity and hope and sometimes even a little happy ending. I wish I could write only happy endings but life just doesn't work that way.

From Silence and Anger
to Love and Vision

INTERVIEW BY DAVID MONTENEGRO

18

Reprinted from David Montenegro, ed., *Points of Departure: International Writers on Writing and Politics* (Ann Arbor: University of Michigan Press, 1991), 110–126

Isabel Allende, born in 1942, was a journalist in Chile until 1975, when she left with her family for Venezuela. There unable to practice journalism, she supported herself with "odd jobs." In 1981 she began writing *The House of the Spirits*. Since that time she has made her living as a writer, though she prefers the title of storyteller, or narrator, to writer. She has one son and one daughter and now lives in the United States.

She is the author of three novels, *The House of the Spirits* (1982), *Of Love and Shadows* (1985), and *Eva Luna* (1988). Her most recent book is a collection of short stories, titled *The Stories of Eva Luna*, published in 1990. She has also written children's stories and several plays that have been successfully produced in Chile.

This interview took place in April 1988, in New York. In November 1990, Allende commented on the end of the Pinochet regime. These comments follow the interview.

" *May we begin with September 11, 1973? A member of Salvador Allende's family, his niece, what happened to you on the day of the coup?*

I think I should start by saying that the fact that I was a member of his family didn't make any difference. Millions of Chileans were affected by that day. There was much pain, much suffering, much fear. And my particular case is not very interesting because other people suffered much more.

Although I belonged to Allende's family, I was not living in his house. I had been with him a week before. We had lunch together. I loved and admired him, and I think he had a beautiful dream. But it's very selfish to talk about my own experience when it was the whole country that was experiencing such a terrible, historical event.

Well, I was a journalist at that time, and that day I got up very early in the morning, as I usually do. I prepared my children for school, like any day, and went to my office. I didn't realize there was a coup, I had no radio in my car, and I reached the center of Santiago. While driving, I saw that the streets were practically empty, except for military transports and trucks and soldiers everywhere. There was a sudden quietness in the air—something very strange. And since we had been hearing about the possibility of a military coup for several weeks—really months—I suspected that it would be that. But we had no experience of such a thing whatsoever; we had never seen that before in Chile. So I continued, and when I arrived at my office it was closed. There was nobody there. So I drove to a friend's house. She was married to a teacher, who would get up very early in the morning and go to his school to correct exams. When I got to her house she was waiting at the door, crying; she had heard on the radio about the coup after he had left, and she couldn't get in touch with him. So I said I would go and pick him up. I drove back to the center of the city where his school was, one of the oldest schools in Chile, the Instituto Nacional. I don't know how I could have crossed all those military barricades. Somehow I got through, but then we couldn't get out. From the school we saw all the bombing of the palace. We were alone in the school when we heard on the radio the last words of Allende. Then finally we could leave the building. Making a big detour, we got back to the upper part of the city where we lived. I couldn't get in touch with my house because it was practically impossible to call on the telephone. All the lines were busy. Maybe everybody was calling at that time. By two o'clock, more or less, I learned that Allende was dead and that many of my friends were in hiding; others were killed; others were in prison. But at that moment it was very difficult to realize exactly what was happening. It was a time of great confusion. And just rumors. On television we only had military marches and Walt Disney movies. It was so surrealistic, so strange.

> *Though there had been rumors of an approaching coup for months, you didn't expect one actually could happen?*

No, we didn't expect it to happen in that way. People talked about the possibility of a military coup because half the population in Chile was against Allende's government. Really the country was divided. The economic crisis provoked by the conspiracy and supported by the United States had really damaged the economy of the country greatly. And the opposition was asking Allende to resign. When I had lunch with him the week before, he said, "I'm not leaving the palace. The people put me there, and I'm not leaving until my constitutional term is at an end, unless the people ask me." But he was talking already—and everybody was talking—of a military coup. We thought, since the armed forces in Chile had a tradition of democracy, and we were not a banana republic, in our case things would be different. That's what people thought. Allende knew better. In fact, in his last speech he announced prophetically what was going to happen because he knew his enemy exactly, precisely. But I think that very few people knew what was going to happen. I was a journalist. I was informed. I had the information, but I never expected it to happen.

> *You are now a novelist. For you, is there a tension between being a novelist and being a journalist, between imagination and objective reporting? What brought you to make that transition?*

Well, that transition was made over many years. After I left my country, I couldn't work as a journalist. I spent many years in silence, and I think that that silence was important for me, in many ways. Literature needs distance and ambiguity. If you are in the middle of the hurricane, you can't talk about the hurricane, not in literature, at least. You can do it in journalism but not in literature. And maybe those years of silence, which were very, very painful for me—those first years of exile with that paralyzing feeling, for example, of being rootless, of having lost all that was dear to me—were important, necessary. And the transition was very smooth because of those years of silence.

There *is* a great difference between journalism and fiction, but I use the techniques of journalism for literature: interviews, reporting, research, working in the streets with the people, participating in a community, talking and listening. That's what a journalist does finally, and that's what I do in literature, too. So sometimes I don't know where the borderline between fiction and reality is. My second novel, *Of Love and Shadows*, is based on a case that actually happened in Chile. Everything in the book was researched; everything is true. But, of course, it's presented as fiction, as a novel, and now I cannot tell you which of the characters is invented and which belongs to reality. I can tell you exactly where the bullets were in the bodies and how the bodies were found. These things I can say are true as I described them. The basic plot is not real; it's fiction, and I don't know any longer how much I invented of the story.

On the other hand, I was an awful journalist. I was always putting myself in the middle of the news and never being objective. I was very emotional, so maybe that helped, too.

Did you feel something was missing in journalism? What does fiction add to the facts?

Interpretation only. In journalism you are not free to look at things from behind because you have to stick to facts. Nobody wants to listen to your interpretation of events. In fiction you feel free to interpret and to pull out the emotion, which, I think, is very much a part of reality. We are not reason only. Facts are never just what we see; there's always something behind, something beyond. And that is an invisible force—reactions, emotions that move us. I think one can put that in literature, and therefore sometimes fiction is more real than objective reporting.

You mentioned the need for ambiguity in fiction. Is this what you also bring to the facts as a novelist? Does fiction show the complexity of a story and of people more fully than reporting?

At least in fiction you have a multiple vision. In journalism you don't. In journalism you're allowed one page, and in that page you have to put everything—when, what, who, and so on. In a novel you can have six hundred pages if you want, so you can tell the events in a much more complex and complete way, I think.

> *You mentioned your silence during the first years of your exile. In* The House of the Spirits *Clara goes through a long period of silence. Is her silence related to your own? Also, what are the dangers of silence for a person?*

Sometimes, when I talk of silence, it's a silence of women, who have had to obey the rule of silence for centuries. Now, recently, we have a voice. We are a choir of different but harmonic voices, feminine voices. We are writing; we are giving our own interpretation of the world on a big scale for the first time in many centuries. Of course, women have done this before, but they have been very isolated, and they have had to pay a big price. The punishment for being different was solitude. Now writing and talking don't mean solitude because we are many women together doing this. Maybe in the case of Clara in the book, and in my case, there is the danger of submission and solitude.

But silence can also enrich you very much. Maya Angelou talks about a long period in her childhood when she was silent, and during those years she turned evil into action. All the evil that had happened to her—she was raped—was turned into a positive strength, into energy, because of those years of silence. She reinterpreted the world, recreated reality. In a way, I think, that happened to me, too. Not as dramatically as it happened to her, but those years of silence were very necessary. Now that I've been talking and talking and talking in these lectures and in these seminars and courses and teaching, I have the feeling that all my energy is gone out, so I've decided that I will stop all interviews, all lectures. I will only do those I've already agreed to do. I will finish these obligations on October 1. And then it's my time of silence, because I need silence. Without silence I can't write.

> *Silence puts the genie back in the lamp, in a sense?*

Yes. [*Laughs.*]

Chile is relatively exceptional for the amount of education available to women there. Until 1949, however, women could not vote in national elections. What is the progress of women's rights in Chile? And are there special difficulties for women in Latin American countries, where the culture is often paternalistic?

Patriarchal and *machista*. It's difficult to talk about Latin America as a whole. Every country is different. The law or the constitution is different in each; the race sometimes, the traditions, are somehow different. But more important than any other thing is social class. Everywhere in Latin America, if you belong to an upper-middle class of educated women, you are more or less equal to men—not equal, but more or less. But if you belong to the middle class or if you are a peasant or an Indian woman, the situation for you is much more difficult in every country.

In the case of Chile, women have traditionally been very strong, although the law does not help them at all. We have no abortion, no divorce. Always, the father is the caretaker of the children, except in those cases where a judge determines that the mother will have custody of them. Women are not protected by the law or are less protected in Chile than in other countries. That makes them very strong, because you have to be strong to survive.

Chile's a poor country. Men have to travel a lot to get jobs. In the life of a woman there can be many men, and with each man she can have a different child. Sometimes women don't marry; very often they don't marry. I'm talking about poor women. And they learn very quickly to be strong. They are self-denying, very generous, very . . . with a great sense of motherhood. I would say that Chilean women are great mothers. They are not so only to their own children but to other people's children, too, and to their men. They always consider men as being a little bit childish. For example, you will always find among poor women in Chile the excuses for men. When a man abandons them, when he drinks, when he beats them, they have the feeling that he's just like a grown-up child, and they are very forgiving.

But they are very strong; they have organized themselves at the base of the society to set up soup kitchens, schools, and to care for the old and children. Because the state, the government, doesn't do much for them. On the contrary, authority is always the enemy—especially in a military dictatorship, which is the most macho society that you could possibly imagine. You can't imagine anything more macho than a soldier with impunity. And that is the government we have. In the slums, in poor neighborhoods, everywhere, in factories, in their working places, they have organized themselves, for survival.

And that organization, I think, will be extremely interesting, when we have democracy back. Because, until the military coup in 1973, we have had a legal, a political, democracy in Chile, but it was not really a *social* democracy. The democracy was not at the base of the society; it was more a political structure than a reality. Now I think we will be able to build a real democracy because, for survival, the society has organized itself in a very democratic way. People vote in the slums to choose their representatives to take positions. They can't vote for a president. They are living in a dictatorship, and yet they vote on every decision at the base of the society. And that's something that women have done.

What other effects has the dictatorship had on women's organizations?

All social and political organizations in the country suffered greatly after the dictatorship began. Many were forbidden or eliminated. Women's organizations are part of that social and political process, so they have also had to suffer great repression. Women have been acting in the opposition very strongly. They are in the first line in the protests on the streets because they have nothing to lose. They have already lost everything. A man always has to take care of his job, if he has a job. Women have nothing, so they can risk everything. And they are usually very courageous.

The military dictatorship has taken away things that women had before, many things. There is a new morality, which I hate, a strange, old-fashioned puritanism, which is very hypocritical. It's very corrupt in its soul, I would say. And that has affected the women very much.

I think the worst part of the dictatorship is that it fragments society. Terror works, isolating people. It is effective, as long as you can't communicate, as long as you are isolated, as long as the society is fragmented. If you are a nuclear family sitting around in a small apartment watching TV, terror works. But if you can get together, unite with other people, talk, express your feelings out front, then you become strong. And that is what the dictatorship fears the most. Prisoners are isolated; people are isolated; gathering is forbidden; and that has affected the lives of women very much because, if women are not united, they are silent. They have had to become very strong in order to get together.

> *Can you give an example of this and also of the puritan fundamentalism you mentioned?*

Yes. For example, the very day of the coup, soldiers would cut the pants of women in the streets with scissors because they wanted ladies to wear skirts which was proper. All movies that were considered erotic were forbidden. There was great censorship and self-censorship. Books . . . *everything* was forbidden. And then on TV we had this sort of fundamentalist righteousness. That was the message. And at the same time you knew that they were torturing, raping, abusing, and that there was extreme corruption. It wasn't even hidden; it was *there*, obvious.

Women were supposed to stay at home and be quiet. How and when could they overcome silence? In the beginning it was very difficult, practically impossible. They were desperately trying to help their men, looking for the disappeared ones, burying the dead, visiting prisons—that's what women were doing, and surviving, working, trying to make a living for the children. Then, after this artificial economic boom that happened at the beginning of the dictatorship and lasted until sometime between 1981 and 1983, the economy collapsed. This economic boom occurred because the United States and other countries injected money into the country, and people could buy anything on credit. But when the minute came when they had to pay and when, added to repression, there was poverty, hunger, lack of jobs, well, the whole economy of the country collapsed.

Women then began protesting in the same way the opposition had protested against Allende—that is, by beating pots and pans. It's difficult to explain, but, when you have to go out in the street and protest in front of a soldier who has a gun, you have to be very brave. But if you are at home and you beat a pot and pan, and you know that your neighbor is doing the same and the other neighbor is doing the same and that it's impossible for the soldiers to stop it, because they can't bomb the city or shoot everybody inside their houses, that's a way of protesting that is somehow safe. And when you beat pots and pans and hear that everybody in your neighborhood is doing it, you know that you're not alone. Fragmentation of society doesn't work any longer. You become part of the community. You know that there are thousands feeling as you do, and so you become strong. And that's how the protesting started.

So the silence and isolation were broken?

Yes. And now everybody knows in Chile that eighty percent of the population is against the dictatorship. They talk about it freely in the streets, in the buses, everywhere. If you go to Chile as a tourist, you will hear it everywhere because now people dare to talk. They didn't five years ago.

In Chile censorship places strict limits on the media. Is there also an undefined censorship of the public that triggers self-censorship? When limits on speech are undefined, do people then become even more silent?

One of the main characteristics of this dictatorship is its ambiguity in certain aspects, which makes it even more dangerous. They can change the rules in one minute. What was allowed yesterday could be forbidden today, but what you did yesterday you have to pay for today. So the rules that were for yesterday do not keep you safe. For example, if you thought that you were allowed to speak against the government in your school yesterday and today the rule suddenly changes, you will be punished for what you did yesterday. That is very perverse because that means that people exert self-censorship to a great extent, I would say.

On the other hand, now there is a space that the opposition has won during these years, a certain space. For example, you can see very outspoken and very brave plays in theater. All books are now permitted. They're not published in Chile, but you can buy *Missing*, *Labyrinths*, Antonio Skármeta's books, my books. You can buy them everywhere; you can read everything. There's no censorship for books. Why? Because books are very expensive, and only very few people can read. But nothing is permitted on television because that's a great mass media. Very little is published in most newspapers but a lot in two newspapers and some magazines that the opposition has been able to keep alive. Why? Because they reach only a few thousand people, and the government believes that they are not really significant. That is an underestimation because they have been very important in the resistance. *But* the rule can change any minute. And the directors of any of those magazines can be killed any day or put in prison. And this has happened during these years. So you have to be extremely courageous to say: Okay, I'll go on and do it, even if I know that tomorrow I will have to pay the price. So it's a very subtle line, and the line moves all the time; the rules change all the time.

Arbitrary rules?

Absolutely. And, with absolute impunity, they can do whatever they want.

So people feel cornered, surrounded?

No. You learn how to live with that. I mean, after fifteen years, there's a whole generation that has been brought up in that situation. They don't know what it is to live in another world.

People have *learned.* They have learned through clues, a sort of special language. Chile's an extraordinary country. During these fifteen years of oppression and terror, there are many groups of people—although groups are forbidden—that are studying its own reality, studying the country, studying our history, studying the dictatorship, preparing for the future, working on an intellectual and, I would say, also emotional, level for the future. So I have great hope that Chile will be a great country after the dictatorship. We've learned a lot about ourselves during these years. And the dictatorship has not been able to destroy those essential values that were always with us. Even if the government is a dictatorship, the society's democratic, multipartied, tolerant. It's only a group that was always intolerant that now has power; they were always brutal. We were afraid to see it. Those fascists were *always* in the society, but we—as people who are very tolerant—just lived with that. And we will continue living with that. And I think that, when democracy has come to Chile, there will be a spirit of forgiveness. Not forgetting, we will shout to

have justice, but I am afraid that most people who have been so brutal during these years will probably be forgiven.

*As a writer, how have these fifteen years affected you? Is there an
evolution in your work parallel to the political events?*

I don't know. It's very difficult for me to talk about my own writing
because I can't explain it. It happens as if in a state of trance. I've
written three novels already, and always the first impulse to write is
a deep emotion that has been with me for many years. I need years
to internalize it. I recreate the pain or the anger or the love. Writing
for me is always a very emotional process. So it's difficult for me to
explain.

Sometimes I'm asked: Do you belong to the post-Boom? I don't
know what that is. I never learned about it or studied anything about
literature. And I don't even care to. I only want to communicate. I
want to tell people what I think is true. I want to change the world. I
know it's very ambitious and very pretentious, but that's what I want
to do. I don't like anything else but that.

*In what way does writing change people or change the society we live
in? How does the writer help?*

Sometimes a writer is a foreteller of the future, has a prophetic gift,
has the ability to speak for others who have been kept in silence.
That's our job. I think it's a gift; it's something that simply happens to
certain people. And if you have that, you have to use it. I'm aware
that, in this world where the majority is illiterate, where only a few
people can buy books and only a very small minority has the habit of
reading, a book has very little impact. But sometimes it's a seed
planted in fertile soil, and you never know what the effect will be or
when you will be able to measure the effect.

Take the books of Charles Dickens. They told people about children working in factories. And many years later people realized that
child labor was obscene and perverse. Or at a certain moment a
group of writers talked and wrote about slavery. It was a seed planted
in the souls of people. And all of a sudden we were able to reach an
agreement; humankind was able to reach an agreement against slavery and say: This is obscene and perverse. I think we have the ca-

pacity to reach that agreement about war, for example. And I think in some years we will be able to look back at ourselves and say: How was that possible? We were building weapons for peace. It's like fucking for virginity. I mean, how could we be so stupid? Or we are going to say: Many years ago people tortured each other. That was obscene and perverse. How could we do that? And we will have the same reactions we have now against slavery. I think that a book can defy the passage of time and somehow change the mind of certain people, and that has an effect, if a small one, but it can grow.

I know some books that have changed *my* life. And if I can do that for one person, I have done enough. I received a letter the other day from a man who is eighty-six years old. He said, "I've read your books, and I've changed. It's not too late for me." Well, I've done something then. I mean, if by talking or writing I can reach a young person and tell him, "*You* have the responsibility as much as I have it of changing the world"—because we don't like the world as it is— and he believes me, he wants to do this with me, well, I've done enough. A lot.

> *When you write a novel, you have to live with your characters for a long time. How do you feel about them? Do you feel differently about each of them?*

First of all, I have the feeling that I don't invent them. I don't create them; they are there. They are somewhere in the shadows, and when I start writing—it's a very long process; sometimes it takes years to write a book—little by little they come out of the shadow into the light. But when they come into the light, they are already people. They have their own personalities, their clothes, their voices, their textures, their smells. I don't invent them; somehow they are there. They always *were* there. I mean, half of those persons were very easy because they belong to my family, so I just had to recreate something that had existed or exists.

In *Of Love and Shadows* the story is real. I needed the characters to tell the story, but those characters could be real; maybe they are. And they were always there, waiting for me to bring them out into the light. The book begins with a small paragraph. I don't remember it by heart, but it's something like: This is a story of a man and a woman who loved each other so deeply that it saved them from a bare existence. I know that's possible—that a great love can save you from a bare existence. I know that there are courageous people who will risk their lives for truth and justice. I know that those people in that book, Irene and Francisco, were always there; I just had to take them out of the shadow, as I took that horrible plan of murder out of the shadow into the story.

But my third novel, *Eva Luna*, is a very joyful, extravagant tale. It's like *The Arabian Nights*, a story of a storyteller who saves her life by telling stories. And Eva Luna's character was always there. I know that the character was within me. She doesn't resemble me; it's not my biography. I'm not her. But somehow she was inside me, as if I were a glove and she were the hand inside the glove. By writing, the hand got out of me and existed by itself.

There's a character, for example, in that book called Riad Halabí. Riad Halabí is an Arab. He's completely invented, if you could say invented. That is, I didn't have a live model for him. First of all, I didn't have to invent the name; the name came to me, and when I wrote Riad Halabí immediately he appeared, and he had a cleft lip. Why was he like that, I don't know, because when I saw him I said: I don't *want* him to be like that. I want him to be handsome because he will have a very important role in this book. He's very important for Eva Luna, so I want him to be handsome. But he was not. He was ugly. I tried to change him, but I couldn't because he was already there. He was a presence in my house.

So that's my relationship with my characters—very strange and very powerful. At the beginning of the novel sometimes they are ambiguous, but by the end they are so real that my children play with the idea that they are living in the house. And we talk about them as if they were part of the family.

> *Some of the characters still live, in a sense, after the book is finished. What, for example, would Irene from* Of Love and Shadows *be doing now or Alba from* The House of the Spirits?

All of them are making love. [*Laughs.*] I'm joking. That's the happy ending for me [*Laughs.*] Some characters live with me, like Clara, like Professor Leal in *Of Love and Shadows*, like Irene, Alba, Eva Luna. They travel with me somehow.

> *Are there any of your characters you would rather not have imagined? You mentioned at the end of* The House of the Spirits *that Colonel Garcia is part of the whole, implying that he had to be included.*

Yes. I think that all the characters have to be there. Some of them I don't love, but I know that they are necessary. And I always try to be fair with them. At least, if I don't like them, I try to understand them. And that's what I try to do with people in real life, too. I try to understand why people think and act the way they do.

In *Of Love and Shadows* I had one character that, when I finished the book, I felt was a stereotype—Gustavo Morante, Irene's fiancé. I hate militarists, and anyone who wears a uniform is scary for me. So I put in him all my prejudices. And when I finished the book I realized that was not a character—that was not a person. That was only all the bad things I thought about soldiers. So I looked for a real model, for a real militarist, someone I could learn to understand, maybe to love in certain aspects. I found someone, and I interviewed him for weeks until I got out of him . . . I think I got his soul, the way he moves, the way he acts.

> *What did you find when you actually interviewed him over that long period of time? What did you discover as a writer about this person?*

I discovered that there is a code of honor, a twisted and perverse code of honor, but it *is* a code. And I learned to understand why they act that way and how their brains work. I learned about all these ridiculous ceremonies, this childish attitude toward the world. These are people who have been trained for death and destruction yet think of themselves as saviors, as owners of the truth, as righteous people. I learned also that they don't act that way—most of them—out of being bad or perverse themselves; it's the system that perverts them, that trains them to think, to not see reality as it is but to interpret it in a perverse way. For a militarist the goal justifies the means, and that's perverse in its very soul. I don't believe in that. I believe that the goal is determined by the process. If you want to have peace, for example, you have to act peacefully. You can't have a war for peace. If you want to be loved by someone, you have to be loving. If you want someone to be violent, then you must accept violence somehow. It's a process. For the militarist it's not. The goal determines everything. And I think *that's* the greatest perversion of that system.

There's another thing that is also terrible about these people: obedience, blind obedience. You have impunity because you are not responsible. Someone else is responsible, someone who is above you.

And then there is the way they use words. Great words that for me have no meaning for them are everything, like—in Spanish, the word is *patria*—fatherland. Fatherland. What is *patria*? *Patria* is people. It's not a territory; it's not a flag; it's not a childish ceremony of soldiers walking in a straight line. That's not fatherland. Fatherland is a language, a tradition. We are all living on the same planet. We have no more land, no more territory than this planet. And we share it. So who cares if the boundary is here or there? Who cares about boundaries, about nationalities, about ideologies? That is crazy, absolutely crazy. And *that* is the perversion of the system. These people are brainwashed to think that that's important. They make wars, and they've been killing each other for centuries for this illusion of having control of a certain part of the globe which belongs to everybody. They will never own anything else but a little piece of this globe, and we *all* own it. We are all part of the same planet and the same human race. I think it's so childish.

> *Your title* Of Love and Shadows *brings to mind Carl Jung, who says the "shadow"—as he calls the capacity to commit atrocities—is collective. How do you react to this? What do you think?*

Yes, I think there is evil in every one of us, in the same way that there is good in every one of us, and therefore in the world, in the society. And there are moments in history and moments in our lives when evil seems to have control of everything. That happens during very violent processes or during a war. The Nazis are a very good example. The dirty war, or what has been called "the process," in Argentina is another. Those are moments in which evil seems to have control over everything. But I think that, just as we have that evil part in us, we have the capacity to control it. And there is a great force that can be opposed to that evil: love. You have to be loved when you are a child to overcome that evil. And you have to love all the time to be able to relate to other people in the world. *Love* is a word that has been so ill-treated that it sounds campy, kitsch, sentimental. You can't talk about it without sounding like a Christian or— I don't know what. Or people laugh, scorn you, when you talk about it. But in my life—I'm forty-seven—I have experienced this force, this energy, this positive strength which love is in such a strong way that it's only fair that I talk about it all the time and write about it all the time.

Of Love and Shadows was meant to be a book about death and torture, repression, crime, horror. And when I started researching and interviewing and talking with the people, the victims of that crime, I realized that I couldn't afford being angry or feeling hate because they didn't, because that was a story of love, of solidarity, of generosity. For one torturer you have a thousand people who have risked their lives for freedom, for justice, to help each other. So how could I talk only about the bad, about the evil, if in confronting that evil was so much good, so much solidarity, so much love? You have to talk about love. And that has been the experience of my life.

I didn't have a father. My father disappeared when I was so young that I have no memories of him. But I had a mother, and she loved me in such a way that I have felt love in my life always. I've always had men in my life that loved me; my children love me, my friends. I feel that I'm a good person because I've been loved. So I want other people to be good because they are loved. Evil is just lack of affection. In those moments evil takes power, takes control.

> At the end of The House of the Spirits *Alba says, "And now I seek my hatred and cannot seem to find it. I feel its flame going out as I come to understand the existence of Colonel García. . . ."*

Yes. Hate, in my case, and fear are paralyzing emotions. But I've been able to overcome them when I've tried. Not before. And those years of silence were years of fear and hate—and anger. I think that anger is good. It's somehow above emotion. It brings action, if you can control it. If you can't control it, it can destroy you.

I think that this love, this understanding, is the only possibility we have to build a different world, a more gentle world, a more entertaining world, a more merciful society. If we give back all the violence that we have received, that only creates more violence. We can't torture the person who has tortured us because then it's a never-ending chain of fear and hate and anger and violence. We have to stop it because we are better. And I think that that is the great difference.

This is not something that I invented or I have felt myself. I learned it from other people who have suffered much more than I, who have *really* suffered, and those people don't have any wish for revenge. They want justice. They want to keep alive the memory of the Holocaust, for example, or of what happened in Argentina. They want the disappeared ones back. They want at least to be able to bury the corpses. They want graves so they can go there and pray—at least that. They want justice. They don't want to forget, but they want to forgive. They are not willing to kidnap the children of the kidnappers or torture the torturer or kill the criminal. No. Because they are better. And that's a great lesson. They are better. And I think the good ones are going to win finally.

> These atrocities, what do they do to the human voice? When you know of such things, is there any loss of confidence in language, since language seems to promise the best things for people, the ability to build, to envision the future, to make changes? When you describe a coup, for example, in your chapter "The Terror" in The House of the Spirits or, in Of Love and Shadows, the discovery of the bodies in the cave, is there an undercurrent that brings language down?

No, I think it gives energy to language because at that moment one has the illusion that maybe by putting it in words it won't be repeated, that you will register history and therefore keep alive the memory and avoid the same mistake or the same evil. Of course, that's not the case, but sometimes it works. And, at least in my case, I have the feeling that language is so powerful that just by saying things you can provoke them or induce them.

Eva Luna—and, in a way, Clara does it too in *The House of the Spirits*—narrates the world. She has the feeling that by writing things down and narrating them she makes them real, that then they exist.

There is an Indian tradition in some tribes in South America in which the Indians don't name certain things because they believe when they pronounce the word it becomes real. Don't name evil. Or name what is good to keep alive what is good. Language has a tremendous power, I think. So I don't feel that there is any contradiction between evil, between these atrocities, and the fact that we have to tell about them.

> *What about the younger generation who have never experienced the democratic tradition in Chile? Has the dictatorship created a deep freeze for cultural and political life?*

It's like a pressure cooker. The lid is tight, but underneath, you know something is boiling. Young people who have been brought up in the dictatorship, and don't know democracy, can dream of it and invent it, imagine it. Most of the letters I receive are from very young people, people who couldn't be aware of democracy as it was when we had it because now they are nineteen, twenty, and they were very small children at the time of the coup fifteen years ago. But it is young people who are protesting, young people in the universities and the schools. They are very subversive; they are irreverent. They defy terror. So I think there is hope for that generation, great hope. Maybe that generation will overcome all the weaknesses and errors of the old political leaders in Chile. And then, as I pointed out earlier, there is democracy operating in the society, real in everyday life.

> *In your books you seem to suggest a moderate political course. For example, in* Of Love and Shadows *Professor Leal goes to collect his son from the revolutionaries in the south. In* The House of the Spirits *there's a similar episode. Would it be correct to say that you believe a moderate course is the best way to achieve the return of democracy in Chile?*

I think that's the case in Chile. But I have great respect for people who take arms against the status quo. I have great respect for those people who can't wait any longer. And there are certain moments in the history of humankind, in the history of certain nations, when the only alternative is violence. Take a look at the history of Nicaragua, for example. Nothing could be expected out of moderation. They have been invaded by the United States thirteen times in the twentieth century. They have had a tradition of dictatorships propped up by the CIA. How could they have anything else but a revolution?

Chile tried to do something very original in Allende's government. We tried to build up socialism within the democratic constitution, without changing the constitution. Allende was elected in popular elections, free elections, and he tried, within the constitution, to make profound reforms that would really mean a social, political, and economic revolution in the country, without eliminating any of the liberties, any of the rights, that the constitution guarantees for any citizen in Chile. That was very original; that was a beautiful dream. And he could have achieved it, but the size of his enemy was too great.

I think that Chile has the tendency to moderation historically, so maybe we will get out of this dictatorship without violence, without more violence. Of course, we have had fifteen years of violence. Therefore, I respect the guerrillas in Chile, armed if Pinochet doesn't leave. If the plebiscite doesn't change anything, if he stays in power for another eight years, we will have a civil war in Chile. That's unavoidable, absolutely unavoidable. Violence will become greater and greater every day.

What do you think the prospects are that he will leave?

I don't think he will leave willingly, that just because he's a nice grandfather he will decide to go and take care of his roses. No, that will not happen. The militarists only understand the language of force, of violence. That's a language they know; they don't know any other. So they will have to be forced out of power. But there are many ways of doing it, not only with weapons. There's a tremendous moral strength, moral force, growing in Chile. And there comes a moment when you can't oppose that with any army.

On the other hand, everywhere in the world the image of Pinochet and the dictatorship is awful. Even in the United States now. And, in spite of Reagan's administration, in spite of the CIA, people don't want Pinochet anymore. Of course, they would love to prolong the right-wing, conservative, military regime, but not with Pinochet. You can't defend Pinochet any longer. He's just awful. So there are many different forces that are conspiring against him at this point. And he's not immortal. He will also die. I hope that he will die very soon.

Two other people, Chileans of a different type: Gabriela Mistral and Pablo Neruda—what do they mean to you?

Those two poets, and some others—I'm talking about poets, not novelists—have been the voice of the people in Chile, I don't know why, but they have been able to interpret the people much better than any other artist or intellectual. Personally, I relate much better to Neruda because in Gabriela Mistral there is metaphysical pain. She's always in pain. She's a solitary person, defeated by pain. And I'm a very sensuous person, usually very happy. I'm very energetic. For me very rapidly pain is transformed into something else. So I relate much better to Pablo Neruda because he has a very sensuous voice and a political voice.

When I left my country I could take only twenty kilos in my suitcase in the airplane. I took some clothes, a small bag of dirt from my garden, some photographs—of my grandmother and my grandfather and friends—and a book by Pablo Neruda, the only book that I took with me. And now fifteen years later, when I recently moved to San Francisco, I brought the same book with me.

Whenever I need to recover my landscape, the feel and smell of my country, I read Neruda. Somehow he represents it, synthetically. I don't know how. He describes Chile by saying, "It's a long petal of snow and wine." A few words: *petal, snow, wine*—that's it.

Which book of his was it that you brought with you?

His *Obras completas*, but it was not his complete works because it was a very old edition. The last work is not there. I bought that afterward. But I like the book very much. I've read it so many times, I can find the pages in darkness. I can find *the* poem I'm looking for.

Is there a particular poem that is most important to you? For example, Canto general?

No, some lines. It's more than a poem; it's a line or word, an image or metaphor that all of a sudden opens a window to me. Sometimes it's the name of a tree that I had forgotten, and, when I read the word and I name the tree, the tree appears. The power of words; they make it real.

> *You mentioned that one of the things you brought with you was soil from your garden. One of the characters does the same in* Of Love and Shadows, *who closes with the words: "We will return. . . ." What are your hopes about returning and what are your feelings in exile?*

I'm sure that I will return. I'm younger than Pinochet. And I will return to a wonderful country. We will be living a very special moment of our history. It will be a time of confusion and making many mistakes but also of creating, and it will be really a renaissance of everything. It will be a very joyful moment to know that the country has changed very much, and I have changed very much. I don't expect to go back to the past. I will return to the future. We have to invent the future in Chile.

My feelings toward exile are very ambiguous. On one hand, I have this nostalgia for my country that I'm not aware of until I'm confronted with something—for example, a movie, a book, a name, a person, a photograph, a memory. Sometimes it's just something so stupid. For instance, at one time I went to Texas and happened to look at the flag, which is exactly like the Chilean flag. When I saw the flag it had this tremendous impact on me, and I said to myself: But you're stupid; it's only a piece of cloth; it doesn't mean anything. And yet it does.

So I have this nostalgia, but I also am very happy to have lived these years out of my country. Now I don't consider myself Chilean only. I have the feeling that I can speak for Latin America, that Latin America is my house, my home, and I have a responsibility to care for everything that happens on that continent to everyone, not only to Chileans. Our circumstances are very much the same. We have five hundred years of exploitation and colonization in common. We have the same Catholic religion, Spanish and Portuguese colonization, that heritage of Spanish and Portuguese cultures. We have the

Indian cultures; we have the African. We have the same demons and the same nightmares and the same dreams. So I think that I've learned a lot. Before I thought that Chile was the beginning and the end of the world. Now I know it's not.

AFTERWORD
November 1990

Allende: The election was held in December 1989. Since March of 1990 there has been a democratic government in Chile. But the old military and economic structure created by the dictatorship of Pinochet remains practically intact. So the democratic government must be very cautious. They can't provoke this structure, these people, because they are there, waiting in the shadows.

Immediately after the election, censorship ended, and there was a great sense of freedom, some sort of river of strength welling up, especially in the arts. Many writers had returned to Chile right after the plebiscite—José Donoso, for example, who has just won Chile's highest literary award.

I think, during all those years of the dictatorship, culture continued with astounding tenacity. In spite of all, it was impossible to destroy. Even though they could not publish or show their work, writers went on writing, painters went on painting. Now there is a kind of renaissance spirit, a very joyful spirit in Chile. This renaissance I can only compare with the time of Salvador Allende's government, when, even though there were difficulties economically, socially, and politically, there was a real renaissance of the arts and of folklore. People were in a very creative mood. People were in the streets creating things. Chile is a very creative country.

A Sacred Journey Inward

INTERVIEW BY ALBERTO MANGUEL

19

Reprinted from *Queen's Quarterly* 99, no. 3 (Fall 1992): 621–626

Although she was a professional writer before the 1973 military coup that would forever change her life, Isabel Allende did not find her true "writer's voice" until she had endured a long exile from her native Chile. In conversation with Alberto Manguel, the novelist reflects on her work and on her recent visit to the country that banished her twenty years ago.

" *She was born in Peru, spent most of her life in Chile, settled in Venezuela for thirteen years, and now lives in California, in a town called Peacock Gap. To most North Americans, this small, quick, bright-eyed woman represents the confusion of countries and traditions encapsulated in the label "Latin American." Her best-known novel,* The House of the Spirits, *has been reviewed again and again as a story about the whole continent. In her own mind, however, Isabel Allende is firmly Chilean, and her stories, however universal they may seem, are firmly rooted in the terrible history of her country over the past two decades.*

Before the CIA-supported coup of 1973, in which Allende's uncle, President Salvador Allende, was murdered, politics was not her concern.

I lived in a bourgeois neighborhood and did all the things a bourgeois wife was supposed to do. I was also a journalist and a playwright, but the social reality of my country was something ghostly, seen at a distance. My social class was strongly opposed to Salvador. The only poster celebrating his victory was in my house. And that because he was a relative.

Allende does not consider her work before the coup as "real writing."

Writing is an inward journey, a sacred journey. Playwriting is something external, a collaboration. You put words on paper, but it is the others—the actors, the director—who bring them to life.

This is why she hasn't accepted offers to publish her plays.

They belong to other people, those who created them with me, on stage.

> *One of her most successful plays,* The Ambassador, *deals with the kidnapping of a diplomat by a group of* guerrilleros. *The two opposed ideologies confront one another for the first time, recognize their human faces and, in the end, through dialogue, become friends. Then the* guerrilleros *are forced to kill the ambassador. Allende laughs when I suggest that, at least in North America,* The Ambassador *would not be considered an "apolitical" play.*

The coup of September 11 was the turning point in my life. Before that I was an adolescent, a little girl, even as the mother of two. Twenty-four hours later I understood that my childhood was over. The reign of terror started, and I felt I could no longer be indifferent to my surroundings. When the curfew ended (the army had forbidden anyone to go out into the street) the person who walked out of my house was another woman. I had friends who had been arrested. We began to record what was happening, getting the information out to Europe, to the States, the names of those captured by the police, and the names of the torturers. We became our memory.

I had no idea that what I was doing was dangerous. I hadn't realized that even using a certain word, "compañero," for instance, meant that you could be arrested. I was told that unless I left the country, I'd be thrown into prison. I fled to Venezuela. At first I thought it would be only for a few weeks. But soon we realized it would be much longer than that. My husband at the time, even though he was not a socialist, opposed the military dictatorship. When he saw that I couldn't return, he left as well, bringing my children with him. He became an exile not as much out of political conviction as out of love for me. I will never forget that.

The exile lasted thirteen years. When Allende left Chile, she took with her a handful of soil from her garden; in Venezuela she placed the soil in a pot and planted seeds in it. The Chilean soil became strangely symbolic of her own life because, she says, in Venezuela, that foreign country, her writer's voice came to her for the first time.

In exile, in an alien place, you have to observe carefully, and you see things that the natives no longer see. Being an exile is maybe the best training for a writer.

On January 8, 1981, Allende sat down at her typewriter and began the story that was to become The House of the Spirits.

Since then, I have started all my books on January 8. I look forward to that day with joy and anxiety, and ritually lay out all my things— my cup of coffee, paper—and start. I always think I know what I'm going to write, and I'm always wrong. A first sentence appears, and the story flows on its own.

The House of the Spirits *became an international best-seller.*

I can't understand why. It's been flying round the world for eight years now, and there are still readers who write to me and tell me how it has touched them. Maybe it's because I speak of emotions that are in us all. All our lives are heroic lives, even the smallest. And all our lives are part of a huge universal epic from which our collective memory draws its dreams. And that universal flow explains the complicity between writers and their readers. Because the writer asks questions which the reader knows have no answers. It is because of the questions that literature is so powerful. It is because of the questions that we read.

Allende's second novel was Of Love and Shadows, *which did not meet with the same success.*

Maybe because it was a plainer, political book. But the man who is now my husband read it and fell in love with me because of it. So I owe much to this book.

Of Love and Shadows *is a fierce indictment of the Chilean military government's crimes.*

I wanted to articulate an anger that was burning me, an anger I still feel. I think of that book as a long reportage. I researched every detail very carefully, in fact I had started collecting my material as early as 1978. So the story was there. But many details were, of course, unavailable.

For instance, in the section dealing with the murder of several Chilean workers in one of the mines, Allende had found most of the circumstances of the event, but no details about the actual discovery of the bodies. The government had sealed up the mine, but the information about the crime had leaked, and the Catholic Church made it public. Allende invented the character of a priest who, after hearing of the murders in confession, sets off on his motorcycle, enters the mine, photographs the bodies, and then delivers the photographs to his bishop. Allende's mother read the manuscript and complained that this was unrealistic. Allende, however, left the section untouched. Of Love and Shadows *was published in 1982.*

Two years ago, after Pinochet stepped down, Allende returned to Chile.

A man called me at my mother's house and asked if he could come and see me. When he came, he told me he was a priest. He was the one who had gone on his motorcycle, photographed the bodies, and delivered the photos to his bishop. Only the bishop and this priest knew what had happened. How, he wanted to know, had I been able to find out the truth? Well, I couldn't tell him. I had invented it all, every detail. Or at least I thought I had. I suppose that, if you tell a story exactly as you feel it, truth will take over. I thought that writing creates reality. It's the other way round: reality dictates your writing. Literature happens to you, like falling in love. Or catching a cold.

Her third novel, Eva Luna, *is almost autobiographical.*

Eva's story is invented, of course, but I am Eva. Eva is the woman I want to be. We are so different, in every way but one: we both tell stories. But she is my dreamself.

Allende's dreamself makes up stories, but in the novel none of the stories (with one exception) are transcribed.

So people started asking me what those stories were. At last I decided I would publish a book of the stories of Eva Luna. I selected twenty-four, and then, because I didn't like the number, dropped one. I'm glad I did, because it was not a good story.

The Stories of Eva Luna are wonderful in every sense: because they are beautifully crafted and because they look upon the wonders of the world, the world as a magical place.

Novels are their contents, they are what you tell. Short stories are how you tell them, they are much more difficult to craft. In Chile I'm called a "storyteller" as opposed to "writer." "Writer" is a label reserved for men.

The male writers of Latin America have, by and large, refused to acknowledge Allende's importance.

I don't belong to their club. I have met most of them—Vargas Llosa, Fuentes, García Márquez—but I don't know them well. My friends in the literary world are women, minorities: black women, Latino women, Chinese-American women, native women. In Latin America women are not respected. You have to make twice as much effort as a man for half the recognition. And if you are a writer, ten times as much effort. In a male-dominated society, women are not allowed to have a creative role. They can be interpreters—singers, dancers, actors, they can play an instrument—but they are not seen as composers, writers, painters. If a woman had written García Márquez's brilliant *Love in the Time of Cholera*, her novel would have been branded mushy, over-sentimental, full of sweet female sentimentality. But because it's García Márquez, a male writer, it's all right. Only men can afford the luxury of being sentimental. And if a woman writes historical works, or political works, then they are labeled "pamphlets." The male literary community in Latin America would be delighted if women wrote only cookbooks, children's books, poetry—but let them not fuck around with the rest, with "real" literature. They, the men, are the only ones allowed to write novels, even novels about women. And when they do it, they do it terribly. Except Jorge Amado. As a writer, he understands women. But the others have no idea what female sexuality is.

> *Allende's own depictions of female characters are powerful and convincing.*

But I had to learn about myself late in life. I was brought up a Catholic, a bourgeois. I never even heard the word "sex" until I was seventeen. The first naked man I saw was my husband. And let me tell you, it was a shock! And then I had to learn that my sexual needs were legitimate, that it was all right to seek my own pleasure. Let me tell you something that happened to me recently in San Diego. I was signing at a bookstore, and a little old lady came up to me, blinking at me through two-inch-thick glasses. "I have a question," she said. "All those love scenes you describe, did you really experience them or did you make them up?" I looked at her and I didn't have the courage to disappoint her. So I told her, "Of course I made them all up! These things never happen like that!" "Thank God!" she said, and shook my hand.

> *I had corresponded with Allende over the past few years, but we had never met. I am surprised by her energy, elegance, and sense of humor. But the book tour (promoting* The Stories of Eva Luna*) is exhausting her.*

I love it, but I will be glad when it's over. I want to get back to my new novel [begun, like all the others, on January 8] which I feel I've abandoned. A novel is like a tapestry; the design reveals itself as it

progresses, but you have to keep at it or the design vanishes, the co-
herence is gone. Now, while I'm here in Toronto, the voices keep on
talking and I'm not there to take them down. I feel like a traitor when
I'm not writing.

NOTE

Alberto Manguel is author of the prize-winning novel *News from a Foreign Country Came.*

An Overwhelming Passion to Tell the Story

INTERVIEW BY ELYSE CRYSTALL, JILL KUHNHEIM, AND
MARY LAYOUN

20

From *Contemporary Literature*, vol. 33, no. 4 (Winter 1992): 585–600. Reprinted by permission of the University of Wisconsin Press.

On March 14, 1991, Isabel Allende gave a talk at the University of Wisconsin in Madison on politics and literature in Latin America. We had planned our interview with her for that same day. But the indomitable weather of late winter in the Midwest intervened with a snowstorm that kept Allende in the Chicago airport until just before her talk. What follows, then, is a telephone interview with Isabel Allende, conducted some two months later when she returned from a national speaking tour to her home in San Rafael, California.

Allende took up residence in the United States some four years ago, after almost fifteen years in exile in Caracas, Venezuela. Born in Lima, Peru, where her mother and father—a Chilean diplomat—lived at the time, she returned with her mother to Santiago, Chile, when she was a small child. She grew up there, spending much of her time in the home of her maternal grandparents—Isabel Barros Moreira and Agustín Llona, whose fictional "spirits" reside in her first novel, *The House of the Spirits*. She lived as well in Bolivia, Europe, and the Middle East, where her diplomatic family was posted. At the outbreak of the 1967 war, she left Lebanon for Santiago, where she finished school and worked for the

United Nations Food and Agriculture Organization. Later she worked as a journalist and interviewer for Chilean television, wrote for magazines (including a women's column—"Civilice a su troglodita" ["Civilize your troglodyte"]—in which she developed a fine comic voice), and wrote plays and children's stories. In 1970 her paternal uncle and godfather, Salvador Allende, was elected president of Chile. The overthrow of his democratic government in a bloody military coup three years later marked a turning point for Allende. "I think I divide my life before that day and after that day," she has said. Although she remained in Chile for the first few months after the coup seized power, her efforts on behalf of some of the thousands of people the junta had imprisoned and tortured endangered her own safety. And so she left Chile for Venezuela. It was there that she wrote her first four books: *Casa de los espíritus / The House of the Spirits* (Plaza & Janés, 1984; Knopf, 1985); *De amor y de sombra / Of Love and Shadows* (Plaza & Janés, 1984; Knopf, 1987); *Eva Luna* (Knopf, 1988); and *Stories of Eva Luna* (Macmillan, 1991).

There is a noticeable lacuna in the interview that struck all three of us—that is between Allende's account of her relation to the political and social situations in Latin America and of her relation to writing itself. Repeatedly citing her distance from what is happening in Chile and in Latin America, Allende defines her writing as a (genealogical) remembering-to-forestall-death. She tells the story of the beginning of her first novel, *The House of the Spirits*, as a letter written from exile in Venezuela to her ailing grandfather in Chile. One hundred years old, he had decided to die and so stopped eating. Allende began writing to him to demonstrate that the "spirits" of their life together—of her grandmother, of her grandfather himself, of her uncles and aunts—would not be forgotten and, in the forgetting, "die." It is to and for this familial community that Allende insists her writing is primarily directed. In an attempt, perhaps, to avert a too-easy bracketing of her work as "political," Allende insists on its "literariness." The extent, however, to which these are not necessarily two separate and distinct categories is perhaps most evident in her fiction itself.

❝ *We thought that, instead of beginning with a question about what you have written, we'd start by asking you about what you haven't*

written—things you haven't written either because you haven't had
the opportunity or because you haven't felt able to.

Well, I began writing very late in my life. I was nearly forty. And I
have the feeling that I've wasted forty years of my life; there are so
many things that I want to write about, so many stories that I want to
tell. I never have the problem of sitting in front of a blank page and
not knowing what I'm going to write; it's usually the other way
around. I have to cut a lot. I have to make a choice finally. And when
I make a choice about a story that I want to write, I always have the
feeling that there's so much left that is *there*, waiting. So there's a lot
that I would like to write about. In general, it's not I who choose the
story; the story chooses me. In a way, it isn't just the characters or the
plot; it's there in the air. And it's knocking at my door. And I just can't
refuse it any longer and have to sit down and write.

Are there other genres that you've been interested in exploring, or do
you feel that you're going to continue working with narrative?

I wrote theater plays when I was young and I loved it; I loved to
work in a team. I also loved the fact that you're not really responsible, that you can always share the responsibility. And if it doesn't
work, you can always blame the director or somebody. When I
write a novel or a short story, I can't blame anybody. I've also tried
children's stories when my kids were small; I told them stories every
night. It was wonderful to be trained for that. Now I think that it's
too late for me. Maybe I'll do that with my grandchildren, but for the
time being I don't have anyone to tell stories to—children, I mean—
so I'm not doing that anymore. I wrote humor for years and I think
that is the most difficult genre of all. I don't think I can try that again;
it's really difficult. I've never tried poetry and I don't think I will.

Do you read poetry?

Yes. I'm very fond of Pablo Neruda. But I'm not good at that. A poet
is someone who can say in six lines what takes me six hundred
pages.

You said earlier that there is so much to write and you feel the need to
make certain choices—on what do you base those choices?

Passion. The overwhelming passion to tell a story. Usually a novel is a very long process. You have to be sitting there in front of your type-writer or your computer for months in a row, sometimes years. So you really have to be very committed; you have to be in love with the story. Without that passion, that love, you just can't do it. I can't. I'm a hard worker and I have discipline, but I need the passion. I know that all of my books have come out of a very strong emotion that has been with me for a very long time. Only *that* triggers the story, gives me the strength to go through the whole process—a process usually long and stressful.

> *And so for each different work there is a different passion or emotion that motivates you?*

Yes. My first book—*The House of the Spirits*—was born, was triggered I'd say, by nostalgia, by the desire to recover the world that I had lost after I had to leave my country and live in exile. My second book—*Of Love and Shadows*—was triggered by anger, anger and sadness, at the abuses of the dictatorship. *Eva Luna* had a wonderful, positive feeling. That was the discovery that finally I liked being a woman; for forty years I wanted to be a man; I thought that it was much better to be a man. When I was in my forties, I discovered that I had done all the things that men do and many more, that I had succeeded in my life. I was okay. And that's what the story is about; it's about storytelling and about being a woman. And then in my recent collection of short stories [*The Stories of Eva Luna*]—a selection of twenty-three stories—all of them were triggered by a different emotion. By something that I had read in the news. By a story someone told me that stayed with me for a long time and in a way grew inside me. And then one day, it was ready to be written.

> *Do you feel that Eva Luna's narrative voice is different in the novel as compared to the short stories?*

I think that it's her voice [in both], but it's a maturing voice. I think that is because I've grown also; I'm older. And I've been living in an English-speaking country for three years. When I came I had "restaurant English." But the fact that I've had to speak English all the time, go to the movies in English, read the newspapers in English, has changed my approach to language. English is more precise, a more pragmatic language; Spanish is more baroque. In a way, when the only tool you have in writing is language and you learn to use that tool in a different way, something changes. I don't know what it is, but it's something very deeply rooted that slowly changes. And I think that the approach to reality changes the stories because of the change of the language. The language is more precise; the sentences are shorter; there is less ornamentation than in my previous books. Personally, I like it better; I don't know what the readers or the critics will say, but I do like it better.

Do you feel that you're writing for a different audience now?

No. I always write for the same person; I write for my mother.

So the change in language doesn't affect that?

The change in language is inside myself. I only discovered it after the book was published when I read it in the English translation. The book was published first in Spanish. When it is published in Spanish, I've been with the book for years, so I don't have any distance to look at it. I just can't see it; I can't even read it. But when I see it in English a year later, when it's been translated, then I have a fresh approach to the book; I can see it better, with a new eye. That happened with these stories [*The Stories of Eva Luna*]; when I read them in English, I realized that there was an audible change.

Do you work closely with your translator? I notice that Margaret Sayers Peden has translated several of your books.

I don't work closely with her. She does a splendid job. And then she's very kind and gives me the translation and I read it. But my English is not good enough to even suggest anything.

Eva Luna says that she writes "the way she'd like life to be." Do you think her stories could be called utopian?

Utopian? No. I think that the stories are about people. Most of the stories that I write are based on real people and real things that have happened, events that I read in the newspaper or have seen on television, or things that people have told me. I just try to go deeper and deeper into the stories to find the motivation. When Eva Luna says that she writes the way she wants life to be, that's what she means: try to understand what is deeply rooted, what is really inside each human being and each event. That's what writing is about; it is trying to understand.

So you feel that your stories are uncovering a deeper reality instead of projecting a different one?

Absolutely.

You once said that "a revolution is always an act of love." I wonder if you could comment on that and talk about the relation between revolution and love, and love stories, and maybe also the role of "spirituality" in your writing.

These are two different subjects. Political revolution is an act of love; it's a total commitment. You will sacrifice your life; maybe you will have to give up your life for something. And maybe you won't even see the results of something you do for others. You're willing to fight, to lead a terrible life, because you think that you have to make changes, not for yourself but for other people. Usually, or very often, the people who make revolutions have good lives; they are students or middle-class people who, out of idealism, decide to cross the line and enter into a violent world where they will be marginal. They will be outlaws; they will have to fight for every square inch of their territory and perhaps even die in the process. So I think that this is an act of love, an act of extreme love and generosity. The problem with the revolution is that, if they succeed, they become very rigid and soon *they* are the power. They are no longer revolutionary; they are the authority. And then we get into the same kind of problem with power. And that is a long discussion.

Now, about spirituality. I am not a religious person in the sense that I don't belong to any religious group or church. But all my life, I've been determined by—this will sound very stupid—I would say that my life has been determined by the illusion that my grandmother lives with me. My grandmother died when I was very young; I was a little girl. She was a very beautiful person; she was clairvoyant; she was a funny, wonderful human being. Very imaginative and creative and generous. The kind of person who is wonderful for a book but really can't live in this world. She died very young. My grandfather said that people only die when you forget them. So he tried to keep her image alive; I think he succeeded very well because more than forty years have passed and she still lives with me. Now, this idea that I can communicate with her, I have extended to the rest of my approach to life. I believe that there is a spirit, a spirit of life in everything that surrounds me—in plants, animals, people, towns, in the air, in the water, everything. And, in a way, like the ancient Indians, I try to be in touch with that. I have the feeling that if I damage anything that surrounds me, it will come back to me. So I am very careful about the world that surrounds me and the people that are around me.

> *It sounds as if there is a connection between the two themes, because in some way you are rejecting revolution when it becomes institutionalized and maybe also religion when it becomes institutionalized.*

Well, I never thought of that.

> *It reminds me of Nívea at the beginning of* Casa de los espíritus *when she says that she wants to have a more direct relationship to God, that she doesn't need the institutionalized religion of the* cura *[priest].*

I've never needed it; I feel very, very awkward in any church. According to my mother, I'm an old-fashioned anarchist.

> *That's a good description. This question changes the subject a bit: how would you characterize the relationship between your fiction and what's happening in Chile now, thinking about the recent political changes?*

Well, my last two books are not related to Chile at all except one of the stories in the collection of short stories. That is the story of two young people who have been tortured; they find out that they have shared this terrible experience when they are in bed together; they try to make love and it doesn't work. That story is about Chileans, about people I have known. The rest of the stories are not based in Chile. I have not lived in Chile for twenty years, for nearly twenty years. Although I still feel that I am Chilean and I only feel at home there, I am not participating in what is happening in Chile right now, Chile is living a wonderful process of giving birth to a new form of democracy after seventeen years of terrible dictatorship. I'm not part of that process. So, although I'm informed because I'm permanently in touch, I'm not there. I'm not doing anything for Chile and I'm not participating. So it doesn't come out in my writing either.

So you don't participate in any groups in the U.S. that support Chile?
Yes. But I do also for El Salvador or Nicaragua or human rights, or women's rights. It's not specifically because it's Chile.

I asked that question because I was thinking of the authors and critics who have spoken recently about the differences between the artistic and cultural responses in Chile and Argentina to their respective dictatorships. And I wondered if you've thought about, or if you have any ideas about, what might be at the root of this difference. The theory is that there has been a more active response in art and in cultural production to what's happened in Chile than there has been in Argentina.

I don't know the reason. Argentina has always been a country where art, especially the theater and literature, has been extremely powerful. They have had the best movies in Latin America. So, they are very good at that; Chile is not. We are a country of poets, mainly. I think that it's too soon to make a judgment; right now we've just come out of a dictatorship, a very long dictatorship, a very repressive one. For a time it seemed that nothing could be written about it that was fiction or that was a recreation of a reality. You could only write documentaries, testimony, chronicles of what happened, journalism, but not real fiction because we are too close, too near; it's too soon. You need a lot of time to exorcise the demons and take enough distance to be able to write with ambiguity and irony—two elements that are very important in literature. Without that you can't write good fiction. But I think that is what's happening right now in Chile. There is a response; during all the seventeen years of dictatorship there was always a very important cultural movement, an underground one, that was dealing artistically with reality. But it takes a while to be able to see it with enough perspective.

> *Given these kinds of changes in cultural production in Chile in particular, and in Latin America in general, and also given the fact that you are no longer living in Latin America but here in the U.S., would you say that your literary community and/or your political community has changed? Is there a different community that you're involved in?*

That is a very difficult question for me because, first of all, I have to tell you that I'm very happy in this country. I'm very happy because I have a wonderful husband, to begin with, and I've been very well received. I feel that I'm more connected to people now than I was before. I was rather isolated in Venezuela for a long time—which is not bad for a writer, by the way. On the other hand, I'm marginal; I'm a foreigner, and I will always be a foreigner here. A foreigner in the language, in the culture, in the way people live, in the values, in everything—which is also very good for a writer. You can stand unsheltered by the system and look at it from a certain distance. You appreciate all the ironies; you are always surprised by reality. That is very stimulating for anyone who writes or even for any creative job. I can also look at my continent and especially at my country with distance, and that's also good. On the other hand, I'm always traveling; I go to Latin America. I'm always in touch; I still speak Spanish at home; I write only in Spanish. So only time will tell.

> *So you think this distance is good, with an occasional check-in to see what's happening?*

As long as I don't lock myself in an ivory tower and start living in a bubble, I think it's good. This idea that I'm always on slippery territory and that I don't belong—in my personal life it can be stressful. But in my writing, it's good. It's that feeling of insecurity—it's great in the writing. You're never sure about anything; you have questions and don't have answers. I think it's very dangerous to think that you have the answers.

Because it closes things off?
And then you become "preachy."

And "institutionalized"?
Yes, that's true; that's why I don't belong to any literary club.

Has your readership changed over the years?
It has become wider. Yesterday, my agent called me saying that I have two new "pirate" editions in Turkey; and somebody said that there is another "pirate" edition in Vietnamese. So my books have somehow spread a lot, but the audience hasn't changed very much I think. It's mainly young people, more women than men I'd say. It's usually very old people or young people. There's an age in between—especially males, white males—who don't relate to my writing very well. I've discovered that because of the lecturing tours where I face an audience and can more or less see if there are more women or men, the age range, and how they look—lots of students, very young people all the time.

By "young people" do you mean in their twenties and younger?
Yes. Up to thirty, I'd say. But it's a lot of students, and very young people. And women, all sorts of women, from every social class and cultural group. In the U S. it's very obvious because I've been on lecture tours and really know who the audiences are.

But I don't think about that when I write. I don't think of a large audience or of how the audience is composed. I don't. I just think of one person and I try to tell the story in a very quiet and private voice to that one person. I want the story to be believable, to be entertaining, and I want to share questions with my reader. I want to take my reader by the hand and say: "Look. This is happening. Let's try and find the meaning; let's see if there's a particle of truth in all this."

You say that now that you're living in the U.S. as a foreigner, you have some distance on life here, but also that you're at a distance from Latin America. Will that double perspective give rise to differ-

ent kinds of subject material in the future—in terms of changing lo-
cations, for example? Will some of your stories start to take place in
the U.S.?

I suppose that will happen, yes. It took thirteen years of living in
Venezuela to write about a tropical country—and I *shared* the language. But finally it did happen, and I wrote *Eva Luna* and all the
short stories which are in the same environment. So, sooner or later, I
will be writing about the U.S., I'm sure.

You sound regretful when you say that.

Regretful? No. Not at all. On the contrary. You know, for me, the
most fascinating part of my job is the challenge that every book is
different, that every time you have to invent everything again. You
don't learn anything in this job; the only thing you learn is a little bit
about language, but nothing else. You're always improvising, always
recreating everything. So the idea of writing about this country or
any country, this reality or any other reality, is wonderful because it's
a new challenge and it keeps me going, keeps me strong.

You don't feel inclined to write novels that begin to connect with each
other and create a world among themselves, where there are charac-
ters that are the same in different works?

I think that that is very artificial. I always have that temptation because there are characters in my previous books that people always
talk about. They come to me and say, "What happened with this person?" "What happened with the Arab, Riad Halabí, in *Eva Luna*?"
"What happened to Alba from *The House of the Spirits*? Why isn't she
back in a sequel?" It's a great temptation to create a literary universe
where you are God and do everything; you make all the decisions
and you are the only one who knows about the characters. But in a
way, it's very artificial for me because I'm always trying to portray reality, something that is going on. So I don't want to find refuge in a
world that I've created that can become very detached from reality,
very much a private planet where I make the rules. I don't want to do
that; I want to stick to the rules of the world and talk about real
people.

Now that you've become a best-selling novelist, it seems that you're also beginning to become a best-selling interview subject. There are so many interviews with you that I wondered what you thought about the format of the literary interview. Why are people so interested in literary interviews?

I don't have the slightest idea because I would never read a literary interview. I don't even read reviews. I'm not interested in what other writers have to say, only what they write. You know, if I go to see a ballet I don't want Nureyev to walk onstage and tell me how difficult it was for him to train for this jump that he is going to do. I just want him to jump, and jump all the way up through the stage without explaining. Just do it! It's like the magician who reveals the trick— I don't want to know it.

Perhaps if storytelling is what you do and what Eva Luna does, then the interview is a kind of storytelling for readers interested in literary interviews.

Let them read fiction. On the other hand—well, not in this case with you because this really is a literary interview in which we are only talking about literature. But most interviewers ask personal questions about my life. And I have a terrible memory. I'm always inventing my own life, so I find that in different interviews I tell different stories about the same subject. My husband says that I have twenty versions of how we met, and I'm sure the twenty versions are true! His version is not true! So I can't tell you if they are accurate or not. My life is fiction too.

I'm thinking of interviews also in terms of how they connect to storytelling, your telling stories to your mother, and just talking in general. Do you have a particular affinity for oral creation, the oral tradition, folktales?

My stories have often been compared with folktales, and maybe that is the voice of my mother, my grandmother, the maids at home, those women telling stories—the oral tradition of storytelling that I was brought up in. So maybe that's the voice.

It's also very present in your fiction. There's a strong tradition of storytelling in Casa de los espíritus, *with Nívea telling stories to Clara even when she's not talking. It's the way important family history is passed down.*

I was brought up listening to the gossiping and the stories, and not only the stories we told at home. My grandfather had forbidden the radio at home because he thought it was an instrument of vulgar ideas. But, of course, we had a radio hidden in the kitchen, and it was blasting all day with "novelas," "radio novelas"—those incredible . . .

Soap operas?

Yes, like soap operas on the radio that would go on for years, and you would feel that those characters were part of your family; they were always there in the kitchen with their passions and their likes and everything. I was brought up in that; I like that. I don't like to listen to them anymore, but I like the idea that you get involved in that kind of thing.

You are certainly a mesmerizing storyteller. Is the interview another way of telling stories, a way of creating another kind of narrative?

No. The truth is I'm a born liar. And on the other hand, I never know where the truth is. After I tell one story two or three times, I'm totally convinced it happened that way. So who knows? Not long ago in this country, a man who said he was a doctor came over after a lecture and said he'd listened to several of my interviews, read several interviews, listened to me on the radio, and now he'd heard me in this lecture, and he was convinced that there was something wrong with me. That I didn't have a line between reality and fantasy; that that had a name in psychology; and that I should see a therapist! And I said, oh my God, if I see a therapist, what am I going to write about? If I could trace that line, there would be no writing.

You mean you'd be "cured"?

I'd rather be sick.

Now that we're talking about the fine line between truth and fiction, could you elaborate on the idea of writing fiction, of telling a truth, of telling lies, of uncovering some kind of reality, and of how these ideas might work together or against each other?

When I was teaching creative writing in Berkeley, I tried to tell my students that in order to write fiction, you have to allow yourself to lie. This was a class of fourteen students and each one was trying to write a novel, a long narrative. Several of them were totally blocked because they tried to approach the story from a "Calvinist" perspective—that is, you have to stick to the truth no matter what. And fiction is not that; fiction is lying. The first lie of fiction is that you're going to put in some order the chaos of life. That is the first lie. You are going to put it in chronological order, in whatever order you choose. You are going to select some part of a whole variety of things; you will decide that *those* things are the important ones and the rest of it is not important. And you will write about those things from your perspective. All that is a lie because life is not that way. Everything happens simultaneously, in a chaotic way, and you don't make choices. Things do happen. But you are not the boss; *life* is the boss. So when you accept as a writer that fiction is lying, then you become extremely free; you can do anything. Then you start walking in circles. The larger the circle, the more truth you can get. The wider the horizon, the more you walk, the more you linger in everything, the better chance you have of finding a particle of truth.

It's sort of an inverse process?

Yes. In fiction it is. It's connected with my life in a strange way. I spend ten, twelve hours a day alone in a room writing. I don't talk to anybody; I don't answer the telephone. I'm just a medium or an instrument of something that is happening beyond me, voices that talk through me. I'm creating a world that is fiction but that doesn't belong to me. I'm not God there; I'm just an instrument. And in that long, very patient daily exercise of writing I have discovered a lot about myself and about life. I have learned. Maybe other people do this through therapy; they go to a therapist for years to talk about themselves and to talk about the world and about life and about the pain of living. I do it through my writing. Those things are very much connected to me. I'm not conscious of that when I'm writing. But later, when I get the reviews—not the reviews, mainly the papers that students write—I discover in these papers things about myself that I didn't know I had discovered. But they came out in the writing and other people pointed them out to me. So it's a strange process; it is as if by this lying-in-fiction you discover little things that are true about yourself, about life, about people, about how the world works. But that's very little; I know very little.

>   *It becomes a less isolated process when you get this response from your readers through teaching.*

Yes. The process is very lonely, but the response connects you with the world. The idea that so many people read a book is fascinating, that something that one creates alone would have this ripple effect. And years later it comes to you in a strange way, in a very distant and remote place where you never thought you would ever be. You find that there is someone who has read your book—it's incredible—and how every reader writes the other half of the book. You only give them half, and they provide the rest with their own biography, with their experiences, their values. It's amazing; it's always a different book.

>   *And so by not writing sequels, you leave the works open for people to fill in those gaps.*

Well, maybe that happens, but I'm not trying to do that. Stories have their own life, their own length. Let's say that I have a plan and I'm heading in one direction and, all of a sudden, halfway, the book is finished because the *book* decides when it is done. And then all the rest that you write, you won't publish. Sometimes I do get to the end of the story that I had planned and then I cut it because *that* was not the end.

>   *So what makes a good end to a story?*

I don't know. In a short story it's different from a novel. A short story is like an apple; it comes whole; there is only one appropriate ending for a short story. All the others are not. And you know it; you feel it.

If you can't find that ending you don't have a story—eliminate it because it's useless to work on it any more. To me a short story is like an arrow; it has to have the right direction from the beginning and you have to know exactly where you're aiming. With a novel you never know. With a novel, it's patient daily work, putting together something that is like a painting or a tapestry creating many colors. You go slowly; you have a pattern in mind. But all of a sudden you turn it and realize that it's something else. It's a very fascinating experience because it has a life of its own. I think that in the short story you have all the control, and therefore it's more dangerous. I think that there are very few good short stories. Very few. And there are many novels that are wonderful, with a plot that you always remember, always remember. In a short story, it's more important *how* you tell it than *what* you tell; the form is very important. In a novel you can make all the mistakes you want and very few people will notice.

Spirits on the Big Screen

INTERVIEW BY JUDITH UYTERLINDE
Translated for this book by John Rodden

21

First published in Dutch in *Handelsblad* (Rotterdam), October 26, 1993, p. 6

This week marks the premiere of the film adaptation of *The House of the Spirits*, the well-known novel. It is directed by the Danish filmmaker Bille August. A conversation with the writer Isabel Allende follows.

The House of the Spirits was the first in a series of best-selling novels by the Chilean writer Isabel Allende, born in 1942. With this debut in 1982 she joined her [late] uncle Chilean president Salvador Allende as an international figure and established herself as a literary successor to Gabriel García Márquez. Her novel is a family chronicle, derived from the history of the family of Isabel Allende. It can also be read as a contemporary history of Chile. The plot culminates in the period around 1973, when [Salvador] Allende allegedly committed suicide and the dictatorship of Chile began. The Danish filmmaker Bille August has recently put the novel on the screen, with the starring roles filled by Jeremy Irons, Meryl Streep, and Vanessa Redgrave.

" *What did you think of the production?*

I was deeply impressed. Some of the success has to do with the quality of the actors, who performed the roles differently than I would have imagined. I think that they improved the book, at least insofar as they have correlated it closer with social reality. In *The House of the Spirits* there are four family histories: Clara is my grandmother, Esteban is my grandfather. My grandmother was a little woman with dark eyes, small as a dwarf. She appears in the film in the person of Meryl Streep as tall, blond, and with blue eyes. And yet it felt to me, as I watched the film, that Meryl Streep was my grandmother.

Do you like films?

I'm a film fanatic. The fascinating thing with film is that all your senses are addressed at the same time. In books, you must work with the word: you must carry the reader along, word by word and paragraph by paragraph, into your world. In film, however, you have many more ways to seduce the audience: sound, light, color, images. There's no escape with all that power at your disposal!

Because of my experience with the filming of *The House of the Spirits*, I'm now starting to think about writing film treatments and screenplays myself. I can do that—I'd like to do it. I think in images, and that's an advantage. On the other hand, I do write in a narrative way, and I use little dialogue in my books—whereas a film is built up from dialogue. So I'll need to study that more, so that I'll be good at it.

But you do already write successful books.

The attractive feature of film is that you can reach an incredibly large audience via it. The more people you can share stories with, the better.

Do you know before you're done how a story will end?

When I start a book, I don't know how it will proceed or how—or even when—it will finish. *Eva Luna*, for instance, had a happy ending. The main characters found each other and loved each other. When I wrote the final sentence and wanted to celebrate the happy ending, I felt, all of a sudden, that it wasn't finished. I had to return to my writing desk, and I then wrote a different ending. I wrote that love had passed and that the couple separated. Many readers, especially women readers, don't like that I changed the ending, but I couldn't help it. When I write, I'm directed by the characters and the story itself—they decide how it proceeds and ends, not me.

Do you invent the first sentence yourself?

I always write the first sentence on January 8, the day that I began to write *The House of the Spirits* twelve years ago. That book was such a tremendous success that I decided, from then on, always to start the book on that date. I go early to my office on that day. And I have a ceremony in which I ask the spirits for help and inspiration. When I've lighted the candles and turned on the computer, I write the first sentence, which I let bubble up from my intuitions, not from reason. That first sentence opens the door to the story that's already there—only it's hidden in another dimension. It's my task to enter that dimension and to make the story appear. When I wrote the first sentence of *The House of the Spirits*, which is "Barrabás came to us from the sea," I didn't yet know who Barrabás was or why he had come. The book ends with the same sentence. It's something magical that I can't explain very well, because I don't control it myself. On January 8 of this year [1993], my daughter Paula had just died. I was in shock. But I did want to start something new, because I had the feeling that I'd go crazy if I didn't. I had already thought a great deal about the new book, and I had the germ of it clearly in mind. But after I wrote the first sentence, I saw that the story was going to go in a totally different direction than I expect. Now I've completed four hundred pages. The book has become something completely different from what I originally had in mind.

There is no sharp line of separation in your books between death and life. Your characters accept the death of their beloved as something natural. Do you think that such an attitude is possible in real life too?

Yes, it's possible. During my previous visit to Amsterdam, I stayed with my daughter in the same hotel—in fact, in the same room. Memories come back to me, memories of things that I did here with her and that I talked about with her. Precisely because she's living so strongly in my memory, I can accept her death. I always talked a great deal with her, and I still do. Writing helps me to come to myself. It helps me accept the pain. Maybe other people do that via therapy, but I do it through my writing.

> *Your latest book,* The Infinite Plan, *is, for the first time, not set in Chile, but rather in the U.S.A. Have you lost some of your interest in Chile?*

I live in California now, and I was inspired to write that novel because I fell in love with the U.S.—and with the stories there, and with a particular man. That doesn't mean that I'll never write about Chile again. My mother still lives in Chile, and through her I still keep abreast of what's going on there. For years we've written each other almost daily—very extensive letters. We just began last week to write each other by fax!

My mother is the first person to read my books. Her judgment weighs very significantly for me—not in all matters, however. When I write sex scenes, she always says, "How can you write that?! Everybody will know you're doing that!!" But I don't care about that. After all, I also describe wartime conditions, in which people murder each other, and that doesn't mean I've killed anybody myself! I'm not the same person as any one of my characters. They are figures in a novel, but my mother can't seem to accept that.

Love and Tears

INTERVIEW BY IGNACIO CARRIÓN
Translated for this book by Virginia Invernizzi

First published in Spanish in *El País Semanal*, no. 145 (November 28, 1993): 48–59

22

Much like her style, which gave her international fame, she herself is baroque, and a "magical realist." She is a fifty-one-year-old grandmother, and she wants to invent more stories to tell her grandchildren. The film version of her novel *The House of the Spirits* was only recently released in movie theaters.

We met in San Francisco, California, in 1988, when Isabel Allende wrote only with a pencil and as fast as she could. She did not have a computer, a library, or an office of her own. She had nothing, not even residency in the United States. She only had her lover, William Gordon, a lawyer and an American. Every morning Isabel stole away to William's office, and there she filled endless pages in her yellow notebook. Naturally she lived unwitting of the success that she would reach in only a short time. Her primary concern was not an adventure in the world of literature, a world that she never truly took seriously, but another: her adventure as a woman, an odyssey into which she ventured blindly at the age of forty-five. "I am hopelessly in love," she told me then, "and I am afraid." She was beginning a new stage in her life, suddenly closing the last, and leaving behind twenty years of a boring marriage and a painful exile in Venezuela. Allende took refuge in nearby Venezuela (along with her son and daughter) when her uncle, Salvador Allende, was overthrown by a military junta. In Chile, except for her passion for writing, all had fallen apart in her life.

But in this warm and sunny November morning, on Sausalito Road, the most beautiful and privileged spot in San Francisco, I wondered what Isabel Allende I was going to find at the other end of the Golden Gate Bridge: a cold and pompous writer marked by her success, or the uncertain and apprehensive woman I had known? In just a few years her work and her fame grew spectacularly. The movie version of her first novel *The House of the Spirits* is due out in Spain December 22. Another of her novels will also soon come out as a film. The sales of her books, translated into many languages, continue to boom. Yet among all this success, an unexpected tragedy shattered the bliss where Allende had found herself in the last few years: on December 6, 1991, her twenty-eight-year-old daughter, Paula, was admitted to a hospital in Madrid.

Two days later she entered a coma and remained in that state until her death one year later. It was a tragic and devastating experience which radically altered Isabel Allende's life: "I have aged ten years in one, but I welcome this aging. I do not want to stop crying because I feel that the tears make me a better person."

" *This is no longer that office to which you stole away and wrote in pencil. This is the perfect office. I see that you work with the best Apple computer and that your printer is laser. . . .*

Yes. Back then I was writing a collection of short stories on a yellow pad. At times I wrote in William's office, at others at his house in San Rafael. I didn't know then that I would remain here or that I would move in with him. It was a time of great uncertainty in my life— until we married.

You married? Tell me about that.
We married in July 1988.

Why?

Well, because I needed the green card. That was the reason. Otherwise we could have gone on living together without marrying and without any problems. I come from a country [Chile] where there is no divorce. There I lived my mother's tragedy: she wanted to marry my stepfather and he never obtained the annulment of his previous marriage. So you could say I have a somewhat personal attitude towards marriage.

What do you mean?

Well, I believe that marriage is a spiritual contract between two people, an understanding which has nothing to do with the church or the law. Yet, since I married William, I feel that on his part there has been a more complete commitment which was not there before we married. Before we married, he was always on the go. But the moment that he said "Yes, now I will marry," and he said it because I put him between a rock and a hard place, his attitude changed.

You did not give him any alternatives?

No. I put him between a rock and a hard place because of a joke about marriage that he told at a dinner in front of other people. I was very mad.

What was the joke?

I don't remember exactly, but it was a joke about marriage. He said that he would never remarry unless there was no other choice . . . and right then and there I became raving mad. I told him that I had made a formal commitment to him when I gave up my house in Venezuela, my children and my friends, all that I had. I had left everything in Venezuela after thirteen years to come to live with him. I asked him that if that was not total commitment, what was it then? I told him that he had done nothing of the sort. I told him he had gone on living in his comfortable abode, in his same lifestyle, and that I was just something that had fallen into his organized life.

Well, this is quite powerful!

And I also told him that I had legal problems. My visa was about to expire and I was going to have to remain as an illegal immigrant in the U.S. Furthermore, I said that if I stayed I would have to find work and that if I worked I would not be able to write, and I was not prepared to give up my literature. So I gave him twenty-four hours to think about it.

And what were those twenty-four hours like?

They were very easy. I did not say one word to him, we did not even hold hands. Before the twenty-four hours were up, he said yes.

I suppose that now you feel secure and protected in the United States, which is where you want to live. Is that right?

Naturally. To begin with, this cleared up the situation with my visa. In a situation like mine, you cannot remain illegally in the U.S. You have problems every time you enter or leave. You have problems of all different types: with the contracts, with the banks. Marriage also gave me stability. I have the feeling that he is my husband now, and not my concubine. It also made my mother very happy because, as you remember, she could never marry my stepfather.

What exactly happened with your father? Did he abandon your family? I understand that it was Salvador Allende who took care of you. Who paid for your education?

I don't know the details because my mother had always kept this secret. I do not know exactly what happened. But I have the impression that my father had to have done something very shameful at that time, in that place. He gradually fled from that something and then he never dared to return.

Did he die?

Yes.

Do you mind if I ask you how he died?

He died on the street of a heart attack. I remember that my father left when my mother was about to have another baby. She already had two children and he abandoned her in Lima—we lived in Lima then. And so you see, my brother Juan, the third child, was born after my father left. Later my mother returned to Chile with her three children when my youngest brother was gravely ill. She never saw my father again. Somehow she had the marriage annulled without ever seeing him, and my father, in order not to have to support us, gave up all his paternal rights. I always thought that he probably did not live in Chile because Chilean society is very small and everyone knows each other. If he had lived there, someone must have seen him. But he never even left Santiago. He simply descended one step in the strict Chilean social classes and we never saw him again. I believe that he lived downtown only a few blocks from where my stepfather worked, near where our dentist had his office, also close to where my grandfather lived. Yet as far as we knew, he did not exist.

It's like a novel.

Yes, with the only difference that it is already a novel.

And how did he die?

When I was twenty-seven or twenty-eight I used to work for the magazine *Paula*. I was quite well-known in the country because I also appeared on a television show. So one day a man died on the street of a heart attack. When they took him to the morgue, they checked his papers and saw that his name was Allende. They called me because they thought that we might be relatives and they asked me to go to the morgue to identify the body. When I arrived, the first thing I thought was that it was my brother Pancho (his name was Francisco Tomás—the same as my father). At that time my brother had become a member of a sect and we had not seen him for a few months. The truth is that we thought he was dead. So when they called me to come and identify the body, the first thing I thought was that it was my brother. But when I arrived and they showed me the body, I could not identify it because I had never seen a picture of my father. It did not even occur to me that it could be my father. I never thought about my father. I did not know anything about him for twenty-eight years and I never thought it could be he. All I said was that it was not my brother; it was not my brother.

Then, who identified the body?

My stepfather. I called him, he saw the body and said, "Isabel, this is your father."

What did you feel then?

I took a good look and I did not feel any of what one could say is the call of the blood. I felt a total void.

Do you feel any resentment towards your father? Do you miss him? Do you hate him? I ask you because they say that it is when a father dies that the son or daughter feels something different towards that person. It could be tenderness, I don't know. It could be a total void. . . . The fact is that when the parent dies something happens, it's a sort of . . .

Yes, a sort of encounter.

Have you tried to analyze in what way all this could have affected you?

I have never been psychoanalyzed so I don't know in what way it could have affected me. Besides, I am not concerned enough to find out. I come from a family where no one looks back. We don't have the time for that. Since I never saw my father, I think I was somewhat curious as a child, but my mother fully replaced the paternal figure. My mother was mom and dad. She has loved me unconditionally. I never felt orphaned. What did stay with me, though, and I cannot totally blame my father's absence, but the powerful patriarchal figures in my family for this, was a sort of rebellion towards male authority, a considerable mistrust towards the male figure. In my personal and professional relationships I rarely trust a man enough to tell him about my intimate life. I even rarely trust a lover.

Not even a lover?

No. It is very difficult for me to open up, to fully abandon all in an intimate relationship. I begin from the premise that I will be betrayed.

That is very difficult, even though the relationship with your mother was so intense. I suppose that she must now be delighted. You are now married, you are successful. . . .

Yes, she is delighted. She still lives in Chile, but I've bought her a fax machine and every day we send each other messages. At last she is proud of me.

You were also very proud of your daughter Paula.

Yes. Very much. What happened to my daughter is a terrible tragedy. She became ill in Madrid December 6, 1991, and she died December 6, 1992.

Exactly one year later?

Yes, she fell into a coma two days later, on December 8, when I was presenting my novel *The Infinite Plan* at a gathering in Barcelona. We were celebrating with champagne and taking pictures. Everything was very elegant, and suddenly I saw Willie coming toward me. He whispered in my ear that Paula had been hospitalized. I believe it was the Clinic, the biggest and oldest in Madrid. Everything ended during that flight from Barcelona to Madrid. I was in the hospital for one hundred days. I suppose the book took on a life of its own. I had no idea what was happening to it. I entered quickly into that world of pain, of illness, of daily humility, that makes us all equal. Sooner of later we all pass through there. At the hospital you are a number, a parcel that goes from hand to hand without the least bit of respect. So many are suffering that it really does not matter. No one cares about the relatives of those who are suffering because there is no time to take care of them. There was such anonymity all around in that place. I bought myself a white smock and white clogs and that way I could be taken for a nurse and walk anywhere I liked. I was eventually just one of the staff. No one asked where I was going or coming from.

No one knew who you were? No one knew that that woman in the white smock with a daughter in a coma was the writer Isabel Allende?

No, I never told anyone who I was.

Why?

Because I didn't want the press to arrive. Carmen Balcells, my agent, helped me very much. We did everything in the most anonymous manner possible.

And your daughter never came out of the coma.
No, I saw her just hours before she lost consciousness.

What was wrong?
She was lacking an enzyme in her metabolism. It's a genetic condition that everyone in my ex-husband's family carries. It's called porphyria. Normally, the other enzymes tend to compensate for the lack of that one enzyme that is missing. But, this time it went too far, she fell into a coma, and when they could not pull her out of the coma, for whatever reason (and it was most probably a mistake made by the people in intensive care), she suffered irreversible damage to the brain.

Were you always by her side?
All the time. I lived with her, day and night, at the hospital. I sat in the hallways with my mother waiting for the two times a day that I could go in to visit her in intensive care. When they disconnected her from a respirator in early May, I brought her home with me to California. I set up a bedroom for her in the living room.

Could you communicate in any way?
No, I believe that she perceived sound, even though she could not differentiate it. She would become startled if something fell on the floor, but if you called, she did not look. I took a course to learn how to take care of her. I hired people to help me. I had to feed her through a tube they put in her stomach. We had to do a number of sordid things. . . . But life went on—the grandchildren all around, the cat wandered about, my husband cut roses on the patio. Everything was so drawn out and slow. She was very well taken care of and everything went very slowly.

What did the doctors say? Did they suggest going to another hospital?
They said that the most we could do was to find an institutional home

where she could die in peace. And I lived with this dilemma, that the more I took care of her, the longer she would last, and the longer she would suffer—and I couldn't stop taking care of her. She was taken care of like a princess. She was a sleeping beauty in a glass urn. Paula was a beautiful woman. She was the most intelligent one in the family. She had a master's in psychology and worked in a school in Madrid. She was twenty-eight years old.

Could you write at all during that year?

I took notes in a yellow notebook. I wrote many letters to my mother. Exactly one hundred days after my daughter fell ill, my mother also had complications with her health. She is over seventy years old and could not stand any more. I put her on a plane and sent her to Chile. I wrote her every day—even several times a day until November when I noticed that something was happening to Paula. I communicated with Paula through dreams—I felt her. When I entered the room I knew whether Paula had a fever without having to touch her. I knew if she was uncomfortable, if she had cramps. And, suddenly, in late November, I could not feel her any longer. I would enter the room and see a body, but I could not feel her call telling me, "Mom I'm cold; move me, Mom." And then I felt terrible fear. I called my mother in Chile and told her that I felt Paula was dying. And I know that she began to pray so that would happen. She wanted Paula to stop suffering. And when I stopped dreaming about her, and stopped feeling her, and she would not call me any longer, I went insane. I consulted witches, psychics, shamans, homeopaths, magnetic beds, miraculous waters, saints, everything that you can imagine. . . .

No one interfered?

No, my friends observed me with tremendous compassion, but they could do nothing. On December 6, at four in the morning, Paula died. I was in a total state of commotion. They told me that I had to go to therapy, that I needed antidepressants, tranquilizers. They told me to go on vacation. And then my mother came from Chile with the only idea that would save me. She brought a package in her hands with all the letters that I had written her. She said: "This is a tunnel through which you must walk until you reach the other side. There is no way to avoid the pain, there are no pills, there are no therapies, there are no vacations. You must walk through this pain until you reach the other side. You must relive the pain bit by bit and assimilate it all. You must know that it will never disappear, that it will be part of you from now on. And you must accept this."

So she gave you the letters?

Yes. She told me that those letters would help me relive every day, minute by minute, everything that happened. And she asked me to read them in order. She had arranged them in chronological order and tied them with a yellow ribbon. There they are, on top of my desk.

And so, you read them?

I read all the letters with my mother by my side. I relived every stage, and when I finished reading them I accepted that the best thing that could have happened to Paula was to die. I resigned myself to that. I understood that I had done all that was humanly possible to save her. And I understood something else, which is the most important in all this. I realized that I had left behind my work, my family, all that without which I thought I could never live. Everything disappeared from the horizon. Only she and I were left, face to face. She with her open eyes but without seeing me. She with a brain that no longer functioned. And I accepted that it was that way. I understood that no matter how much I worked on her body, no matter how much I massaged and loved it, it was deteriorating—it was becoming disfigured. There was no way of avoiding it. And I said to myself: Paula, my precious, my daughter, is gone.

What did you do? Did you let her die?

I locked myself up in the room with her and said: die Paula, die, it is over. I adore you. I will always love you. You will always be with me, but, please die in peace. I will not fight any longer. I do not want to retain you forever.

And she died?

Yes. What I learned from so much suffering was that all that is left at the end is the love that you give. Not even the love that you receive, because Paula could not give me anything. She only received. But I was left with the everlasting treasure of the love that I gave her and that I know I am capable of giving.

You had never felt that before?

Never. Up to then all my relationships, even the relationships with my children, had been a two-way road. If you are a good son/daughter, I will adore you. If you are a good mother, I will have a good relationship with you. If you are a good lover, I will marry you. And what I learned that year was that the only love, beyond those that are conditional which one day dry up, the only thing that remains and does not exhaust itself is that love that does not expect love. And so I realized that the richest person in this world is Mother Teresa. No millionaire is richer than that woman.

But that woman, Mother Teresa, has faith in God. . . .

I believe she has boundless love towards humanity.

Has all this brought you closer to a religious experience?

No. If I searched for a religion it would be Buddhism. I believe that the spirit, which is not exclusive to the human being, can be found in all of nature. I have a spiritual life. I write about spirits all the time. I believe that those who die somehow still hold our hand. I used to ask my grandmother and my mother-in-law, who died fourteen years ago, to help me communicate with Paula. But I don't believe that there is a God up there who punishes us and rewards us and who observes our actions. In any case, if I had to pray to a god, I would pray to a benevolent and compassionate goddess, with breasts bursting with milk, and not to a punishing god who selects certain peoples and needs to be adored. What a ridiculous thing!

Do you feel bitterness?

It is not bitterness, but I have aged ten years. I welcome them. I do not want to forget pain. I do not want to stop crying.

You really do not want to stop crying?

No. And I want to clarify that it is not masochism, because I laugh and play with my grandchildren. But I do not want to lose this pain. It makes me a better person.

Will you some day publish those letters? I imagine that they must be moving. I would guess that your readers, now that they know the letters exist, await them.

They are of no interest to anyone. My mother's letters, the ones she wrote to me, are very moving. She is the true writer. But she lived in a country, Chile, and a time when women were oppressed. I belong to the first generation that rebelled against that straitjacket that machismo and the church imposed on us.

And so those letters will never be published?

Never. I have a pact with my mother. If one of us dies, the other will burn all the letters. These letters are like Clara's notebooks in *The House of the Spirits*.

Let's talk about your success.

Success? What success? What is success?

I am referring to your literary success.

It surprises me that my books sell so well and in so many languages. But here nothing has changed. Success happens outside my circle. I am the same. Here my grandchildren grow up and diapers have to be changed, someone has to go to the market, and write eight hours a day with the same humility that I wrote the first sentence of my first book. And I must do all this with the certainty that I know nothing, that each time I have to invent it all because I learn nothing from each book.

You mean that here, in the U.S., you do not actually feel your success?

Very little. My books are more popular in Europe than in the U.S. Much gets published in the U.S., but Americans like to read thrillers. And I don't write that type of book. Americans also like to read po-

litical books. Besides this, the U.S. is a country that is constantly observing itself and does not show much interest in translated books.
Very few foreign writers have any success here, even if they live in
this country. It could possibly be different if I wrote in English.

Do you like this country?

I like it very much. I am fascinated by its complexity, its flexibility.
The fact that the worst and the best can happen here; that there is
possibility for quick change. Europe is different. It has rigid structures that are three thousand years old. It has problems that are three
thousand years old. It is overpopulated and it is much more difficult
to make significant changes. The rest of the world exists at a level of
subsistence. What they call the Third World still struggles for basic
food and there isn't much possibility for change because it is all basically at an emergency level, while in the United States that possibility
does exist. Besides, this is a mixed salad with all races, languages,
much land, and a youthful history. All this allows for great changes in
short time spans. I want to be part of all those changes.

Are you planning to lead a movement?

I feel I have a mission. I belong to the lowest of the low in the social
classes in this country. I am Latina and I am a woman. But I have a
platform to speak in English about my culture. I first had it with my
books and now with the movie, and soon with the other movies that
they will make about my other books. All that places me in a position
of responsibility and privilege that I plan to use and abuse.

Do you want to make more politics than literature?

I don't believe that literature is an end in itself. I don't believe in art
for art's sake. I don't have any respect for literature and I treat it with
the minimum seriousness. I believe that literature is a magical way of
shaking someone and saying: look, this is the way we live, this is
how it is.

You don't take literature seriously? You laugh at it?

I work seriously, but I don't take it seriously. I cook seriously. I cut onions and lettuce very well, but I don't take the kitchen seriously. And I do the same with literature. I write meticulously and patiently, but I don't believe that literature in itself is something serious or important for anybody. I used to attend conferences and listened to writers talk about themselves, their work, their entire oeuvre, and I felt ashamed for them. My skin itched. I couldn't take the self-congratulatory atmosphere. I couldn't stand how they spoke about themselves, their work . . . I felt ashamed. And I couldn't stand how they analyzed each other and threw roses, that is shameful.

Do you feel that the universities are better places than those conferences?

Often I visit universities and I find that there is a group of thirty youngsters whom they have tortured during a semester looking for symbols and metaphors in a book of mine where there were no symbols or metaphors intended; where all that I intended was to tell a story. I ask them why they don't yield to the pleasure of reading in the same way that I yield to the pleasure of writing instead of analyzing, forcing parallels, and searching for influences. . . .

I have read in an interview that you gave, that when you were twelve years old you carried books by the Marquis de Sade in your school bag. . . .

I read everything back then. Everything that fell into my hands.

And what did you think of de Sade at that age, and later?

I don't like him at all, and he has had no influence in my life. I have not ended up a sadist or a masochist for having read his books.

What writers do you admire?

Many. Right now I am reading a group of women writers that belong to ethnic minorities in this country. They are great writers, Chicanas, Japanese, Latinas. They are writing extraordinary works, and they are taking over the world of literature that the white men in New York monopolized. Minimalist literature is dying. And it was about time. We are seeing a return to great narrations, to the baroque narrative. We are seeing a return to artistry in words, in sentences, in the extravagance of the story itself. I am very attracted by that.

Are you attracted by extravagance? What do you think of Toni Morrison's work? As you know, she received the Novel Prize for literature not long ago.

She is a good example of what we are speaking about. She is a black writer who publishes books of great interest to the public, where she also tells things that had to be told about slavery. She talks about poverty and the female condition. Toni Morrison heads that movement.

Now, you are darkly complected and a small woman. You said a couple of years ago that you would exchange all that to become a tall, blonde, twenty-year-old woman with large breasts. Do you still feel that way?

No. I would now trade all that to become a tall, blonde woman with large breasts, but remain a fifty-year-old.

Why not younger?

What a catastrophe to have to live those thirty years all over again! No, no, not one more day! I've already accumulated fifty years of experience and I have only a bit of wisdom. It would be hell to have to go through the frustrated loves, to have to cry over the first wrinkles, to have to lose all that I've lost all over again. No, no, not one more day!

You also said on one occasion that until you were forty, you had always wished you were a man. Do you still feel that way?

No, I don't. I don't feel that way any more because I have done everything that men can do and some things that they cannot do: like having children. No, I would not trade my place for a man's. But I still believe that men have things easier than women—all over the world. Even though now they say that the most threatened, vulnerable, and persecuted group in this country is the white males. They are attacked by everyone: feminists, blacks, everyone.

And do you believe this?

I believe that ultimately what is being attacked is the value system of the white male, that which they defend and represent. But I don't believe that it is each white male that is being attacked.

Am I right to think that you are a woman who dreams a lot?

You are right. I do dream a lot. And I have premonitory dreams. They are very precise dreams. For example, I can predict the sex of my children and grandchildren before they are born. I also see them the way they are going to be in the different phases of their lives.

Were you right with your children?

Yes. Absolutely. I also write down all my dreams so that I can relate them to life and interpret them. I have recurrent dreams, and they also help me to solve problems when I write. Sometimes I am just stuck and can't go on, and that same night I resolve the problem in my dreams.

Did you also dream about the illness and subsequent death of your daughter?

No, and that's why I never believed she would die. I never saw her ill or dead.

Can you tell me one of those recurrent dreams?

Well, for example, I dream about a very large house with many rooms and many doors, and behind every door there is a dirty and disorderly room. So I begin to clean the rooms, but there are always more dirty and disorderly rooms. That means that there is something in my life that isn't working well; something that I have to resolve. Other times I dream about anonymous babies without faces, and that baby is always the book that I am writing. What happens to the baby is what happens to the book, and I realize this as I write—I realize it in the dream.

What happens to the baby?

For example, it is locked up in a room and cries, and I try to reach him and I can't. That means that what I am writing hasn't yet captured the essence of what I mean to say. It means that there is an obstacle of some kind. I also dream about a baby that cries in the voice of an old man, an animal, or a parrot, and I know that has to do with my narrative tone. I am not writing in the appropriate tone.

> *It is very curious, and I suppose very useful that you dream in that way.*

Yes. Since I write my dreams in a notebook, when I turn on my computer the next day, I correct what I wrote the previous day.

> *What are you writing now?*

I don't want to talk about that.

> *Why? Is it bad luck, or do you want to give us a surprise?*

All of that together.

> *Do you write every day?*

Yes. And I live every day with the sensation that life will end tomorrow. I have no plans for the future.

> *Does it give you a certain inner peace to live like that?*

Absolutely. If you have no plans for the future, you cannot fear it. You are not afraid of being unable to carry out those plans. I try to live today as best I can. That way I have the feeling that I have finished everything. I can die tomorrow in peace. I would leave no one in absolute desperation. It is very pleasant to be my age. Being a man or a woman matters little because all those things that are intimately tied to sexuality, that is, menstruation, birth control, lovers, passions, all seem insignificant. They are all gone. And now all that is left is an unpleasant aftertaste, if anything at all.

> *You speak as though you were truly elderly. Have you really said good-bye to sex and other interesting things?*

I have entered a stage in which I am now grandmother, guardian, and witch. I am here to care for the children as long as I have the strength, to care for my family, for the planet. I am no longer in the market for sex. I am not trying to seduce anyone.

Not even William Gordon?

No, not even him. We are very much in love and I have no need to seduce him. It is no longer a matter of seducing him, but of sharing.

"Something Magic in the Storytelling"

INTERVIEW BY JAN GOGGANS

23

Reprinted from *Writing on the Edge* 6, no. 1 (1994): 127–142

When I walked up to the law office Isabel Allende shares with her husband, a Latino family came spilling down the steps, blinking into the sunshine, talking and laughing. "Just like in the book," I thought, for in *The Infinite Plan*, Gregory Reeves dedicates his legal skills to California's Mexican community. Allende's real-life husband, Willie, ushered me back to her studio—a bright, sunny room full of flowers, its walls lined with books—and as we settled in, she chatted about some of the women writers she had met since moving to the United States. Louise Erdrich was coming for dinner, and when I mentioned Erdrich's unfailingly exotic earrings Allende brightened and wondered if she should call her friend, who designs earrings. "Just like in the book," I thought again, as Allende talked about the real-life version of Carmen, the joyously sensual jewelry designer in *The Infinite Plan*.

Since her shift from journalism to fiction writing in 1981, Allende has written five novels, one a collection of short stories "written" by Eva Luna, the heroine of her third novel. Her writing is characterized by a seamless interweaving of reality and fiction; she creates worlds which ignore boundaries of death and life, in which characters move easily from the "real" world to the spirit world. Yet Allende shrugs off the title of magical realist, saying she is writing her reality—with perhaps a little exaggeration. For one magical hour on a January afternoon, I sat while Allende wove her worlds together before my very eyes. We talked about geography, politics, gender, and love, and the way each had affected her writing; we talked particularly of the way perspective affects the storyteller's magic.

> **"** *You have a very individual writing process. Could you talk about the specific rituals you follow when you begin a novel?*

My ritual for beginning a novel is always to start on January 8th. That is in a few days—Saturday. So I am preparing myself for Saturday. I began my first novel on January 8, 1981, because on that day, we received a phone call in Venezuela saying that my grandfather was dying in Chile. I'd promised my grandfather that I would be with him in his last moments and that I would help him to die. I felt that I had betrayed him terribly because when I left Chile, I did not say goodbye. I didn't dare tell him that I was leaving. I always thought that I would leave for a few weeks and then come back, but as the circumstances were, I could not come back.

Hadn't you received death threats in Chile?

There were many things, many combined threats and circumstances that forced me out. And I didn't want to talk about these things with my grandfather, who didn't know what was going on in Chile at the time. I also didn't want to say goodbye because we were so close. I saw him every day. And I was convinced that I was going to return very soon. So, years later when he was dying in 1981, I felt that I had betrayed him because I could not be with him. And I began a letter to him that later turned out to be *The House of the Spirits*. That book was very fortunate in the way that it opened a door for me into literature. It changed my life in many ways. I started my second novel the same day—because it was a lucky day and a lucky book. And the second book did very well, too, so with the third book I didn't dare change the date, and now, six books later, I still don't dare change it. This year, I have to start a first sentence on January 8th.

That day, which is a sacred day for me, I come to my office very early in the morning, alone. I light some candles for the spirits and the muses. I meditate for awhile. I always have fresh flowers and incense. And I open myself completely to this experience that begins in that moment, that day, which I know nothing about. Because I never know what I'm going to write, really. I have plans. I may have finished a book months before and may have been planning something, but it has happened already twice that when I sit down at the computer and turn it on, another thing comes out. It is as if I was pregnant with something, an elephant's pregnancy, something that has been there for a very long time, growing, and then when I am able to relax completely and open myself to this experience of the writing, with no prejudice, then the real book comes out. Although I may have planned something, I try to write that first sentence in a state of trance, as if somebody else was writing it through me. That first sentence usually determines the whole book. It's a door that opens into the book. And slowly as I write, the story seems to unfold itself, sometimes in spite of me. It just happens.

I'm not the kind of writer who can have an outline, talk about the writing to anybody, or read parts of my writing in process. Because I don't know what's happening. I really don't. Until the first draft is ready—and that first draft can take months, and it's usually very long—I don't know what the book is about. I just sit down every day and pour out the story. When I think that it's finished, I print it, and I read it for the first time. At that point I know what the story is about, and I start eliminating everything that has nothing to do with it. On the second draft, I start working with language, form, tension, rhythm, tone—those things that are part of the craft of the writing but not the story.

So you are a storyteller first and only later become a writer?
Yes. The storytelling is the fun part; the writing can be boring.

I also know that you've said that writing is fun. Your background in journalism, your facility with language, your ability to shape people and sentences—while that's work, it clearly is fun for you as well.
There is a part of the writing that is fun. I work with emotions; lan-

guage is the tool, the instrument. But really, the story is always about some very deep emotion that is important for me. When I write, I try to use language in an efficient way, the way you do as a journalist—you have little space and time and have to grab your reader by the neck and not let go. That's what I try to do with language, and that part is fun, to try to create that tension that sometimes I feel in myself. Very often when my daughter-in-law Celia comes here in the morning she finds me crying or laughing because I'm so involved in the story that I have become part of it. When the day is over and I am ready to go back home, I need some space, some time, before I confront the family, and I go back to normality. This place, this cocoon here, seems to contain the characters so vividly that they are part of the air here. I don't work at home because it would be a haunted house.

> *When you talk about opening yourself up to the experience, are you opening yourself up to a magical world? Do spirits actually come in and suggest words or images or scenes for you?*

Yes. In a certain way. There is also an intellectual process, of course. But there is something magic in the storytelling. You tap into another world. The story becomes whole when you tap into the collective story, when other people's stories become part of the writing, and you know that it's not your story only. I have a feeling that I don't invent anything. That somehow I discover things that are in another dimension. That they are already there, and my job is to find them and bring them into the page. But I don't make them up. And in these twelve years that I have been writing, things have happened in my life and in my writing that prove to me that there is another world. And when you spend too many hours—as many many hours a day as I do—in silence and alone, you are able to see that world. I imagine that people who pray or meditate for long hours, or are just alone in a convent or some place, end up hearing voices and seeing visions because solitude and silence create the ground for that.

Sometimes I write something, and I'm practically convinced that it's just my imagination. Months or years later, I discover that it was true. It happened somewhere, to some people. And I'm always so scared when I have that happen. . . . "What is this? What if things happen because I write them? I have to be very careful with my words." But my mother says "No. They don't happen because you write them. You don't have that power. Don't be so arrogant. What happens is that you are able to see them and other people are not because they don't have the time, they are busy in the noise of the world." My grandmother was like that, she was clairvoyant. And although she did not write, she could guess things and tap into those unknown events and feelings. She could discover things because she was aware. I imagine that it's just a question of being more aware.

Your stepfather called you a mythomaniac.

Yes. A liar. [*She laughs.*] He says that I am liar. I am currently writing what is a strange book for me because I write fiction and this book is a memoir. It's the first time that I'm not writing fiction, and I know that my stepfather and my mother are going to object to every page because from my perspective the world of my childhood, of my life, is totally different from the way *they* see it. I see highlights, emotions, and an invisible web—threads that somehow link these things.

> *Joyce Carol Oates talks about a luminous memory, as though it comes in and glows on a certain spot. I'm thinking of the difference in what you remember from your childhood—being hung upside down in a contraption intended to encourage your growth—and what your stepfather remembers as being some kind of safe device. Perhaps you are just remembering what you felt: while you were in a safe device, it actually felt like you were being strung up by the neck.*

There's a lot of that in my writing. For example, I will remember a story but can't remember a place or a date or a person or a name. But I remember something striking about the story.

> *Whereas some people will remember the date or what they were wearing.*

Or they remember the truth. I will perhaps only remember what I fantasized about the event.

> *But in the end, as in* Eva Luna, *first you say one thing and then you say—*

"Maybe it didn't happen that way." I always have the feeling that maybe it didn't happen that way. I have fifty versions of how I met Willie, my husband. He says they are all true.

> *In your earlier novels, in the political chaos of Latin America, the government is untrustworthy, inconsistent—there is that Kafkaesque feeling that no matter what you do, you won't understand the government. There is even inconsistency within the government; the government isn't predictably evil. The world is shifting, undependable. Do you see the spirit world as being a more dependable place? Is it in the spirit world that the infinite plan makes sense and in the real world that it doesn't?*

It's a difficult question. The spiritual world is a place where there is no good and evil. It's not a world of black and white as the real world seems to be. There are no rigid rules of any kind. There are no rules. In that sense it is totally different from the infinite plan—which is a joke—proposed by the preacher in *The Infinite Plan*. In the spiritual world there is only intention, there is just being. And there is no sense of right or wrong. Everything just is in a sort of very steady and still way. And because things are so ambiguous in that sense, so delicate and so unfocused, it's a safe place. You don't have to decide anything. Things just are, and you somehow float or—I don't know how to express this—you are just there. In a very, very delicate form. For me, it's a very safe place. That's the place where the stories come from. That's the place of love.

This sounds very corny. My life has been determined by two things that have been extremely important: love and violence. Violence and death and sorrow and pain in my life—always, I've always had those. But there's another parallel dimension, and that is love. There are many forms of love, but the kind I am talking about is unconditional. For instance, the way we love a tree. We don't expect the tree to move or to do anything or to be beautiful. The tree is just a tree, and we love the tree because it's a tree. You love an animal that way. We love children that way. As life gets more complicated and relationships become more complicated, you start demanding things.

You want things in exchange. You have expectations and desires and you want to be loved as much as you love.

In this spiritual world, which is a world of love, there are no conditions. Like the way I love my grandchildren. I think they are perfect. It doesn't matter whether they grow or stay the way they are because I can see them, know what they are, the infants they were when they were just born. The fetuses they were inside my daughter-in-law. The persons they will be when they are adolescents, the persons they will be when they are adults. The soul has no age. Maybe that's what I wanted to say. When we love something deeply and completely, we love the essence. And that doesn't age. It doesn't look this way or that way. It's not fat or thin or tall or blonde. I think that is the condition of the spiritual world. The condition of the essence of things.

> *The condition you describe sounds very Buddhist. Weren't you raised Catholic?*

I was raised as a Catholic, and I'm not a religious person. I don't have formal faith. I don't believe in God. It's that simple. I do not believe in the gods that I have heard about or the God I was raised in. I don't believe in a creator who decides our lives and punishes or rewards. I have a sort of horror of all religions, although I do respect people who have faith, and I think it's a gift that makes your life very easy. You can always explain everything and justify everything through faith, and I have never had it.

Although I'm not religious and I'm not a Buddhist either, I feel very connected to something that is beyond the mind and the body. I'm convinced that life is just a pause, a sort of stage in a journey. We have to be in this body for a while because we have to learn things that we are capable of learning only through the senses. And then the soul moves over to some other plane, and souls do something else. I feel very powerfully that way now because of my daughter's death. Although I can't communicate with her—I can't pick up the telephone and call her as I did every day before—she is present in a very real way. What is essential of her is here. Her death is an accident; her life was an accident. The fact that I was there to bring her into this world and I was there to usher her into another world is also an accident. She didn't belong to me and never did. That part of her soul that is connected to my soul is real to me, a very powerful reality. I feel the same way about my grandmother. My grandmother died when I was very young. My mother says I so badly needed a grandmother that I invented one. But the truth is that I have never needed any other grandmother. She has been a wonderful grandmother, and the fact that she is dead is just too bad. But it didn't change the fact that she is my grandmother and she's great! I feel the same way about my daughter.

> *I think transcendence is what you are talking about, the ability to move above and beyond this real world to a transcendent understanding of feelings and emotions. Would you say your novels are defined by that characteristic more than any other?*

It's strange that my work has been classified as magic realism because I see my novels as just being realistic literature. They say that if Kafka had been born in Mexico, he would have been a realistic writer. [*She laughs.*] So much depends on where you were born! Sometimes I use tricks that are literary devices to exaggerate something in order to make it more funny or outstanding or spectacular. But the essence is always true. When I say that Clara Del Valle could play the piano with the lid on, that's an exaggeration, of course she couldn't. But in real life, my grandmother could move objects. Not big things. She couldn't say "Okay, we have to move the furniture today" and start moving the furniture from her chair. No. But sometimes the ashtray would move a little on the table, or something like that. So something that is perhaps minor I exaggerate. And it looks weird in the book.

But in real life, a lot of things are strange. I have a very good relationship with my husband, though we have only been together for six years. We come from different cultures, from different races, different languages. We look so different. Sometimes when he is shaving in the morning and I'm putting on my makeup in the same mirror, I think, "Gosh, this guy's like a Martian. What am I doing here?" And I feel I have just been cast in a movie! It's so strange. However, the intimate communication we have is so accurate that sometimes we will be driving in silence, and he will say something that is absolutely connected to what I am thinking. And vice versa. I know he can read my mind. He doesn't know he is reading my mind, that our thoughts and our dreams are connected the way our flesh is. I feel that sometimes with my kids. Or with my mother. So there's a reality there. In literature I exaggerate it, I transform that into telepathy, but there's something that is true.

> *Irene and Francisco in* Of Love and Shadows *have to be completely remade at the end of the novel. They get in the car and look at each other wondering who the other is. They don't recognize each other physically, but they still recognize each other's souls. That's an important statement that the novel makes very realistically.*

Of all my books *Of Love and Shadows* is the one that had the least success. It was accused of being sentimental and too political. But I have sympathy for that book. First of all because the story is true. The main story concerns a political crime committed in Chile, which I researched. The characters are true. And also because it brought Willie to my life. Willie read that book, he fell in love with it, and eventually he fell in love with me. And finally because it brought to my life the awareness of how powerful the written word can be: how you can tap into that world that we are talking about and discover things that would have been impossible to know if you didn't have that connection to a collective knowledge that comes through the writing.

> *In an earlier interview you defined yourself as a troubadour. You said: "I want to go from village to village, from person to person, from town to town, telling about my country, telling about my continent, getting across our truth, that accumulated suffering and that marvelous expression of life that is Latin America." Do you still feel that way?*

Yes, I do. That's the only thing that I like about lecturing and reading. I don't like to travel very much, but when I go on these tours and find myself surrounded by people and can tell them something that I have seen or lived, I feel like the storyteller that goes from village to village telling the stories.

> *Music runs through the lives of your characters. Eva Luna, for ex-*

ample, hears a street singer and thinks that rhyming would be a good way to remember her stories. Is your storytelling a musical experience?

No. It's not. Unfortunately, I don't have any musical ear. It's closer to poetry maybe. For me, it's easy to remember a story when I can visualize the place, the smell, even if I have not been there, and somehow imagine it as a poem, as Pablo Neruda's poems, which are always loaded with sensuous feeling. That's how I see poetry, and that's the way I try to remember my stories.

I'm surprised to hear you say that you don't have an ear for music. Your prose is very musical.

Well, I read my writing aloud. I read it aloud because I can feel it when a word doesn't fit there, when a sentence is too long or too short, when I have to balance something in a paragraph. When I say that I have no ear for music, it's because I can't compose music, I can't sing, I can't remember music. It's too bad because being musical would really help.

You describe your grandparents' cellar as having "a cavernous silence, in which even your most tentative sigh sounded as strong as a gale." Do you hear your novels as well, when you write them?

I write in the voices of the characters. For me, the best example is Riad Halabí in *Eva Luna*, who had a harelip. I remember that when that character really appeared in my life, I had never known anybody with that problem, I didn't know how the voice would sound. But from the beginning I was struck by how strange the voice sounded. And when I began researching and found out what kind of voice a person with a cleft palate would have, it proved to be similar to what I had imagined—that kind of strange voice that cannot articulate consonants.

Is that an example of tapping into a collective truth?

Yes.

When you would move into Gregory Reeves' voice did you feel as though you had been possessed by him, as though you were an oracle for his essence? Is that how it felt?

Sometimes. And I tried to convey the chaos in his mind and in his life. The confusion, the terrible confusion, and the many choices— the wrong choices. I tried to convey that even with the writing, so the writing is very chaotic in certain parts.

He is certainly a man characterized by wrong choices.

He survives. He is a survivor. In real life Willie is too. He's a survivor, and the people who bend but never break are always fascinating to me. They can be on their knees today, and tomorrow they get up.

At what point in the novel did it become clear to you that Gregory and Carmen would not end up together?

To me, it was clear all the time. Because I knew the story. But I wanted them to get together.

Everyone does!

[*She laughs.*] I wanted them to get together. However, I had to be true to the characters. The same thing happened to me in *Eva Luna*, with Huberto Naranjo and Eva Luna. I wanted them to get together! But I would have betrayed Eva Luna profoundly if I had not yielded to the reality that they could not be lovers. And there I was, stuck, in the middle of a novel that I had planned in a certain way (well, I never planned much). I had these two characters I had been following from the very first page, these two orphans in the street who would eventually get together and become lovers—it was just obvious. And when it happened, it didn't work.

But she gets the German boy.

I didn't have the German boy then. I was stuck in a dead end. Then I was invited to tour Germany, and I ended up in Hamburg in the winter, an awful day. After the reading, a man came over and said he was a journalist and wanted to have a cup of coffee with me. I said I was really very tired and not ready for another interview. He said, "It's not an interview. I just have something to give you." And I thought,

"What is this?" So we went to a bar and had a beer while he told me the fabulous story of his life. He was the son of a German SS officer who was a sadist and had tortured his children and everybody around him. He had a sister who was retarded and who was brought up under a table covered with a white tablecloth. He gave me the story and I wrote it down on a paper napkin and asked, "Can I use this?" And he said, "I'm giving it to you." So when I went home, I just introduced the paper napkin into the computer, and there I have Rolf Carlé. I didn't have to make him up; someone gave him to me.

I think synchronicities happen when you are working on something and you are really very much into it. The world conspires to make it happen. The fact that I was stuck at that very moment with Huberto Naranjo allowed me to be open to the story of Rolf Carlé and bring him into the book. He became such a powerful character that he reappears in the short stories. He is somehow always in the back of my mind, he is so real.

> *Something about the red shoes that his mother has to wear is particularly frightening. Probably because it is disturbingly erotic, it is one of those horrible experiences, like when you read a rape scene and are at some level aroused. There is something so coldly powerful about the way she has to wobble around on those high-heeled boots. Is that real?*

No. I tried to think of something that would symbolize in few words how the mind of this man worked, and how the family was trapped in the mind and the horror of this man. I came up with the shoes. I don't know how.

> *They're really scary. Don't you agree?*

Now that you say it, yes. But to me, the most scary part of that character in that book is the child under the table. And in order to write that, I put a tablecloth over a table, and I spent a day under it because I wanted to see the world from down there, under the table, and through the tablecloth.

> *All of the horror of Evangelina's maggot-ridden corpse in* Of Love and Shadows *is not as bad as Katharina under the table. What can*

you do for Evangelina? She's dead. That's why it's so appropriate that Irene and Francisco make love after they see her.

Everybody objected to that scene so much! I think it's the only thing they could do. Fortunately, when I saw the scene in the movie, it worked great. The director originally had a lot of problems with it. She said, "I just can't take the audience from the mood of the corpses and all that to an erotic scene. It won't work." So we talked about it, and when she tried it, it worked fine. It seems to be the only thing that they can do to save themselves. It reaffirms life.

You once said that you came from such a repressed background you have a hard time writing erotic scenes. In comparing Francisco and Irene's lovemaking—which is heavily metaphorical, very beautiful and floaty—to Carmen and Leo's—which is very real and earthy—it seems fair to say that you've lost your repression, that you've developed the ability to write sensually. Is that conscious?

No, I think it has to do with the book. Every book has a way of being written. Every story has a way of being told. The story determines the tone in which we should tell things. Francisco and Irene are two very young people who lust for each other in the beginning and then they fall in love. By the time they have sex, they are really in love. They are also two young people who have been touched for the first time in their lives with the brutality of death and torture and repression and violence. They have entered into the evil dimension of the world down in hell. Making love brings them back from hell to life, to the paradise of love, in which they are safe; in that cocoon they are safe for a few moments only. Later, they will be destroyed by events, by life. The scene is told in such a way because, without even me being very conscious of it, it's like the myth of Eurydice. It's like something that happens in hell—Orpheus goes down to bring her back to life.

Carmen and Leo are just two middle-aged people. Like you and I and everybody else. There is nothing metaphorical about them. They are totally earthy. There is also that element of carnality, of being forty, that is not the same romantic thing of being twenty.

It is strange. Yesterday I was writing another scene, an erotic scene, and was finding it difficult. I always find it difficult. Some people say the best parts of my books are the erotic parts, but I find it very difficult to write them because I always think my mother is going to read them. My mother will say, "You've done this?" So I will have to explain it to my mother, and that really paralyzes me.

> *At a lecture last spring, you mentioned you were not going to write any more short stories. Are you adamant about not returning to that genre?*

I don't know. I should never say I'm never going to do something. Short stories come to you whole, like gifts. A novel is work—work, work, work—and then one day it's over; it's finished. But a short story is something that happens to you like catching the flu. You just go through it, and you don't decide anything. You don't create anything. The short story is really inspiration. All of a sudden, you have a flash of lucidity which lets you see an event from another angle that is totally unexpected. And you can't provoke that. It happens to you. You go to a place, you see some people dancing, and all of a sudden in a flash of inspiration you see the relationships between those people, or you seem to see something that is there that nobody else in the room can see. And then you have a short story.

I'm scared of short stories, very scared. I was teaching a creative writing course at Berkeley, and I said please, not short stories, because how can you teach a short story? It's impossible. A novel you can teach because once you have an idea, you can teach the craft of writing, of creating tension. But you can't teach that wonderful thing that a short story is. A gift. How can you teach that?

> *Do you write your stories as Eva Luna? Or do you write them and rewrite them as her?*

No, those were written as Eva Luna. Except the last one ["And of Clay Are We Created"], which is the story of how Rolf Carlé finds the little girl in the mud and helps her to die—that was not written from Eva Luna's perspective. It was always written from his point of view and then at the end, I turned it around, so that it's her, watching him through the TV. That really happened, in 1985 in Colombia. There was an eruption of a volcano called Nevado Ruiz, and a mud slide covered a village completely, and thousands of people died. They never recovered most of the bodies, and finally they declared the whole place a cemetery, a sacred land. Among the many victims was a little girl, nine years old, called Omaira Sánchez. This girl—who had very short dark curly hair and black eyes, huge black eyes—agonized for four days, trapped in the mud. The authorities could not fly in a pump to pump the water and save her life. And the television cameras came to the place in helicopters, planes, buses.

All over the world, for four days, the audience could see the agony of this child.

When that catastrophe happened in 1985, I turned on the TV and all of a sudden I saw this girl. There was a connection between those eyes looking at me from the screen and my own life. I was fascinated. I realized that she was trying to tell me something, teach me something. Later, I had her photograph on my desk for years, and I thought that by writing the story I would exorcise Omaira Sánchez, take her out of my mind. It has not happened. She has always been with me. When I wrote the story, it was the story of the girl who was trapped in the mud. And then I realized it was not her story. It was the story of a man who was holding her. And so I wrote the story from his perspective, him holding her. And then I realized that it was not him, either. It was me, watching. It was Eva Luna in this case, but it was me watching from the other side of the world what was happening there. We were separated by this enormous distance, and there was nothing I could do. Like in Greek tragedy, you know the ending, you know what is going to happen, and you can't stop it.

In 1992, my daughter fell sick. She was in a coma for a year, trapped in her body the same way that Omaira Sánchez had been trapped in the mud. From the very first moment that I saw my daughter in intensive care, the image of that girl came back to me. And I realized what she had been trying to tell me all these years about patience and courage. And death. And what it means to be trapped in a place from which you can't get out and you can't die. There you are—waiting. And what happens to the people around you who are determined and conditioned forever by this event. So when I think of my daughter, I always think that maybe some place she walks hand in hand with Omaira Sánchez. Her story and the fact that her eyes haunted me for so many years was a premonition. Life was telling me that I was going to have to go through this, and that man holding Omaira Sánchez was me holding my daughter, years later. That man helping her into death is me helping my daughter into death. I always make that connection: through the writing and through things that happen in your life, you're aware, you can see what is going to happen. You're being prepared. You never know what you are training for. I have that feeling all the time. So I try to be open to these lessons, to these teachings that make me more aware.

> *Your ability to stay open to experiences and carry them with you is matched by your ability to then sit down and through your writing make those things real, even through a very distant perspective. How much has geography affected your writing?*

I don't think it has because I always write from a long distance. That distance can be in geography. My first novels that are about Chile were written in Venezuela. I needed to get away from Chile to see Chile with some perspective. In Chile, I would never have been able to write them. *The Stories of Eva Luna* was written in the United States and it's about the Caribbean, Central America, and Venezuela. I also needed to get away from there in order to recreate the space, the color, the smells, the heat—everything. And *The Infinite Plan* was written from the greatest distance of all: the distance of not belonging. I will always be a foreigner in this country. I am first of all a foreigner to the language, which, for a writer, is something that determines your life. Because for me, life begins when you can tell it. If you cannot tell something, it has not happened. When my daughter died, I had to start talking about it in order to make it real. It was not real until I was able to say it in words, until I was able to say the word "death" instead of saying "passed away," or instead of saying "She's not here with us anymore." When I said *dead*, it became real and I could deal with it. So for me, language is very important, and the fact I am living in another language creates a tremendous distance that allows me to see this country with the same perspective that I would see it if I was living in Nepal. I don't belong, and everything for me is awesome. In a way, I am always asking the wrong questions. Fortunately, I seem to find the right people to ask the questions of. So I get wonderful answers, and from those answers the stories come. But there is that distance, which is essential. So I don't mind where I live. If I would have met a man from Kenya instead of from Marin County, I would be living in Kenya, and that would not make much of a difference. Now I'm writing a book that has nothing to do with the United States. It's a book about Chile. The fact that I'm living here and that I wrote *The Infinite Plan* doesn't mean at all that my future writing is related to this part of the world.

> *I'm struck by your ability to take something the majority of the world sees as a disadvantage and make it an advantage. Most people would see living in a second language as being marginalized.*

But that's great! Who wants to be in the mainstream? What are you going to do in the mainstream? The other day I heard something wonderful on TV about the problems this country is going to face in the next ten years—crime, violence, education, the lack of values, the destruction of the family, teenage pregnancy, drugs, AIDS. Someone said something extraordinary: "Have you noticed that immigrants don't have these problems? These are problems of born Americans, not of immigrants. Because immigrants come to this country with the same ideas and the same ideas that our great-grandparents came with. The first Puritans came with those tools to toil in this new world." This is related to what I've always said, that being marginal is like being a new immigrant, that you can reinvent everything. If you can transform marginality into something positive, instead of dwelling in it as something negative, it's a wonderful source of strength. It really helped me in Venezuela. When I first left Chile, I thought I was going to die. I just couldn't adapt. Chileans make terrible immigrants.

> *Margo Glanz has written that "hair is one of the things that most identifies a woman with her body and her sexuality. So hiding it was the worst kind of repression, and caring for it is the best way to show love . . . and a very feminine way of organizing the world." Are you making a statement about the strength or marginality of women through your characters' hair?*

No! I did not have the slightest idea that this person had written this thing. And I have never thought of it. My daughter had wonderful hair. Brown hair, down to her waist—a mane of beautiful hair. I remember braiding her hair. When she got married she wanted to have curly hair and so we did a thousand little braids, and then afterwards, when we undid the braids, it was just this incredible thing. And I never thought that it was a sign of power or sexuality or anything; it was just hair.

We often talk about the woman's voice in literature, and that is a perspective from which you write very successfully. Was it difficult in The Infinite Plan *to write in a man's voice?*

No. I also wrote from the perspective of a man and with a man's voice in *The House of the Spirits*. Some of the parts of the book are told by Esteban Trueba. I don't find that difficult at all. With *The Infinite Plan* it was easy because I had my husband. He was the guide. First of all, he helped me with the research. I was just overwhelmed by the research. I could not separate what was important and what wasn't in his fifty years in California. He helped me with that. He lent me his life. So he's the model. Although the book is fiction, he's the model for Gregory Reeves. For four years we talked and talked about the story. He told me his life. I automatically became his voice because I was listening to his voice in my ear all the time. We would talk in the car, we would talk in bed, we would talk everywhere, and anything could trigger a conversation about the book. We would see some event in the street or somebody, and then he would remember something that I could later use for the book. It was always his voice talking. And it became very easy. Then I realized also that the similarities are much more than the differences in gender. That men and women are very similar. Essentially, human beings are very similar, and we are stuck in the differences instead of highlighting the similarities. When I got into his skin and became him, I got to know him much better than if I had lived with him for thirty years. I came to realize what parts in him I could identify with and what parts in me he could identify with. That was a good experience.

That seems like a good place for us to turn back to the world of the spirits, to the place we started. Would you add to the characteristics of the spiritual world that it is genderless?

Maybe it contains gender. I have been a feminist all my life, fighting for feminist issues. When I was young, I fought with terrible aggression, giving aggression and receiving aggression. So there's a fighting time. I was a warrior when I was young. And now, more and more, it gets harder and harder for me to see the differences. More often I see the similarities, as if the angle were just drifting away, and I am becoming more aware of those essential things we have to explore that could really bring us together.

NOTE

Jan Goggans teaches at the University of California, Davis.

Writing from the Belly

INTERVIEW BY MICHAEL TOMS

Reprinted from *Common Boundary*, May/June 1994, 16–23

Most of us in the United States live lives isolated from the rest of the world, separated not only by geography but also by media filters. Unless we travel outside our nation's boundaries, there is precious little information about other lands and cultures. Our cultural bias has brought us numerous problems, including war. However, a growing number of writers from other cultures whose works have become popular in the United States are helping us to transform our mind-sets about other peoples of the world and leading us into the global society. Not the least of these is Isabel Allende.

The niece of Salvador Allende, former Chilean president, Allende was born in 1942 in Lima, Peru, where her diplomat father was posted. Her parents divorced when she was three, and her mother returned with her to Chile, where they moved in with Allende's maternal grandparents in Santiago. She spent many of her childhood years in that house, which would later become the basis for the family mansion described in her first book, *The House of the Spirits*. Following her mother's second marriage, again to a diplomat, Allende lived in a number of European and Middle Eastern countries, as her family followed her stepfather's diplomatic career.

Her first job, at age seventeen, was as a secretary for the United Nations Food and Agricultural Organization. Assigned to the Information Department, Allende immediately began to work with journalists. While there, she married her first husband, an engineer, with whom she had two children, Paula and Nicolás. In 1965 she became a freelance journalist in her own right.

In 1973, Allende's world changed irrevocably: Her uncle was assassinated in a military coup against his Socialist government. Describing the effect of this event, Allende once said, "I think I have divided my life [into] before and after that day. . . . In that moment, I realized that everything was possible—that violence was a dimension that was always around you."

Forced to leave their homeland, Allende and her family eventually settled in Venezuela. It was there, in 1981, that she began *The House of the Spirits*, which chronicles three generations of a family caught up in Chile's recent brutal history. Since her impressive debut, she has published *Of Love and Shadows*, *Eva Luna*, *The Stories of Eva Luna*—all international best-sellers—and, in the spring of 1993, *The Infinite Plan*, her first novel set outside of Latin America. Divorced in 1987, Allende now lives in San Rafael, California, with her second husband.

" *You began your writing career as a journalist. How did you become a fiction writer?*

I didn't have a choice. I had been silent for a very long time, paralyzed by the experience of exile and the losses in my life. Then one day—it was January 8, 1981—I heard that my grandfather, who lived in Chile, was dying. When I was little, he was the most important male figure in my life. So I began a letter—it was a sort of spiritual letter—to say goodbye and to tell him that he could go in peace because I had all the anecdotes he had told me, all his memories, with me. I had not forgotten anything.

I started writing the first anecdote he ever told me—the story of my Aunt Rosa, who everybody said was very beautiful. But the letter became something else. I started stealing from people's lives, and other characters stepped in. All of a sudden I was writing fiction. But I didn't know what it was; to me it was still a letter. When I had five hundred pages, it didn't look like a letter any more. Then my grandfather died, so he was never going to receive it.

> *When you realized you had a book on your hands, was it easy to get it published?*

No, it was very difficult. I didn't know it was a book. I gave it to my mother, who said, "I don't know, but this looks like a novel to me." She helped me to correct and edit, and then I submitted it to several publishers in Latin America. No one wanted to read it. This was a first novel—a very long, very dirty manuscript. No one knew me, and I had a very political name, so it was a risky thing for any publisher.

Then one day a secretary in one of the publishing houses called me and said, "They are not going to publish this book here, but they're not going to tell you. I think it is good. Why don't you send it to an agent?" I didn't know that agents existed for books. I thought they were only for sports. So I sent the book to the person she recommended in Barcelona. The agent had the book published, translated, reviewed, and distributed. So I was very lucky.

> *You write in Spanish, don't you?*

Yes, only in Spanish.

> *Have you tried writing in English?*

No. I can write a speech in English, or a letter, but I can't write fiction. Fiction is something that happens to me in spite of myself. It happens in my belly, not in my mind. It's like making love or having children; it only happens in your own language, I suppose.

> *How do you start writing a book?*

I always start my books on the same day—January 8—and I have a ceremony that has become more and more complicated. You know, writing a novel is a long pursuit; it can last two or three years. You have to be in love with it; you really have to befriend the spirits of the book. The characters have to walk into your life, into the space where you're going to write, and you have to welcome them. I need help and inspiration. My mother, my daughter, who died recently, and my grandmother, who died long ago, help me. In this ceremony I welcome them; I ask them to help. Every morning when I write, I light a candle for them. They're there; their spirits are with me.

I get in the mood by writing a letter to my mother every morning. Then I just open my heart. It sounds tacky, but that's the way it is. When I start a book, I write a first sentence. Usually I don't know what the first sentence is. Sometimes I think I know what I am going to write, but when I start I realize that something totally different has been growing inside me. So I let myself go; I'm very open to the experience. I pour out the story in a first draft that is very messy and very long; I don't know what the story is about until I print it and read it. Then I say, "Ah, this is what it is," and I start cleaning it up— eliminating, editing, correcting. When I think that it's more or less okay, I send it to my mother in Chile. She reads it and comes here with a red pencil. We fight for a month at least. Then she leaves. Of the six hundred pages I had originally, I have maybe fifteen left. Then I start working again.

Was your mother always an editor?

No. But she is a tough critic, and she loves me unconditionally and is very honest with me. She doesn't have to be careful; she can say anything she wants. I know that it's always with the best intention. Although I don't pay attention to everything she says, I know that if she doesn't like something, there is something wrong. She can say, for example, "I don't like the ending," but she can't say what would be a better ending. But if she doesn't like it, it's because it's not working. So I write it over and over again until I feel that I've found what is best—or better, at least.

Would you say your books have a message behind them?

No. I don't intend to deliver any sort of message, because I don't have any answers. I just have the questions, and these are the same questions that everyone asks. Maybe what a writer has to do is just tune in to the question and repeat it in such a way that it will have a ripple effect and touch more people. I'm always moved by the same themes, so by going over and over the same questions, I ask myself who I am. It's like a journey inside myself. I suppose people do that in therapy; I do it through my writing.

> *It strikes me that your work emerges from deep feeling. Do you see your work coming out of your own pain, your own anguish?*

I think that every book is triggered by a very strong emotion that has been with me for a long time; usually that emotion is painful. However, the process of writing is so joyful—it's like an orgy—that I can't complain. I have a great time writing. I can write fourteen hours a day and not eat anything in that time, and yet I feel wonderful because the process is so exhilarating. But what triggers it is painful. I often cry when I write.

> *Do you think that's true for most writers, that one has to suffer in order to be creative?*

No. I think that you are more creative when you have free time, when you have met your basic needs, when you have affection and support, and when you are free. I think that's the best creative mood.

> *You're a great believer in solitude for writing. Tell me about that.*

Writing requires concentration and silence, and I can only get that in total solitude. If I don't have a sort of womb where I work, where I can retreat completely, then I can't write. I can write journalistically, I can write letters and speeches, but I can't write fiction because fiction is like embroidering a tapestry. You go little by little with a very fine needle, with threads of different colors. You need concentration because you don't know the pattern, and you can't leave any threads loose. You have to tie them all, and that requires that you have everything in your mind. Maybe other writers have an outline and follow it, and in that way they don't need this kind of concentration. But I'm incapable of doing that. Writing happens one line at a time. So I have to keep in mind the previous line and the first line that I wrote three months ago so that the whole story will be clean in the end.

I recall a story you told about one of the accounts in one of your books. You wrote about a mine where peasants had been murdered. There was a kind of psychic thread that moved through your writing process.

That story is from *Of Love and Shadows*. What triggered that book was anger at the abuses of Chile's dictatorship. They had killed many people. Many had disappeared. The story you are referring to is of a political crime that happened in 1973. Fifteen peasants were murdered, and their bodies were never found. Five years later, the Catholic Church opened an abandoned mine and found the bodies. No one knows how they got the news and how they opened it before the police could stop them. It was in the media, and there was a trial; that is how I learned about it.

When I wrote the story, I had some partial information, but only what the Chilean government released. I had to fill in the gaps with my imagination. When I finished the story, my mother read the book and she said, "This is totally unbelievable. The fact that a priest learns in confession that the bodies are in the mine, takes his motorcycle, goes to a place that has been closed by the police during curfew, opens the mine, finds the bodies, photographs them, and brings the photographs to the cardinal—that's impossible!" And I said, "Well, Mom, it's a literary device. I have no other way of solving the plot."

The book was published in 1984. In 1988, I was able to return to Chile. While I was there, a Jesuit priest came to speak with me, and he said he had learned in confession that the bodies were in the mine. He had gone there during curfew on his motorcycle; he opened the mine, photographed the bodies, and took the photographs to the cardinal. That's how the Catholic Church opened the mine before they were stopped by the authorities. He asked me how I had known, because the only people who knew about this were the cardinal and himself. I said, "I don't know. I thought I had made it up—but maybe the dead told me."

So it's like you are tapping into another level of consciousness, another reality.

I had the feeling with that book that the women in the story, the women who were looking for their husbands, sons, and brothers, forced me to write the story. There was a clamor that I heard, and that's why I wrote it with so much anxiety and anger. Often during the writing, I had the feeling that people were telling me things. I heard voices—not real sounds, just voices in my mind—and I would have dreams related to the story. I suppose that always happens when you are very concentrated on a project; you end up hearing things.

For example, when my daughter was sick for a year in a coma, I took care of her at home. She couldn't communicate in any way and was totally paralyzed. Yet I had the feeling that I could hear her voice, especially when I was asleep. I could hear her talking to me; I could see images. I knew exactly when she was going to die, because the communication became very strange, very foggy, blurred. I realized that she was just drifting away, although nothing had changed—there was no infection, her lungs were clear, and the doctor thought that she could live a long time. I knew that was not the case. The day she died, I knew the moment had come. She actually died the next day at four o'clock in the morning.

When you're concentrated on something—when your energy, your mind, and your emotion are focused on something—then you become aware of other signs, other languages, that maybe are always there, but you don't realize it when you are busy in the world.

How was that process for you, being with your daughter while she was in a coma?

There were stages, different stages. At the beginning, I had hope and struggled like a samurai to bring her back to life. Then I slowly gave up. I first gave up her body and said, "Well, she's not going to be the beautiful, graceful, wonderful girl she was." Then I said, "It doesn't matter. We still have the rest." Then I gave up her mind. When I learned that she had severe brain damage and that she would never recover, I said, "Okay, the mind is not so important. I'll take care of her. We have her alive; she's still here." Then I gave that up also and said, "Okay, she can go, and I will not love her less for that." I told her that she could go, that I loved her very much, and that I was going to be with her here and somewhere else in the future. She died and I had some ashes, and then I didn't even have that.

Is there something else that you'd like to say about your daughter?

I get very emotional when I talk about this, but I know that many people have relatives or people they love who are dying or are very sick. My experience may be useful to them: After a while you lose the fear of death, not only that your daughter will die, but that you yourself will die. You realize that death is like being born. It's like a threshold that you cross into another world. You don't carry any memories with you; that's why it's so frightening. But there is nothing frightening in the fact that you die.

Paula died in my arms. I got in bed with her and held her for a day and a night until she died. When it happened, I had a feeling of peace so profound that I fell asleep. I still remember the dream I had when I was holding her and she was dead. My son woke me up because Paula was already rigid, and he said, "We have to dress her and clean her," and we did that. Then I said, "We are not going to take her out of the house until her husband comes." Her husband was in Chicago. So Paula's body stayed with us for two days. In those two days, I got acquainted with death. There's nothing frightening about it. It's painful for me now to know that I will never talk to her again and never hear her laugh. But she exists; the spirit exists and is connected to mine. I'm not scared of her death or mine.

That's a powerful experience. I don't know what I can say other than I can imagine another book or two coming out of the experience you've gone through.

It's difficult for me to write when I'm in the middle of a hurricane. Literature needs ambiguity, irony, distance. Right now I don't have any of those.

But you think it is important to tell stories. Why is that?

I think that stories are to the society what dreams are to individuals. If you don't dream, you go mad. Dreams somehow unclog your mind and keep you tuned in to the unconscious world, from which you can draw experience and information. I think that's what stories do. There are hundreds, thousands of stories, but we always repeat the same ones. All the great plots have already been told innumerable times. We can only tell them again in a different way. Every time we do that, we tune in to the myth and somehow we make society dream.

The power of storytelling is amazing. Just try saying, "Once upon a time . . ." in an elevator. No one will get off. They remain until you finish the story.

At one point you wrote or said something about the contract between the reader and the author. Can you talk about that?

In Sudan, the storyteller sits in the center of the village and says, "I'm going to tell you a story," and the people say, "Right." She says, "Not everything in the story is true." They say, "Right." But then the story-teller says, "Not everything is false, either." "Right." They have a con-tract, you see. She tells the story, and the listeners know the rules. Not everything is believable, but we are going to pretend that it is. Well, that's how I feel with my reader. I'm proposing something. I'm saying, "Hey, this is the story I'm going to tell. Not everything is true, not everything is false, but maybe in this bunch of lies we can find some particles of truth. Let's both enter into this dimension of litera-ture, which is similar to reality but not altogether real; let's pretend it is and find our way together." That's what writing is. I can't imagine writing for myself, or writing and not publishing because I feel that a book doesn't exist in itself. It's not an end; it's a way of communicat-ing, a bridge. If I don't have a reader and I don't find someone to hold my hand and explore the space and time of the book, then I'm not in-terested. I would rather do something else.

Do you think about the reader as you write?

I think about one reader. I don't think of large audiences or millions of copies. I want to touch one person's heart; I want to grab that per-son by the neck and say, "I'm not going to let you go until the end of the book. You will read until the last page." That's important, very important.

Are there any Latin American writers who have influenced your work?

All of them. I belong to the first generation of Latin American writers to be brought up reading other writers from our continent. The pre-vious generation grew up reading European and American writers in translation. But I was influenced by all of them—by García Márquez, by Carlos Fuentes, Jorge Luis Borges, Julio Cortázar, José Donoso, so many of them—some of my own generation, like Eduardo Galeano. It's easy for me to write because I don't have to invent anything. They already found a voice, a way of telling us to ourselves, so it's easy.

What about Pablo Neruda?

I don't know if he influenced my writing but he's a big influence in my life. Pablo Neruda is a poet of the senses. For example, I think of his "Ode to Oil." You may have used oil all your life, but you've never seen the transparency or the color, felt the texture, smelled it; you don't know where it comes from or how it's made. The beautiful nature of oil becomes real when you read Neruda.

That's one of the gifts that Latin American writers give to us who live in North America. There's a quality that reminds me of the rain forest, the richness and luxuriant quality of the rain forest.

But I think that you find that in many North American writers, especially minority women—black women, Chicano, Chinese American, Japanese American, Native American. You find that kind of writing all the time. It's the WASP literature that is dead.

In The Infinite Plan, *you have a chapter about Berkeley in the '60s. You weren't here then; how did you find out about Berkeley?*

I have a friend who was in Berkeley in the '60s, and she took me back there. We walked the streets and talked to the street people who have been there for twenty years. She told me her story and allowed me to write about it, and many other people in the street told me their stories, too, so it was easy.

Vietnam was more difficult. I wrote the chapter about Vietnam twice. I felt that I was ready to eliminate it from the book because all the information was there, but no real feeling. I can't relate to the experience of war. Being a woman and being so anti-militaristic, it's very difficult to understand that. But I'm lucky. At the point when I was ready to take it out, a Vietnam veteran walked into my life and gave me the wonderful gift of his experience. I recorded it, and my job was only to translate it into Spanish.

You've described yourself as an insatiable story hunter. What do you mean by that?

I'm always stealing other people's stories. I meet someone, and I want to know what has happened in their lives and why. I always ask the wrong questions, but I am lucky and I ask them to the right people, so I get stories.

So the people who appear in your books are real people?

I always write fiction, but I can't trace the boundary between reality and fantasy anymore. The stories are always based on real people or real life. But I turn them around and twist them and deform them, so it ends up being fiction.

You do this with your friends? You take their stories?

Yes. I take my friends' stories, but I'm careful not to betray them. For me, a person is always more important than a character. I never use another person's story unless I've been authorized to do so.

So you tap into other people's stories.

Yes. But again, it's fiction. I take many things. For example, I have taken some parts of my husband's life, but Gregory Reeves [the main character in *The Infinite Plan*] is not my husband. Now, fiction is sometimes more powerful than reality. Who knows? Perhaps my husband will start believing that he is Gregory Reeves. That happened with *The House of the Spirits*. When I wrote the book, my relatives were very angry at me. But then the book became very popular, and they started playing the roles. The book has replaced the family's real memory. Now they talk as if these things happened. But movies are more powerful than books, and as soon as the movie is released everybody will think that Meryl Streep and Jeremy Irons are my grandparents.

You're talking about the movie of The House of the Spirits.

Yes.

Tell us about it.

It's directed by a Danish director, Bille August, who directed *Pelle the Conqueror* and *The Best Intentions*. He has done a super production. He filmed all the exteriors in Portugal because at the time when he started the negotiations, he could not do it in Chile. We still had a military dictatorship, and this is a very political movie. The interiors were filmed in Copenhagen. The movie will be in English, and the cast also includes Glenn Close, Vanessa Redgrave, and Winona Ryder. I have a wonderful photograph of myself sitting on an armchair surrounded by the stars in costume.

How about your other books? Do you see those getting onto film as well?

Well, they started shooting *Of Love and Shadows* in July 1993 in Argentina. It's an American production with an American director, Betty Kaplan. I'm signing the contract for *Eva Luna* and have some offers for *The Infinite Plan* but don't want to rush it.

Do you see any more Eva Luna stories emerging?

In every reading, someone from the audience asks that question. Writing short stories is very difficult. I find them much more difficult than a long novel. A short story is closer to poetry. You need inspiration, and I don't feel very inspired right now.

What advice would you give to someone who'd like to write a novel?

I don't know. I can't give any advice, but I tell my students that writing is like training to be an athlete. You're never going to break the record if you don't train every day. There's no way that you will write a novel by chance. There's a lot of daily work involved.

Then I think you have to be very cruel with the editing. Don't have any compassion for what doesn't work. Even if you've spent months working on a chapter just eliminate it. The best advice I ever received is, "Cut, cut, cut." You do that in journalism all the time. You are looking for an adjective, and all of a sudden you realize that you don't need it; you leave the noun alone. You can do the same with a sentence, a chapter—with a lot of stuff. Cut.

Speaking of journalism, I once heard you say that you were a bad

journalist because you always got too involved with your stories.
How can anyone write about anything without being involved in it?

Yes, that's true, but there are limits. My limits were far-fetched. I think I was a lousy journalist. I was always putting myself in the middle of everything, writing in the first person, never being objective. I lied all the time. If I didn't have any news, I made it up; that's a bit too much.

But don't you have to immerse yourself in something to be able to
understand it? How can you distance yourself?

You have to pretend that you are objective. I was never able to do it. But I loved journalism. What I loved about it was the feeling of participation; you're in the streets talking to people. That feeling of belonging is wonderful.

How does it feel to be away from your home country?

It was terrible when I couldn't go back, but now I go every year. My mother is there. I have the feeling that I have one foot there and one foot here. The terrible time was when I was living in Venezuela and felt that I could not return. Maybe I could have returned, but I was afraid. Fear is such a strange thing. It makes you totally irrational; you make the weirdest decisions because you are afraid.

I once wrote a story of two people who are tortured ["Our Secret"]. They find out when they are making love that both have had the same experience. One of the characters says [*she paraphrases*], "Fear is stronger than love. Fear is stronger than death, than hatred, than everything. Fear can make you do the most awful things." When I wrote that story, I thought that was true. Now I would change that. I don't think that fear is stronger than love. I think love is stronger.

What created that change?

Paula, my daughter.

Life is amazing, isn't it?

Yes. It's very complex and wonderful. But I have the feeling that life is like a very short passage in the long journey of the soul. It is just an experience that we have to go through, because the body has to experience certain things that are important for the soul. But we shouldn't cling to life and the world so much: we shouldn't cling to the material aspects of the world, because you can't take them with you. You will lose them no matter what; you will lose your own body.

Do you see that tendency more in the United States than in Latin America?

I see it everywhere. But I think there's a change. I'm very optimistic about the '90s. I think that there's more awareness, more sense of community. I tried to portray that in *The Infinite Plan*. My protagonist goes through life running after the materialistic American Dream. The '80s betray him, and he ends up on his knees. He has to start all over again; he has to find his roots and go back to basics, and he does that. I feel that's what's happening to this society. We've reached a point where violence, crime, loneliness, and despair are so terrible that people are looking for answers in other places now.

You're hopeful.

Oh, yes, very hopeful. I don't think that we're going to destroy ourselves with the ozone layer or a nuclear holocaust. I think that we're going to survive and be better.

What about community? Do you see community taking a new form in the '90s?

I think that humanity's capacity for survival is amazing. When we reach a point that we are going to destroy ourselves, we somehow wake up and make changes. I think that there are new forces in this society that are leading to change. More and more women have been able to get away from the cultural pattern that they received when they were children. These people are raising children who are different. So I'm hopeful, very hopeful.

What about urban violence?

In a lab, if you have too many rats in a cage, even if there is enough food, they will kill each other. So there is a point when we will have to divide the big cities into small villages. We are going to do that, because there is a point when these mega-cities destroy life and the environment. Mexico City has nineteen million people who live in chaos. You can't live there. The birds fall dead from the sky because of the pollution. So we have to find solutions for that.

Where do you see your work taking you?

I don't have any plans for the future. I may die tomorrow. That's what I told my husband when I met him. It was October, and he said, "I'm going to visit you in Venezuela in December." I said, "What are you talking about? December? I may be dead by December." He said, "Why? Are you sick or something?" I said, "No, but who knows? I can be dead." That's how I feel. I feel I can be dead tomorrow, so I don't have any plans. I want everything now.

NOTE

Michael Toms is cofounder of New Dimensions Radio. He also serves as senior acquisitions editor for HarperSanFrancisco and is the author of *At the Leading Edge*. This interview is from the transcript of New Dimensions program 2384, broadcast nationally on public radio stations. Copyright © 1993. New Dimensions Foundation, P.O. Box 410510, San Francisco, CA 94141. All rights reserved.

Writing to Exorcise the Demons

INTERVIEW BY FARHAT IFTEKHARUDDIN

25

Reprinted with permission of the University Press of Mississippi from *Speaking of the Short Story: Interviews with Contemporary Writers*, ed. Farhat Iftekharuddin, Mary Rohrberger, and Maurice Lee (Jackson: University Press of Mississippi, 1997), 1–26

Isabel Allende was born in Lima, Peru, in 1942. She currently resides with her husband in California. Her career covers a wide range of experiences including journalism and teaching. As late as 1989, she taught creative writing at the University of California, Berkeley. She is the author of the international best-sellers *The House of the Spirits* (1985) and *The Infinite Plan* (1991). Her works also include two other novels and a collection of short stories: *Of Love and Shadows* (1984), *Eva Luna* (1987), and *The Stories of Eva Luna* (1989).

This interview was conducted during the Third International Conference on the Short Story in English hosted by the University of Northern Iowa, June 4–7, 1994.

    ❝ *Critics have drawn comparisons between your works and other Latin American writers. They readily compare Gabriel García Márquez's*

> One Hundred Years of Solitude *with your novel* The House of Spirits. *Some feel that it is a remake of Márquez's novel replacing patriarchal authority with emphasis on matrilineal strength. How do you respond?*

I belong to the first generation of writers of my continent who have been brought up reading other writers from Latin America. The previous generation, which we have called the Boom generation, included such writers as García Márquez, José Donoso, and Carlos Fuentes. The phenomenon of the Boom started in Barcelona. I was very privileged to be a part of the readers of the writers of that time. I grew up reading them, and when I started writing, I think that all those wonderful words, those images, that tone to narrate our continent was so deeply rooted in me that it just came right out in a very natural way. It was not my intention at all to create anything ironic about *One Hundred Years of Solitude* because I really admire that novel very much. I have read it a long time ago, and I don't remember it very well. But comparing *One Hundred Years of Solitude* in the way that it is compared is totally unfair.

> *What were the compelling reasons for writing* The Stories of Eva Luna *after the novel* Eva Luna?

Well, several reasons. The first one was that many people questioned, when I finished the book, that Eva Luna is a storyteller, this is *her* story but where are the stories she tells? I had never considered the short-story genre because I think it is very difficult, and at the time, after I finished *Eva Luna*, I divorced my husband in Venezuela and went on a crazy lecturing tour that brought me to the United States. I ended up in northern California where I met a man and fell madly in love, so that's the reason too. I had to move to this country following a passionate heart; it was a very hectic time. The only advantage of short stories is that you work in fragments. I thought that since I had to go on working, the only thing I could do then was something that was brief. So, I thought that writing short stories that Eva Luna didn't tell in the book was a good idea. So that's how I did it.

> *Almost every story in* The Stories of Eva Luna *has an epiphanic*

ending. Is this sudden awareness simply an awakening on the part of the character, or is there an embedded socio-political message?

I don't try to give a message in anything I write. Sometimes there is a sort of surprise for me too because the characters come out with these endings; they come out with these things that happen to them, that happen in spite of myself. In some stories, I seem to know from the very beginning what the ending will be, but I know it at a gut level; I don't know it intellectually. If I would have to tell you the story before writing, I wouldn't know, but when I start writing, everything seems to flow in a very natural way and ends up in a surprise for me, except in one of the stories. It's called "The Little Heidelberg." When I finished that story, my mother read it and said "I like the story, but this is a crappy ending." I thought she was right; there was something wrong with this ending. She couldn't tell me what was wrong, but I realized that I had not followed the instincts of the characters; I had tried to impose a happy ending, and it didn't work. So I just let the characters talk for themselves, and I got a very strange ending that is difficult to explain, but that's what they wanted.

Was that the only story where you felt that you were being an intrusive author?

Yes, except for one other. The last story in this collection, which is the most elaborate story in the book, is called "And of Clay Are We Created" and is based on a real story. In 1985, there was a volcano eruption in Colombia and a little girl was trapped in the mud, and she died there after four days of terrible agony. I saw her on television in Venezuela, and I wrote this story. When I finished the story, I realized that I had tried to tell the story from an intellectual point of view, very passionate but it was my mind working. And then I realized that is wasn't the story of the little girl; it was the story of the man who was holding the little girl. So I rewrote the story once more, and when it was finished, I realized that there was something phony about it too. It wasn't the story of the man who was holding the girl; it was the story of the woman who is watching through a screen the man who holds the girl. This filter of the screen creates an artificial and terrible distance but also a terrible proximity because you see details that you would not see if you were actually there. And so, the story is about the change in the woman who watches the man holding the girl who is dying.

> *Do you feel that aspiring short-story authors should attempt to create that kind of a screen in order not only to distance themselves but also give themselves the ability to be introspective without being intrusive?*

I think each author has a different approach. You cannot give a formula or a recipe because it won't work. What works for one story may not work for the other story. I think that in a short story the most important thing is to get the tone right in the first six lines. The tone determines the characters. In long fiction, it's plot, it's character, it's work, discipline—a lot of stuff that goes there. But in short stories, it's tone, language, suggestions—it's inspiration. So I don't have a recipe. That's why I don't like to write short stories; I hate them. I like to read them, but I don't like to write them. I would much rather write a thousand pages of a long novel than a short story. The shorter, the more difficult it is.

> *Why don't you elaborate on what it is exactly that you find difficult about writing short stories?*

The fact is that everything shows. In a novel, you can have a lot of knots and bad stitches, and if you are lucky, the charm of the tale will carry the book, and the reader will be trapped in the plot and in everything that happens there; it's like a party, an orgy. A short story is not; a short story has very brief time, very condensed concentrated plot, if there is a plot. The subtleties are important; the suggestion is important. You work with the reader's imagination, and your only tool is language, and there is no space or time for anything else. Everything shows. This is how I compare these genres: the novel being a very elaborate tapestry that has a lot of details, and you embroider it with threads of many colors without even knowing what the finished design is. A short short story is like an arrow; you have only one shot, and you need the precision, the direction, the speed, the firm wrist of the archer to get it right. So, you do it right from the very beginning or just abandon it. Get it right the first time. How does one do it? I think that's where inspiration comes in, the muse. That's why I feel so uncomfortable with short-story writing because I am not an inspired person; I am a hard-working person. So, I don't mind spending twelve hours a day for a year writing fiction, but if I need the inspiration and I don't have it, I feel very distressed.

Do you feel the impulse that it is time to write another short story?

I have not felt the impulse since 1987. But it may happen again in my life, depending on the circumstances. People are always asking me for short stories for some reason. The publishers don't like short stories. They think that they won't sell. However, the students seem to like them a lot. I get a lot of letters from them, and they always ask me for short stories. And you know what? The movie people want short stories because it is much easier to create a movie from a short story than from a novel.

In the short story titled "Interminable Life," you write:

> *There are all kinds of stories. Some are born with the telling; their substance is language, and before someone puts them into words they are but a hint of an emotion, a caprice of mind, an image, or an intangible recollection. Others are manifest whole, like an apple, and can be repeated infinitely without risk of altering their meaning. Some are taken from reality and processed through inspiration, while others rise up from an instant of inspiration and become real after being told. And then there are secret stories that remain hidden in the shadows of the mind; they are like living organisms, they grow roots and tentacles, they become covered with excrescences and parasites, and with time are transformed into the matter of nightmares. To exorcise the demons of memory, it is sometimes necessary to tell them as a story.*

> *Is this your definition of short story and also your process of writing short stories?*

This is how I feel about fiction writing. I have had a tormented and long life, and many things are hidden in the secret compartments of my heart and my mind. Sometimes, I don't even know that they are there, but I have the pain—I can feel the pain; I can feel this load of stories that I am carrying around. And then one day I write a story, and I realize that I have delivered something, that a demon has come out and has been exorcised. It's not something that I do consciously, except in very few occasions, but when it happens, it's such a relief. That's how I feel about fiction. Some people do this in therapy, some people do it in meditation, some people do it drinking. My way of getting rid of the pain, my way of exorcising and understanding the world, is writing fiction. Maybe that paragraph is about that; it's about all the demons and the angels that I have inside that I don't know that I have, and I have to bring them out into the light and talk to them and see them in the light.

What are the sources of the experiences that you describe in your stories?

Most of them come from things that have really happened. Newspapers, television, radios, those are the great sources of inspiration for me. For example, that story we were talking about, "And of Clay Are We Created," is something that I saw on television. Sometimes, it is something that I see very briefly in the news, and I start asking myself questions about it. In *The Stories of Eva Luna*, there is the story— I don't remember the title ["If You Touched My Heart"]—of a woman who is kidnapped by a man and put in a cellar where she spends fifty years. She never talks to anybody and becomes like an animal in the darkness. When she is finally rescued, she is transformed, sort of, into a horrible beast that has spent all her life in that cellar. I got this from a spot on television (in the news) in Venezuela. A jealous man had kidnapped a young woman and put her in a cellar where she spent fifty years. I saw her on television when they brought her out wrapped in a blanket. That was it; she was never again in the news. So, I started asking myself, why did it happen? Why didn't she scream? Why didn't she try to get out? How did she survive? By asking myself those questions over and over again, the story came out; the motivations of the story were in those questions. Other times, it's people who tell me things, and I look behind whatever they have told me. They tell me something that they think is a story, and I realize that that is not the story. The story is something that lies behind that or beyond that. Often, it's something that I guess. I have one story called "Our Secret." It is a story of two young people who meet, make love, and in the lovemaking they discover that both have been tortured in the same way. The experience of torture has marked them so profoundly that they can't completely make love and cannot relate to the world; they have been destroyed. This came from something that I saw once. I had just met a couple of young people, Chileans, in Venezuela. I saw that both had similar marks on their wrists. At the beginning, I thought that they had tried to commit suicide. Then I realized that they were both from Chile, both were exiles, and both were from the same generation: I started asking myself more and more questions about them. Finally, when I came up with the story, I thought this is just pathological. I am imagining these awful things; this can't be true. Later, I confronted my theory with the reality of their lives, and it was true.

How do you then cloak fiction with truth or truth with fiction?

I can't trace the boundary. I think that everything is true, that fiction is just a way of saying something that is truthful from the very beginning. What is fiction? A bunch of lies, but it wouldn't work if those lies didn't come from a very honest truthful place inside you. Why do you want to write that story? Why do you want those characters and no other characters? That plot and no other plot? Because you are tapping into something that is your own experience, your own sentiments, your own emotions, your past, your biography, or a collective soul. And because you tap into that, the story is true and it works. When you don't, you have created this artificial fiction that is reassuring—the romance novels, the thrillers, and the mysteries—which are genres that don't work with truth, but they are also categorized as fiction, entertainment. But we are not talking about that; we are talking about something that is much deeper.

Is Agua Santa your mythical town like William Faulkner's Yokna-patawpha or Sherwood Anderson's Winesburg, Ohio?

No. I feel much better with an undetermined place and undetermined time. I like the ambiguity when the story happens in a landscape that the reader can invent. If you think about it, the only thing that you know about Agua Santa is that it's hot. You don't know anything else about it; you don't know where it is; you don't know how it looks or how many people live there because I want that place to be not my mythical place, but the reader's mythical place. And that's the same treatment that I give my characters. Very seldom is there a physical description of a character in my writing because I want the reader to create the character. So I only describe what is absolutely essential for the story. The fact that a person is retarded, or has a harelip, or is very tall, is told because, in a way, that is important to the story; otherwise, I wouldn't even say that. I don't even mention the age; you don't know whether they are young or old.

> *How about those characters who are highly sensuous. There is overt sexuality in stories such as "Wicked Girl" or "Toad's Mouth." Are you asserting the notion of female body as text in these stories?*

I wouldn't say that my stories are sexual, I wish they were. I really would like to write erotic novels. Unfortunately, I was raised as a Catholic, and my mother is still alive, so it's difficult. However, I feel that there is a part of me as a person that is extremely sensuous and sexual. Through that part of me, I can express certain truths that I cannot express otherwise. When I say sensuous, I don't mean sexual: for me sensuous includes food, texture, and smells. In all my stories and novels you will find smells because that is extremely important to me. A few days ago, I was given a doctorate in Maine, and the person who was putting the hood on me smelled wonderful. I got totally distracted; I couldn't think of the fact that I was receiving this doctorate, only of his smell. I would have followed that man to the end of the world because he smelled a certain way. Smell is very important to me; it's like nature, like sounds.

> *In your stories the real and the hyperbolic blend. That puts you into the field of magic realism. You also have an acute female sensibility that we can detect. Some have observed the parodying of perhaps Pablo Neruda and Marquis De Sade. If you were to characterize yourself, would you call yourself a feminist writer?*

Yes. First of all we should agree on the term feminist. Right now it is loaded with negative meanings for a lot of people. Because I am a woman and because I am an intelligent woman, excuse my arrogance, I have to be a feminist. I am aware of my gender; I am aware of the fact that being born a woman is a handicap in most parts of the world. In only very privileged societies, very privileged groups, have women achieved enough freedom and enough awareness to be able to fight for their rights. But in any circumstance, a woman has to exert double the effort of any man to get half the recognition. I want my daughter, my granddaughters, and my great-granddaughters to live in a more gentle world. In a world where my son, my grandsons, and my great-grandsons will also live in a much better place and where people can be companions and partners, where sex can be something that we will both enjoy greatly, and where love for ourselves, love for each other, and love for this planet will prevail. I think that is what being a feminist means, the awareness and the strength to fight for what you believe.

> *The epigraph to your novel* The House of the Spirits *is a poem by Pablo Neruda where the poet raises the question, "How long does a man spend dying?" Addie's father in Faulkner's* As I Lay Dying *may have already responded to that when he said that "the reason for living was to get ready to stay dead a long time." How would Alba, Eva Luna, or even you respond?*

I don't know about Alba or Eva Luna, but I know what I would respond. I think that the reason to live is to learn. We come here to experience through the body things that the spirit could not experience otherwise. So we need this body, and we have to transform this body into a temple of learning. It is difficult because our culture does not promote that at all. But I try to use my senses, my imagination, my body, my mind, and all the things that I have in this life to make the spirit grow. That's what we come for. If you think about it, there is silence before we are born and silence after death; life is just a lot of noise.

> *Elvira in* Eva Luna *tells Eva, "Your mother must have had a liquid womb to have given you that inventiveness you have to tell stories, little bird." Is that the secret of writing short stories?*

That's one of the many dirty tricks. It's amazing. Sometimes these things just occur to me, and I write them down without ever thinking that anybody will even notice. For example, I write a food recipe. I just make it up and then people call me and say it didn't work. If I provide a beauty recipe saying that if you do this or that, it will make your hair blond, people believe it, but it's not true. It's just part of the tricks, and after all, all wombs are liquid when you are pregnant.

> *Going back to the issue of asserting yourself as feminist, what is it that you don't want readers to view your work as? I hope it's never negative in the sense of not reading a piece of literature simply because it is viewed as feminist—that would destroy the essence of literature.*

I don't know. Each reader has a different approach. I want my readers to be entertained. I want to grab them and seduce them into the reading. I want to invite them to this wonderful place where we can share a story, and I only give him or her half the story; the other half has to be recreated or created by the reader, and that is the space we are going to share. Sometimes in the stories there are political elements, social elements, feminist issues, or environmental issues. All the things I believe in come out, but I don't want to deliver messages. I don't have answers; I just have the questions, and I want to share the questions. On the other hand, labels are unavoidable when you have critics. Critics are terrible people. They will label you no matter what, and you have to be classified. I don't want to be called a feminist writer, a political writer, a social writer, a magic realism writer, or a Latin American writer. I am just a writer; I am a storyteller.

> *Scheherazade not only saved her life though her stories, but also received the recognition of the Sultan. In essence, she brings herself into existence with words. Is Eva Luna your protagonist who brings "the female" into existence through words?*

Yes. I also think that in a weird way Eva Luna is me or I am Eva Luna. She is a storyteller, and she creates herself; the reader doesn't know if he or she is reading Eva Luna's biography, what Eva Luna invents about herself, or the soap opera that she is writing. So there are three levels of writing and understanding this novel. I believe that in a certain way that's how my life has been. If you ask me to tell you my life, I will try, and it will probably be a bag of lies because I am inventing myself all the time, and at the same time I am inventing fiction, and through this fiction I am revealing myself. So these are the three levels through which my life happens. I can't say who I am because the boundaries, as I said before, between reality and fantasy are totally blurred.

Are those the three levels that readers must also keep in mind when they read the collection of stories, The Stories of Eva Luna?

Don't keep in mind anything, just enjoy it.

I think you are looking at a critic here.

Critic, just enjoy it.

What do you think your narratives lose in translation?

My books have been translated into twenty-seven languages that I know of, but I also know of other translations that have not been authorized, for example, Vietnamese and Chinese. I have no control over the official translations, let alone the ones that are not authorized. In English, French, and German, the translations I know are very good. Now, every time that I read aloud in English my own stories, I feel very uncomfortable. I think the translation is great; sometimes it sounds much better than in Spanish, but it's another story. I can only be myself in my own language. It's like making love, you know; I would feel ridiculous panting in English. I really need to express it in my own language. When I play with my grandchildren, it's always in Spanish. There is something that is playful and sensuous; it happens at a gut level, a very organic level that can only happen in your own language; it's like dreams.

Is there something you cannot write about, a "demon of memory" that you cannot "exorcise"?

I don't know because I have been trying to exorcise them all and in the long run, I may achieve that if I have enough time, if I live long enough. I have a lot of demons. There are certain things that appear over and over in my writing that I can't avoid: they seem to be love and violence—two very strong issues in my life.

You have written four novels and a collection of short stories. You have reached fame with these works. Is it time for another collection of short stories, you think?

You know, I have just finished another book that will be published soon. Now it's being translated. It's a sort of memoir. I think it's non-fiction; however, it reads like fiction. After finishing this book, I felt so exhausted, so drained, that I thought, well, I will spend six months without doing anything, and let's see what happens next. And there is a certain voice inside me saying why don't you just spend these six months thinking about short stories? But as I told you before, I really need inspiration and if it doesn't come . . .

What's the title of this new work?

It's called *Listen, Paula.*

What would you tell aspiring short-story writers about writing short stories?

Don't. Write a novel; it's much easier—the longer the better. You will get a publisher, you will get an agent, and it will be much easier. It's much easier to write. Short stories are closer to poetry, to dreams, than they are to long narratives. And I think that you need a very skilled writer. How many short stories can you remember? How many are memorable? How many have been transcendent? How many short-story writers are really important writers only for their stories? It's because it's a very difficult genre, very difficult. So I would tell them, try with a novel first and when you have the skills, then you can write a short story. But people think it's the other way around. People think that if they can write a short story then eventually they will be able to write a novel. It's actually the other way around. If you are able to write a novel, someday with a lot of work and good luck you may be able to write a good short story.

You started off your career as a journalist. Has that made writing fiction easier for you, particularly the short story?

Yes, because I still use many of the techniques that I used as a journalist: for example, interviewing people. As a writer of fiction, I believe that it is much better to research with interviews of real people who have experienced the event, whatever that event may be, than going to a library and looking at books. Through interviews you can come up with things that you will never find in a book. Journalists are in the streets hand in hand with people talking, participating, and sharing. Writers are very isolated people. They usually live under the big umbrella, protected under the big umbrella of a university or some institution, and they are disconnected from real life in the world. They end up writing for professors, students, and critics, and forget that there is the world out there. So, my background as a journalist helps me in that way. And there is something else that helps enormously. As a journalist, you know, you have a few sentences with which to grab your reader, and you are competing with other media; you are competing with other articles in the same newspaper or whatever media you are using. So you have to be very efficient with language, and you have to remember that the first important thing is to have a reader. Without a reader, there is no text. Writers forget that; writers write for themselves. I am in that sense much more of a journalist. I will not write something that is just for myself except the last book which I recently wrote, a book that I wrote out of extreme pain. I could not have written anything else. When I wrote it, I was not thinking of publishing it. My daughter died recently; she was in a coma for a year, and I took care of her. During that year, everything stopped in my life. I had a year to revise my life, to ask myself the questions that I had been avoiding and go through the most excruciating pain. I think that I am still in that tunnel of pain, but the fact that I finished the book has been like a catharsis in many ways. So, when I started writing *Listen, Paula*, my only goal was to survive; that is the only time that I have written something without thinking of a reader.

"An Orgy of the Senses"

INTERVIEW BY PILAR ALVAREZ-RUBIO
Translated for this book by Virginia Invernizzi

26

First published in Spanish in *Revista Iberoamericana* 60, no. 8 (1994): 1063–1071

Clara del Valle, the indefatigable grandmother of *The House of the Spirits*, suggests to her suffering granddaughter that writing will help her survive the torment to which she is being subjected by her torturers. Now, in one more of those cases in which life imitates art, the writer Isabel Allende, much like her character, manages to endure moments of profound pain through her own writing. Today her writing is a palliative for the recent death of her daughter, much the way it alleviated the pain of exile at the beginning of her literary career.

The selection that follows is part of a conversation that I had with Isabel Allende in Corte Madera, California, on January 28, 1993. This conversation was postponed twice, once due to the death of my companion of many years, and the second time due to the death of Allende's daughter. These circumstances gave our conversation a very personal tone which dissipated all my apprehension of interviewing a personality of the stature of Isabel Allende: a well-known journalist, the most widely published Latin American woman writer, and the niece of the late president of Chile, Salvador Allende. The importance of what we had both just experienced erased all the unnecessary barriers that separate human beings, and so Isabel Allende was no longer the internationally known novelist, but the woman, the mother, the compatriot. The public personality became the very personal woman and the conversation flowed naturally, sometimes reaching mutual disclosures that I have not included in the published interview. At other times there were charming moments of laughter, yet always following the line of her work.

> " *Due to the circumstances and the process that this interview has followed, I cannot avoid asking you about absence, loss, and about the theme of motherhood that seems so present in your first novels.*

It must be because in my life, the oldest, most powerful, and strongest relationship is the one I hold with my mother. She has also been the greatest love of my life. My mother distinguished me among her children by granting me unconditional love. This love has served me as a type of take-off runway for everything that I have done in my life, and to have a sort of audacity, because no matter how much trouble I get into, I can always run back to my mother. I have not done it, but I always have that marvelous feeling that she is there for me. I have the sense that if my mother loves me, the rest of humanity loves me too. I love my children in the way that my mother loved me; I love the men in my life with an intensity similar to the love of my mother.

Have you felt the absence of a paternal figure?

I thought I had not, but now with the death of my daughter and with everything that has happened recently I realize that I carry with me many losses, many separations; from the first separation which was my father's leaving, to the fact that my mother married a diplomat and we were always traveling. As a child, I spent my childhood saying goodbye to schools, friends, places, landscapes, and climates. And that relentless farewell had its effect on me. When I had to confront the last and most severe separation in my life, which was the death of my daughter Paula, I was invaded by a sense of loss, of solitude. All the feelings of exile returned, the loss of Chile, the loss of family, the loss of roots. It is difficult, but I think it is good. It is good from the perspective of the soul, first of all, and then possibly also from the perspective of writing itself.

> *I have noted a strong biographical component throughout your writing. I was thinking, for example, of your last novel,* The Infinite Plan, *dedicated to your husband, and with an ending where one can identify an encounter, almost directly, between William Gordon and Isabel Allende, and not between the author and the character as in* Niebla, *for example.*

Yes, but that book is fiction, and Gregory Reeves is not Willie. Even though there are many episodes from Willie's life and parts of his personality, I also stole from other people's lives.

> *Yes, but how important is the autobiographical or the relationship between reality and fiction in your writing? Do you take much from life?*

I don't have much imagination. What I do have is a certain capacity to take things from reality and transform them, but most of what I write has a basis in real life; not so much from the lives of other people, but from events. For example, I read that in Los Angeles adolescents run with the trains in a sort of a challenge against each other, and many of them die. I then imagine that my child could be there, and I get into the story and I start twisting and turning it. Then, all of a sudden, I realize that I can use it for the novel that I am writing. Other times something has a great impact on me, and I don't use it immediately but I take notes and I save it for later. I have a folder where I keep newspaper articles and after a while I look inside and discover real jewels.

> *And so that is your method for writing?*

I also interview people when I need something specific. I needed a Vietnam veteran for *The Infinite Plan* and the right person appeared in my life just at the right time. We were locked up in a room for hours, days, with a tape recorder and that was how the chapter on the war was born. I developed the character of Carmen based on two people from real life to which I also added elements of fiction.

> *I found Carmen Morales a very interesting character. Do you ever think of taking your characters and continuing on with them in other novels the way Galdós did, for example?*

I don't think so. A novel never ends; but there comes a time that you give up, you can't go on any longer, you have become saturated with the characters and the story. And I suppose that is the moment to end it because you can always go on correcting and adding more. A story never ends, life goes on, but the author gets tired of narrating. When I close a book with its last page I do not ever read it or think about it again. It leaves my head.

> *In any case, you have to reread in order to correct.*

I hardly touch the galley proofs because the final manuscript that I send has been over-corrected. I could spend two years correcting the original.

> *I have heard that your mother is one of your literary critics.*

My mother is my harshest critic. She is the only one I would allow to tell me the terrible things that she tells me. [*Laughs.*] When I finish a book, I send it to her in Chile. She immediately gets on a plane and comes armed with her red pencil and we lock ourselves up in the dining room and begin the battle. When she leaves, of the six hundred pages in the book, I am left with about fifteen that have no red marks on them. She is my most ruthless critic. She reads everything of mine with patience, prudence, and she is painstakingly fastidious in her work. I then rewrite the book and no one sees it after this final draft. That draft goes directly to the press. I have no editors who correct my work, except for my mother.

> *Again we see that strong connection with the maternal . . .*

And with the grandchildren! I have a very strong connection with my grandchildren. With my grandchildren the connection is one of being in love. When one is in love (I am in love with my husband, so I know) and they don't call you on the telephone, something inside hurts. You feel that you are going to die, and if you don't see them one day the feeling of restlessness is so strong that you cannot rest . . . that's what I feel with my grandchildren. [*Laughter.*] If I don't see them one day I feel the same anxiety one feels before an absent lover. I am totally in love with the children.

About your writing, do you have a project in mind at the moment?
Yes, but I cannot speak about that.

Can we talk about it some other time then?
No, I never talk about what I am writing because I am very superstitious. I believe that if I talk about it, it will disappear into thin air. The wind will steal my words and then I cannot write them down any longer. I need to save up all my energy to write.

When did you finish writing The Infinite Plan?
In October 1991.

And you have already started something new . . .
I should have started in 1992 but my daughter became ill and I did not do anything. I spent all year with her. I have just begun another book; I don't know what it will be exactly yet.

Let's return to the relationship between reality and fiction, which is an often-debated issue in Latin American literature. The critic Fredric Jameson believes that in general, the fiction coming out of the so-called Third World countries tends to be allegorical of the socio-cultural and historical situation of the countries. He sees this as the opposite of what would happen with the literature of the First World countries where the writers can have the luxury of playing with form, fantasy, and art. Based on this idea, some critics accuse Latin American literature of a lack of artistic autonomy. What do you think about the matter?
Well, if independence means fleeing reality and entering an ivory

tower that is generally protected by the great umbrella of the universities and the foundations, and if that also means writing for the critics so that they study your work, I am not interested. I prefer a thousand times to stay with my "underdeveloped" literature that grabs the reader by the neck and makes her/him think and feel a reality that possibly at that time is not hers/his, but could be.

> *Do you believe that the Latin American writer has the responsibility to reflect upon the reality that surrounds her or him?*

I don't feel literature as a responsibility. When I began writing, and when I was much younger, I felt that every Latin American writer had a certain responsibility before the reality that one experiences in our continent. Besides that, it was the worst years of the dictatorships. But now I am much less pretentious. I realize that writers don't have all the answers. Often we don't even know how to denounce happenings; we are but witnesses before events and among all the lies we discover particles of truth. That is our task: merely to ask the questions that everyone asks themselves. We don't have an answer; at least I don't know anyone who has an answer.

> *Nevertheless in Latin America, traditionally the writer has been assigned the role of interpreter of reality.*

I think that all artists in Latin America feel very committed to reality. You and I come from Chile, where all one talks about is politics and food . . . and nothing else. And in many places it is like that. Reality is so strong, there are so many contrasts, so much violence, so many things that one needs to examine. Questions are inevitable in writing and in life itself.

> *In order to write about Chilean reality, you had your own personal experience. So what was your creative process in order to represent a Chicano family, or the sixties culture in Berkeley in* The Infinite Plan?

When I arrived in this country I felt very marginalized, very foreign. I didn't know the rules, I didn't speak the language well, I couldn't even go to the movies because I didn't understand what the actors were saying. I felt very isolated, and then I realized that there were millions of Latinos in the same situation and that there was a sort of subculture, or parallel culture, which was our own, to which I had not integrated myself. Something that fascinated me was that relationship of love and hate that has existed between Latinos and Anglo-Saxons in this part of the world. It is a story laden with greed, violence, excess, and hope, which inevitably will end with integration. Because there is no doubt that it will happen sooner or later. And in spite of the barbed-wire fences and the police dogs, millions of people cross the border from here to there and from there to here every day. It is an extremely rich phenomenon in its nuances and very interesting for a writer. I decided one day to write about California and the clash between the Latino and the North American world. This happened like a flash the day I was married. I married Willie and we had a very small, private ceremony for our friends. The man who married us had gotten a certificate from the Universal Church for twenty-five dollars, and so had the authority to marry us. My husband, a lawyer, couldn't find a judge to marry us. Well, Willie and I seem so different that it is as though we belonged to different species. Willie is a tall, very fair man with eyes so blue that they seem transparent . . . together we look like a Saint Bernard next to a Chihuahua. That adorable man who married us said, "You have come together to form a bridge between two cultures." It was like a flash of lightning to all-of-a-sudden understand that it was a wonderful mission. Willie speaks Spanish perfectly. All his life he has lived among Latinos and attempted to bridge that gap. I bring part of our culture to this part of the world. I have the privilege of having people who want to publish and read my books. That allows me to speak for those who don't have a voice or those who have not been heard. Writing a book about that seemed a fascinating project, but I did not know how to do it. One day, Willie told his story as a white boy in the Latino ghetto in Los Angeles, and I thought it would make an extremely original tale. Instead of telling it from the point of view of the immigrant, I inverted the situation, and so the perspective changes completely. The American part was much more difficult for me to write than the Latino part. I did a lot of interviews. I went to Los Angeles to speak to people. I went to almost all the places mentioned in the book, except Vietnam. Willie's experience in the ghetto when he was a child was very helpful to me. Families that Willie had met at that time were also cooperative, and served as a model for the Morales family. There was a lot of material. The American side was much more demanding for me to write not because the information was hard to find, but because it is difficult for me to write about that from the heart.

So you feel comfortable within the Chicano culture?

Yes, I feel comfortable with the Latinos in this part of the world. I don't know if it would be the same in Florida, but here I feel very comfortable.

It seems that within the United States, in general, the interest in Latin American literature was concentrated within the academic community. Because on a larger scale it seems readers only know authors like García Márquez, Puig, and Allende. How do you explain this, specifically in your case?

People in this country don't like to read translation. The same applies to French, German, or Scandinavian literature. People don't read translations, and editors don't publish translations if they can avoid it. That is one reason. Nevertheless, Latin American literature has entered the market in England and the United States recently. During the decade of 1973–1983, the decade of the dictatorships in Latin America, of the people that left, very few came to the United States or England. But many went to Germany, France, and the Scandinavian countries. Those countries are more receptive to our culture. Now the writers, the music, the Latin American food begins to be known more and more. You always start with the food. Have you noticed? The food, the music, and then other expressions of art.

And speaking about the international recognition of your work, I have read that The House of the Spirits *is being filmed in Europe. Have you had any part in that project?*

Yes, the filming has already started. The director is Bille August, the Danish director who directed *Pelle the Conqueror* and *The Best Intentions.* They say he is Ingmar Bergman's successor. There are many great artists playing roles in the movie. It will cost thirty million dollars. The cast is composed of such great artists as Meryl Streep, Glenn Close, Jeremy Irons, Winona Ryder, Vanessa Redgrave, Antonio Banderas, and other well-known actors. Such a cast has elicited much attention from the press because it is unusual to have gathered so many wonderful artists. The other day they called me from a radio station in Chile to ask me how I felt about the fact that a Chilean work of art had reached this level of acclaim. I answered that it was not that it was Chilean or mine. I do not feel that the credit is in any way mine. It is all Bille August's and if he had chosen another book he would have created something just as spectacular. This movie will be solely to his credit.

> *As the creator of this story, do you feel comfortable giving him* carte blanche *to recreate it for another medium?*

Absolutely. It is an entirely different product. At this very moment they are producing a play in England that does not belong to me either. *The House of the Spirits* left my hands twelve years ago and does not belong to me any longer. Possibly, it never belonged to me. I believe that the writer puts in about half; that is why every time a book is read, it changes. Every reader remakes the book according to his/her biography, life experience, feelings.

> *So it is as though the book became an autonomous entity.*

Of course. Why is it then that there are people who hate it, others who adore it, and still others who don't care much one way or another about it? Wouldn't it make sense to say that every one puts a bit of themselves in it?

> *How do you face the blank page? Do you plan much, or are you more spontaneous about it? For example, there is a critic that says that* Eva Luna *is a picaresque novel, another that says it is a* Bildungsroman. *Were you thinking in those terms when you began the novel?*

Not at all. I don't plan anything. I write for the infinite pleasure of writing. I turn on my computer and write the first sentence with an open heart. The characters and I will create something and I have no idea where it will all lead. I often have a plan, but I am not able to follow it because the characters themselves take over the story. This happened with *Eva Luna*. I had created those parallel lives, Huberto Naranjo and Eva Luna, who would naturally get together at some point in order to become lovers or something like that. When I got to that point, it didn't work out because Huberto Naranjo had turned into a very unpleasant macho. He unfolded that way as a character, and there was nothing I could do. He was stronger than I was. I finally came up with a character from Austria, Rolf Carlé, and I incorporated him into the story. Rolf Carlé, who was really my way out, began to grow and grow and even returned in *The Stories of Eva Luna*. He became a very important character for me.

> *So we could generalize and say that you are more of a spontaneous author, rather than a deliberate one.*

That is the way I am for everything in my life; even my cooking. [*Laughter.*]

> *Writing is never burdensome for you then.*

No, it is pure joy. Life tends to be a burden because it has very grave moments, with a very heavy karma. But the process of writing, even if you are writing the most painful piece, is always an orgy of the senses.

> *Do you believe that there is a karma?*

I believe that there is a destiny. I also believe that you can do much to modify it. There are things with which one is born and over which one has no control. Why are you born male or female, ill or healthy, black or white, in China or the United States? I don't believe that it is coincidence, but that it all belongs to some mysterious design. Now, thinking about what happened to my daughter, I can tell you that one controls very little. Free will is something very personal, part of your conscience. There is not much freedom in how you can fabricate your life.

> *One notices a great interest for marginal characters in your books. To what do you attribute that fascination?*

To the fact that they are much more fun than people with common sense. [*Much shared laughter.*]

I agree, that is one reason . . .

And also, because I believe that writers are almost always marginal. I feel that way in any case. I never really belonged anywhere. I didn't belong in Chile with my family. I didn't belong within my social medium; I was always a misfit. I never felt that the values of my social class fit me in any way. I felt I was outside the church, outside the family, outside society.

And how did you function then within that society?

As a rebel. My sense of humor made people overlook the rebel in me, my aggression and my differences, because I laughed it off. No one took me very seriously. For example, I married a very good and tolerant man. I was a most atypical wife, but since I did it all with a sense of humor, it all seemed as though I were very original. I wasn't a threat for my marriage, for society or anyone else, but in the end, all those things that I referred to with humor I actually felt very deeply; and I still feel them very deeply. I frequently spoke against machismo. All my life I have questioned authority, all types of authority, starting with patriarchal authority. Ever since I was a child I have questioned the authority of the church, the government, of hierarchies, of social classes. Imagine how much aggression I have experienced!

Your work has been applauded for the female characters that break the silence imposed on all women since time immemorial. On the other hand, it has also been said that your heroines reinforce stereotypes, and here I paraphrase: women and their attraction to magic and spiritism; the "normal" capacity for procreation; the passivity of the raped female peasant. Alba, standing before her tragedy, awaits and endures, but does not actively participate (except with her writing). Others are painfully naïve like Irene. Can you comment on these critics' questioning of your own feminist stance?

I believe that the majority of my characters resemble real life very much. I don't invent characters so that they serve as models for radical feminists or young women who want to be feminists, but I simply tell how life is. Life is full of contradictions. I, myself am full of them. I have been very liberal, a feminist, and very daring to do all the things that women of my generation were not permitted to do. Yet I use lipstick, high heels, and what I am most proud of is motherhood. I think that I am an exemplary daughter and mother, and I am extremely proud of that. What does feminism have to do with that? Absolutely nothing! Alba, Irene, and other protagonists are naïve women who slowly wake up to reality. You tell me how many people go through that? It even happened to me in Chile. I wasn't born with my political ideas absolutely clear and having decided what I believed was correct. No! I was full of doubts and very confused and it took me a long time to realize what exactly was happening in Chile. And when I realized it, I was already deeply involved in it and had to leave the country. But it all happened slowly. It wasn't that the day after the military coup I knew what was happening and began to do heroic acts, no. Life is not like that in general. Now, about the peasant who was raped and passively accepted the fact. You tell me, how many peasant women would rebel before such an act? Because what kept her from rebelling was an entire social, political, and economic infrastructure which has held her in a humiliating position for generations, for centuries. And then, are you going to make her come out and defend herself? One woman may possibly do it, but she is not the character that I need in my novel. I need the one that corresponds to reality. Of course there are good military men, lots of good military men, but the one that I need for my novel is not good. I need the torturer who is also part of reality.

> *Feminism is a movement of great breadth in Chile, with considerable social support and even official support. There is even an Office for Women's Affairs. Are you in contact with Chilean feminists?*

Yes, I am always in contact with Chile. I go every year if I can. I have many journalist friends and I receive a lot of information. It's quite curious. Women in Chile have always been very strong and well organized, very independent within the private sphere and communal organization, but when it means taking charge of power, I don't know why, but they always take a step back and the power always ends up in men's hands. The men have the economic and political power in Chile and women (barring some exceptions of course) have not yet taken over.

We were speaking before about the marginal characters in your novels. The last one is Gregory Reeves, who spends part of his life in Berkeley, which is also a marginal place within North American culture (the sixties, "The Day of Indigenous Peoples," instead of "The Anniversary of the Discovery of America," etc.). Can you comment on your teaching experience at Berkeley? Would I be correct in saying that Berkeley as a marginal space seems fascinating to you?

Yes, fascinating. The part that takes place in Berkeley is written with a lot of love and care and that is evident in the book. My experience teaching there was fantastic. I taught a course on "Creative Writing Long Narrative" and I learned a lot. But at that time I couldn't work on my own writing because I was so involved in the fifteen novels that my students were writing. Those novels were forever in my head. One of those students, a woman who didn't work very hard but was extremely talented, is now about to publish her first novel.

The House of the Spirits and Of Love and Shadows were written in exile and about the socio-political reality in Chile pre- and post-coup. Did you have the Chilean reader in mind when you wrote these novels?

At the time when I wrote those two novels, there was a young Chilean woman who had read everything I had written and was my unconditional fan. I had the sense, then, that anything I wrote was for her. In many ways I felt a sort of responsibility towards her. I wanted that utopic or potential reader to feel good while reading as well as come along with me in my search for something. Now I don't think about her specifically, but I do imagine that I am telling a story to a small handful of people, all sitting in my living room, all listening to a story. And that is the way I write; using an intimate and familiar tone. If I thought about the millions of readers and translations, I would feel blocked. It would be impossible to write.

What Chilean writers do you read today?

I think that Chilean poetry is very good. I am interested in what is being published in Chile. Yet, right now I am reading much more literature written by North American Black, Chicanas, Japanese American, and Native American women writers. They are writing very different books from the ones I was used to; the ones by North American male writers. How refreshing to go from Norman Mailer to Toni Morrison!

> *And again your attraction for the marginal. These are writers who are attempting to interpret certain cultures and lives that have been dismissed for generations.*

I feel that we are sisters, in the same search, in the same tone.

> *At this time you are not in exile, but an immigrant. What is the worst and the best of Marin County, U.S.A.?*

The best part is a scenery and certain security that I did not know. I had never felt so secure. There is much less crime here than in other parts. You can leave your car unlocked and nobody steals it. The children can play out on the street. That is possibly the best . . . well, except for the fact that I live with Willie. I could live with him anywhere. The worst part of Marin County is the isolation. One feels so comfortable that you can begin to think that this is the world, and then become totally detached. That is a great danger for me as a human being and as a writer. The world is not Marin County!

> *Do you still have that little bag of earth that you took with you when you left Chile?*

Yes. I have that and also another bag with five one-cent coins that my mother gave me when I was a little girl and we had to part. When the Civil War began in Lebanon in 1958 they asked the families of the diplomats to leave, and so my stepfather and my mother sent me back to my grandparents' house in Chile. When we said goodbye my mother gave me a little bag with coins inside and said to me "Take these, keep them, because as long as you have them you will not lack food to eat." I always have it with me because the part of not "lacking food to eat" seems so symbolic to me. And the truth is that except for one time in my life, and only for three days, I have always had enough to eat.

Immigration, Integration, and Blending Cultures

INTERVIEW BY BOB BALDOCK AND DENNIS BERNSTEIN

27

Reprinted with permission from *Mother Jones* magazine, © 1994, Foundation for National Progress

Isabel Allende went into exile after her uncle, Chilean president Salvador Allende, was overthrown in a CIA-assisted coup in 1973. She traveled, worked as a journalist, and wrote her books *The House of the Spirits*, *Of Love and Shadows*, *Eva Luna*, and *The Stories of Eva Luna*. Her latest novel, *The Infinite Plan*, is set, as is she, in Northern California.

> **"** *You've lived all over the world and traveled extensively. Now that you've married an American and you live here, what do you find surprising about the United States?*

I realize that there is much more to it than I ever thought. It is a very complex society—multiracial, multicultural, with many languages. Americans have a warrior's mentality, most of them. That's how this society was built. The fact that you can own a gun and shoot to defend your life is a very American way of thinking.

There is also this spiritual quest, mainly among women. You can afford that, because that's something you can do when you have passed the stages of survival. In other cultures, women are at the stage of feeding their children. There are many people in this country who also have that as their first priority, but there are many who don't. And those people can afford the luxury of searching for the god or goddess, and worrying about the body, and vitamins, and organic chicken, and the perfect cappuccino.

> *Given the power of your feeling for women in your writing, especially for the connections they sustain over generations, what do you make of tendencies here for generations—families—to drift apart, to become disconnected?*

One of the characteristics of North American culture is that you can always start again. You can always move forward, cross a border of a state or a city or a county, and move West, most of the time West. You leave behind guilt, past traditions, memories. You are as if born again, in the sense of the snake: You leave your skin behind and you begin again. For most people in the world, that is totally impossible. We carry with us the sense that we belong to a group, a clan, a tribe, an extended family, eventually a country. Whatever happens to you happens to the collective group, and you can never leave behind the past. What you have done in your life will always be with you. So, for us, we have the burden of this sort of fate, of destiny, that you don't.

There are advantages and disadvantages to both situations. In the United States, the fact that you can start again gives a lot of energy and strength and youth to this country. That is why it's so powerful in many ways, and so creative. However, it has the disadvantage of loneliness, of individuality carried to an extreme, where you don't belong to the group and where you can just do whatever you want and never think of other people. I think that's a great disadvantage—a moral and spiritual and ethical disadvantage.

> *So how do you see the future for this country, with its separate, isolated peoples and cultures?*

I'm very optimistic because I think that the real strength of a nation like the United States comes from blending cultures. There's no way that you can close the frontiers, anywhere. The borders are there to be violated permanently. That is what humankind has been doing, at least during the last century. We are living in an era of communications, of masses of refugees that go back and forth crossing all lands. We see these dark—what they call brown—people all over, and you can't stop them, why would you?

I live in Marin County, where a part of the community is fighting against the Latin American immigrants. People are terrified because they see these dark men standing in groups waiting for someone to offer a job. That's very threatening. Because they don't know them and don't understand their ways or their language, they feel that these men are criminals, that they don't pay their share in this society and yet they benefit. That is not true. They don't pay taxes, but they don't benefit.

They come here to do the kind of work that no American will ever do. You will not be able to stop them. They will integrate. Sooner or later, their children will be with the white children in the schools. It's unavoidable: In twenty years they will be part of this society, just as the Jews are, the Irish, everybody.

> *How do you work against this fear that people have of foreigners, of threats to their way of life? How do you prevent fear from interfering with growth and expression and learning?*

The biggest straitjacket is all the prejudices that we carry around, and all the fears. But what if we just surrender to the fear? There are things greater than fear. The great, wonderful quality of human beings is that we can overcome even absolute terror, and we do.

In Venezuela, when I was living there, crime was growing. You couldn't feel safe anywhere. You couldn't leave your car in the street, because it would be stolen. You couldn't live in your house if you didn't have a high-security alarm system, because you would be burglarized seven times a week.

Well, all the family got together after someone had broken into the house for the seventeenth time and everything had been stolen. And we said, well, how are we going to live? Are we going to put bars on the windows and install an electric alarm system? Are we going to buy guns? We decided we were going to leave the house open and let people come in and steal everything, because we couldn't live inside our own prison.

Fear is like a black cavern that is terrifying. Once you enter the cavern and explore it, you realize that you can get out of it, go through it and get out of it. Then there's another cavern that is just as big and terrifying, and you just go in and dwell in it and see what is the worst that can happen.

Last year was a very, very difficult year for me because my daughter was very sick. She was in a coma. If you had told me the day before she fell into the coma that such a thing was going to happen, I would have killed myself. If I had known the amount of pain I would have to endure, I would have killed myself because I would have thought I would never be able to survive this thing—and I wouldn't have wanted to survive, I would have wanted to die before.

But then, one day at a time, you take it. You go through one week, and the next week; the whole year goes by. And things happen that are so horrible, and they get worse and worse. You think that you are going to die at every step, but you don't die. You survive. Then one day, you are holding your daughter because she's dying. You hold her, and you hug her, you spend the day and the night with her, and she dies, very peacefully, and you realize that you have not died, that you are there. And the fear is gone, the fear of pain, and the fear of death.

Is your view of the millennium, then, generally positive? What do you envision?

I see a more feminine world, a world where feminine values will be validated, the same as masculine values are. A more integrated world.

I see that in the future, things that we have lost in the past will be recovered. There's a search for those things, a search for spirituality, for nature, for the goddess religions, for family and human bonding. All that has been lost in this industrial era. People are in desperate need of those things. I don't think the world will destroy itself in a nuclear cataclysm. On the contrary, we have the capacity to save ourselves and save the planet, and we will use it.

NOTE

From an interview by Bob Baldock and Dennis Bernstein for "Skirting the Brink: America's Leading Thinkers and Activists Confide Their Views of Our Predicament," a public radio project in progress.

Magical Feminist

INTERVIEW BY JENNIFER BENJAMIN AND SALLY ENGELFRIED **28**

Reprinted from *510: East Bay Arts and Culture Magazine*, no. 3 (December 1994): 18–19, 48–50

With her blend of politics, spirituality, and magic fused into novels that are both moving and memorable, Isabel Allende is an important literary voice in the Bay Area. Though often brutal, her four novels, *The House of the Spirits, Of Love and Shadows, Eva Luna, The Infinite Plan*, and her collection of short stories, *The Stories of Eva Luna*, are written with beauty and love. Allende challenges us to examine the politics of fascism and the horrors it creates in the psyche, and how that pain can gradually be transformed into powerful art. She is someone who has actually lived through the fascist takeover of Chile's democracy, and with the unsettling events that seem to be popping up in increasing frequency in the United States, her story serves as a lesson and a warning to us all. Allende's latest book, *The Infinite Plan*, takes place partly in the East Bay and Allende, as an outside observer, reconfirms the unique magic of the area.

❝ *Do you have a regimen for your writing?*

Because I don't have a boss I really need to discipline myself, and everything pulls you away from the writing. People don't seem to understand that writing is a job, they think it's a kind of vice or hobby or something. If you give them the excuse that you're writing, no one respects that. In the beginning it was easier because I didn't have as many demands as I have now. Now I'm pretty strict. I'm more creative in the morning, so I get up very early and come here and I write all by myself, no telephone, nothing, until around two or three in the afternoon. Then my assistant comes. We sort the mail because every day I have a pack of mail. I answer all the fan letters by hand. That's a lot of work, but I feel it's important. If a person has taken the trouble to write a letter and to find my address to send the letter, the least I can do is answer, and it's always a pleasure, really. So that takes a while, and then I spend some time correcting or reading or researching.

Do you have techniques that you use if you come here in the morning and draw a blank and don't feel inspired? Is there anything that gets you going?

I think that this is like any other job. Not always do you feel like doing it, or feel thrilled because you're going to the office, but I don't believe in inspiration, I believe in training. I think that this is like being an athlete, that you have to do a lot of training in order to beat the record or to be able to reach your own expectations and your own demands. What I do is start every day with a little ceremony, and then I start writing. And sometimes I know that what I'm writing is awful, but I do it anyhow. I have to go through this stage of learning something in order to reach another stage where I will be able to use what I write. This is important. You have to lift the weights every day in order to box. On the other hand, I very seldom feel that I don't have anything to write about. Except if I'm very depressed, which seldom happens. I don't even remember that it has ever happened.

You never planned writing The House of the Spirits. *Once you had this pile of pages how did you pursue getting it published?*

I showed it to my mother and she said, "This is a book." So she started correcting grammar, and then the family got together and decided it was a novel and that I needed a title. Everybody proposed a different title—no one had read it yet—and we couldn't agree so we tossed a coin in the air, and that's how *The House of the Spirits* was named.

Then my ex-husband said, "Well, let's find a publisher." I knew one person who worked in a publishing house, and that person told me where to submit the manuscript. I sent it to several publishing houses in Venezuela and Argentina, and no one wanted to read it. I didn't even get rejection letters, nothing, just a void and silence for some time. Then one day a secretary from one of the publishing houses called me. She had this manuscript lying around and had taken it home and read it. She thought it was a great book but that it would never be published in that place, and she said, "Why don't you find an agent?" She gave me the name of someone in Barcelona—at the time I was living in Caracas. The agent read the manuscript—because she was curious about my name, probably, and the fact that I was a woman writer and so very few women writers from Latin America were known in Europe at the time. In a month, she signed a contract with me, and in six months the book was published and translated in Europe. But it took some time for it to be published in Latin America.

> *You've said it's very hard for you to write about eroticism in your novels, but it's in all of them. It seems very natural for you.*

There are themes that are always present in my books. Birth, death, sex scenes, and violence. I didn't plan it that way, it just happened. Somebody noticed this and told me the other day. I had noticed the violence part, but the birth and death and sex I hadn't noticed that much. I imagine that it comes naturally as part of what the fabric of life is to me. All that is related to the strongest emotions that people feel and that motivate people. When I was a journalist, my job was to ask what happened. My job as a writer is to ask why did it happen. And when you look for the motivations you always go to the basic instincts, to the basic emotions, the basic things that have moved humankind always. That's what all writers write about, ultimately. What did Shakespeare write about? Jealousy, love, sex, power, greed, the same stuff that soap operas and the Bible are made of. It's always the same. So I imagine that it comes in a very natural way to me.

What I find difficult often is the wording. How to write it in a way that will be effective. Let's take, for comparison, a torture scene. I know a lot about it, but if I as a writer try to describe exactly what is done to a person, who does it, and what the effect is on that person, you can't take it as a reader. I destroy the effect that I am trying to create. I have found that it works better if you create the climate of terror. You force the reader into the mood of terror and let him imagine the details. Just give a hint of what is going on, the smell, maybe the sound, and let the reader do the rest. It's usually much more effective.

With the sex scenes, it's the same. It's easy for me to describe what a sex scene is because I'm fifty and have had some experience about sex. However, you destroy the effect if you go into the details. The reader, unless you're writing pornography, doesn't really want to know what happened and who penetrated whom. They want the feeling of eroticism, the sensuality. They want to use their own imagination, their own experience, their own sense of what sex is about. Let them add to the scene whatever they want. That's the way I try to do it. Now, it doesn't always work, because sometimes you can get carried away and end up writing very corny scenes, sometimes it can even be funny. So there is a fine line that you have to find. And I find it difficult—I joke that it's because of my Catholic upbringing, but that's not true, it's more than that. It is the strict environment in which I was brought up, and my mother, who's still alive, will read the book.

Do you have to put her out of your mind when you're writing those things?

Yes, I do. Because my mother will read this, and she won't like it. And of course that doesn't stop me, but I do think about it. Yes. My mother's a strong lady. We get in these awful fights.

Did it bother you that the actors playing your characters were not Latin in the movie, The House of the Spirits?

The fact that they are not of Hispanic origin doesn't bother me. For many reasons. First, no Latin American director ever wanted to make the movie, so I don't feel that I have taken it away from anybody; they were not interested. People who don't live in Latin America have this impression that all the continent is Indian or black; the people who are in power and the high social classes are always European-looking. Even in the countries that brag of not having racial problems, like Brazil, you will never find a black president or a black chief of the armed forces. The structure of economic, political, and social power in Latin America is very racist. We don't say it's racist, we say it's classist, but it's the same: the power is in the hands of the white, the males, the rich, and the military, so the higher you are in the social scale in Latin America the more European-looking you are. *The House of the Spirits* is a story of an upper-middle-class family, what would be considered aristocrats in Latin America though we don't have any aristocrats there. They all look white, and you will find a lot of blond people because they have British, German, and French influence. The lower you go in the social scale, the more you will find the Indian features and, in the Caribbean and Brazil, the black features. The composition of the casting is not strange, because when you watch the movie you see the social classes. You see, for example, that the high-ranked militaries are whiter than the soldiers. You see that the peasants look totally different from the owners of the land, and [director] Bille August had an eye for that. That was the first thing he noticed, and he reproduced it, so the movie looks very Latin American.

> *How would you compare the racism in Latin America to the racism in America?*

I think that racism has the same awful face everywhere. It looks and acts exactly the same everywhere. This is a more sophisticated and educated society so there's more awareness, and being a racist is not welcome at any level now. We're educated not to be racists, although most people are. In Latin America we don't even think that it's bad to be a racist. We think it's perfectly okay. My mother is the worst racist I've ever known and she thinks it's perfectly okay. But there has been a change in the world in my lifetime. When I was born it was much worse. Racism and feminism are the two big issues that have changed in my lifetime.

As far as being a feminist and a woman writer, do you find it easier to be respected here than in South America?

I find it easier to be a woman here. Probably a writer also, but being a woman is much easier in industrialized societies in Europe and the United States. The rest of the world is a terrible place for women in general and Latin America is no exception. If you belong to an educated class and you live in a city you have a better chance, but if you live in the country and you belong to a non-educated family, you are handicapped. It's very hard for a woman—very, very hard. We're born in servitude.

You've spoken about fascism in the U.S. What do you mean by that?

I mean that this is a very complex society and that the best and the worst is given in this country. Everything can happen and everything really significant passes through the filter of North America. The composition of this society has a large number of people who are potential fascists, very nationalistic, very provincial. They are the ones who have the weapons, who are willing to exert violence and take the law into their own hands and who are racists and believe that they are the best of the world. This is exactly the same feeling that promoted fascism in Europe during the Second World War in Italy, in Spain, and of course in Germany.

The advantage of the United States is that it's a country of immigrants from many forces that move and interact constantly. The democratic forces in this country have always been more educated and more powerful; you can have a very fascist government in this country. Let us be aware of it and be very careful, because people take things for granted. That's exactly what happened in Chile and I witnessed it.

Chile was the longest and most solid democracy in Latin America. Chile had 160 years of democracy before the military coup. It had the oldest constitutions, it had the most advanced social laws, and everything ended in twenty-four hours because those forces took over. It's not that it happened in twenty-four hours; they had always been there and we failed to see them. We failed, we underestimated them. We thought that it would never happen in Chile—that that kind of thing only happened in banana republics and places with dictator-

ships and chieftains. It was other people, not us. And it did happen
to us because we were not aware, and we paid a terrible price: seventeen years of the most brutal dictatorship. That can happen in the
United States, as it can happen in London and it can happen in
France. It can happen anywhere and history proves that. So what is
our role as communicators? Be aware that that's a possibility. As
you're aware of the environment, as you're aware of feminism, as
you're aware of racism, be aware of the political circumstances and
prevent them.

You've said that "there are no rules in terror." How does terror work?
The way terror works is by first separating people, isolating them.
When you have a regime of terror, the first thing that they censor or
forbid is communication, all forms of communication. The press, of
course, is censored and all political and social and sometimes religious organizations that bring people together. Unions are forbidden.
You can't gather in your home more than six people without a permit
from the military. Even in a restaurant you can't have a big table.
When you are in a group of people somehow you get the strength and
energy of the group, and when you are isolated you are very scared.
That's why they also isolate the political prisoners—that way they are
weaker and cannot spread their energy or get the other people's
energy.

The other thing that happens in a time of terror is that torture, or
disappearances of people, or murder, is not most of the time to get information, as we think. We think that people are tortured so that you
will learn something from them. You will force them to talk. That is
not true. People are sexually harassed and tortured for humiliation
and punishment. They are not killed most of the time, they are tortured and released. Why? Because those people will talk and other
people will know what can happen to them if they don't comply. So
you spread terror. You give the message very clearly: this will happen
to you. Those are the known rules at the beginning, but then afterwards, the other important rule is that you change the rules all the
time. Because if people learn the rules they will learn to get around
the rules. You can be punished for something that was legal when
you did it. That also changes. It's a state of confusion in which you

don't know how to act. You're like an animal that is in a place where everything is threatening and you don't know where to run to. There is no safe haven for anybody.

How did you become an expert on torture?

I lived in Chile during the military coup. I was a journalist and some journalists decided at the time—you couldn't publish anything—that our job was to learn what was going on, record it, and smuggle information out of the country. At the time it was impossible to make a video, but we did a lot of tapes with interviews. And that was part of what I did. Some of my friends were tortured. I have piles of interviews. For a year and a half that's what I did. Unfortunately. I say unfortunately because all my nightmares are about that. That's one of the few issues I can't deal with. It's always sad. It's devastating to learn what people can do to other people. You are in touch with the raw evil, and there's no way you can justify a little baby being tortured in front of the mother. People do that and then they go home and they have dinner and they watch TV. That's a job. It's hard to understand how bad we can be.

I always think that if someone out there is capable of doing that, I am too, given the right circumstances. People are very similar, so what is potentially saintly in another person I can achieve, and what is potentially most evil can happen to me too. That knowledge, that torture is something that is potentially human and therefore mine, is horrifying. It's a constant nightmare because I don't think that I'm better in any way and that it would never happen to me and that I'm never going to do that. I don't know. I hope I will never do it, but I don't know.

Are you familiar with the Colonia Dignidad? *And is it still in existence?*

Yes. As familiar as you can be, because it's a big mystery. It's a colony of German immigrants that came [to South America] after the Second World War. They were all ex-Nazis from the hierarchy. They bought a large piece of land in Chile and somehow, because Germans are powerful in Chile, they obtained special guarantees or protection from the military and the government. It became a scandal. Once in the late '60s a young woman who looked German but spoke Spanish escaped. She had been born there, and she told horrors of what was going on in Colonia Dignitad. It was a big scandal in the press and Salvador Allende, who at the time was the candidate for president, said that in his government he would open Colonia Dignitad. He never could. He never could because the military was involved. After the coup it became a torture center and a concentration camp. And it is still there protected by the military. So as long as General Pinochet is the chief of the armed forces, Colonia Dignitad will be there.

Who was the character Rolf Carlé of Eva Luna *based on?*

That character was given to me like a gift. I had written *Eva Luna* and I had two characters. They were two orphan children raised in the streets who were uneducated, two marginals. My idea was that these two characters would grow up to be lovers and be the protagonists, but by the time they became lovers, like on page 120, the guy was a jerk. I mean, I wouldn't want him. Really. He just developed in that direction in spite of me. And there I was, in the middle of my book with no male protagonist.

I went on a lecturing tour to Germany, I was in Hamburg, and a man after the lecture offered me a cup of coffee. He said he had a story to tell me, and I can really get hooked with that sentence. So I followed him, blindly, to a coffee shop, and he told me that his father was a Nazi officer, that he had died the way [Rolf Carlé's father] died in the book. He told me that he had a retarded sister who was brought up under a table covered with a table cloth. He gave me a few things about his life and I wrote everything on a paper napkin. When I went home I just introduced the paper napkin into the computer and there was Rolf Carlé. So it was a gift, a real gift. He was a journalist like the one in the book.

At the end of Eva Luna *you talk about how Eva and Rolf are lost together and meant to be together, but then you say maybe they'll end up not being together. I wanted it to be a sure thing.*

I feel more and more uncomfortable with certainties. Because there's a lot of ambiguity in the world and things can be one way apparently and maybe they're not that way at all. I'm more and more aware of that as I get older, the uncertain thing. Especially love.

> *Was it harder to write magically about the United States in* The Infinite Plan?

I'm living in California—how could it be difficult? When I moved here, I was in a state of shock. I couldn't believe it. There is so much going on. There's a whole California language that you have to learn. Words like "empowerment," "primal," "support system," "organic." Everything is "organic." All those things were very striking to me. I'm still in awe of everything I see. This is a magic place. The crazier you are the more west you go—apparently that seems to be a rule. All the lunatics end up here and also wonderful people. All the new ideas of the last fifty-eight years have somehow germinated here. It's a wonderful place and I didn't find it difficult to write about because being an outsider is the best position for a writer; if you're in the middle of a hurricane you can't write about the hurricane because you can't see it. You need to get out of it in order to watch it from a certain distance and have enough irony and ambiguity to write about it.

> *The character Carmen in* The Infinite Plan *seems not to try to control her life at all, just lets things happen when they happen. Do you think things happen when they're supposed to?*

I'm a fatalist in the sense that I do believe in destiny. I do believe that you can control only so much. Of course, given the game, you can play it right. But there's a lot that is given—your sex, race, age, whether you're healthy or you're not, the place where you're born, the family in which you're born. Most of who you are is determined before you are even born. Those factors are there and you have to deal with them. I believe that there's a certain amount of control you can have over your life, but there are many things that just happen and no matter what you do they will happen anyhow. The older I get, the less I try to control. I just try to float. I feel that everything moves under my feet and I try to be on my feet, but it's like riding a horse. You have to follow the rhythm of the horse in order to be able to ride the horse properly.

Is Carmen based on a real person?

I made Carmen with two people. One is an old friend my husband had in his childhood called Carmen. She lives in a Mexican ghetto in East L.A. and she's very much like the character in the first part of the book. The second part of Carmen, when she becomes a jeweler and is successful and she's in the streets in Berkeley and all that, is Tabra, a very famous jeweler in the Bay Area who is also my best friend. So you see I don't have a great imagination. [*Laughs.*]

In The Infinite Plan, *Olga says, "the dead go hand in hand with the living." Do you believe that?*

I do believe that. The first loss in my life was my grandmother, and she has been with me for fifty years. When I say she has been with me it's true, not in the sense that she appears like a ghost, floating and moving chains around, no. But every time that I'm at a cross-roads and I'm lost and confused I think, what would she do given the image I have of her? The answer is she would do the most original and unexpected thing, and the most generous. And I try to follow that rule. When I'm really frightened, I ask for protection and I feel that she has protected me. She has saved me from situations I have put myself in that were pretty risky.

I feel that I have a guardian angel with me. My daughter died, and she's with me in a way that she never was when she was alive because she had a life of her own and she had a destiny of her own. She still has them, in the spiritual world she's doing things, but the memory of her lives in me. I carry it with me and it's part of my life in a very vivid way. So vivid, in fact, that when I come here every morning I light a candle for her. I have her photograph and her ashes there and I feel her presence very strongly. There's a lot of sadness still going on, but I know that I will get over that and there will be a point when I will understand the spiritual life better and will not be stuck in the loss. I will probably be connected better to who she is now.

Not only the dead walk hand in hand, but, when there is a strong connection, the living walk hand in hand too. That's how I feel with my son, my daughter-in-law, and the babies. That will probably not last because life will separate us sooner or later, but as long as it is there, it's a very profound feeling of being hand in hand, and that whatever happens to you happens to them, and whatever happens to them happens to you.

Have you ever felt that with people who are living over distances?

My mother. I feel that constantly with my mother very, very strongly. And of course I feel it constantly with my husband. But I think that connection has another quality because it is also sexual and that gives a totally different tint to it. Sexuality is something, in my case at least, that I only practice when I'm in love, and that creates a sort of intimacy that makes a relationship totally different from any other relationship that I have in my life.

You've mentioned that Americans haven't really come to grips with death too well. How does that change us? How would it affect us if we were to come to grips with death?

Well, the first thing you have to know is that you're going to die. That's the only certainty that everybody has: the minute you are born you are walking towards death. If you are not aware that death is over your shoulder permanently you don't have a feeling of how precious life is to begin with, and life becomes something perfectly disposable—other people's lives, I mean. That's why we have so much violence and crime and people dying on the screen. Death has no significance because it is filtered by the archetype of the image. It's not real because we really don't think we are going to die unless we are confronted with it, as I have been.

When you get in touch with the fact that you are going to die and the people you love are going to die and that's part of the cycle of life, your approach to the world is different. First of all you become more detached. You are not so materialistic because you realize you are not going to take anything with you and your body will disappear. So you gain a sort of spiritual dimension that opens up completely your world. You are aware of that spiritual world and then everything that happens in your daily life has a different meaning because what happens in daily life is only part of reality, a small part. There is much more than we can see and feel and describe.

It's hard to talk about these things without sounding religious, very hard, so I seldom do it. I feel it very strongly and I live it, but I'm not a religious person in the sense that I don't belong to any traditional religion, not even Buddhism, which I think is wonderful. So it's not something that could be described as religious, but it is spiritual, and I think that it is different when a society, a culture, accepts and honors death.

Do you think that we ever will?

Yes. This country's funny. Now that the baby boomers are reaching fifty, menopause is cool. Wait until they reach seventy, and everybody will be into death. The older the population gets, the more they will be talking about death. It's only the young who can deny it. The very young.

What about the power of dreams? How do you use them and how do they help you in everyday life?

I write them down when I feel they are important, if I wake up with a strong emotion. Sometimes the dream is so vivid and so clear that I don't need to go into a lot of thinking to understand what it means. Sometimes I need to repeat the dream several times in order to understand that my mind is trying to tell me something. When a dream comes back, and very often they do, I know that there is something that I have to solve, something that is telling me, hey, pay attention to this.

And you meditate?

Yes. Not a lot, I'm not a fanatic. I like frozen yogurt a lot, and I know there's a certain point when it's not even good for you. No matter how nonfat it is there's only so much frozen yogurt that you can have, so I have made myself have a frozen yogurt a day but not more than that. It's the same with meditation. It's great to meditate, but too much is like frozen yogurt. You end up sitting down with your mind blank and not doing anything productive. So I do meditate because I need it and I like it, but not a lot. I do it everyday in short periods of time. I have a meditation group and sometimes when I'm in need I just go on a bench and I sit in the forest and meditate for hours, and I like it.

Does it help you write?

No. It doesn't help me write. What helps me write is talking, when people talk to me and tell me things. It's like all of a sudden I realize that I'm making a connection. Something that is confused to me becomes clear because someone says something. Meditating helps for other things. It helps to calm me down. I'm very hyper most of the time, and it settles me down.

You've said that literature is "premonitory, like dreams." Can you talk about that?

I spend many hours by myself in silence connected to the story in the book. I feel like when that happens during a long period of time, your mind opens up to connections that you don't have in your normal state of mind. Because you are very busy in the noise of the world. When you are in silence you tune into another dimension of reality, and you start to perceive things that you don't have time to perceive when you are in the world. What happens to me is that sometimes I write things that I think are just my imagination, and later I find out that they happened that way, and I didn't have any way of knowing that it was that way. I had that several times in *Of Love and Shadows*, which was a very premonitory book.

Sometimes I just make weird connections. You were asking about Rolf Carlé. The way I found the name for Rolf Carlé is strange. I wanted a name that wouldn't sound too German, because it would be too obvious, so I went through my ex-husband's library and I found an author called Rolf something. I liked the word Rolf, which means wolf. Then I was looking for something that wouldn't be too German for the last name, and I remembered the driver who had driven me in a limousine to Hamburg. He was of French origin, and I thought, I'll put the two names together. When I went to Germany many years later I found out that the name of the father of the man who told me the story was Rolf Carlé. And he didn't use his father's name because he had rejected his father's name so I didn't have any way of knowing. That kind of thing happens a lot when you're writing, not only to me.

This is something that writers talk about all the time. Jean Shinoda Bolen has a book about synchronicity in which she says there is no such thing as a coincidence. When you are in a project, no matter what that project is, the world conspires to make it possible, and there are a lot of things going around that come together to lead you in the right direction, if you pay attention and you listen. And, as a writer, many things happen that force you to pay attention. For example, I'm writing now something about the military coup in Chile. The military coup happened twenty years ago. I do have the memory of what happened, but often you don't have the emotion, and by one of those synchronicities I was writing on the twentieth anniversary of the coup, which was September 11. On September 11 all the country revived what had happened. There were TV shows, videos, the press, everybody was talking about it, and the emotion of what had happened twenty years before was there in the streets. It was exactly the same day that I needed that and it came to me as a gift. Often things coincide in such a way that you have to ask yourself what are these synchronicities? Why do these things happen to help me with the writing?

A Mother's Letter of Loss

INTERVIEW BY ROSA PINOL

29

Reprinted from *World Press Review* 42, no. 4 (April 1995): 47. Copyright © 1994, *La Vanguardia*.

"Listen, Paula, I am going to tell you a story, so that when you wake up you will not feel so lost." With these words, Isabel Allende begins the long letter she created for her daughter Paula while she was in a coma. An attack of porphyria, a rare inherited disorder, complicated by other factors, left Allende's older child in a coma that endured for twelve months before she died in Madrid on December 6, 1992. That letter is now *Paula*, the most recent book by the author of *Eva Luna* and *The House of the Spirits*. (*Paula* is scheduled to be published this spring in the U.S. by HarperCollins.)

Paula is not just Allende's story of living with her sick daughter. It is also a reconstruction of the novelist's life: the fundamental experiences of her womanhood, her relations with men, and her career as a journalist. Paula reveals, for example, that when Allende earned money translating romance novels, she altered the dialogue and changed the endings to improve the images of the female leads. And that she once worked as a chorus girl in order to write a story about the women who worked in cheap theaters.

"Many people have told me that my life seems to come out of a soap opera, but it has always seemed absurd to me," says Allende, a Chilean born in Lima, Peru. She is the niece of Chilean President Salvador Allende, who was ousted and killed in a bloody coup in 1973.

Now fifty-two, Allende says: "I would not trade my life today for that of any younger person. With the years, one gains in wisdom and one becomes enriched as a person. I think that we women are beginning to . . . realize that maturity is a stage of life full of surprises."

Allende was interviewed at her home in California.

---

66 *Was it your idea to begin writing this letter to Paula?*

Carmen Balcells, my literary agent, told me that I ought to write about what was happening, that it might serve as an escape valve. One of the terrible things about those first months was the waiting: waiting and hoping that on the next visit, my daughter might open her eyes, waiting for the doctor's report, waiting to see the neurologist, waiting, waiting. . . .

This was creating a terrible tension inside of me. Writing meant being able to concentrate on something else; it made the time pass more quickly. In addition, I thought that Paula would wake up with huge memory gaps, and this would be how I would tell her who she was, who her family was, who her mother was, and what had happened.

You reveal, in Paula, *your most intimate experiences. Was this painful?*

No, because in the beginning I was not thinking of publishing it, and I did not think about the fact I was stripping myself bare. My daughter and I had such an intimate relationship that there was nothing we could not have discussed. I trusted her just as much as I do my mother.

What led you to decide to publish it?

After my daughter died, many people who had undergone similar ordeals came up and spoke to me, and I realized that my experience was one that I shared with the better part of humanity. Sooner or later we all lose someone: Abandonment, loss, and death are part of life. And I thought that, during this period, I had not read any book that helped me and that publishing *Paula* might help other people share such devastating pain.

Death has always been a great motivator for writers. Wasn't the death of your grandfather the reason behind The House of the Spirits?

My books have always been born from a separation, a loss. To lose Chile and all of my past because of the military coup and being forced into exile pushed me to write *The House of the Spirits*. The loss of political innocence, when I became aware of the disappeared, the tortured, the dead, the brutal repression throughout Latin America, impelled me to write *Of Love and Shadows*. *The Infinite Plan* was inspired by the love of my present husband.

There must be only a handful of very privileged people who can believe that life is a party, all celebration. But they are wrong. I am not a pessimistic or sad person, but accepting this has made me able to enjoy the good moments all the more.

"Listen, Paula"

INTERVIEW BY ALFRED STARKMANN
Translated for this book by John Rodden

30

First published in German in *Focus Magazin*, March 20, 1995, 122–125

Paula, the twenty-eight-year-old daughter of the Chilean writer Isabel
Allende, fell sick in December 1991. Almost immediately she slipped
into a coma, from which she never again awoke. Isabel Allende sat
several months, for endless hours, in a Madrid hospital and in a hotel
room—and then at Paula's bedside in her house in California, in the
summer and fall of 1992. She also began to compose a long letter to
Paula, so that she shouldn't feel so lost when she awoke. Alfred
Starkmann spoke with the world-famous writer of *The House of the
Spirits* in Sausalito, California.

" Is Paula *your most private, your most sincere book?*

Yes. I don't think that I'll ever write something so personal again. In the beginning, I never envisioned it gaining publication—it was only a long letter to Paula. Therefore I wrote it with a totally open heart, without any kind of precautionary measures. Only later did I pursue the possibility of publishing it, and I then thought I'd simply drop parts of it that weren't very flattering about me. But somehow I felt that dropping them would damage the spirit of the book. Therefore I've left the text of the book just as it was.

> *In one place you say that you have, until now, never shared your past with anyone. Does that mean that your revelations about your past in your earlier books did not correspond to the truth?*

They did correspond to the truth, but not to its depths. I simply left out the really important things. I talked about my past, but not about my feelings, my doubts, my mistakes. I gave instead anecdotes without the dimension of feeling.

> *One has the impression that this new book was written breathlessly, as if in a single great agony of composition. Have you laid less value on aspects of form and style than in earlier work?*

I never thought about form and style. In the beginning it was just a letter. When Paula died, my mother brought me the letters from Chile that I had written to her when I was in Madrid. And my son-in-law Ernesto gave me letters that he had exchanged with Paula. I've taken many paragraphs out of them literally and simply included them in the book. The result is a mix of different elements. There are many narrative voices in the book. I speak directly with Paula, I speak with her in the third person, I speak with myself. I haven't polished up anything.

> *So you never even sat down again and, with a cool editorial eye, worked through the manuscript?*

Naturally I read it through again, but I changed very little. I think that the value of this book lies in the feeling that it transmits, rather than in its literary claims. It's existed already for a little while in Spanish and Italian, and I've received hundreds of letters from people who have been moved by the emotion of the book rather than feeling impressed by the form. That has special value for me, given my present emotional situation [i.e., still in mourning over the death of her daughter].

How have the professional critics reacted to the book?

Very positively. I think they've all recognized that the point of the book is the theme. Maybe on that account the critics are willing to forgive me the many mistakes in the book.

The doctors constantly assured you that Paula felt no pain. She didn't feel it, but you felt pain and may have projected her pain into yourself. Do you feel that is somehow a punishment for your guilt?

Not so much that. What dominated me was a feeling of helplessness. Whatever I did, I couldn't save her. I couldn't even make her life a bit less miserable. Yes, I thought back then that I was experiencing the pain of guilt. But not because I had earned a punishment.

Was it a providential stroke of fate?

I have a pretty fatalistic attitude. There is a destiny, a karma, and this was for the opportunity to learn a great deal. It was a painful process, but not absolutely bereft of happiness. I could share deep feelings with Paula that I would never have before experienced if she had been healthy and conscious.

The military coup in Chile in 1973 and the death of your uncle and godfather Salvador Allende signified according to your own statements a turning point in your life. The second turning point came in Madrid after a conversation with the doctor responsible for your daughter.

Before, I was a very spontaneous person, always directed outward toward people and activities. On that day in the Madrid hospital it became clear to me that I possessed no kind of control over things, that life flows like a river that I can't ever stop and whose course I can't alter either. Something had changed in me and I can see it properly only after two years. I preserve more distance, I'm not so open for meetings with other people, I'm not so curious, not so well-disposed toward public engagements. That doesn't mean that I've lost my love of life or my energy. I've simply withdrawn a step. I know now that everything happens by accident.

> *You are not a believing Christian, but your book leaves the impression that you have traveled the path of the Cross.*

Oh, you've just clarified something for me, and you're right. Yes, I imagine that the stations of the cross, of suffering, have a universal meaning and significance. I had to travel them first, in order to discover them.

> *Compared to eternity is the life of the human being less than a drop in the ocean? Do we not sometimes overvalue the significance of a single destiny?*

Yes, in a certain sense. Somewhere in the book I write that life amounts to just about nothing. But millions of people are born, live, and die. In that regard it doesn't make a difference whether Paula died at twenty-eight or if she lived until seventy-eight, as far as the history of humanity is concerned. But I must at the same time say that, in my life, this single life was important—namely, hers. And you are bringing this to my awareness again, and that also marks a part of my new distance: I've lost my fear of death.

> *What is your conception of life after earthly death?*

I am convinced that there is a life after death. But I don't think that Paula has an individual soul that is striving to gain entry to heaven. I imagine a kind of ocean of knowledge, consciousness, and spirit, and we possess drops of it in our bodies. I can't identify my daughter in this great spiritual container, but I can identify with my memories of her. The memory is my link, but the feeling of connection comes also from the body.

> *Why don't you explain anywhere in your book the nature of the sickness of porphyria, of which your daughter evidently died?*

Because there was no necessity to do that. She was an expert insofar as her condition was concerned. It's just as unimportant that Paula actually didn't die of porphyria, but rather because of an error in the intensive care unit in Madrid. One can grow old with porphyria. It is a large hospital, and somehow the list of medications to which she was allergic—which she always carried on her person—got lost. Her brain damage was caused by the administration of the wrong drugs.

> *Back to you yourself. You have two lives, you've said, a waking and a dreaming life. And you can decipher your everyday life with the help of dreams. How does that work?*

When I go to bed at night, I prepare myself to dream and to record my dreams. I get up right away, during the next morning, and I write down the dreams if they appear significant to me, and enter them into the computer. In this way I've been able to recognize patterns. It may sound completely crazy, but my theory functions.

> *One can hardly speak of a dream when one speaks of the death of Salvador Allende. You portray him as if the terror were almost palpable.*

Strange that you mention that. I suffer from nightmares, which again and again bring these events before my eyes. Soldiers enter in—and weapons, bullets, screaming too. So it's easy for me to remember, but perhaps the memory is sharpened by the experience of another death.

> *You are well known for your commitment to feminism. Is the claim true that, in the case of Paula's illness, you battled against a male-dominated world of medicine?*

I am generally guarded about health care because of the ignorance and arrogance of the medical establishment, where a kind of authority and power rule that won't let itself be doubted. I fear that attitude greatly, because it resembles a military authority and power that never questions itself.

> *In closing, another question about your book. Why was the German edition called a novel?*

That didn't come from me. The book is my memoirs, if one wants to introduce a genre concept. The fundamental theme circles around death and loss, but it is at base a book about life and love—and about the twenty-eight years that Paula spent with me. The fact that she was born out of my body is more important for me than that she died in my arms too. I remember more the moments of the birth than the moments of the death. I don't know whether I've succeeded to communicate that in the book.

After Paula

INTERVIEW BY JOHN RODDEN

31

Not previously published

On April 11, 1995—the date on which the English edition of *Paula* was officially published by HarperCollins in a first print run of one hundred thousand—Isabel Allende kicked off her twelve-city American promotional book tour with a visit to the University of Texas at Austin.

Dates are important to Allende—above all, January 8, the date on which she began to write her first novel, *The House of the Spirits*, and on which she started all her other books. But after publication of *The Infinite Plan* in 1991, Allende unexpectedly found herself at a hospital bedside in Madrid on January 8, 1992. She had gotten word just a few weeks before—at a Barcelona book reception to launch *The Infinite Plan*—that her daughter, Paula Frías, had been rushed to intensive care.

Allende would soon find out that Paula's influenza had taken a disastrous turn. Suffering from a rare, hereditary enzyme deficiency known as porphyria, Paula underwent complications, was misdiagnosed by Spanish physicians, and sustained severe brain damage. "I love you too, Mama," Paula murmured, just before she lapsed into a coma from which she never recovered. Allende began jotting notes to her daughter. As she would later record in her memoir: "On this January 8, 1992, I am writing you, Paula, to bring you back to life."[1]

But the prognoses were dark and Paula's condition deteriorated. Still hoping for a miraculous recovery, Isabel Allende took her daughter to her San Rafael, California, home in mid-1992, whereupon the ironies of dates and fates again intertwined for the Allende family: Paula died precisely one year—to the day—after falling into the coma: December 8, 1992.

Although *Paula* is Allende's sixth book, it is her first work of nonfiction. "Listen, Paula," the memoir opens. "I am going to tell you a story, so that when you wake up you will not feel so lost." Originally entitled *Para Paula* [*For Paula*], the story that Allende tells her daughter is the story of the Allendes' life and the family's history. Written "for Paula"— the Spanish edition featured a heart-rending photograph of Paula on its jacket cover—*Paula* tells the story of the Allende family rather than just that of Paula herself. Indeed, *Paula* introduces the extraordinary family members who inspired Isabel Allende's fiction, especially *The House of the Spirits*. And like *The House of the Spirits*, the memoir begins as a letter to a family member. But that first letter of January 8, 1981, began as a goodbye note to a one-hundred-year-old grandfather who wanted to die, whereas *Paula* represents a farewell letter—and an anguished love letter—to a twenty-eight-year-old daughter who had everything to live for.

And Fate would soon intervene in Allende's life in yet another unforeseen way—via the publishing success of *Paula*. A fortuneteller had once told Allende that Paula would become known in many parts of the world. Throughout the tortuous year of Paula's illness, Allende had derived hope from this prediction, originally believing that it meant that Paula would recover and go on to great accomplishments. But the prophecy—like so much in Allende's life—was to come ironically true in another way: By the end of April 1995, *Paula* was #8 on the *New York Times* best-seller list, after having already become a best-seller throughout Europe.

Petite and vivacious, Isabel Allende, fifty-two, is down to earth and forthcoming. Although she carries the pain of her daughter's death with fortitude and dignity, she acknowledges that the pain is always there—and she looks forward, after the book tour, to a less public life that will grant her the solitude to grieve: even though writing *Paula* partly served this very purpose, Allende has only just begun, she says, to mourn the loss of her daughter.

"Children, like books, are voyages into one's inner self," writes Allende in *Paula*, "during which body, mind, and soul shift course and turn toward the very center of existence."[2] In the following interview, conducted shortly before her lecture to a campus crowd of more than a thousand at the University of Texas, Allende speaks with remarkable directness and openness about her books and her inner self and her shifting fortunes: about her writing habits, her family's involvement in her work, and above all the changes in her outlook on life and death after *Paula*—and Paula.

❝ *You are known for starting to write all your books on January 8, including your recent nonfiction book,* Paula. *You've said that you do this because* The House of the Spirits *was begun on that date. January 8 also just happens to be the birthday of Elvis Presley.*

Is this your "lucky date"? Is the practice of beginning on that date superstition?

January 8, 1981, is a sacred date for me. But there's nothing in the stars about January 8th, though I've heard that it was Elvis's birthday. I was never a great Presley fan when I was growing up. The significance is not astrological but very personal—even though the personal dimension does include a superstitious element.

To understand all this, you must understand my life. I stayed in Venezuela thirteen years. I went into exile from Chile [in 1975] and ended up in a school with four hundred kids, teaching every day. I did that four and a half years. I hated it!

On January 8, 1981, I received a phone call that my grandfather was dying. And I decided to write a letter about all the things he told us when we were young. I was working two shifts, twelve hours per day, and I wrote at night. I had five hundred pages by the end of the year. And it was *The House of the Spirits*.

My mother sent it to the publishers. I heard nothing, and finally a receptionist called. *She* had read it and liked it. She gave me the name of an agent in Barcelona. She was interested in my name and in politics: in Chile and Allende. I sent her two envelopes, the first with pages 1–250 and a cover letter, and the second with pages 251–500. But she only got the second one. It took a while to figure out what was wrong. Finally, I sent her another copy of pages 1–250, and in less than a month, I got a contract. And less than a year after that, the novel was translated into every European language.

I began my second novel also on that date. So, for me, the date has a superstitious significance, because it's the date on which I began my first novel and it is the date on which my career as a fiction writer began.

Today, I start all my books on January 8—not just out of superstition but also discipline!

Discipline? Do you mean that the ritual of starting to write on January 8 imposes discipline on your writing habits?

Yes. If I didn't have this date, I might never begin! I would always want to be pushing the beginning further and further off. I would always have some excuse or rationale to think about just waiting a few more weeks or months. And it would stretch out even further.

I suppose that urge to delay is because of the anxiety about beginning a new book. About beginning anything that is going to be so large and demanding as writing a book. I know it is going to be painful and take a great deal out of me. But at the same time, I'm excited about it.

So, in a sense, January 8th launches me. It's something that I have that points me forward and lets me begin. Once I've begun, then I'm into it. And I can respond to the demands and begin to feel excited and enjoy the process. So this bit of "superstition" actually has very realistic and practical aspects to it. It lets me get down to working. Without it, getting started would be much more difficult. I only work on one project at a time. If I finish a book in October, I'll take a four-month vacation!

So you look forward to January 8—and also fear it.

Can you imagine what every January 7 is like?! I'm hysterical! The whole family goes crazy! I get locked in a room and prepare for the next day.

On January 8, I try to write a first sentence that comes from the heart. I have no outline, just a plan. I try to write a first sentence that comes from the womb, and it becomes a door that opens to a different place. It may not remain the first sentence in the book, but I keep it somewhere in the book. When I began writing *The House of the Spirits* and wrote "Barrabás came from the sea" [the first sentence of *The House of the Spirits*], I didn't know who or what "Barrabás" meant—most dogs in my grandfather's house had biblical names. That sentence just sounded good. In *Of Love and Shadows*, the first sentence that I wrote wound up in the second chapter. Sometimes the first sentences remain the openers, and sometimes they wind up elsewhere, but I always keep them in the work. "My name is Eva, which means 'life.' . . ." I left that in *Eva Luna* [as the opening sentence]. "Listen, Paula. I'm going to tell you a story, so that when you wake up you will not feel so lost." That [first sentence in *Paula*] came to me in the hospital, and I kept it because I wanted to tell Paula all that she had been missing.

In general, though, I usually wind up writing something different than planned. I proceed from what the first sentence suggested and then it's a continual process of discovering and uncovering, of peeling away—just as it is for a sculptor. The statue exists already in the stone; the story exists already in me.

So it's just a matter of sculpting or unveiling it.

Right. I just let the first draft emerge. It's just a storytelling draft. When I'm writing that draft, it is about anything and everything. Then I print it out and read it, and only then do I really know what it's about. But it's still so messy at that stage. The second draft is to straighten out the story. And the third draft is stylistic, to get the language right.

Then it's done, and I give it to my mother to read.

> *Your mother has always been a valuable critic of your work in progress.*

My mother is actually my only critic: she is my first and most serious critic. We have had some real knock-down battles about what to include and exclude from my books! She is the first person to read my work and she is a very sensitive and intelligent reader. But most important: she feels free to tell me anything and everything! She is especially concerned with my use of language—not just with the development of plot or the portrayal of different characters.

So we fight over the draft. In a six-hundred-page manuscript, maybe fifteen pages will survive unscathed. She fights over characters, telling me I'm too closely identified with a character. She tells me to go deeper into a character. And although I don't, by any means, follow all her suggestions or preferences, I pay great attention to her comments.

After we fight, I rewrite the book. And I finish it. The first draft takes me about four months. The whole process takes about two years. I don't show her the last draft. She feels she's worked so hard that she can't take any more. She's seventy-four, after all.

> *So she focuses on your use of language. Does she have any characteristic criticisms?*

My explicitness! She doesn't like sex scenes! I censor all those scenes when I show her the early draft—I take them all out. I also cut out all passages about the Pope and the church in that draft. Then I put some of them back in. She never reads the final version or the published book itself, so she never encounters the sex scenes or the anti-Catholic criticism.

> *Do you also share your work in progress with friends or colleagues?*

My husband also reads Spanish and he is a very valuable critic of my work too. But his Spanish is not at a level at which he can help with questions of literary style. He doesn't have a native speaker's ear for the precise use of language. I also used to share my work in progress with my daughter. Now I share it with my daughter-in-law.

After it's published, neither my mother nor I read it again. We have been through so much up until the moment of finally completing it that it's over for us. It's no longer the world that I have inside me. I've moved on.

> *Apart from the fact that* Paula *deals with the tragedy of your daughter's illness and death, it is an autobiographical memoir and quite self-disclosing—one might almost say self-exposing—about your own private life and your past. How did you feel writing about yourself and other family members in* Paula*?*

I talked with everybody in the family mentioned in *Paula*—we had many family discussions. And everyone accepted to be in the book. My mother wanted some changes, but I didn't make them. She wanted me not to reveal so much. But I didn't feel comfortable taking anything out.

Yes, I felt exposed all the time. I expose facts of my life in *Paula*—for example, facts about my lovers. I also expose the influence of religion and politics on our family.

And there was also an even deeper level of exposure: of my sentiments. I took the risk of appearing sentimental. A writer uses emotions in an artful way to provoke a reaction in a reader. A melodramatic action—exile, the death of a child—will usually provoke a strong reader response. And some readers will find the exposure too great and react defensively. But what I wrote is true, the raw truth.

But, you see, my candor and expression of strong emotions in *Paula*—that also felt like exposure.

> *And yet, you felt that you had to go through this exposure as a way of confronting and expressing the "raw truth." And after going through this ordeal—which is also, given that you are now on a book tour, a quite public event—where do you find yourself? Has the experience of writing a book about your daughter's death altered you greatly— as a writer, a woman, a human being?*

I've asked myself countless times: Why her? Why her and not me? If I pray, maybe it will happen to *me* and not her—that's sometimes what I thought. I asked, Why didn't she die at the beginning? Why did she stay for a year in a coma?

It was tragic, but I learned a lot in that time. It would have been much easier if she hadn't fallen into the coma. The pain was much greater because she stayed a year.

Because Paula stayed, I learned a lesson. My destiny was to lose a child. I believe in destiny! I did all that I could to save Paula, and I could not protect her from her condition and from the world. I believe that we are not just body and mind. We are spiritual too. We come from some place and go to some place, and this world is just a stage. So this disease and death were Paula's destiny. Some people leave the stage in just twenty-eight years, like Paula.

What do I do *now*? I can be angry, I can try to make it a transcendent experience, I can write a book. What do I do with these cards? She was given the card of porphyria—and her life lasted just twenty-eight years. But it is not less valuable because it was brief.

I'm less passionate now than I used to be. I held Paula for many hours until she died. She died on December 8, 1992. And just seven months later, a girl who was a drug addict and HIV-positive had a premature, seven-month baby in the same room in which Paula died. I thought at first that this is Paula come back! There was a stillness, a sacred space there.

Yes, there was a strange air in that room; it was a sacred moment. Paula's spirit was still in that room. I wanted to ask the baby: "Tell me where you come from, before it's too late!" I felt her mother was a door! The baby was from another world, I thought.

Jennifer [the baby's mother, daughter of Allende's husband, William Gordon] lived in Oakland, in the poorest neighborhood. If she had given birth there, it would have been a dead baby. In Santa Rosa, a rich neighborhood, she was taken care of. The baby couldn't be taken out of the hospital. It was kept in an incubator. She is an adorable, HIV-positive baby and will die. But more important is this: she is alive. Her name is Sabrina.

I still ask myself: What if this *is* the soul of Paula in this baby? I hope this is another soul that will have its own, different destiny.

I feel I was training to learn to love.

All this is behind *Paula*. When I was writing it, I had the feeling that I'd trained all my life to write this book. Now I can't find the passion to do anything else. Maybe I'll get the passion back to write again.

I hope that the book is useful for people who have had losses.

Does the loss of Paula affect your attitude toward your writing and your identity as a writer?

I started another book on January 8. I'll soon see if I'm a changed woman.

But I know that I've already changed a great deal. I'm letting things happen more, not forcing them. I'm not as goal-oriented as before. And not only because of Paula's death, but also because of my own aging. I've learned a great deal more about myself and about living than I once knew or was able to accept.

Now I realize that life is really a process. Perhaps my grandchildren have taught me some of this. Now I enjoy the present moment more. I used to live a great deal in the future, with plans and dreams and goals. But I came to realize that life is now. Life is this moment.

Before, I always wanted things *to get done*. Fast and well. I always wanted a *finished* book. I wanted to come to the end and to have something. Now I enjoy the process far more. I've discovered in a much deeper way the joys of writing itself. I've really learned to enjoy writing, which means to enjoy living and being present to it. This is especially true of my feelings about storytelling. Sometimes I have readers who say: "I'm reading the ending very slowly because I don't want the book to end! I want simply to dwell in the story a little longer."

And I have come to feel the same way when I'm writing. Sometimes I simply like it to last a little while longer, because I'm so enjoying it. Rather than focus on the finished product, I'm enjoying each moment in the process.

So I'm less concerned with achieving a certain product than I am with valuing and entering fully into the process of what I'm doing: in this case, the activity of writing. Just letting go and enjoying it. That is the most difficult task for most writers. Most of us have a goal-oriented attitude because, finally, the book is a product. It gets delivered into the hands of publishers, editors, and readers. And we are concerned about their opinion of it.

The experience of writing, however, is a process. What gets shaped from that experience is in the form of a product, but the experience is fundamental. Remembering that is the difficulty.

And reading is also an experience, and it is often related to the writing experience: the sharing, during the reading, is also an experience. A reader knows if a writer has enjoyed the act of writing. Partly what gets shared between reader and writer is the experience of what has happened in the act of creation. That is somehow bound up in the world that the writer has created and which the reader enters.

Yes, I enjoy the process of writing more now, and maybe that also has something to do with the fact that I also appreciate my grandchildren more. I simply enjoy seeing them growing.

Yes, I find my life purposes altering. After Paula, everything is different.

Nothing will ever be more significant than this loss. And now I know: I could die tomorrow.

> *You mean that you now know that in a visceral way, not merely in an intellectual or abstract sense?*

I know it as a mother who has lost a child knows it. As a mother, I feel the instinct to protect my child. And I couldn't do it. I couldn't. During that year, I loved her more than ever before. She went back to being a newborn baby—there was even a tube in her stomach to feed her.

Paula was the genius of the family. But in the hospital, I just hoped she was comfortable. I re-learned to love with the unconditional love of a mother for a newborn. And even more than that—because I had no expectations of even a smile from her. And yet, she left me with a wonderful gift! If I could just love everyone—with a joyful love and no attachments—everything would be all right.

It's so hard to do that! I still tend to keep an accounting of what my husband and I owe each other!

That must be stressful.

Yes! And so I hope reincarnation is not true! I don't want to come back! It's too stressful! Who wants a body again? I dream that my daughter is free, like a drop of water in the ocean, free of all attachment.

Paula's death reminded me that we think we are immortal—but we are not. But there's nothing awful or unnatural about death—even the stars and the trees die. We need to remember all that.

What feelings does that insight evoke?

Strength, courage, peace. When Paula died, I lost the fear of death completely. It was as if life and death were not opposites but complements.

I had written about death since *The House of the Spirits*, but not *experienced* it. Only in my imagination. But now I see it's a wonderful feeling of liberation and detachment. Now I can love freely. I can now be the perfect grandmother, with no desire to control anyone's life!

So this feeling of fearlessness in the face of death has remained with you.

Yes, in the sense that I know I'm not immortal—that's the deception by which most of us live. We think that nothing will ever change. But I've discovered that there is nothing awful or unnatural about death. It's part of life. It's part of creation and dissolution. It is all a process.

And so it isn't to be feared. It's to be understood as something that comes in its own time. So what I finally learned was acceptance. I lost fear and I gained acceptance and understanding.

You mentioned a moment ago that the fact of your aging had contributed to these feelings of acceptance and understanding. Could you elaborate on what you've learned?

The greatest lesson is simply that life is lived in the present. The value of life is chiefly in the present. It's not in all the plans and strategies one has about what might happen in the future. I've lived so much of my life in the future, hoping to realize certain plans, hoping to be successful in certain ways!

Many of my plans have been realized. I've had some success in realizing my career ambitions.

But with aging I've come to see that life never quite turns out as you plan it. That gives me less of an urgency to control or direct it and more of a willingness to accept it and understand it and enjoy it for what it is in the present moment.

> *Politics and social justice have been major concerns in your work. Have you found that your politics has changed? Are you less interested in politics, now that your concerns have become more otherworldly?*

I'm still concerned about social justice, just as much as ever. The spiritual insights have added to, not taken away from, my political concerns. Paula's death, or the fact that I now reside here in the U.S.A. with my family, doesn't mean I've changed my attitudes toward American foreign policy or toward immigration, Proposition 13, and America's responsibilities in the world.

My views on social justice have not changed. I'm still angry about many aspects of American foreign policy and the U.S. role in the world. I've simply come to know America better—and so I understand why American politicians and many American people believe what they do. I've had my understanding of America deepened but not changed.

NOTES

1. *Paula* (New York: HarperCollins, 1995), 10.
2. Ibid., 231.

"I Leave My Books to Their Fate"

INTERVIEW BY JOHN RODDEN

32

Not previously published

The following interview, conducted at the University of Texas at Austin, addresses Allende's views on translation and adaptation. It occurred after Allende's informal talk to the Texas Center for Writers and continues the previous interview of April 11, 1995.

> " *You mentioned this afternoon the close working relationships that you have with family members during the process of revising your books. You also have a very close relationship with your English-language translator, Margaret Sayers Peden.*

Yes. But I only share the completed books with her. I show her all my work even before the Spanish edition is published—often even before I have an American publisher.

So you're pleased with the English translations of your work.

Very pleased. My first English translator [Magda Bogin] did not get on well with my editors. But my second translator [Peden] is a friend of mine. She is the only translator whom I personally select. Otherwise the publishers of all other foreign-language translations decide on the translator.

I wish I could write in English. But my work probably reads much better in Spanish, because it addresses Latin or Spanish themes—and the style is more expressive, partly because Spanish prefers longer sentences. English sentences tend to be shorter and English is a more prosaic language.

Do you like to do English-language readings from your work?

Very much. When I do readings from the English, I find that it's always a new and different experience. In fact, I have that experience whenever I look over translations of any of my books—in French or Italian, for example. I have a slightly different experience of the book I've written.

Your books have been translated into more than a dozen languages and have topped the best-seller lists in Italy, Germany, and Scandinavia, as well as having done extremely well in English-speaking countries and throughout Latin America. By some estimates, you are the best-selling female writer of serious fiction in the world.

How do you account for your popularity in translation?

There's nothing much to do, after all, in Oslo or Hamburg except read!

The northern countries generally like my books more, except Britain. The English only read English authors—it's practically impossible for a foreign author to break in there. But yes, if I were living in Germany or Scandinavia, I'd be a national celebrity. Most of my royalties come from there. I'm really popular there.

Why? Probably because they think Latin America is exotic—and with Germany, it probably also helps that there were close ties during the Communist era between East Germany and Chile. I sign copies of my books for German booksellers—four thousand copies. People in Germany read books!

Oddly enough, though, I'm also very popular in Italy at the moment. *Paula* is now #1 on the Italian best-seller list, and already in its seventh printing. I always think: It's crazy to read in Rome! Go out, enjoy the sun, sit and have a cappuccino! But they're reading me.

Do you ever consider the possibility of writing in English?

Well, I do write some essays and other short pieces in English. And I do most of my interviews in English. But I couldn't write the novels in English—for the reasons I've told you.

And yet, it's harder than ever to write in Spanish. It's hard to write in Spanish and live in the U.S.A. for me. My husband thinks he speaks good Spanish, but he doesn't! He invents words and then I use them in a novel! So I'm not able to write in English and my Spanish is deteriorating. It's a difficult situation.

How about the translation of your work from print to celluloid: Are you pleased with the film adaptations of The House of the Spirits *and* Of Love and Shadows? *Some reviewers have criticized them very harshly.*

I loved the movie of *The House of the Spirits*. It's not a Latin American movie, but it works as a story. The problem is that the people think it's supposed to be exotic. The director [Bille August] went to Uruguay and Chile, but the film doesn't have a Latin American feel. Some Americans were disappointed that it doesn't look exotic. But the only nation it wasn't successful in was the U.S.A.

Of Love and Shadows was a hugely successful movie in Latin America. It was filmed in English because of the big English-language market, but the accents of the characters are very strong.

I don't mind my books being filmed. The stories aren't mine. The filmmaker interprets them anew. I don't even remember the story [of *The House of the Spirits*] from twelve years ago! I let it all go. I leave my books to their fate.

Some Latinos have criticized the production of The House of the Spirits *for relying exclusively on white "name" actors.*

I'm no chauvinist. I don't think only Latinos can play Latin characters.

I selected the director for *The House of the Spirits*—Bille August. He's Scandinavian. *Of Love and Shadows* was directed by a man brought up in Latin America, and it was filmed in Argentina and Chile. I think it's a great movie. Although *The House of the Spirits* cost twenty-six million dollars and was filmed with celebrities, *Of Love and Shadows* cost only four and a half million dollars and was filmed in a private way. I like it even better than *The House of the Spirits*, because it's very faithful to the book.

You've occasionally said that you'd like to write screenplays—either for film or for TV soap operas.

Yes, I would. I'm really tempted to write screenplays. But that's another craft. I find it hard to write for commercial purposes. I don't have the same way of thinking if I'm concerned whether something will sell.

Part of the attraction for you is the obvious power of film and TV.

Yes. And the abuse of that power. For example, soap opera has been terribly misused. It controls people's imaginations—but it could be used constructively. For instance, a leading character on a Venezuelan soap opera once developed breast cancer and got a mammogram. And thousands of Venezuelan women went straight out and got mammograms.

And you've sometimes referred to the power in your own life of a kissing scene in Niño, *the Chilean soap opera of your youth.*

Yes, the kiss in *Niño*. There was a kiss, a famous kiss that felt to me so powerful and alive that it still seems to me more real than any kiss I've been given or received. But I mention *Niño* because it shows that fiction—whether in print or on the screen—can be more powerful than reality. A world that is created and designed with a certain power and symmetry can be more memorable than the real world in which we have lived.

And in some ways that's what has happened to me as a creator of fiction. Those fictional worlds that I enter and inhabit have an extraordinary power that is so well-ordered that, in some ways, they are deeper and more gripping or vivid than life itself. They imprint themselves more dramatically on one's consciousness than does the so-called real world.

The Writer as Exile,
and Her Search for Home

INTERVIEW BY JOHN RODDEN

33

Not previously published

In April 1995, Isabel Allende, already one of the best-selling writers in the world—more than eleven million copies of her books are in print in thirty-five languages—published her sixth book and first work of nonfiction. The new book was a searingly personal memoir titled *Paula*. Written in the form of a letter to her daughter, Paula Frías, who was hospitalized with a rare enzyme deficiency known as porphyria, *Paula* chiefly relates the story of Allende's tumultuous past life and her daughter's losing fight with death.

   Paula is thus an account of Isabel Allende's year of agony with her twenty-eight-year-old comatose daughter; Paula died on December 8, 1992, a year to the very day she slipped into a coma in a Madrid hospital. But the book also introduces the reader to the dramatic events and larger-than-life family members that have formed the basis of Allende's richly imaginative world of fiction. The memoir shows that Isabel Allende has led a life as adventuresome and dramatic—indeed tragic— as any of her numerous heroines and heroes. Or as one British critic wrote of the memoir: "[It] gives magical realism a human face."[1]

"People die only when they are forgotten," Isabel Allende's beloved grandfather, Agustín Llona, once told her. In 1981, when she found out that her grandfather was dying at home in Chile, the exiled Allende began a five-hundred-page letter to him that would become her first novel, *The House of the Spirits* (1982). A decade letter, she started a similar letter in response to family tragedy—but this letter was aimed at saving Paula, not mourning her. Allende finished the memoir, however, in the spirit of her grandfather's pronouncement: *Paula* would help a mother to remember: never to forget the past, never to forget Paula. "The word for 'remember' [in Spanish] is *recordar*," Allende noted in 1995, "—which literally means 'pass it again through the heart.' So memory comes from the heart and not the mind."[2]

Possessed of a strong heart filled with love, Allende still hoped in early 1992 that a mother's love could triumph over the shadows of sickness and death. Allende expected Paula to wake from the coma— most porphyria patients begin to recover after one month—but Paula had suffered severe brain damage as a result of a misdiagnosis. Rather than leave her daughter to the care of the Madrid hospital staff, Allende daringly decided to fly Paula to her home in San Rafael, California, which became Paula's final resting place—and for Allende another "House of the Spirits." When Allende's second grandchild—and one step-grandchild—were born in the house not long after Paula's death, the house felt to Allende even more a home for migrating souls. "Sometimes when I am alone, I can sit there in my daughter's room and feel her presence," Allende said in 1993. "The house is alive in a wonderful way."[3]

Paula's death occurred shortly after the publication of Allende's fourth novel, *The Infinite Plan*. That novel is based on the life story of her husband (San Francisco lawyer William Gordon) and his itinerant, Bible

Belt preacher-father, from whose breast-beating religious tract of the 1930s Allende takes her title. Formerly, says Allende, she agreed with her hero Gregory Reeves: "There is no infinite plan, just the strife of living."[4] After Paula's death and the composition of *Paula*, however, Allende thinks a "personal destiny"—if not a grand design—may indeed exist. Caught up in our daily round, however, we humans seldom glimpse it. And Allende admits the same of herself. As she writes in *Paula*: "Through forty-nine years of a life of action and struggle, I have run after goals I can no longer recall, pursuing something nameless that was always a little farther on. Now I am forced to inaction and silence; no matter how much I run I get nowhere, and if I scream, no one hears. You, Paula, have given me this silence in which to examine my path through the world. . . ."[5]

In the following interview—which occurred on May 24, 1995, just days after Allende returned home from a grueling, whirlwind, twelve-city book tour to promote *Paula*—Isabel Allende examines aloud, courageously and openly, her evolving path through the world. In a radical, unflinching act of self-scrutiny, she discusses her demons: her anger, her drivenness, her perfectionism. "I will never again be the person I was," Allende wrote in *Paula*. The interview is devoted to her new-found spirituality and self-understanding, to the differences between who Allende was and is becoming: before and after Paula.

A person of strong moral principles and values, Allende acknowledges below that she is sometimes a prisoner of a stern, unrelenting conscience. She shares how its commanding "shoulds"—what she calls her internalized, piercing, "critical voices" of Authority—have affected her work. These voices—whose origins she traces to her rearing and, specifically, to her grandfather's teachings—have inspired her extraordinary self-discipline, industry, productivity, self-control, and professionalism. But they have also instilled a level of perfectionism—in work and daily life—that torments her.

The confrontation with Paula's death has awakened Isabel Allende to the reality of her own mortality—and to other, less purposeful aspects of Life. Success does not bring inner serenity: Allende experiences this revelation as a return from an imposed exile of self-alienation. In the aftermath of Paula's death, Allende finds herself less goal oriented; she is trying to relax and savor life. She is attempting to relinquish emotional distance and to accept intimacy. She is more at peace, both with Paula's departure and with herself. Life—not just fiction—unfolds in miraculous ways, Isabel Allende allows. If there is no "infinite plan," Paula's life and death still belong to a miracle—to the wonder of being and becoming.

> **"** *Now that you are back home from your book tour [for* Paula*], and at work again, have you found that the passion for writing and for life itself are returning?*

I don't know yet. I've just started [to work again]. It may be that I'll never write another book again.

> *You once said: "A writing career is like a long marriage. The danger is that you'll lose the passion."*

Yes, but what I meant by that is that I'm more critical of myself as a writer now. I used to write on the strength of passion alone. But a writing career is like a long marriage insofar as you start seeing the defects after a while. And you lose the passion. I've started to see the defects of my own work.

Like with another lover, with the work of another writer, I surrender and let go. I want the story to be told to me. But when I write, I have to tell the story myself.

> *But you also believe that the reader gives you a great deal back.*

Definitely. I was trained to be a journalist. And I believe a book is not a work of art, but a way of communicating with people. It's like lovemaking in a private place. You are alone with a reader. And the reader gives the story its other half. It's not the author's story any more, it's a shared experience in the reading act.

> *How have you become "more critical" of your work? What "defects" have become conspicuous?*

For instance, I'm more accurate with language today. My preoccupation with style and word choice has become so strong that sometimes a critical voice takes over. It tries to control the creative process. I want to simply let the creative process flow. I want to let it continue and not interrupt it with the voice of the critic in me. Letting it flow means letting the storyteller tell her story and not, as it were, looking at it from the outside and seeing its blemishes.

So I'm more of a self-conscious critic of my own work. The critical voice in me has increased in volume. It's very difficult for me to tone it down or silence it now. I've always been an extremely demanding person of myself. And as a result, the critical voice is louder than ever.

> *Do you worry that your book tours, or your occasional association with academe, threaten the integrity of your creative process by making you even more self-critical? Or more likely to approach writing in a conceptual or self-conscious way?*

No. I don't feel as if association with the publishing industry or the academic world makes it more difficult to click off the critical voice in me—because I really have very little association with either of them. I don't have an academic appointment. I only deal with the publishing world when my books appear. I don't even socialize with other writers.

So it isn't a matter of concern about the judgment of the publishing world or the reviewers, or a fear of compromising my work in responding to their criticism. The critical voices involve primarily me and my own nature. I've always been a very demanding person of myself and in some ways that tendency only increases when I perform well and have a great success, because then I expect even more of myself. I want to do even better the next time.

So it's simply me. Despite everything I've said about learning to let go after writing *Paula*, I still struggle with this critical voice inside me. It has to do with my drive to succeed and the way in which I've increased my demands on myself.

This critical voice of mine always seems to be intruding! It always seems to be insisting, to be demanding that I perform up to a certain level. Or interrupting the flow of my energies by pointing out certain shortcomings or inadequacies in one sphere or another.

I need to learn to let go. I need to learn to simply be in the world that I create. And when I'm in that world of my creation, I'm free and the writing flows.

Where do you think this critical voice comes from?

A lot of it has to do with my upbringing. And my relationship to my grandfather. I grew up with all his proverbs about hard work and struggle and effort and diligence. I grew up in a home with no games, no music, no fun. It was a male-dominated family, in which work counted above all.

> *So your upbringing developed your diligent work habits, but also instilled a puritanical, even tyrannical voice of authority that makes it hard to relax.*

Well, I now see that my upbringing is the source of my success, but it's also something I need to grow out of. I want to let go of some aspects of great responsibility and independence that are linked to a reluctance to trust. My mother still can't understand that. She has the old values. Whatever will make you successful—that's still her chief concern. "Don't you want to be successful?" she asks. That's her attitude.

You see, my grandfather's proverbs have gone in so deep. He was a major factor responsible in my upbringing for the first ten years of my life. He constantly gave me proverbs such as: "Don't trust other people"; "Don't expect of them what you couldn't expect from yourself, or from those in the family"; "Keep on your guard"; "Be wary of those who seem to have good motives"; "Don't get taken." Above all, he would say: "Count only on yourself and those in the family."

And these kinds of proverbs taught me conditional love. That is, no one ever said to me, "I just want you to be happy." The message instead was, "We want you to be a great success. We want you to perform well."

So I turned into a performer, I became a great performer and I sought to succeed. And those proverbs were not bad. But they can and did, in my case, have some negative influences on me as a child. I have spent my whole lifetime attempting to work my way beyond them. My goal recently has been learning to let go and just be in the flow. But I've always set very high standards for myself and tried to reach them. I've always been something of a perfectionist. I've sought to perform extremely well. And so it's very hard for me not do that, and just to experience the joy of living.

But all this is not black and white, it is gray. That is, the proverbs have made me a very self-sufficient person. I rely on myself during times of crisis. Fortunately, I have resources within me to act alone and to transform my circumstances. So they make me a very independent person.

But, once again, that autonomy has a negative side to it. I was never asked, as a child, about what activities and goals made me happy. People didn't think like that back then. In fact, that is really a very American notion. This is precisely what I now ask about my grandchildren. I ask them: "What will make you happy?" Not what will make you successful or what will make you capable of impressing others. But simply: how do you want to be happy?

So the proverbs are partly responsible for the great demands I've placed on myself, but also for the successes I've had, as well as for my strength and resilience.

Could the voices also be responsible for the intensity of your work—and maybe even for the passion?

Yes, but when the voices get too loud, they suffocate the passion.

But apart from worrying about the critical voices, I worry that I'm getting less fresh in my thinking. And that is probably every writer's challenge in a long writing career. The danger is that, after a while as a writer, you lose the joy. I feel that sometimes.

After a while, the passion of courtship goes elsewhere. I wrote *Paula* with passion because I was in such pain.

That is my nature. When I'm reading a story, I forgive all the defects of a book if a writer tells a story with passion. So, for me, it doesn't compensate if a story is more precise or better crafted. If it has no soul, no heart, it's no good. That's why my more critical orientation doesn't feel to me as if it will be enough to compensate for a loss of passion in my work. Some writers are craftspersons—and others are not. I'm not. For me, it's not a matter of finding a new form of commitment that is not based in passion. The only way for me to continue to write or continue to be in a relationship is if the passion remains. Because that is what keeps it alive, that is what preserves the vital connection.

But after writing Paula, *the task might be to find a new rhythm in your life.*

True, one needs to learn to relax. If you don't discover your own rhythm, and learn that there's an ebb tide and a flood tide, then you may mistakenly think your ability and passion to write are gone. And that they're gone forever.

But my point is that, whether or not the passion comes back, I'm not the kind of writer who can substitute something else for the passion—in writing or in life. There are other writers and other partners who can find a different source of commitment or energy, a different way of being in the marriage or of being a writer, but I'm the kind of writer and partner who also needs the passion. For me, it is maintaining the passion, it's finding some way of tapping into the passion that is the key.

Perhaps it must be in a different way than I did it before. But without the passion, then my personal relationship or my work begins to die.

In what aspects of the activity of writing does your passion reside? In creating your characters? In the storytelling?

Yes, above all in the storytelling. I have the feeling that stories are our connection to the world. There are only a few myths and stories, but we can retell them differently, and then they feel fresh and new again.

In our psyche, we are all part of the same story. That's why storytelling is so important: it keeps us connected to the whole. We know then that we're part of a larger story, still unfolding, and that the language that we all use is the web providing the connection. When we see that, we see that we're not individuals—it's as if the self goes away and I open up and am part of everyone and everything. And the story keeps us together. We're all searching, all searching for connection—for home.

Might a part of a new rhythm be a turn toward more nonfiction? You began your writing career as a journalist, as a nonfiction writer. In the aftermath of the success of Paula, *do you plan to write more nonfiction?*

Someday I might do more nonfiction. But I enjoy fiction much more. I don't want to have to be concerned about adhering to standards of accuracy. I want to be able to create my own world and to fashion it as I please. So I enjoy fiction because it allows me to unleash my imagination completely, without any limitations that would enter if I had to be concerned with getting the facts right.

> *That was precisely your frustration with journalism during your years as a reporter in Chile.*

Yes. I hate being limited by the facts! Until *Paula*, I was never tempted to write nonfiction. I'm too imaginative. I'm always imagining different dimensions. That's why I don't set the story in real places or use historical dates—I'd have to be so accurate.

But with *Paula* I didn't mind being accurate, because it's not a novel and the circumstances were special. Still, there are parts of it that feel like hallucination. I started writing it in a hospital. I wrote 190 letters, mostly to my mother. And Ernesto [Paula's husband] gave me the love letters from Paula to him. That material formed the basis of the first draft. In the second draft, I used some of Ernesto's letters to Paula. But there was very little editing after I wrote it out the first time. With nonfiction, everything is just given to you.

> *But ironically, so much of your fiction is, in a sense, also "given." You derive a great deal of your fiction—plot, characterization, setting, leitmotifs—from history and current events.*

That's true. But as a journalist, I sought to explain *what* happened. As a writer and storyteller, my job is to ask *why* it happened—and *that* becomes the story itself.

I find my stories in the experiences of people. They've all happened, or they will happen. They're derived from common human experience. Eighty percent of my short-story collection [*The Stories of Eva Luna*] came from newspaper accounts.

For instance, a thirteen-year-old girl in Columbia in 1985 in Tomero got trapped in a mud slide. She died a slow, anguished death. I saw this on TV in Venezuela. TV cameras had filmed it all but nobody saved her. Then I wrote a story about it ["And of Clay Are We Created" in *The Stories of Eva Luna*].

I feel I don't really "make up" anything. I just tell people's stories. I have an ear for stories. I don't remember faces or places, but I have a mind for storytelling. I get the main plotline of the story from others and then I create the details.

I think my first obligation is to make the story believable—no matter how weird it may seem. For instance, I write that Rosa [in *The House of the Spirits*] has green hair. And readers accept that. My family believed that our Uncle Pablo flew over the Andes with his wings. And so I elaborated further [in *The House of the Spirits*]: I made Uncle Nicolás an inventor equipped with different devices for flying.

The weirder the real-life story, the better. I hate normality! I want to be with weirdos! I get my stories from their experiences.

For example, you derived the plot for The Infinite Plan *from the life of your husband and his family.*

Yes. When I met him, my husband talked to me at length about Berkeley in the 1960s. But I didn't live through that. No matter how much I research it, I'll never get it. Or the Vietnam War. It's all in *The Infinite Plan*, but I wasn't here in the States and didn't live through it. I can't get inside the humiliation that millions of Americans felt.

Did your distance from events also afford you advantages?

Yes, because it's good for a writer to be outside, to be marginal. I couldn't have written about Chile if I had remained *in* Chile. The distance helps, whether in terms of geography or time. Or if there's a cultural gap, as in *The Infinite Plan*. My husband tried to write a book about much of the content of the novel, but he couldn't do it.

I could do it, both because I had the distance and because I became a journalist again. I interviewed my husband and a friend named Tabra who makes my jewelry. I went to all the places, I "researched" California: there really *is* a man who invented a religion called "The Infinite Plan."

So there is an "infinite plan"?!

Yes—marry your man and get the story! [*Laughter.*] No, the truth is that I needed a green card! [*Laughter.*] No, the *real* truth is that I met this gringo lawyer in San Francisco—he was the last heterosexual

male in San Francisco—and I'd been living in chastity for too long—
about two weeks! [*Laughter.*] And we "locked in": I got his story and
he got me.

Well, no, I don't believe there is an "infinite plan." But I believe
there is a personal destiny. We're dealt the cards, and the cards are
marked. But there's no exact plan as to how they get played. What
can we do? Just play the cards as best we can.

> *Being "outside" or "marginal" raises the question of exile, which has*
> *been an important dimension of your life, both as a child and an*
> *adult. It sounds as if you believe that the writer in exile has special*
> *opportunities, the creation of a world that becomes, as it were, his or*
> *her spiritual home.*

Exile is better for a writer, I think. Not for his life, but for his work—
it's best for your work if you must confront a situation you don't understand and make sense of it through your work.

I might not be able to write at all if I had led a safe, predictable
life! I've had an adventurous life: I've been through one coup, a military regime, three revolutions, and the death of a child. Some writers
might regard this as a hindrance, because they would understandably
see a more stable and peaceful life as providing the serenity that allows their creative worlds to merge. But somehow the turmoil and
the upheaval in my life, and my role as an observer and exile writer,
have all contributed positively to my creative capacity.

> *Do you consider the writer to have a kind of divine power—to create*
> *a world?*

I feel I'm like God as a writer: I make up the story. The act of creation
is a God-like act. And yet I'm not capable of simply having the characters behave in a certain way or even say certain things that I would
prefer. It's as if the characters have free will. As if they are living out
their own lives and I'm simply observing it all, as if I were merely a
radio and I *hear* the voices and simply record them. And the characters do really have free will, in that they have an existence of their
own. I am capable of giving voice to the story, but not of altering it or
manipulating them in such a way as to have them say or do what
they fundamentally would never say or do.

So my task is to listen very, very closely and to observe—very, very precisely. To listen closely—so that a world can emerge. I want to be sensitive to the most delicate vibrations of that created world. I want to notice all that there is going on. Especially because most of the characters in my work are not created out of whole cloth. They're people that I've known, or they are composites of people who I'm acquainted with, and the stories are invented from events that have really happened or from lives of people I've known.

And so I feel as if my life has furnished the material, in a very direct way, out of which my fictional worlds have come. If I hadn't lived this life, I wouldn't be able to create these fictional worlds. Perhaps I wouldn't be a writer at all. Or at least not a fiction writer.

NOTES

1. E. Jane Dickson, "Death and Dancing Sugar Bowls," *The Independent* (London), September 23, 1995, 6.

2. Mike Bygrave, "My Country, My Child, My Passion," *Sunday Telegraph*, September 10, 1995, 3.

3. Margaria Fichtner, "Latin Vision in U.S.: Passionate Author Brings Dreams to America," *Arizona Republic*, June 7, 1993, C1.

4. *The Infinite Plan*, 379.

5. *Paula*, 162.

"I Remember Emotions,
I Remember Moments"

INTERVIEW BY VIRGINIA INVERNIZZI

34

Not previously published

I conducted the following interview with Isabel Allende on June 29, 1995, in Sausalito, California. My interest in Allende as a writer began in 1986 when she visited the University of Virginia, where I was working on my Ph.D. in Latin American literature. Allende had been invited to teach a short, three-week seminar on creative writing, and I enrolled in the course. It was interesting to work with Allende in a small group, yet what made the experience even more engrossing was that her daughter Paula helped her teach the course.

Paula was, at the time, a graduate student in psychology at the University of Virginia. We all came to know Paula well and she soon became one more member of the group.

During those inspiring three weeks we worked with Isabel Allende the writer, the teacher, the mother, and the friend that she soon became. It was a unique experience that only a handful of students were fortunate enough to have.

In the course of those three weeks, we wrote, read, laughed, played, and came to know the woman who was quickly becoming the most widely read female author in Latin America. My own interest in Allende's work was sparked by her exceptional popularity (no other Latin American female writer has received such great accolades), and I have since then attempted to fathom the phenomenon of her unique popularity in some of my own work.

After Allende wrote *Paula,* I wanted to interview her. Allende has given numerous interviews, yet, as John Rodden and I discussed in the course of my research, there were too many questions that had not been asked, and which I wanted to include as part of this volume.

I flew to San Francisco and met Allende in her quaint and charming office in Sausalito. On my way to Sausalito I remembered that Allende loved flowers, and I asked the taxi driver to stop at a flower shop. I bought a bunch of big yellow lilies. As I gave them to Isabel when I arrived, she hugged and kissed me in the typical Latin American fashion, asked me to make myself comfortable, and rushed out of the room. A few minutes later she returned with five calla lilies which she had cut from her own garden, and which she placed in a vase, together with the yellow ones I had brought, in a beautiful arrangement. It was remarkable to observe the way in which the white calla lilies brought out the beauty in the yellow ones I had just given her. I watched her place the vase on a nearby table and was suddenly struck by how much her everyday life so closely resembles her art. As I gazed upon the beautiful yellows and whites in the vase, I thought how this is precisely what Allende attains in her writing: she embroiders, she turns the daily reality into magic. She takes the simple yellow lilies and offers the reader the much lovelier contrast of the yellow against the white.

What follows is the conversation that Isabel Allende and I had on that June morning in 1995. Imagine, if you will, a warm, gentle, and extremely focused woman speaking about her life and her art.

" *It's interesting, but after reading* Paula *I very much wanted to hear more about the parts of your life that you recount in the book.*

You are a scholar, interested in writing and literature, but most people are not. And I am not such an interesting subject. I thought there was too much about myself.

Well, for example, I wanted to know more about Isabel Allende the child. I wanted to hear more about the everyday occurrences in your life.

That's the problem with memory, with my memory anyway. I remember the highlights and the very dark moments, but I don't recall the grey in between, the routine of everyday life. It seems to fade away. I can tell you a little bit about how I looked and what my personality was like. I was a small child. I was the smallest in the class and the smallest in the school. I was extremely sensitive. I was hurt all the time by things that happened and I was hurt by the social injustice in the house where I lived. A hungry dog, a hungry beggar on the street, all this hurt me. All this created within me a permanent state of pain. As a young child I loved to read. I was a sullen child, you could say. Later it became a form of anger, and if I had had a therapist, as children do today, it would have been different. I ended up writing because my childhood was not a happy one. Everything comes from that, from the anxiety, fear, and loneliness of childhood.

Your books give one the impression that you have a cheerful personality. You seem a happy person when one meets you.

I *am* a happy person now.

What made you change from the sullen and unhappy child you once were?

I think mainly the fact that I am in control of my life. Very early on I wanted to be in control; ever since I was a child I didn't want to depend. I didn't want to be a victim, I didn't want to be like most women in my family had been in the era when I was brought up. I needed to have a feeling of power in my own life.

*There is a part in the book that left me with a special sense of aston-
ishment, of wonder. Could you comment on the time when you saw
the seer in Buenos Aires and she told you that one of your children
would be known all over the world? You mention it, and in retrospect
we know what a dreadful prediction that was. Yet you do not comment on what you thought about it at the time.*

The seer in Buenos Aires, María Teresa Juárez, predicted several
things. She said there would be bloodshed in my country for many
years. She said that I would be paralyzed, or incapacitated, that my
only calling was literature, and that one of my children would be
known in the world. Then my mother held out two photographs, one
of Paula and one of Nicolás (my son), and placed them on the table
face down. María Teresa had not seen the faces. She placed one hand
on each photograph and said, "This one," and she turned it over and
it was Paula's. So there was a joke in the family that Paula was the genius among us, and that she would be known all over the world. This
was long before I became a writer. And when I was writing the book,
I was writing to Paula and thinking that Paula could not die because
she had not fulfilled the prophesy. She had not yet done what she had
come to the world to do. After the book was published, many people
have said that it may have been through this book that Paula was to
become famous.

And now what is your reaction to that prediction?

Now I am scared. And I also say this in the book. Many times I think
that what I write becomes true, in twisted, strange ways. So I have to
be very careful with what I write.

Do you feel a certain sense of spiritual responsibility because of this?

I feel a sense of responsibility, yet at the same time the temptation to
write is stronger than the feeling.

Do you ever want to change things so what happens is good?

Yes, but then I can't. Sometimes in a story, I want a happy ending,
and I have this superstitious feeling that if I write a happy ending
something good will happen to the people who inspired the story.

But I can't do it. My calling as a writer is stronger than anything else; and the critical eye of the writer prevails. Let me give you an example that has nothing to do with a good ending, but pertains to this point. When I was writing *Paula*, and afterwards when I was considering publishing it, my mother said that I had to take certain things out that were too revealing about myself. "You don't want to expose yourself like this," she said, "you don't have to be your own character. You can make yourself look a little better." I had the vain temptation to make myself look good and create a sort of legend about myself. But the critical eye of the writer prevailed, and I said, "No, this is the way it is going to be, because this is the way the writing has to be."

Do you think that is the "critical eye," or is it your own humility?
No, I think it is the eye of the writer, the eye of the storyteller that looks for the story. I feel that even if the story makes me look bad, and the story is good, I want the story. My mother asked me, for example, why I wanted to write about the episode with the fisherman. "It makes you look bad," she said, "it is not relevant." And to me, as a writer, it *is* relevant, because it explains all the seduced children in my writing. I think it is a good story. It is a story you can take out of the book and it would work all by itself. So my eye as a writer prevailed. I just wanted the story; I didn't care if I didn't look good.

You say you believe in destiny. Now, do you believe in destiny or providence? Destiny meaning that humankind has no free will, and providence meaning an existence that does include free will. You often mention destiny in Paula, *and my recurring question was how, or if, you differentiated it from providence.*
I have the feeling that we are given a set of cards to play the game, and often the cards are marked. And you, as the player, can play well, or not. But there is limited space for the game. The fact that you are a woman or a man, in one place or another, in one time or another, part of one race, or another, whether you are educated or not, all this determines your life. That is predetermined. That is destiny. Now, it was written in my destiny, in my marked cards, that I would lose a child in the most awful way. That was given to me. That I could not

control. I can react to that in different ways. I can commit suicide, or I can write a book. That is my choice. But the fact that Paula would die, and I could not avoid it, was given to me.

> *So, for you, then, providence is intimately linked to destiny. Some things in life are dealt to you. Yet you have the free will to react as you are able.*

Yes, and you can always exorcise the demons, and call the angels, and change pain into something else, and have a creative life. You can create something good out of all the mess that is dealt to you. But the raw material is given to you, and with that you do what you can.

> *Have you made your life fascinating, or has it come to you? Was that dealt, or constructed?*

In a book like this, in a memoir, you only talk about the things that are relevant; the good and the bad things that determined your life. It always sounds fascinating because you're telling it like a story and you highlight the things that you think are important. And it will always look like a wonderful soap opera. Anybody's life could look like a soap opera when you choose the right parts to tell. So I don't know if I have lived my life like a novel, or if I have lived a common life, a banal existence. But because I remember only certain things, it looks fascinating. You know, I've lived fifty-two years, and this is only 360 pages. There's a lot of grey in between, long spaces of nothing! [*Laughter.*]

> *If you wrote an autobiography, how would it differ from what you have written about yourself in* Paula?

I would never write an autobiography because I am not interested. An autobiography would be about name dropping, dates, awards that I have received. Of course, it would also be about moments of defeat and failure, about moments of success and the great things that have happened to me. In other words, I would be letting the world know how important my life has been. I'm not interested. I think that is boring.

> *After reading* Paula, *and after hearing the interview that you recently*

gave on National Public Radio, I felt that as a woman I could learn so much from you and your experience. I felt that you spoke to me in a special way. I felt that you had learned greatly, especially spiritually, from your very difficult experience, and that you were now very much of a model for other women. You have learned; now you are giving to the reader. Wouldn't you be doing that, too, in an autobiography?

The problem with autobiography is that I don't remember anything. I suppose that if I look through my files my memory will be sparked, but I really don't remember much. I remember emotions. I remember those moments in my life that I have already related in *Paula*; the moments that have carved me into the person that I am today. The goals, achievements, those things are not what have made me what I am.

At the beginning of Paula, *you say that part of it is fiction and part nonfiction. Is your reader ever to know which parts are which?*

No—because I don't know. I am convinced that everything is true. But I'll tell you something. My mother, for example, says that my childhood was not that unhappy. And I say to her, "Mother, this is how my heart remembers." In Spanish the word *recordar* (to remember) means to pass once more through the heart, *volver a pasar por el corazón*, and that is what memory is about for me. It is something that is filtered through the heart, and not the mind. And even if my mother thinks that my childhood was much better than what I remember, in my history, in the story of my life, my childhood was an awful period. A period of darkness and pain. I wouldn't want to live one minute of that childhood again. And this is what I remember in my heart. So what is fiction and what is not, I don't know. Maybe my unhappiness was fiction, but that is how I remember it, so for me it is real.

There is fiction in the fact that I eliminated so many of the things that happened because they are not interesting to me. For example, I chose not to mention the fact that I had four step-siblings, that I had a stepsister who lived with us. She was not significant in my life, and she still is not. So, I do not mention her. On the other hand, people who may seem absolutely irrelevant, are not. I mention in the book the small part one of my uncles played in my life. And why do I do that? Because I remember him in my heart. I remember him as important.

So, what is fiction and what is not is very relative. I think that all the facts in the book are true.

> *I see* Paula *as initially an interweaving of a life, yours, and a death, Paula's. But towards the end, I, as a reader, realized that it was really two deaths. It was her physical death, in order to become a spirit, as you say at the end, and it was the death of the old you in order to become someone new, someone more spiritual.*

I think that you may be right, but let me phrase it differently. I would like to see Paula as being born to another stage of her life, and me being born to another stage of mine. I don't feel it is like a death in my case, and it is difficult for me to feel it is like a death in hers, because death is terminal. I still carry with me everything that I was before, and in many ways Paula lives in my memory not only as the spirit that she is today, but as everything that she was before. It's hard to explain, but the feeling is one of continuity, not of conclusion. It is just a continuation in another form. I am basically the same person that I was before, but something has changed. I still carry with me the child I was, the young woman that I was, all the aspects that are really the seeds of the person that I am today.

> *Critics repeatedly mention the circular structure of your works. . . . That term "circular structure," you have often talked about how silly, or awful it sounds to you . . . [laughter] while you explicitly say that you dreamed the ending to some stories, or the spirits came to you about the ending to others. I wonder, what does it feel like to have critics label this very spiritual side of your writing?*

It's their job! [*Laughter.*] And it seems to be a respectable job! It's okay with me, but I try not to get hooked on that, because I don't want to end up writing for them as some writers who are sheltered by the big umbrellas of the foundations and universities end up doing. They write for those people and others within that small circle. And that is not what I want to do with my writing or my life.

> *You've said in the past that you write because you need to. In* Paula

you say "each word is like a wound." And in interviews about Paula *you mention that you were much more critical about your writing in this book. Can you talk specifically about writing* Paula *in that context?*

I said that each word was like a wound because I wish so much that I had never written this book. I wish the circumstances had never existed for me to write this book. I would give everything that I am, and everything that I have, to have Paula back. The book helped me to go through mourning and survive. Word by word, and tear after tear, I retraced every step of that horrible year. And by doing so, I retraced every step of my life. And I was able to put everything together in these pages in such a way that I could then see a light at the end of a very dark tunnel.

I would come here every morning. I wrote that book here. Well, no, I wrote the first part at the hospital, but when I decided to rewrite all that, I thought of it as something I would leave my son and my grandchildren. My son has also tested positive for porphyria, you see. We still don't know about my grandchildren because they cannot be tested until puberty. So I wanted to write this book for them. And I would come here every morning, and I would sit here. Sometimes Celia, my daughter-in-law would come, no, often she would come and find me crying. And she would hug me, and try to save me from the pain of writing. And it was very hard for me to explain that this was necessary; this wound was necessary. I had to go through that pain again. And while it was painful, it was also joyful because I was . . . I was . . . walking. I was not stuck, paralyzed in the pain. I was walking through the pain.

And the critic in me came at the end, when I read it and realized that this was a totally unusual book; that it was too revealing about myself and it would not be interesting to anyone. I also thought it could be too sentimental, and I am always afraid of corniness. This book is very emotional, and it is always difficult to draw the line between what is emotional and what it sentimental. Now I know where the line is. The line is a gender line. If a woman is writing, it is sentimental; and if a man writes, it is emotional. So, there was a critical eye at the end, but during the writing process, it was just raw pain, and celebration of the writing. It was celebration of the fact that I had this wonderful tool that allowed me to define the boundaries of the pain. I was saying, "This is me, this is my life. This is Paula in me, this is Paula in my life."

Most people go through this awful experience (because there is nothing unusual about losing a child—it happens all the time) and they go through it without the tool I had. They go through it without the possibility of exorcising it, without the catharsis of the writing. They do not have the time and the silence. They do not have the possibility to stop, and mourn, and remember. People tell you, "You have to get over it. You have to go on with your life. You have other children." You are not supposed to dwell on the mourning, on the love. I was able to do exactly what they say not to do; I was able to stop. For a whole year I stopped, and cried as much as I wanted, and wrote as much as I wanted.

> *You write in* Paula *"Tal vez la etapa de la literatura ya se cumplió" [perhaps the age of literature has already passed]. Are you still writing, since in that quote you imply that you may not write any more?*

I started writing on January 8, but I haven't gotten far because I am swamped with mail. People are writing me about this book from all over. Besides all the mail, I have also been doing interviews for Europe and all over the United States. The promotion for the book has taken three months. But by June 15 I hope to be free and in peace, and be able to go into a sort of a long literary retreat in order to write. And we'll see if it happens. I feel totally dry. I don't have a story inside me. But it often happens that I don't even know that I am pregnant with another story. And only time and silence allow me to feel the child moving inside—and the voices begin to speak.

> *You also write in* Paula, *"No quiero seguir viva y morir por dentro. Si he de continuar en este mundo debo engañar los años que me faltan" [I don't want to continue to live and die inside. If I am to continue in this world, I must seize the years that lie ahead of me]. In other words, you say you do not want to remain physically alive, yet dead inside. These are words that will ring true for so many readers who may have gone through an experience such as the one you endured. Did you mean to share what you have learned with your reader as*

well as purge yourself through this writing? Did you ever think that this would help your readers?

I wrote those words when Paula was still alive, though at the end. I was talking to her. I already knew that she was leaving. But this is the kind of conversation that we would have had with Paula. We talked about these things all the time. We talked about aging often. My mother, Paula, and I always talked about the fact that there were twenty years between each generation among us. My mother was opening the way, and I followed. So Paula could see herself at forty, and sixty in us.

I often talked to Paula about how things felt at my age, and she would tell me how she felt about her age, because you tend to forget. Also, things change from one generation to another. I often talked with her about being a fifty-year-old woman, and all the spiritual changes that come with the physical changes. And this was very interesting to her because we talked a lot about spirituality in these talks.

Paula was a very spiritual person. She was a religious person who was endlessly searching for God within the setting of the Catholic Church. And I was spiritual in a very different way. I was always looking in other places.

Do you feel that your search for spirituality away from organized religion, and hers within it, had something to do with the difference in age?

I believe that eventually Paula would have turned away from Catholicism. But this is just an intuition. Paula needed desperately to believe in something, but she was not satisfied with the answers that she got in the Catholic Church. She would say, "Mom, there must be people who understand, and are part of the ethos of what this is all about. I want to be one of them. I don't want the dogma. I want the real thing. How can I reach the truth?" And she studied theology and she searched for her truth. And I would say to her, "Even within the essence of today's dogma, you have to start by an act of faith and believe in what is the basis of this religion." She always felt torn by that. She found certain aspects of the dogma very difficult to overcome.

I felt that same conflict when I was sixteen. But I did not have any doubt about leaving the Catholic religion, because I was not a religious person and did not have the needs that Paula had. I have those needs now, but Paula started much earlier.

So you did not have those spiritual needs before?

Well, yes I did, and they are evident in all my writing. But my spiritual needs of before were much less than they are now. And I had much less of a spiritual awareness than I have today.

You don't allow life to get you down. You paint, you paint life in different colors, you embroider. What drives you to see it all that way? Is it effortless? Is it difficult to see life that way?

I think it is chemistry in your body. Some people are depressed. I know many such people because depression runs in my family, and they see everything in dark colors. They stay at the bottom and tend to be unhappy all the time. And because of the chemistry in my body, I have an incredible amount of energy and I am very healthy. Because of this I tend to see things in bright colors. But I compare my life with my mother's life, for example. My mother is a depressive person, very depressive. And although she is very creative, has a great sense of humor, and can pull herself out of the depression often without help, she is depressive, and comes from a depressive family. Why I am not that way, I don't know, because both my brothers are. I am sure it has to do with my metabolism.

Is it then a conscious decision on your part, to see things from a cheerful perspective?

No, it's in my body, the same way that I can eat anything, sleep anywhere and I am never tired. When I go on my five-week tours, I go everywhere. I have escorts who accompany me at times, but I run out of escorts because they just can't keep up with me. I have enormous energy, and this allows me to see the world in bright colors and do things that most people don't have time to do. I never quit.

In Paula *you mention that a woman taught you the social codes of*

Venezuela; you knew the social codes in Chile, but had no idea they were so different in Venezuela. I am intrigued; what did she teach you?

Oh, yes! Chile is a sober country made up of Basque and Castilian immigrants, and our Indians who were very dark people, very sad people in a way. Chile is a country where nature, the weather, and race determine the character of the people. We live practically on an island. We are separated from the rest of the world by the Andes, the Pacific Ocean, and a great desert to the North. Then the country ends to the South in Antarctica. We are always looking at ourselves with a sense of shame, of embarrassment. We don't dance, we don't sing, we dress in discreet colors. If a woman is beautiful, she will hide it. We don't wear makeup. All Chilean women (who are usually very beautiful) look alike, because they dress alike, and there is something very understated about the way they carry themselves.

Venezuela, on the other hand, is a Caribbean country made up of immigrants. The country was experiencing a sort of airborne euphoria at the time when I went. All the races have mixed there, and the result is beautiful people. The women win all the beauty pageants in the world; the most extraordinary beauties are there. And they know how to show their beauty; if you have breasts, you exalt them, if you have hips, you accentuate them. They wear high heels and show their legs. We don't do that in Chile. Venezuelan women dance, and joke, and have time for everything because they are never punctual. Life to them is long, and beautiful. There is warm weather and no one wants to become stressed because of formalities. There is no sense of embarrassment if you drink too much, for example, or if you are loud on a plane, or at a party. It is perfectly acceptable to be extravagant. In Venezuela people are kind; they will never say no. In Chile we are very precise and legalistic. If we cannot do something, it will be very clear that we are not available. In Venezuela kindness prevails and people want to make you feel good, so they will never say "no," or they will say "tomorrow." And if you don't know the code, you come back tomorrow, and the day after tomorrow. So you have to learn that code. Besides all this, at the time that we were there, Venezuela was a very corrupt place, and we were not used to that. And so there were many social codes that I had to learn, and it took me many, many years.

Leaving corruption aside, when did you become Venezuelan then?
[*Laughter.*] I learned to enjoy life without embarrassment in Venezuela. I am shocking in Chile.

But you were shocking before.
I was shocking before, yes. But for other reasons. I was shocking before because I was very informal, rebellious. My mother says I don't have much respect for social codes, even now, at my age! For example, I will go to Chile to visit my mother and she is very happy to see me, but she is also afraid that I will say something awful on television. So I think that she is relieved when I leave [*laughter*] because she says that I have no respect, that I don't mind saying the most awful things. Well, actually, I used to do that, but now it is all mixed with a sense of enjoyment for life. If I am happy and doing well, I am not embarrassed to say so. In Chile you never admit that you are really doing well. You say "I'm okay or I'm so-so." All this because you do not want the other person to feel that you are arrogant, or showing off, or pretentious, or nouveau riche. Oh, that would be dreadful! [*Laughter.*] I come from a family that had some very wealthy members. And at parties, for example, all the women wore black and white pearls because any more than that would be showing off. That changed though, during the military dictatorship, because the wives of the military did show off. [*Laughter.*] But now we are certainly going back to the sobriety of the past that was deemed so proper.

Let's talk about the movies that have been made based on your books. I know they have only recently made a movie based on Of Love and Shadows. *Is it out? How well has it been received?*
It is out in Italy, Argentina, Brazil, and a few other countries. It's doing very well. But that does not mean that it will do well in the United States.

Did the movie of The House of the Spirits *do well?*

Oh, very, very well. It did very well most everywhere except in the United States.

I could not make much sense of it.
I loved it.

It didn't seem to have much to do with your book.
But it was a good movie. We are not talking about an interpretation of the book. We are talking about a movie. It's a different form. Let's take the plays based on *The House of the Spirits*, or the stories of *Eva Luna*. They are excellent plays, and they have nothing to do with my writing. I am not judging them in reference to my writing, but how they stand by themselves as pieces of writing. In Iceland they made a musical of *Eva Luna* where everyone is blond. And it's their interpretation of something that I wrote. I don't know if they could ever begin to understand what I had in mind, yet it is their interpretation, and in itself, it is wonderful. People have enjoyed it tremendously. There is also a play based on *The House of the Spirits* that was put on in London. It was eight hours long! They cast 150 people. It worked for them. I don't feel that it interpreted the book, but that is my problem. Success has nothing to do with the book. Its success has to do with the fact that it worked as a play, even though it was that long.

There was another play that they did in Denver based on *The Stories of Eva Luna*. They picked out pieces from all the stories, and they created a sort of fog that runs through all the stories. It holds the play together. They recreated the entire thing. I put very little dialogue in my books, and they created all the dialogue, and it had nothing to do with my book, or with the stories in particular. It's a great play, and people loved it. So that is how I also feel about the movie.

The movie based on Of Love and Shadows *was directed by a woman. Do you feel this will have a special effect on the making of the movie? What I mean is, do you feel it will be more in touch with what you meant to convey?*
I think that the fact that the director was a woman did have a special effect. In the book the protagonist is a woman. In the movie, however,

it's the man, Francisco, who is the protagonist. He is played by Antonio Banderas, and has a better role, in my opinion, than she does. But
the fact that a woman directed it means that all the romance and the
sexual parts of the movie are done beautifully. She also understood
the motivation behind each character. And even though the movie
works like a thriller, because it is filled with suspense, it is not the
kind of thriller that a man would have directed. It was made with a
most feminine intuition.

> *You've mentioned that what you write must be very personal, and it
> must change you in some way. It is quite obvious how* The House of
> the Spirits *and* Paula *helped transform you, but could you talk about
> that change through another book?*

Let's take *Of Love and Shadows*. Before I wrote that book, I was full of
hatred for the military. I wanted to kill them all. I could not understand anything about the military, and I was angry at all they represented and all they did. I am still angry. But in the research I did for
that book I spoke with many people who had been victims of terror.

I spoke with people who had been tortured, raped, people who
had lost their children, their grandchildren, husbands or wives. I
never heard anybody say, "I want to torture the torturer," "I want to
rape the rapist," "I will kill the killer." The more you suffer, the more
compassion you have, and the better you understand that you cannot
breed violence; you have to end it. Punishment is not your goal, your
goal is to know the truth. And the process of healing is finding the
truth, not a continuation of the violence.

That is what I learned in that book. I learned how the military
thinks, what their motivation is. I learned about these people who all
dress alike, adorn themselves with ridiculous medals, and use weapons like toys. I learned about these people who are trained for destruction and death. What happens inside those minds? How do you
turn them around? Or is this something that we all have inside? Is
this part of human nature? The writing forced me to research, to interview, to try to understand, to open my heart to this experience. So
in this process, I transformed the anger into something else. I still believe that we have to eliminate the military, but I do understand the

people who are part of the military. I do understand their motivation. With every book I deal with something that is a very strong emotion inside me, and I need to exorcise it.

> *You have said that to you, a book is not a work of art, but a way of communicating with people. You have also said that you need passion in order to write. What type of passion are you referring to?*

My reader is my confidant, my friend. I have something that I am sharing with that person. Recently, well, yesterday to be exact, a Chilean friend came to visit. She spent three days with me. After three days I could speak in Spanish with my old accent. We spoke like parrots, as we say in Spanish. We talked about things that we had not said for years, sharing, sharing stories and emotions, and tears, and laughter. There was exuberance of feeling. This is what I share with my reader, that space that I shared yesterday with Patricia. It was very intimate, a place where all walls come down and so do the defenses. You just surrender to the charm of telling something, and the other, to hearing something. That is what reading and writing is all about to me. It's a space that we share in total confidence. We just surrender, we accept. As a reader and as a writer we accept the most unbelievable things in the writing. During the reading process, we leave behind all that which we cling to in order to feel a sense of security, and we just float in this which we call writing.

> *It seems to me that is what your readers sense and that's why they love your writing. They are allowed to let go. And this brings us to another point. While there are many Latin American women writers today who are published, many people would say that the limelight is on you. You are possibly the best known of them all, especially in non-Spanish-speaking countries. You have also been much more widely translated. Why do you think that is the case? What attracts the reader so much to your books?*

I have had very good publishers. I also think that the fact that I have traveled all my life gives me a sort of nonregional point of view. Latin American literature tends to be what we call "regionalist," that is grounded and steeped in the traditions of the region. And it is not only the fact that we have different ways of speaking and writing Spanish that makes it very local, but we are also very isolated within our own countries and our own environment. Sometimes it is possible for the writer to describe the village, and that village becomes the world. That's an achievement. Especially if you have not been exposed to the world. When you have been exposed to the world, you can talk about a village like Agua Santa (which I invented in my writing) and it becomes the world. But that is because you have been exposed. And this has fortunately been my case; I don't seem to have roots anywhere. I have been a foreigner all my life.

> *Let me preface this question. As you know, Faulkner is seen as an important precursor to García Márquez, and García Márquez is seen as an important literary precursor to you. Let's also think of Emerson's words, "Poetry is born of poetry," and Borges' comment that when you read* Don Quijote *all you are doing is really rereading* Tirant lo Blanc *and* Amadis de Gaula. *In other words, all literature comes from previous literature. In that vein, how much of García Márquez's influence on your writing, do you believe, has to do with the fact that you were both journalists before you were writers?*

I think that it has much more to do with the fact that we were both raised by our grandparents. He tells the stories that his grandmother told him, and I do the same. Also, remember that most Latin American writers have been journalists, so for many of us, that past with journalism has determined the way in which we write, and the way in which we see things.

> *In your writing, at times, it seems that you have female characters who need to find their own private place, or their own selves, and they find that in, or near, water. Another Chilean writer, María Luisa Bombal, who also creates worlds of women, finds refuge in water as well. Has she influenced your work at all?*

I don't think so. I read María Luisa very late. For me, actually, what you mention is more connected to forest, to dirt, and to the land. In my real life it has to do with walking in the forest, and hiding in the trees. In moments of great, great pain, it has to do with eating dirt.

And I can't say why. It is not like the character in *One Hundred Years of Solitude* who eats the adobe house. I just need to feel the dirt on my face and be part of the land, part of the earth.

> *Only very recently a critic has commented on the fact that Neruda's legacy is quite evident in your writing. Can you comment on that? How has he influenced your writing and where do you think that influence is most evident?*

I don't know where it's most evident. But I have been traveling most of my life, and I believe that most of the idea that I have about my own country comes from some of Neruda's poetry. He defines the land for me. In a way he creates my memory of Chile; it's a Nerudian memory. In that sense it's important. Now there is something about Neruda that I think is a great influence in my writing. Neruda is a poet of the senses. He is about texture, smell, color, how things feel when you touch them. When you relate to things not only with your eyes, but with all your senses, and your intuition, and your memory, and your instinct, then you see Neruda's world. When I write I try to imagine a scene or a person with all my senses. And when I don't do that, I see it as flat. It's missing the Nerudian approach to the world through all the senses.

> *You are a writer who believes very strongly in the spiritual aspect of life. I wonder then, how you react to the works of someone like, let's say, Borges, and to encountering the skepticism, the lack of answers, the much colder and more rational approach to searching out answers or posing questions.*

It depends on the writer. I am fascinated by Borges. He creates an intellectual world that you want to explore with him. Other times, I just get bored. I am not interested in little stories, and little lives. I can't relate to minimalist literature, or safe literature. Literature that deals with safe lives, and safe spaces. I just read a book (and I won't mention the title) that I did not like at all. Everything is safe in that book. Nothing happens in those lives. Everything stays the same, except, maybe, a twist in the mind. There is no connection to the outer world. There is no collective heartbeat. They are individuals separated from the world. When everything relates to one individual's experience, and there is no sense of a person being part of a whole; then I am bored. I like to hear the epic heartbeat of the world and of life. I want to see this in a movie, in a play, in a book, and I want to have this in my writing.

In the San José Museum of Modern Art I recently saw an exhibit entitled "La frontera." It was the first time I found myself crying before a work of art. I am always moved by art, but never to the point of crying. This was not a master. I wasn't before El Greco. This was a collection of photographs of illegal immigrants crossing the river. And you see a tire, and people clinging to that tire. It is a collection of pictures of these same people, also children, hanging on to the tire. And hanging from the ceiling were fifty plastic bags, transparent plastic bags filled with dirty water from the river with little baby shoes inside each one. Now that capacity of artistic expression, the ability to concentrate in one image (in one sentence sometimes), the collective pain, a time, a space, a people, an event. That is what art is about and what I look for when I read a book.

> *In 1974, you published some of the articles that you wrote for a magazine coincidentally also called* Paula, *in the form of a book entitled* Civilice a su troglodita *[Civilize your troglodyte!]. A critic has recently said that this book keeps your other work from being taken seriously. How much of your experience as a writer in that magazine influenced your later writing, and, if you could go back to 1974, would you rethink the publication of those articles?*

First of all, that critic is talking for him- or herself. My work is taken seriously all over the world, whether within academia or outside it. Secondly, back in 1974 I was not a writer. I was asked by the publishing house that published *Paula* to put all the articles together and publish them. I would not do it again. I have been asked innumerable times to revise my articles and republish them as a collection. I will not do it.

> *And why not?*

Because I think that they had a certain charm that is intricately linked to the time they were written. You cannot take them out of context or out of the time when they were written.

> *Pablo Neruda said, referring to what you yourself have called "la cursillería" or kitsch, "quien huye del mal gusto cae en el hielo." That is, "he who flees from bad taste falls on the ice." Can you comment on this in the context of your thinking and your writing and its validity for you as a writer?*

I am not scared of some kitsch. I think that at times it is inevitable. You cannot talk about certain things like love without being a little kitschy. And who determines what kitsch is? Men! Men do; not women. No, I am not afraid of some kitsch, but of course there is a limit; and I am careful. I am more careful now than I was at the start of my work as a writer because I wasn't as aware as I am now of all this. I am more aware of my writing in general now. I am aware of kitsch in the same way that I am aware of not repeating adjectives, or of how long a sentence should be. I see kitsch as something that you should use in homeopathic doses.

> *In most of your novels there seems to be a desire on your part for a good, positive, ending. We as readers go through the mystery, the adventure, and the romance with you, and we know that the familiar order will be restored. Why do you think that in the late twentieth century, when many writers tend to convey an opposite sense, a sense of chaos, you, on the other hand, leave us with the perception that all will work out in the end and that order will be restored?*

I don't know. I don't have that feeling about my endings. On the contrary, I have the feeling that usually the ending is unexpected. I want it to be a happy ending. I want those two elderly people who are dancing and have not been able to communicate verbally because they don't speak the same language to live those last few years together. But it doesn't happen that way. She disappears, she turns into lace, she turns into fog, and she is finally just a memory in his mind ["The Little Heidelberg"]. So there is a restoration of order, as you say, but in a twisted way.

A woman has been raped and kept in a basement for fifty years and she is finally rescued. She re-enters the world, and the man is punished and sent to jail. But she finds herself eerily attached to that man, and she goes to the prison where he now is, and feeds him, and keeps him alive ["If You Touched My Heart"]. So there is always something more that intrigues me, and I don't determine that. When I am writing the story I am not thinking in those terms. In my imagination the story ends when the woman is released from her prison and the man goes to his. That is the end of the story to me. I don't know what happens when another sentence appears and the story continues. The story creates itself in a way.

In *Eva Luna* it is very obvious. I have the two lovers get together finally, and they make love, and it is a wonderful day, and the bells are ringing, and it is perfect. That was the end of the novel. I went to bed at this point. But I woke up in the middle of the night and I had the feeling that it wasn't the end of the novel, and I had to get up and write six more lines. And those lines say that maybe it wasn't like that at all. Where did I get that? [*Laughter.*] I don't know! I just don't know where. I have the feeling that within that restoration of order, as you say, there is space for ambiguity.

It happens in my life all the time. I want a certain thing to happen and something very different happens. In the end it's better. When I look back, it's better.

> *The reception of your work is, I believe, among the most intriguing. Some critics love and exalt it, and others pan it. You yourself have said that* Eva Luna *had the worst reviews of any book in the history of literature. What is going on?*

Eva Luna had a terrible review in *The New York Times Book Review*. It was written by a man who is a specialist in baseball. He had been traveling in Latin America and so they thought he could handle Latin American literature. He obviously did not understand the book, and wrote a terrible review. In spite of that the book was on the bestseller list. And it is still doing quite well today. But it did receive a bad review.

Why that happens, I just don't know. I can't worry about that. I can't worry about how the book is going to be received. I can only worry about how I am going to offer it. Every book is an offering, and how the offering will be received is not my business.

> *A final question. Let's say that you are before the Pearly Gates and you must present what you believe to be your greatest achievement in this life in order to enter. What would it be?*

Motherhood.

> *Not a book?*

No, that's not important in the larger scheme of things. People may not read or remember me in a few years. But the memories of my children and my grandchildren, and my love for them, is what is important for me and how I define myself as a person. It is what justifies my existence.

For Further Reading

ANNOTATED BIBLIOGRAPHY

The following items, which have been selected to place the interviews in *Conversations with Isabel Allende* in a wider context, illustrate both the critical and popular reception of Allende's *oeuvre*. Isabel Allende is a serious writer whose work is enshrined in the literary canon, not only in the United States and the Spanish-speaking world, but also in Britain and Germany. Isabel Allende is also the best-selling female writer of serious prose in the world, a public voice whose work has been translated into more than twenty-seven languages and sold more than eleven million copies. Often the critical and popular aspects of Allende's literary reputation go hand in hand. In Germany, for example, where Allende has had her greatest popular success, *The House of the Spirits* is required reading in some states' world literature courses; at the same time, the filmed version of the book had its world premiere in Munich and received the 1994 Bavarian Film Prize. Still, despite Allende's unique status, no systematic scholarly attention has yet been devoted to her remarkable reception.

Allende's work has elicited admiration from academic critics and kudos in the mass media, but it has also been the object of fierce controversy and attack, delivered variously by Latin American scholars, critic-intellectuals, and daily newspaper reviewers. With the exception of *The House of the Spirits*, which was mainly lauded, each of Allende's books has been both praised and damned in heated language, and often on contradictory grounds: Critics variously charge both that Allende traffics in obtrusive feminist/socialist ideology and that she submits to a patriarchal/capitalist *Weltanschauung*. They variously claim both that Allende captivates readers by her magical realist techniques and that she alienates readers with her sensationalist improbabilities in plot and characterization. They variously insist both that Allende risks expression of open, passionate feeling and that she exploits emotions with an annoying, cloying sentimentality.

Such judgments are seldom rendered so pointedly in scholarly exegeses of an author's work, however, and so the bibliography includes a generous sample of magazine and newspaper reviews, which openly engage in such polemical judicial criticism. These reviews offer insight into the development of Allende's extraordinary critical and popular reputation—the latter of which, in the United States alone, has grown so far as to include serialization of her work in *Vanity Fair*, celebrity profiles in magazines such as *Vogue* and *People*, and a feature story on her San Rafael mountaintop home in *Architectural Digest*.

The selection below includes items in Spanish, French, Italian, Dutch, and German, but the focus is on English-language—chiefly American—articles and reviews. Of special interest is the attention—if not always the enthusiastic support—that Allende has attracted from well-known American poets, novelists, and critic-reviewers, including Diane Ackerman, Robert Bly, Carolyn

Forché, Doris Grumbach, Barbara Kingsolver, John Updike, and Jonathan Yardley.

ABBREVIATIONS

APH	Aphrodite	IP	The Infinite Plan
EL	Eva Luna	LS	Of Love and Shadows
HS	The House of the Spirits	P	Paula
IA	Isabel Allende	SEL	The Stories of Eva Luna

WORKS BY ISABEL ALLENDE (IN CHRONOLOGICAL ORDER)

Books

Civilice a su troglodita. Santiago: Lord Cochran, 1974.

La casa de los espíritus. Barcelona: Plaza y Janés, 1982. Translated by Magda Bogin under the title *The House of the Spirits* (New York: Knopf, 1985).

La gorda de porcelana. Madrid: Alfaguara, 1984.

De amor y de sombra. Barcelona: Plaza y Janés, 1984. Translated by Margaret Sayers Peden under the title *Of Love and Shadows* (New York: Knopf, 1987).

Eva Luna. Barcelona: Plaza y Janés, 1987. Translated by Margaret Sayers Peden under the title *Eva Luna* (New York: Knopf, 1988).

Cuentos de Eva Luna. Buenos Aires: Editorial Sudamericana and Barcelona: Plaza y Janés, 1989. Translated by Margaret Sayers Peden under the title *The Stories of Eva Luna* (New York: Atheneum, 1991).

El plan infinito. Buenos Aires: Editorial Sudamericana and Barcelona: Plaza y Janés, 1991. Translated by Margaret Sayers Peden under the title *The Infinite Plan* (New York: HarperCollins, 1993).

Paula. Buenos Aires: Editorial Sudamericana, 1994. Translated by Margaret Sayers Peden under the title *Paula* (New York: HarperCollins, 1995).

Afrodita: Cuentos, recetas y otros afrodisiacos. Barcelona: Plaza y Janés, 1997. Translated by Margaret Sayers Peden under the title *Aphrodite: A Memoir of the Senses* (New York: HarperFlamingo, 1998).

Other

"Los libros tienen sus propios espíritus." In *Los libros tienen sus propios espíritus: Estudios sobre Isabel Allende*, ed. Marcelo Coddou, 15–20. Jalapa, Mexico: Universidad Veracruzana, 1986.

"Writing as an Act of Hope." In *Paths of Resistance: The Art and Craft of the Political Novel*, ed. William Zinsser, 39–63. New York: Houghton Mifflin, 1989. IA on why and for whom she writes.

WORKS ON ISABEL ALLENDE

Selected Books, Book Chapters, and Scholarly Articles

Antoni, Robert. "Parody or Piracy: The Relationship of *The House of the Spirits* to *One Hundred Years of Solitude*." *Latin American Literary Review* 14, no. 32 (July–December 1988): 16–28. HS begins "in the tradition of magical realism, but as it continues it becomes less and less Clara's (or García Márquez's) book, and more and more Alba's (Allende's) book, until finally there is no longer magic but only realism, and the novel becomes the tragic political history of Chile."

Berchenko, Andriana Castillo, and Pablo Berchenko. *La narrativa de Isabel Allende: Claves de una marginalidad.* Perpignan, France: Crilaup, Université de Perpignan, 1990.

Coddou, Marcelio. *Para leer a Isabel Allende: Introducción a* La casa de los espíritus. Concepción, Chile: Educones Literatura Americana Reunida, 1988. An introduction to IA and *HS*.

———, ed. *Los libros tienen sus propios espíritus: Estudios sobre Isabel Allende.* Xalapa, Mexico: Universidad Veracruzana, 1986.

Cohn, Deborah. "To See or Not to See: Invisibility, Clairvoyance, and Re-Visions of History in *Invisible Man* and *La casa de los espíritus*." *Comparative Literature Studies* 33, no. 4 (fall 1996), 372-383. Ralph Ellison's *Invisible Man* and *HS* tell the stories of persons marginalized by their mainstream cultures. In similar ways, the protagonists in both novels transform their political anger into an expression of love.

Earle, Peter G. "Literature as Survival: Allende's *The House of the Spirits*." *Contemporary Literature* 28, no. 4 (winter 1987): 543–554. *HS* joins a "literature of survival" that gives voice to "the ultimate power of testimony through the creative use of memory."

Foreman, P. Gabrielle. "Past-on Stories: History and the Magically Real, [Toni] Morrison and [Isabel] Allende on Call." *Feminist Studies* 18, no. 2 (summer 1992): 369–389.

Galarce, Carmen J. *La novela chilena del exilio (1973–1987): El caso de Isabel Allende.* Santiago: Universidad de Chile, 1994. A study of the experience and themes of exile in the work of IA and other Chilean writers.

Gordon, Ambrose. "Isabel Allende on Love and Shadows." *Contemporary Literature* 28, no. 4 (winter 1987): 530–542. IA's fiction is not technically innovative; she has merely "left the novel genre where she found it." But her novels "strike a blow for freedom and love against the tyranny that still grips her beautiful country."

Hart, Patricia. *Narrative Magic in the Fiction of Isabel Allende.* Rutherford, N.J.: Fairleigh Dickinson University Press, 1989. Analysis of IA's "magical feminism" in her first three novels, which consists of narrative techniques that promote a "feminocentric" vision and distinguish her fiction from that of Gabriel García Márquez.

Levine, Linda Gould. "A Passage to Androgyny: Isabel Allende's *La casa de los espíritus*." In *In the Feminine Mode: Essays on Hispanic Women Writers*, ed. Noel Valis and Carol Maier, 164–173. Cranbury, N.J.: Associated University Presses, 1990.

Meyer, Doris. "Exile and the Female Condition in Isabel Allende's *De amor y de sombra*." *International Fiction Review* 15, no. 2 (summer 1988): 151–157. In *LS*, IA "announces that women must turn silent complicity into outspoken activism," because "women's condition as exile must end."

———. "'Parenting the Text': Female Creativity and Dialogic Relationships in Isabel Allende's *La casa de los espíritus*." *Hispania* 73 (May 1990): 93–100.

McMurray, George. Review of *Paula. World Literature Today* 70, no. 3 (summer 1996): 671. *Paula* "resembles a novel" and is "never dull." It is "a poignant tribute from a mother to her dying daughter."

Moody, Michael. "Isabel Allende and the Testimonial Novel." *Confluencia: Revista-Hispánica-de-Cultura-y-Literatura* 2 (fall 1986): 39–43.

Mora, Gabriele. "Las novelas de Isabel Allende y el papel de la mujer como ciudadana." *Ideologies and Literatures* 2, no. 1 (1987): 53–61.

Otero, José. "La historia como ficción en *Eva Luna* de Isabel Allende." *Confluencia* 4, no. 1 (Fall 1988).

Rivero, Eliana S. "Scheherazade Liberated: *Eva Luna* and Women Storytellers." In *Splintering Darkness: Latin American Women Writers in Search of Themselves*, ed. Lucia Guerra Cunningham, 143–156. Pittsburgh: Latin American Literary Review Press, 1990. *EL* exemplifies how recent women's fiction creates imaginative alternatives to androcentric visions.

Rojas, Sonia Riquelme, and Edna Aguirre Rehbein, eds. *Critical Approaches to Isabel Allende's Novels.* New York: Peter Lang, 1991. Fourteen essays, written in English and Spanish, devoted to textual and thematic issues in IA's first three novels.

Shea, Maureen E. "Love, Eroticism, and Pornography in the Works of Isabel Allende." *Women's Studies* 18, nos. 2–3 (September 1990): 223–232.

Shields, E. Thomson, Jr. "Ink, Blood, and Kisses: *La casa de los espíritus* and the Myth of Disunity." *Hispanofila* 33, no. 3 (May 1990): 79–86. Through "ink," IA "transforms blood and kisses into more than just literal acts of violence and love; blood and kisses also become metaphors for the more abstract ideas of the real world and the fantastic."

Tayko, Gail. "Teaching Isabel Allende's *La casa de los espíritus*." *College Literature* 19, no. 3 (October 1992): 228–233. Pedagogical suggestions on how to approach *HS* in interdisciplinary courses on post-colonial literature.

Wittig, Wolfgang. *Nostalgie und Rebellion: Zum Romanwerk von García Márquez, Mario Vargas Llosa, und Isabel Allende.* Wurzburg: Konigshausen & Neumann, 1991. A historically oriented study of the thematic tensions between nostalgia and rebellion in the work of three Latin American novelists.

Selected Portraits, Book Reviews, Essay-Reviews, and Film/TV Reviews

Ackerman, Diane. "Touchy-Feelie." *Los Angeles Times*, April 26, 1998, 12. Ackerman, author of *A Natural History of the Senses* (1980) and *A Natural History of Love* (1985), criticizes *APH* as "derivative and on too many occasions just factually wrong." Ackerman mentions, for instance, that IA mistakenly claims both that humans are the only mammals "capable of making love face to face" (whales do too) and that it is unknown whether a close "bond between food and sex" exists among animals (courtship feeding is widespread throughout the animal kingdom). Ackerman takes IA to task not only for shoddy research, but for failing to "credit many of the authors and scientists whose hard work she is otherwise presenting as her own."

Adams, Robert M. "The Story Isn't Over." *New York Review of Books* 32, no. 12 (July 18, 1985): 20–23. The women in *HS* are "entertaining creatures," but "after a couple of hundred pages, the reader is likely to develop an irritating sense that Isabel Allende doesn't really know what to do with this cast of picturesque eccentrics."

Agosín, Marjorie. "A Picaresque Ramble through a Land of Magic." *Christian Science Monitor*, November 29, 1988, 22. *EL* "is a novel that goes beyond political ideology and concentrates on the adventure of the powerful protagonist who grows up among antique furniture and ancient books in Latin and who, through the power of the word, invents her own reality governed by magic and fate."

———. "Powerful Chilean Saga Blends Fact and Fiction." *Christian Science Monitor*, June 7, 1985, B5.

———. "Review of *La casa de los espíritus*." *Revista Interamericana de Bibliografía* 35 (1985): 448–458.

———. "Searching for Truth and Finding Love in Today's Latin America." *Christian Science Monitor*, May 27, 1987, 20. *HS* "captivates and holds the reader throughout its four hundred pages."

Allen, Bruce. "A Magical Vision of Society in Revolt." *Chicago Tribune*, May 19, 1985, 37–38. "Along with García Márquez's masterpiece [*One Hundred Years of Solitude*], [*HS*] is one of the best novels of the postwar period, and a major contribution to our understanding of societies riddled by ceaseless conflict and violent change."

Ament, Delores Tarzan. "Grief for Paula Inspires Story Balancing Emotions." *The Seattle Times*, June 18, 1995, 5. Account of Paula's last days.

Anton, Jacinto. "Isabel Allende: Lo primero no es hacer literatura, sino tocar el corazón de la gente." *El País* (Madrid), November 20, 1987, 45.

Arana-Ward, Marie. "Coming to America." *Washington Post Book World*, May 23, 1993, 6. Review of *IP*. "We plow endless, barren chapters looking for the richness of language that has graced her earlier novels." It is as if she has "drawn her characters not from life but from the arid well of Monday night television. . . . Allende is better than this."

Bader, Eleanor J. "A Life like a Dimestore Romance." *Belles Lettres: A Review of Books by Women* 4, no. 2 (Winter 1989): 5. "A life that reads like a dimestore romance [EL] is hardly the stuff that one expects from Allende."

Bahar, Zillah. Review of APH. *San Francisco Examiner*, May 20, 1998. The "directness" of APH "is unlike [IA's] exotic fiction, which spirits the reader off into "a surreal Spanish-speaking world suffused with color, magic, danger, and extreme emotion." But APH's "beauty" and "precious gift" to readers lies in its power to bestow a "heightened awareness" of the sensual, this-worldly pleasures of food and sex.

Barker, Elspeth. "Three Quarters of an Epic Reeves' Tale." *The Independent*, June 20, 1993, 35. "This [IP] is so nearly a great novel. The characters . . . both convince and fascinate" and the "writing is supremely elegant." But the stylistic clichés and pat, happy ending "spoil a work of such potential splendor."

Bautista, Gloria. Review of *De amor y de sombra*. *Discurso Literario* 5, no. 1 (1987), 211–215.

Bell-Villada, Gene H. "Eros Makes War." *New York Times Book Review*, July 12, 1987, 23. The "troublesome secret" of HS was that it "was mostly imitation García Márquez," but LS is a "suspenseful thriller" in which IA "skillfully evokes both the terrors of daily life under military rule and the subtler form of resistance in the hidden corners."

Bellini, Giuseppe. "Attimi di un dolore esemplare." *Il Sole 24 Ore*, March 12, 1995, 26.

———. "Isabel Allende: Per leggere dell'altra America." *La Stampa* (Turin, Italy), November 22, 1992, 23.

Benedict, Elizabeth. "Sumptuously Surreal." *Chicago Tribune*, October 9, 1988, C6. In EL, IA's "bountiful romanticism sometimes spills over into her prose," but "such excesses only match those of the roiling universe Allende describes."

Benesch, Susan. "Mixing Fantasy, Reality." *St. Petersburg Times*, December 11, 1988, 7D. In EL, "the least satisfying thing about Eva is that, although most of her fellow characters are deeply marked by their pain, she tends to stand up and trot off to her next adventure."

Bernikow, Louise. "The Stories of Eva Luna." *Cosmopolitan*, January 1991, 22. IA has "only gotten better from one book to the next." SEL is "absolute magic on every level."

Bianchini, Angela. "Addio a Paula." *La Stampa* (Turin, Italy), January 21, 1995, 2.

Blake, Patricia. "From Chile with Magic." *Time*, May 20, 1985, 79. HS is "full of promise," but IA has failed "to break away from the domination of her unwitting mentor" [García Márquez and his novel *One Hundred Years of Solitude*].

Bly, Robert. "Westward to the New Age Covered Wagon." *New York Times Book Review*, May 16, 1993, 13. IP "has more vision and ambition" than IA's earlier books, but "we can't be sure in our bones that we know the interior life of any one of her characters."

Bond, Matthew. "Canny Self-Revelation vs. Obstinate Reticence." *The Listener*, August 8, 1995. Review of BBC1's *Listen, Paula*, which flounders because it confuses distinctions between portraying IA's intimate relationship with her dead daughter and creating a show for a mass audience.

Bowden, Charles. "Tame as a Novel, Wild as a Book on Pumas." *Los Angeles Times*, December 27, 1990, E2.

Bustamante, Juby. "Isabel Allende: La gran sorpresa literaria del año." *Diario* 16 (November 28, 1982): 22.

Carlson, Lori M. Review of *The House of the Spirits*. *Review*, no. 34 (January–June 1985), 77–78. "The reader cannot finish a chapter without thinking of García Márquez's Buendía family," but HS "does remain compelling, nevertheless."

Carman, Diane. "Recipe of Sensuality Focuses on the Physical." *Denver Post*, April 5, 1998, F5. *APH* is "thoroughly researched and charmingly candid," and it contains many moments "when you just can't help but laugh out loud" at IA's observations about lovemaking or at her recipes.

Cheever, Susan. "Portrait: Isabel Allende." *Architectural Digest*, April 1995, 32–36. A tour of IA's San Rafael home and its furnishings.

Coleman, Alexander. "Reconciliation among the Ruins." *New York Times Book Review*, May 12, 1985, 1, 22–23. "With this spectacular first novel [*HS*], Isabel Allende becomes the first woman to join what has heretofore been an exclusive male club of Latin American novelists."

Cryer, Dan. "A Picaresque Tale of Rags to Riches." *Newsday*, October 9, 1988, 19. *EL* is "an undisciplined mishmash" that "comes to an abrupt end."

———. "Unlucky in Love in Latin America." *Newsday*, January 21, 1991, 46. In *SEL*, "the initially mesmerizing voice becomes cloying; the characters are vividly drawn but too rigidly cut from the pattern labeled 'exotic'; the plotting is energetic but given to soap opera."

Davis, William A. "The Magic Realism of Isabel Allende." *Boston Globe*, April 14, 1991, A40. *SEL* possesses "the quality of legend or folk myth."

"*De amor y de sombra*." *El Europeo* (Spain), January 31, 1985, 14.

De Ferrari, Gabrielle. "Letter to a Dying Daughter." *Washington Post Book World*, April 30, 1995, 10. *Paula* is "filled with fascinating material that brings to light the sources of Allende's writing."

Demarest, Donald. "Allende Left Magic in Chile." *Washington Post Book World*, May 23, 1993, 6. *IP* is "an infinite pain," with a "setting [that] has elements of soap opera that remind one of *The World According to Garp*."

Di Antonio, Robert. "Allende Takes New Direction." *St. Louis Post-Dispatch*, May 16, 1993, 5C. *IF* pays "homage to the Spanish telenovela," but is "a major disappointment." *IP* "may remind many readers of the Italian director Michelangelo Antonioni's hollow attempt to capture the American *Zeitgeist* of the late '60s with his film *Zabriskie Point*."

Dickson, E. Jane. "Death and Dancing Sugar Bowls." *The Independent*, September 23, 1995, 6.

Drake, Sylvia. "Latin Lady of Letters." *Variety*, March 28, 1994, 40–42. A profile of IA in connection with the film adaptation of *HS*.

Dugan, Judith. Review of *Of Love and Shadows*. UPI, June 5, 1987.

Eder, Richard. "The House of the Spirits." *Los Angeles Times Book Review*, June 16, 1985, 3. *HS* "has the material and the sensibility to be an engrossing novel of contemporary history," but in its use of magical realism it "wears a robe of fashion. . . ." IA "rarely manages to integrate her magic and her message."

Feigenbaum, Nancy. "Facts Are Uninspired in 'Paula.'" *Orlando Sentinel*, May 21, 1995. IA's "restraint" has "curbed . . . her sense of storytelling."

Fernández, Enrique. "Send in the Clone." *Village Voice*, June 4, 1985, 51. *HS* is a "knockoff" of *One Hundred Years of Solitude*, marred by its "shameless cloning" of García Márquez's style. IA "writes like one of the many earnest minor authors that began aping [García Márquez] after his success."

Fichtner, Margaria. "Latin Vision in US." *The Arizona Republic*, June 7, 1993, C1. *IP* "wrings enchantment from tension, danger, courage, and style. . . . Allende's enthronement as the most widely read Latin American female writer in history remains secure."

Forché, Carolyn. "Of Love and Shadows." *Los Angeles Times*, May 31, 1987, 1. In *LS*, "we are by turns enchanted and entertained, as in a fairy story."

Fraxedas, J. Joaquin. "'Plan' Tells of Uncommon Journey of a Solitary Soul." *Orlando Sen-*

tinel, May 30, 1993, D10. *IP* is "not only an important contribution to the literature of the world but also a great American novel, a novel we may claim as our
own."

Fruendt, Bodo. "Der chilesische Trauerspiel." *Süddeutsche Zeitung*, October 5, 1994. More
successfully than in the film version of *The House of the Spirits*, the screen version
of *Of Love and Shadows* "links the private love story with the general recognition of
the reign of terror of the Pinochet regime. . . . Thus [the film] familiarizes even politically indifferent moviegoers with Chile's history and present."

Gernes, Sonia. "Lovers & 'Desaparecidos.'" *Commonweal*, August 14, 1987, 460–462.
"This is one of the most memorable novels this reviewer has read in recent years."

Girgado, Luis Alonso. "Isabel Allende: La cuentera y us andanzas." *El Correo Cultural*
(Santiago de Compostela), November 8, 1987, 29.

Glastonbury, Marion. "States of Emergency." *New Statesman and Society*, July 5, 1985, 29.
In *HS*, "magical powers proliferate and become something of a bore"; "Gothic
mayhem" seems to reign "for the sake of sensation rather than sense."

Golden, Gayle. "A Nice, Rambling Trip to Nowhere in Particular." *Dallas Morning News*,
June 6, 1993, 8J. "Allende's narration is superficial and sidetracked. . . . [*IP*] is limited and sometimes lost."

Gonzales, Fernando. "Latin America's Scheherazade." *Boston Globe Magazine*, April 25,
1993, 14.

Grey, Jennifer. Review of *APH*. Florida *Times-Union* (Jacksonville), May 17, 1998, D4.
APH is "a lazily digressive examination of the aphrodisiac value of foods." But it is
also "informative, humorous, and touching . . . a must read for any lover of food or
of life."

Groot, Ger. "Isabel Allende, Het oneindige plan." *Trouw*, November 12, 1992, 4. Review
of *IP*.

Grossman, Ron. "'Infinite' Twists are Fascinating and Frustrating." *Chicago Tribune*, May
26, 1993, C3. *IP* is written in the reportorial style of Theodore Dreiser and Sinclair
Lewis, and its spiritual theme evokes the work of Thornton Wilder. *IP* "will fascinate as many readers as it will perplex."

Grumbach, Doris. "Farewell, My Daughter." *Los Angeles Times Book Review*, April 30,
1995, 3. IA is a "born storyteller," but the "frame" of Paula's sickness is sometimes
"merely a literary device."

Harris, Daniel. Review of *The Stories of Eva Luna*. *Boston Review* 16, no. 2 (April 1991):
28–29. *SEL* is "saturated with a denigrating sort of nostalgia for less complex,
preliterate cultures [with] childlike spontaneity, wisdom, and harmony with nature. . . . [T]he suspicion arises that [IA] performs the old soft-shoe of her lively
Hispanic vaudeville for the amusement of gringos."

Hart, Patricia. Review of *The Stories of Eva Luna*. *The Nation*, March 11, 1991, 314–316.
"Like James Joyce of *Dubliners*, Allende builds each of these stories to a moment of
epiphany."

Hemmerechts, Kristien. "De geest in de gordijnen." *NRC Handelsblad*, December 23,
1994, 4.

Hermsen, Joris. "Isabel Allende verwerkt in 'Paula' dood van haar dochter." *De
Gelderlander*, December 27, 1994, 1. *P* is "an open-hearted and heart-rending"
memoir of a mother's love for her daughter, filled with humor and anecdotes amid
the suffering.

Holt, Patricia. "Allende Returns to Eva Luna." *San Francisco Chronicle*, January 13, 1991,
1. IA is "a sap for romance" in *SEL*, but "this does not mean that her penchant for
morbidity, violence, and the dark side of the human psyche is ever far away."

Hopkinson, Amanda. Review of *Paula*. *New Statesman and Society*, September 22, 1995,
34. *P* is an achievement "unsurpassed by Allende since her seminal" *HS*.

Hornblower, Margot. "Grief and Rebirth." *Time*, July 10, 1995, 65. *Paula* has brought a "new audience" to IA, but IA continues to mourn her daughter's death. In her Sausalito cottage, IA "surrounds herself with mementos: Paula's baby shoes encased in copper; photographs of her, framed in silver; the earthen jar that contains Paula's ashes. . . ."

Hughes, Kathryn. Review of *The Infinite Plan*. *New Statesman and Society*, July 2, 1993, 38. IA "uses report and description at the expense of dialogue to produce page-long paragraphs of unrelieved tedium."

Johnson, Brian D. Review of *The House of the Spirits* (film), *Macleans*, April 11, 1994, 69. The cinematic *HS* is "soap opera." Director Bille August "rarely gets beyond the sheer mechanics of churning through the story."

Jones, D. A. N. "Magical Realism." *London Review of Books*, August 1, 1985, 26–27. "The trouble with [*HS's*] political stance is that it gives the impression that nothing can be done about Chile's notorious government—you know what South Americans are like, ha, ha!—and that Pinochet's regime is no worse than its predecessors. This is surely untrue."

Kakutani, Michiko. "Of Love and Shadows." *New York Times*, May 20, 1987, C27. In *LS*, IA tends to "cast everything in terms of white and black, good and evil, love and shadows. . . . A noisome sentimentality pervades [the lovers'] entire relationship, and combined with the novel's diagrammatic politics, it makes for sticky, predictable reading."

Kaplan, Fred. "Angel of Gluttony and Lust." *The Boston Globe*, April 1, 1998, D1. *APH* is a "romp," a "giddy sequel" to *Paula*. It "restored her contact with the pulse of storytelling" after Paula's death, since storytelling possesses "links to food and sex [that] are fundamental."

———. "Rites of Passage toward Great Unhappiness." *New York Times*, June 25, 1993, C31. *IP* does not treat postwar American historical events "with the least bit of originality or felt emotion: rather, they feel like trite, second-hand orchestrations of old magazine stories and pulp fiction. . . . [A] disappointing and mechanical novel."

Kendall, Elaine. "New Master Storyteller Commences Her Reign." *Los Angeles Times*, December 28, 1990, E5. "There is violence in [*SEL*]—revenge, madness, death, lust, and greed—but also compassion, vitality, humor, tenderness, and generosity, and all in exquisite balance and proportion."

Kingsolver, Barbara. "Fish Fall from the Sky for a Reason." *New York Times*, January 20, 1991, 13. *SEL* is "of enormous value to North American readers," because the stories—unlike most American fiction—are carefully plotted. Such a plot-driven narrative, based on cause and effect, "is profoundly political, since it incorporates at least the possibility of justice."

Kleinmann, Leanne. *Memphis Commercial Appeal*, May 28, 1995, 3G. "Allende is masterful at turning passion into words."

Krich, John. "Rich Little Poor Girl." *New York Times Book Review*, October 23, 1988, 13–14. *EL* is not "believable," leaving the reader to wonder whether IA is writing "magic realism à la García Márquez or Hollywood magic à la Judith Krantz."

Kronsbein, Joachim. "Tante mit Fluegeln." *Der Spiegel*, April 10, 1995, 222. IA has written in *P* an "unreflective mishmash of superstition, naïveté, and esotericism, which makes the book a document on the denial of reality. *Paula* is no argument with her own life, but an escape from it."

Kübler, Gunhild. "*Das Geisterhaus.*" *Neue Zürcher Zeitung*, November 5, 1993. "One can criticize many things in Isabel Allende's hit novel [*HS*], but it doesn't deserve such an uninspired [film] adaptation."

Lagos-Pope, Marie Inés. Review of *De amor y de sombra*, *Latin American Literary Review*

15, no. 29 (January–June 1987): 207–213. *LS* "presents a partial and idealized vision of a problematic and highly polarized situation" in contemporary Chile.

Lambert, Pam. Review of *APH*. *People*, April 20, 1998. *APH* is a "highly literary broth" for a cookbook, indeed a "road map—via the stomach—to the innermost chambers of the human heart."

Lee, Hermione. "Chile Con Carnage." *The Observer*, June 7, 1985, 21. *HS* is "a little too schematic," but "it seems petty to quibble, when there is such cause for celebration and delight."

Lehmann-Haupt, Christopher. Review of *The House of the Spirits*. *New York Times*, May 9, 1985, C29. "One never stops feeling impatient with the symmetry of good and evil . . . there are simply no good right-wingers and no bad revolutionaries. . . . But judged by the standards of the mainstream of historical fiction, *The House of the Spirits* has to be considered powerful and original."

Levantesi, Allessandra. "Peccato." *La Stampa* (Turin, Italy), April 29, 1995, 16. Betty Kaplan's adaptation of *LS* "imprints itself on our memories and consciences" and is a portrait of Chile as "an intolerable collective tragedy."

Lewis, Peter. "Life and Love in a Latin Ghetto." *Daily Mail*, June 24, 1993, 56. "A hopeful, warm-hearted, absorbing novel, affirming life and love but not flinching from exploring the pain that inevitably accompanies both."

Lothar, Corinna. "All about Eva." *The Washington Times*, February 11, 1991, F2. "Like old-fashioned fairy tales, Eva Luna's stories [in *SEL*] are tales of good and evil, and the best have that timeless and spaceless 'once upon a time' quality."

McCabe, Carol. "'Paula' Speaks of Mother's Love and Tenacity of Spirit." *Buffalo News*, May 28, 1995, 8G. A "masterpiece," a "breathtaking tour de force."

Mackay, Leslie. "Isabel Allende: Memoir as Autobiography." *Baltimore Sun*, April 30, 1995, 5F. *IA's* "magical realism" "emerges as self-indulgence" in this nonfictional work.

Mackey, Mary. "Adrift in America." *San Francisco Chronicle*, April 25, 1993, 1. *IP* is a "fascinating portrait of America seen from an Anglo/Hispanic perspective." IA adopts "the viewpoint of a modern Tocqueville," which has "the peculiar attraction of a guidebook aimed at foreign visitors" to the United States.

Maitland, Sara. "Courage and Convictions." *New Statesman and Society*, July 10, 1987, 27. IA is so insistent in *LS* to "get across her Political Message" that "her political themes weigh down her imagination. . . ." *LS* is "the stuff of Girls' Own fiction gone left-wing."

Max, D. T. "A Transplant's Travails." *St. Petersburg Times*, May 23, 1993, 6D. *IP* is "deeply disappointing." Partly this is due to the fact that "translator Margaret Peden . . . has still never matched the superb translation Magda Bogin made for *The House of the Spirits*."

Medwick, Cathleen. "The Amazing Isabel Allende." *Vogue*, March 1985, 506–513. An illustrated profile that introduces IA to her new American public.

Mehren, Elisabeth. "Isabel Allende Weaves Novels of Private Pain, Public Passion." *Los Angeles Times*, February 10, 1988, 10. Portrait of IA.

Mesic, Penelope. "Isabel Allende's Loving Farewell to her Daughter." *Chicago Tribune*, June 18, 1995, C3. IA "obliterates the distance" between author and reader in *Paula*. "It is impossible to stay unmoved, to withhold sympathy."

Mitgang, Herbert. "As Isabel Allende Sees Herself." *New York Times*, February 4, 1988, C19.

Morris, Mary. "Chile Enters the Dark Ages." *Chicago Tribune*, April 19, 1987, C1. "Again and again she confronts harsh political realities" in *LS*. "She has something to say. Her great gift is that she's not afraid to say it."

Mujica, Barbara. "The Life Force of Language." *Americas* 47, no. 6 (November–December 1995): 36–44. Portrait of IA's spiritual struggle after Paula's death.

————. Review of *APH*. *Americas* 50, no. 30 (June 1998): 60. *APH* is "hardly a literary masterpiece," but it is "written with a mirth and animation that make it a joy to read."

Nederpelt, Rob. "Platte toneelversie van Allende's 'Eva Luna.'" *Eindhovens Daglad*, September 23, 1995.

Nieto, José García. "*Eva Luna*." *ABC Literario* (Madrid), September 26, 1987.

Noiville, Florence. "Les mille et une nuits d'Isabel Allende." *Le Monde*, May 10, 1991. IA has both a taste for "commerce" and a "slightly perverse" streak. Her first four books are "a patchwork of miracles and superstitions, stories of saints and sinners and maledictions and carnivals, of civil wars and rebellions."

Norman, Matthew. "Missing Paula, Missing the Point." *Evening Standard*, September 19, 1995, 45. Review of the documentary on BBC 1, directed by Mischa Scorer and titled *Listen, Paula*, which "ostentatiously" fails to "paint a vibrant picture" of Paula Frías, who seems "little more than the peg" on which IA's own history is hung.

Novak, Ralph. "Of Love and Shadows." *People*, June 1, 1987, 11. "None of it rings true, neither the lovemaking nor the couple's eventual flight from government agents."

Paterson, Peter. "Taking the Sting Out of Death." *Daily Mail*, May 25, 1995, 47. Review of BBC2's portrait of IA, titled *The Long Goodbye*. Admires IA's view that "the majority of mothers across the world are familiar with the grief which comes with the loss of a child: it is only in privileged countries that mothers assume that all the children they bear will live."

Pflaum, Hans Günther. "Aufwendig." *Die Woche*, October 21, 1993, 28. "The images and sequencing [in the cinematic *HS*] never get moving and never find a visual rhythm. . . . Only with the *putsch* and its aftermath does the film acquire a dynamic. . . . [A] tame film."

Pierluigi, Battista. "Parolaio." *La Stampa* (Turin, Italy), February 13, 1995, 16.

Pinol, Rosa María. "Eva Luna es la feminidad aceptada, dice Isabel Allende." *La Vanguardia* (Barcelona), November 20, 1987, 20.

————. "Isabel Allende's Letter of Loss." *World Press Review* 42, no. 4 (April 1995): 47.

Powers, John. Review of *The House of the Spirits* (film). *New York*, April 11, 1994, 56. "This picture is prosaic and glum. A well-upholstered star vehicle headed straight to the video store, it offers little more than handsome cinematography and the spectacle of expensively dressed gringos taking the magic out of magical realism."

Prescott, Peter. "Land of the Lotus-Eaters." *Newsweek*, May 13, 1985, 82. Review of *HS*.

Preston, Rohan. "Allende's 4th Novel Falls Short." *Chicago Tribune*, June 4, 1993, 26. *IP* is "a Baby Boomer's guide to magical realism," but it lacks "the exotic patina of her previous work."

Provan, Sarah. "The Shooting of 'Spirits.'" *Europe: Magazine of the European Community*. no. 327 (June 1993), 41–42. An inside look at the filming of *HS*.

Regan, Jennifer. "Riding the Currents of History in the Los Angeles Barrio." *The Buffalo News*, July 25, 1993, 7. IA's "range and storytelling talent are prodigious," but *IP* is "globs and blobs of history and analysis of history, mostly glibly presented."

"Reportaje a Isabel Allende." *El Clarín* (Buenos Aires), May 30, 1985, 3.

Rojas, Maro A. "La cases de los espíritus de Isabel Allende: Un caleidoscopio de espejos desordenados." *Revista Iberoamericana*, July–December 1985, 917–925. Review of *HS*.

Rosetti, Claudia. "Love and Revolution in the House of Trueba." *Wall Street Journal*, June 19, 1985, 35. Review of *HS*.

Ross, Janice. "Night Stories." *Dance Magazine* 72, no. 1 (June 1998): 109. Della Davidson has successfully adapted three tales from *The Stories of Eva Luna* ("Wicked Girl," "Tusca," and "Revenge") in a dance production that forms the leadoff show of an ambitious series titled "The Eva Luna Project."

Rubin, Merle. "Unusual Characters Pursue Their Dreams." *Christian Science Monitor*, June 10, 1993, 14. "Admirers of Allende's earlier work may be a little disappointed by her lack of finesse in this one [*IP*], but will still find much to engage mind and heart alike."

Ruta, Suzanne. "The Long Goodbye." *New York Times Book Review*, May 21, 1995, 11. IA has "eliminated the negative" in her story of the family's response to Paula's illness and "high-flown rhetoric obscures some of her introspective passages."

Ryan, Alan. "Scheherazade in Chile." *Washington Post Book World*, October 9, 1988, 1–2. EL "is a remarkable novel, one in which a cascade of stories tumbles out before the reader, stories vivid and passionate and human enough to engage, in their own right, all the reader's attention and sympathy."

Saladriagis, Roberto. "*Eva Luna* desde Isabel Allende." *La Vanguardia* (Barcelona), October 8, 1987, 49.

Schifferle, Hans. "Es war einmal in Chile." *Süddeutsche Zeitung*, October 21, 1993. "As in the novel, the figures [in the cinematic *HS*] are outsized, alienated, and artificial. . . . [In *HS*], clichés and characters with whom we strongly identify slide into one another."

Schmitt, Hans-Jürgen. "Selbstporträt unter dem Namen der Tochter." *Süddeutsche Zeitung*, May 12, 1995. *P* is "a book with no shame—not in the moral sense, but in the comprehensive sense of an apparently defenseless openness. . . . The autobiography is . . . a colorfully told historical document."

See, Carolyn. "A North American Tale." *Los Angeles Times*, June 6, 1993, 13. IA's realism in *IP* bears comparison with Bryce Courtenay, Ayn Rand, and James T. Farrell, but she "has thrown away images, style, and magic in [*IP*]. . . . I hope I'm wrong about this book. . . . Allende is a genius. . . . She must know what she's doing."

Shapiro, Harriet. "Isabel Allende, Salvador's Niece, Builds a House of the Spirits from the Ashes of Exile." *People*, June 10, 1985, 145–148. Portrait of IA.

Simpson, Blaise. "The Mystical Isabel Allende." *Los Angeles Times*, March 27, 1994, 7.

Starkmann, Alfred. "*Paula*: Ein Hymnus an das Leben." *Focus Magazin*, March 20, 1995, 125. "Is *Paula* a novel? . . . Some images and metaphors graze the line of kitsch. . . . An extraordinary case in modern literature. *Paula* is a melodrama that bears no negative connotation from that characterization, an atheistic version of the stations of the Cross . . . , a gigantic gravestone with many inscriptions, and a hymn to Life."

Stein, Ruthe. "Isabel Allende's Fantasy as Reality." *San Francisco Chronicle*, May 12, 1993, B3.

Stijfs, Jos. "Recensie *Paula*." *De Limburger*, September 27, 1994. *P* is a memoir invested with so much "life" that it makes IA's life of trials resemble that of Job.

Sunen, Luis. "Una excelente novela chilena." *El Pais* (Madrid), January 23, 1983, "Libros," 3.

Torres, Maruja. "Isabel Allende recoge en su primera novela la tradición oral de su familia." *El Pais* (Madrid), November 24, 1982, 19.

Updike, John. "Resisting the Big Guys." *New Yorker*, August 24, 1987, 83–86. In *LS*, which is "smaller, paler, and less magical" than *HS*, "speaking deteriorates into rhetoric" and "fantasy intrudes as a softening veil [that] allows us to take the protest more lightly."

Uyterlinde, Judith. "Familiekroniek 'Het huis met de geessten' van Isabel Allende verfilmd." *NRC Handelsblad* (Amsterdam), October 26, 1993, 6. Review of cinematic *HS*.

Valente, Ignacio. "*Eva Luna*: Entre la calidad y el éxito." *El Mercurio* (Santiago de Chile), October 25, 1987, 6.

van Vlerken, Peter. "Isabel Allende: Een leven als een roman." *Eindhovens Dagblad*, August 26, 1995. Profile of IA.

van Weert, Henk. "Recensie *Paula*." *Eindhovens Dagblad*, December 20, 1994, 22. "More autobiography than novel, this is a strongly romanticized autobiography." *P* is a "dramatic" book, but one carved from the landscape of real events in IA's life.

Weiss, Hedy. "Talented Allende Loses Her Way." *Chicago Sun-Times*, May 9, 1993, 12. *IP* "might pass muster as an elaborate outline for a television mini-series, but as a novel it has all the qualities of a beached whale." It "reads as if it had been composed from a chronologically organized pile of newspaper clippings."

West, Paul. "Narrative Overdrive." *The Nation*, July 20 and 27, 1985, 52–54. *HS* is an "ably done variant of the typical recent Latin American novel." Its echoes of *One Hundred Years of Solitude* are respectful "bows, perhaps, but a book of bows becomes a bow-wow."

Whitehouse, Anne. "Looking at America." (Louisville) *Courier-Journal*, November 13, 1993, 15A. The protagonist of *IP*, Gregory Reeves, is "a cipher onto which Allende has grafted nearly five decades of American life, a 'type' who is frequently undergoing metamorphosis rather than a fully realized individual. . . . His voice is not differentiated from Allende's. . . . The novel might be more successful as a straight third-person narrative."

———. Review of *The Infinite Plan*. *Atlanta Journal and Constitution*, April 25, 1993, M10.

Wilson, Leigh Allison. "The Risks of Passion." *Washington Post Book World*, January 20, 1991, 3. IA's "perceptions of the roles of men and women" in *SEL* "are bothersome," but "her work is a welcome addition to a body of contemporary fiction in which it seems the greatest threat is malaise."

Yardley, Jonathan. "Desire and Destiny in Latin America." *Washington Post Book World*, May 12, 1985, 3–4. *HS* is "a genuine rarity, a work of fiction that is both an impressive literary accomplishment and a mesmerizing story fully accessible to a general readership."

———. "Passion, Politics, and Grace." *Washington Post Book World*, May 24, 1987, 3. *LS* is that rare political novel exhibiting "depths of empathy and compassion. . . . [W]e see the world in miniature. This is precisely what fiction should do."

Zingman, Barbara. "Moonlight." (Louisville) *Courier-Journal*, March 9, 1991, 13A. Review of *SEL*. "Moments of passion, love, anger, revenge, and sweet humor make up these fairly short fictions."

Zuber, Helen, and Swantje Strieder. "Ja, diese Wochen waren fürterlich." *Der Spiegel*, no. 45 (1986), 182–190. Review of *HS*.

Index